Lies, Lying and Liars

Lies, Lying and Liars: A Psychological Analysis delves into the psychology of lies, exploring the processes of lying and its far-reaching consequences.

The author's unique approach considers the ways in which lying sculpts our realities when used by public figures such as politicians, as well as how lying is woven into our everyday life. This book dissects lies in natural social contexts, from the innocent childhood fibs to the more nefarious fabrications of con artists, cheats, and adulterers. Drawing from a rich tapestry of psychology and sociobiology, as well as research and literature from philosophy and the social sciences, this book discusses the role of lying and liars in day-to-day life. It offers profound insights into the strategies of deceit, the presence or absence of remorse, emotion and rationalisations, pathological liars, the development of lying, its connection to narcissism, the functional utility of lies, and lie detection. Lies, this book argues, are a part of the social structures inherent in everyday social life, and there is a need to explore their psychological significance in a range of natural, everyday contexts.

Written in Beattie's unique and engaging style by using elements of personal narrative and self-reflection, this is a fascinating read for students and scholars of psychology, sociology, and politics, and other disciplines of the behavioural and social sciences, as well as anyone interested in the phenomenon of lying.

Geoffrey Beattie is a professor of psychology at Edge Hill University and a visiting scholar at the University of Oxford, UK. He is a prize-winning psychologist, author, and broadcaster with a PhD in Psychology from the University of Cambridge. He was awarded the Spearman Medal by the British Psychological Society for *'published psychological research of outstanding merit.'*

Lies, Lying and Liars

A Psychological Analysis

Geoffrey Beattie

Routledge
Taylor & Francis Group

LONDON AND NEW YORK

Cover image: GettyImages\Boy_Anupong

First published 2024
by Routledge
4 Park Square, Milton Park, Abingdon, Oxon OX14 4RN

and by Routledge
605 Third Avenue, New York, NY 10158

Routledge is an imprint of the Taylor & Francis Group, an informa business

© 2024 Geoffrey Beattie

The right of Geoffrey Beattie to be identified as author of this work has
been asserted in accordance with sections 77 and 78 of the Copyright,
Designs and Patents Act 1988.

British Library Cataloguing-in-Publication Data
A catalogue record for this book is available from the British Library

Library of Congress Cataloging-in-Publication Data
Names: Beattie, Geoffrey, author.
Title: Lies, lying and liars: a psychological analysis / Geoffrey Beattie.
Description: Abingdon, Oxon; New York, NY: Routledge, [2024] |
Includes bibliographical references and index.
Identifiers: LCCN 2023054507 (print) | LCCN 2023054508 (ebook) |
ISBN 9781032495958 (hardback) | ISBN 9781032495941 (paperback) |
ISBN 9781003394563 (ebook)
Subjects: LCSH: Truthfulness and falsehood—Psychological aspects. |
Deception. Classification: LCC BF637.T77 B43 2024 (print) |
LCC BF637.T77 (ebook) | DDC 153.6—dc23/eng/20240207
LC record available at https://lccn.loc.gov/2023054507
LC ebook record available at https://lccn.loc.gov/2023054508

ISBN: 9781032495958 (hbk)
ISBN: 9781032495941 (pbk)
ISBN: 9781003394563 (ebk)

DOI: 10.4324/9781003394563

Typeset in Galliard
by codeMantra

This book is dedicated to my mother, Eileen Beattie with love.

Contents

Acknowledgements

In writing this book, I have drawn upon many sources and many experiences. Some of it is highly personal. But lying is an important topic for us all, and I felt that I had to examine these childhood and teenage experiences of mine as honestly, openly, and carefully as possible. If we are to properly understand how lies work in everyday life, we need to delve into different sorts of experience, sometimes in acts of remembering, sometimes in the memoirs of others, sometimes in what we can see on news film and video, and sometimes on the basis of what is right in front of us. I was fortunate in getting a great education which has allowed me to articulate and frame some of these early memories and experiences in a more analytic way, and I would like to thank St Marks Primary School in Ligoniel in Belfast, Belfast Royal Academy, the University of Birmingham and Trinity College, the University of Cambridge, for the opportunities they gave me. It should be obvious from this book how much I owe to Belfast Royal Academy in particular, it literally marked the 'turn of the road.' *The Guardian* allowed and encouraged me to write about the North under Margaret Thatcher and all of that devastating industrial decline and the personal and psychological consequences. I thank John Course, the Northern Features Editor, who is no longer with us, for his encouragement and incredible support throughout. This opportunity persuaded me that writing about and documenting ordinary lives out there on the street was what I, as a psychologist and social observer, needed to do. *Granta* subsequently encouraged me to write about my working-class Ulster Protestant background, and *Routledge* has been fantastic in allowing this writing to grow and develop. My agent Robert Kirby from United Agents has supported me for many years, and again I am extremely grateful for his support and encouragement. I use extracts from collected volumes published by *Chatto & Windus, Victor Gollancz, Heinemann, Granta*, and *Routledge* in this book, as well as part of an academic article published in *Semiotica*.

For the past ten years I have worked at Edge Hill University, which has been a very supportive environment in which to work, and I hope that I am contributing in my own small way to helping it achieve some of its ambitions alongside Laura McGuire, my co-worker and my rock. What this university does for working-class children in the North West of England is nothing short of remarkable. Whilst I was writing this book, I was also a Visiting Scholar at the Oxford Centre for Life-Writing and Wolfson College, the University of Oxford. This was a fantastic opportunity to learn from other visiting scholars and members of the university, and I am exceptionally grateful for this extraordinary opportunity.

I was raised by my mother in a two-up, two-down in North Belfast. She worked in the local mill. She was a strong woman, but bereft when my father died, far too young. They loved each other very much and I never once saw them argue. I know that I am like her in so many ways. She was smart and as everyone told me 'the best looking girl in Ligoniel,' but she had none of my educational opportunities. Working-class people didn't in those days. Nothing I've ever done would have been possible without her support and her love, and I dedicate this book to her. My own family know how important they are to me.

1 Introduction

Lying is essential to humanity. It plays as large a part perhaps as the quest for pleasure, and is moreover governed by that quest. One lies in order to protect one's pleasure, or one's honour if the disclosure of one's pleasure runs counter to one's honour. One lies all one's life long, even, especially, perhaps only, to those who love one. For they alone make us fear for our pleasure and desire their esteem.

Marcel Proust (1923/1925) *The Captive and The Fugitive*
(Volumes 5 and 6, *A la Recherche du Temps Perdu*)

A lie is the deliberate act of deceiving someone by presenting false information as the truth. It is an intentional deviation from what is real, authentic, or true, with the intention of leading others to believe something that is contrary to what you yourself believe, or know. Lies can take various forms and be expressed in different ways, including not only through words in speech and written statements but also through gestures and bodily actions, dress, and even through silence and inaction, in other words across the full range of the verbal and nonverbal spectrum. Gestures can substitute for words; they can communicate specific meanings like words themselves. Gestures can accompany speech and change the meaning of what is being said (Beattie 2016a). You can also dress in a particular way to help construct and transmit a false impression of who you are, in other words, a lie about personal and social identity, wealth, and status perhaps. Dress is just one example of the 'external support,' which is necessary for so many lies, as noted by the Roman orator Quintilian in A.D. 95. Sometimes, in life, you also have to speak up and speak the truth. In staying silent, in saying nothing when called upon to speak, you may be engaging in deliberate deception. As Robert Louis Stevenson noted in 1881: 'The cruellest lies are often told in silence. A man may have sat in a room for hours and not opened his teeth, and yet come out of that room a disloyal friend or a vile calumniator.' We will consider lies in many different forms throughout this book; the discipline of psychology often has a much narrower definitional focus on what constitutes a lie, and how we should study them. My view is that it is critical to look at the breadth and depth of lies in everyday life.

DOI: 10.4324/9781003394563-1

There are two primary ways to lie – you can conceal information (i.e. withhold true information without actually saying anything untrue) or you can falsify (i.e. withhold true information and also present false information as if it were true). According to one of the pioneers of scientific research on lying, Paul Ekman, liars prefer concealing to falsifying because concealment is easier – you don't have to make anything up or possess a good memory (an attribute repeatedly stressed by Quintilian in the *Institutio Oratoria* or, as the French philosopher Michel de Montaigne wrote in 1602 'Not without reason it is said that no one who is not conscious of having a sound memory should set up to be a liar'). But there is another reason why concealment is preferred, it seems less 'reprehensible' than falsification – liars feel less guilt about concealing information than falsifying. When it comes to adultery, for example, concealing information is much preferred for reasons to do with guilt. Ekman writes 'The liar can maintain the reassuring thought that that the target really knows the truth but does not want to confront it' (Ekman 1985: 29).

There are no tell-tale signs of lying per se, but there are indicators of increased or altered cognitive activity associated with the planning of the lie, and indicators of emotion (both negative and positive) associated with telling the lie – anxiety, apprehension, fear, guilt, shame, embarrassment, and, on the positive side, so-called *duping delight* – delight at getting one over on another person. This is not a complete list. The *strategy* of lying, for example, concealing versus falsifying, may have significant implications for how easy it is to detect the lie because there is less cognitive activity necessary for concealing information (falsification requires both the inhibition of the truth, as in concealment, and the planning of new, false information), and, in addition, the intensity and range of emotions associated with the concealment lie can be reduced because, as we have already noted, it may seem less reprehensible. So, from both a cognitive and emotional point of view, concealment lies are preferable from the liar's point of view (less thinking and cognitive planning, less reprehensible, less intense emotions, less chance of getting caught).

At times, lies may be seen as harmless, employed to spare another person's feelings or to avoid conflict. There are many types of so-called 'white lies' and other lies designed to calm and placate. However, it can be argued that all lies inherently erode trust and undermine the foundations of relationships. Even seemingly innocent fibs, white lies – lies for the benefit of the other person (for example, saying 'You look lovely in that dress' to your partner), can have unintended consequences, as they can create a false sense of reality (your partner keeps wearing the dress, even though they do not actually look nice in it), and the lie can thus hinder open and honest communication. When do you tell your partner that they never looked nice in that dress? What happens when they spontaneously ask 'Do I still look nice in this dress? You never tell me anymore.' How do you respond? Do you confess? Do you lie again?

What defines a lie is the intent behind it – if the purpose is to deceive or mislead, then it remains a lie regardless of its apparent harmlessness and many lies might seem harmless to the sender but not to the recipient. Indeed, there often seems to be a gulf in perception between the liar and the recipient of the lie, a gulf regarding the morality of the lie, the emotional harm caused by the lie, the implications of the lie, and the consequences for the relationship. I start to explore some of these issues in Chapter 2 (and subsequently throughout this book).

Lies are social acts, involving two people (at least), the sender and the receiver, the liar and the deceived, the perpetrator and the victim and in this book we will at times consider both parties. Academic psychology tends to have a very different focus certainly in the experimental work on the subject, where participants are invited into the laboratory and are then *instructed* to lie. There is no receiver of the lie, no deceived, no victim – we only see part of the process in action, and a very artificial part at that.

Lies can range from small, inconsequential falsehoods to elaborate, manipulative webs of deceit, from the personal to the political. White lies, for instance, are considered by most people to be socially acceptable, necessary even, as they are used to protect the feelings of others. But whilst the user of white lies may aim to maintain harmony, their underlying principle is still rooted in deception, and they may have a downside as already suggested, and the boundaries between white lies and other lies may often be blurred in everyday life. White lies do seem to be very common, as we shall see in 'Your Muffins Are the Best' (Chapter 2), when we consider the diary studies conducted by the American social psychologist Bella DePaulo on students. Much of everyday social interaction seems to be based on these sorts of lies. So common are they, that it's hard to think of them as lies at all.

Of course, at the opposite end of the spectrum, there are malicious lies that seek to harm or manipulate others. These may be used for personal gain, to damage someone's reputation, or to advance one's own personal agenda. We have to *learn* to use such lies (although lying generally does begin very early in life, as Charles Darwin noted with his own son, which we will discuss in 'The Innocence of Childhood' in Chapter 3). Some individuals are more suited to using these malicious lies than others, and much better at it. There are many natural liars, pathological liars, and expert liars out there (the boundaries between these categories are often blurred, they certainly overlap). Expert liars have strategies of deceit and ways of dealing with any possible emotional responses, like guilt or shame, and we will consider expert liars in Chapter 4. Then there are 'natural' liars and pathological liars, who tell lies frequently and effortlessly (even more effortlessly than the expert liars), liars who experience few *negative* emotions when telling a lie. Their main concealment goal is often to stop their *positive* emotions leaking out, their joy, their feelings of superiority as they fool us, their duping delight. I consider personality differences in lying in Chapter 5 and consider how the so-called 'Dark Triad' of personality characteristics, non-clinical psychopathy, narcissism, and Machiavellianism might connect to frequent and successful lying. These sorts of lies can have significant and far-reaching consequences, both on an individual level and on a much larger scale within society.

History, of course, has taught us something about the devastating power of lies, from propaganda used to manipulate the masses to false testimony leading to wrongful convictions in numerous legal systems across the globe. In Chapter 7, I consider both contemporary and historical examples of the lies of politicians – how these lies are developed and maintained, how they connect to the construction of the power and authority of the liar (power and authority are always an issue of perception, of course, and thus ripe for manipulation and deceit), how these lies are framed and delivered, and the effects these lies can have on both the rational and emotional mind. Machiavelli understood some of these processes well, but others went even beyond Machiavelli's imagination. Hitler originated the concept of the 'Big Lie' and wrote in *Mein Kampf* that he learnt it all from the British (I suppose that he had to blame somebody) and their very successful use of propaganda in the First World War (he then subsequently blamed 'the Jews – the masters of the lie'). Hitler explained how big lies can be used to manipulate a nation:

> ...in the primitive simplicity of their minds they more readily fall victims to the big lie than the small lie, since they themselves often tell small lies in little matters but would be ashamed to resort to large scale falsehoods.
> (Hitler 1925/2022: 213)

Putin developed the big lie with such arrogance with that expression 'special military operation' to describe his invasion of Ukraine. Trump told us all that climate change was a Chinese hoax (as I write this in the summer of 2023, with Spain, Greece, Canada, and Hawaii all burning, fewer people now believe this particular lie), but I also explore how Trump lies with his body language and attempts to fake the most intimate connection between the verbal and nonverbal channels in a form of *multimodal deceit*.

The significance of the lie goes beyond just the act itself; it extends to the impact they have on individuals and society as a whole. Lies erode trust, creating doubt and suspicion among individuals. When trust is compromised, relationships suffer, and cooperation becomes increasingly difficult. Trust is the very foundation upon which healthy relationships, communities, and societies are built, and thus lies can disrupt the balance and harmony that underpin our very social fabric. At the political level, lies can create scapegoats, they offer simple solutions to complex problems, they can bind people together (as Machiavelli understood) and galvanise them sometimes to horrendous actions, and all in pursuit of a falsehood. At the personal level, they can destroy relationships, friendships, families. I explore the psychological consequences of being lied to within the family home in Chapter 2 ('Please Release Me'), sometimes the response can be highly irrational, but perhaps this is just me (although I suspect not).

Of course, one must always remember that lies are not always born out of malice or ill-intent. Sometimes they may originate from fear, self-preservation, or a desire to protect oneself or others. I consider the lies of gang members in Chapter 3 ('Gangs, Lies, and Belonging'). In these instances, lies may serve as a defence mechanism, a bonding signal to keep the group together, a device to shield the individual members from potential harm or emotional distress. They may offer a degree of security, but I also suggest that these lies can have an instrumental (or even transformational) role in the shaping of attitudes and beliefs, and I discuss this in the context of cognitive dissonance and the effects that what we say can have on what we believe. Lies are not just words after all. While these self-preservation lies are still deceptive, it is important to approach such situations (as analysts) with a degree of empathy and understanding (and overcome our first reactions), recognising the complex motivations behind the lies. Indeed, when we start to unpick and analyse lies, we need a good deal of empathy generally, even when we ourselves are the recipient of the lie, and part of that empathy needs to be directed at the social situation in which the individuals, both the liar and the recipient of the lie, find themselves.

In Chapter 4, I consider lies in an important social context, indeed a critical time in British social history – the 1980s in the North of England under the Iron Lady, Prime Minister Margaret Thatcher. This was the period marked by the closing of the steel mills and the mines (and the miners' strike), and soaring unemployment. Some might say (and many did say) that this was all about the wholesale destruction of the Trade Unions and Northern working-class communities ('no such thing as society,' she famously said, as if to justify the whole thing). This period was also marked by the rise of the *Me* generation, the pursuit of selfishness with quasi-religious fervour, with yuppies in London and the South, but with hundreds of thousands thrown onto the scrap heap in the North. Two nations, one country. But what about the people caught up in all this change up there in the North ('grim up North,' they said), in Sheffield and Doncaster and Rotherham, the once proud steel and mining towns? What became of the steel workers, the miners, and all those communities that depended on them? What did they turn into? Certainly not yuppies with a role in the city, that's for sure. But did they just accept these new roles and positions imposed on them, or did they challenge them? And if they challenged them, did they ever resort to falsehoods? Did they ever lie about their destiny and their predicament and who they were? This seems to me to be an important question because we might want to consider why lies might be important for maintaining self-esteem and happiness, hope even, for creating a positive image of self (even a false positive image), and whether some lies about self-identity can be linked to broader political, social, and economic change. When economic conditions get harder and unemployment rises, do people feel an increased need to lie about who and what they are? How does the psychological need to generate falsehoods or miscommunication connect to the political and the economic pressures from above? What are the drivers of deception in society?

They have an expression in South Yorkshire – 'the ten-bob millionaire.' It's a derogatory term used to describe someone who dresses and acts like they have a lot of money when in fact they have very little. In 'Shadow Lives' in Chapter 4, we meet one ten-bob millionaire. He drove a Rolls Royce but lived in a council house. He lived a lie. When I first met him, he was employed by Yorkshire Water on forty pounds a week, and he siphoned petrol out of other cars to keep the Rolls Royce on the road. After that he was unemployed, but he maintained a sense of optimism and hope throughout all of this, by lying. I was surprised at how important that one external source, a Rolls Royce car, this status symbol, was to his whole façade. He was always vague about his work and his connections, he never gave that much away, indeed he rarely said anything of any significance. The car did all the talking in a city that was down on its luck, and yet, in this place, where they sneer at pretence and showiness and where they coined the term 'ten bob millionaire,' they warmed to John. Being a ten-bob millionaire in Sheffield in the 1980s, after the miners' strike, was a risky business but John rarely leaked any emotional discomfort. After all, what was he lying about? He was just parking his Rolls Royce in the underground car park next to Sheffield's 'top nitespot.' He let others draw their own conclusions and he did have his own internal narrative of hope, optimism, and eventual success, which may have kept him going.

It was a different type of lie to many that people tell. The shiny big car that stood out from the rest in that dark underground car park in that darkest of recessions was far more eloquent than he could ever be. The Roman scholar of rhetoric Quintilian in the first century A.D. wrote about the importance of these types of props – 'Sometimes, too, we get a false statement of fact; these...fall into two classes. In the first case the statement depends on external support...The other has to be supported by the speaker's native talent.' John had limited native talent in the game of lying (he was just very vague about everything), he depended critically on the Rolls Royce.

But there are less ostentatious props than a Rolls Royce, like an academic gown, an honest symbol of student success in a prestigious college. You have earned the gown so now you can wear it and let other people draw their own conclusions about you; let them make their own assumptions about your past and how you got there to that most prestigious of academic institutions. You can see how lies can be spun with few actual duplicitous words in 'Cloaking the Past' in Chapter 4, after all silence is hardly a lie. Or is it? Or that designer suit, and not a fake one either, the men in the know can spot snide goods a mile off. But how do you go about getting hold of a real designer suit on the cheap when you need to wear a disguise in order to play the part – when you need to be taken seriously by the high rollers and the conmen, who get everything on the cheap, the way that men in the know do. They couldn't be seen talking to someone so evidently on a lower rung of the social ladder. We will see this unfold in 'The Disguise.' You may then understand the motive behind this attempt to look the part and you may also feel the embarrassment of the protagonist a little more intensely because, let me assure you, there was a lot of embarrassment.

Some props, on the other hand, are designed to take you in the opposite direction – down the ladder rather than up, but of course 'up' and 'down' are relative terms in this and so many other contexts. Dirt on the face of the now unemployed workers as they sat outside their terraced houses in Crookes in Sheffield, taking a tea break from their home improvements, to signify that they were and *are* still grafters, prepared to get their hands dirty, ex-steel men and miners used to hard graft and dirty, dangerous work. In the 1980s, they were signalling that they certainly were not loafers on the dole, 'dolemites,' one shop owner I interviewed called those who signed on. I think that it was meant to be humorous, a blend of Dolomites (the mountain range in north-eastern Italy), dole, and head lice (mites). It wasn't particularly funny, but he laughed uproariously every time he said it. His customers were the young dolemites. But how was a tea break outside on the street without a wash of the face a lie? It wasn't. But it was a managed stage performance done for effect, done for an audience (the neighbours), and critical to maintaining their sense of self-worth. It was nonverbal rather than verbal, but they would tell you, when asked, how they were working their way round the house, so words could accompany it. Anything was better than being perceived as a loafer – a dolemite.

Of course, not all props are inanimate. People can be props. People can be the external source to back up the lie. And these sources don't even have to speak in order to do this. Inferences are made based on association alone. Cockney Richard knew this well. He was what you might call a 'hanger-on,' the 'best friend' of many of the local Sheffield celebrities, the footballers, snooker players, men who had been on TV once, or maybe twice. His glamour came primarily through association, as we will see in Chapter 4 ('The VIP').

And then, sometimes misunderstandings can arise without any props, deliberate or not. But then again, if you don't correct a misunderstanding immediately, is that a lie? I'll let you decide in 'Home Truths' in Chapter 8. Impersonation can be a serious crime or a tragedy. But is it always a lie?

I am also interested in how lies develop within the individual, the development of lying would seem to be part nature and part nurture, like most human characteristics. Charles Darwin (1877) published a detailed diary of the development of his son, William Erasmus, and he describes the first instances of his son lying to him. He described how his son then aged 2 years 7½ months ate some sugar in the dining room which he had been explicitly told not to do. A fortnight later, Darwin describes how his son was looking at his pinafore which he had carefully rolled up as he came out of the dining room, and Darwin notes that his manner was just a little odd. Darwin asked to see the child's pinafore, but his son *commanded* him to 'go away.' The pinafore, it turns out, was stained with pickle-juice, which his son had been forbidden from eating, so Darwin concludes that 'here was carefully planned deceit.' When you read Darwin's diary, it's almost as if these actions of his young child (who Darwin clearly doted on) have taken him completely by surprise, having witnessed what he interprets as the *pleasure of lying* in one so young.

And Darwin emphasises that this child was being brought up in a household where he had 'never been in any way punished,' so there was no necessity to lie. Furthermore, his son's lies were carefully planned. Darwin does not say so explicitly, but he clearly cannot seem to find any explanation in the child's upbringing or early childhood experience which it could be attributed to, and on that great seesaw of nature versus nurture, you can see that he's grappling with lying tipping in the opposite direction, towards a non-learned instinctive response to the world.

In other words, lying seems to be part of our DNA but can be, and clearly is, augmented by experience (Darwin seems very keen to tell us that his son turned out okay in the end). I discuss how children learn to lie and how it correlates with intelligence, and what happens in those mysterious hard to observe teenage years when teenagers are left to their own devices and lie repeatedly (all in Chapter 3 'Gangs, Lies, and Belonging'), and what the consequence might be.

Of course, in a world where lies can be spread rapidly through technology and social media, distinguishing truth from falsehood becomes increasingly challenging. The prevalence of misinformation and fake news highlights the need for critical thinking, research, and fact-checking. Some well-meaning people would say that fostering an environment that encourages open dialogue, respect, and understanding can contribute to reducing the temptation to lie and promoting honesty. But clearly lying can give the individual a powerful advantage in many situations. The sociobiologist Robert Trivers in his book *'Deceit'* shows why this is so, and why self-deceit is so critical. He argues that self-deceit makes lies more convincing and more effective and therefore more advantageous from an evolutionary point of view. Nietzsche (1895) in the *Anti-Christ* had commented that 'The most common lie is the lie one tells to oneself; lying to others is relatively the exception.' But the two may be intimately connected for good reason.

In Chapter 6, we turn to 'Lie Detection' and consider how good professional lie detectors *and* the public are at identifying lies. The answer is that both groups seem to be very poor at this and I want to try to understand why. Are they looking out for the wrong things? Are they inadvertently influencing the suspected liar's behaviour so that they can then spot the cues they're looking for in the first place? Are cues to deception too unreliable, too faint, too quick to be reliably spotted? Are we just too different from each other with so many different internal strategies in place to disguise our various lies? I will consider all of these and more.

There is nothing new about lying, of course, or nothing new about commentary, critical thinking, and the analysis of lies. Plato (375 BCE) considered whether the Gods can lie in the *Republic* (in the dialogue involving Socrates and Plato's brother Adeimantus; the conclusion seems to be that 'God has, then no reason to tell lies...God is therefore without deceit or falsehood in action or word'). In the *Republic*, Plato also introduced the concept of the 'noble lie' to preserve social harmony; Aristotle, on the other hand, wrote about the social qualities associated with truth and falsehood, stating that 'Falsehood is in itself bad and reprehensible.' Lies appear many times in the Bible in both the Old and the New Testaments. Jacob pretended to be his brother Esau to receive the blessing from his father Isaac; Samson lied to Delilah about the source of his strength; Peter denied that he knew Jesus after his arrest, not once but three times ('Woman, I do not know him,' Luke 22: 54), as Jesus himself had predicted. In Peter's case, it was a lie of self-preservation that was reprehensible and caused great remorse, and Peter, of course had denied that it would ever occur. Samson's lie was also about self-preservation. Jacob's was a more strategic lie, although self-preservation lies are, it must be said, also very strategic.

Lies have been with us from the beginning. In the story of the Creation in Genesis, lies are told in the Garden of Eden and responsible for *The Fall*. God forbids Adam and Eve from eating the fruit of one particular tree (God says, 'You must not eat fruit from the tree that is in the middle of the garden, and you must not touch it, or you will die.'). But the 'serpent' (figuratively, one imagines, the dark side of human nature) tells Eve that this is a lie, and Adam and Eve both eat the fruit and consequently both acquire self-knowledge. But they fear that they have disobeyed God. They then

> heard the sound of the LORD God as he was walking in the garden in the cool of the day, and they hid from the LORD God among the trees of the garden. But the LORD God called to the man, "Where are you?" He answered, "I heard you in the garden, and I was afraid because I was naked; so I hid." And he said, "Who told you that you were naked? Have you eaten from the tree that I commanded you not to eat from?"

Of course, Adam was in fear because he had disobeyed God and was naked as a consequence, not just because he was naked (his nakedness was the sign that he had disobeyed him). So, his response was a lie. In the Bible, lies are at the very beginning of Creation, as are the justifications for wrongdoing, with Adam blaming Eve for his action, and Eve blaming the serpent. It seems that both lies and justifications have been there from the very beginning, at least in our constructions of our beginnings in the book of Genesis.

But lies do seem particularly prevalent at the present time. We live in precarious and perilous times with climate change and all its consequences (including mass migration), and war in Ukraine that could turn nuclear (we are constantly being 'reassured' about the possible use of tactical or battlefield nuclear weapons in the conflict). And lies are central to many of the issues we face, exacerbating the problems – lies about the origins of climate change generating doubt and indifference in the public as the crisis grows, lies about the invasion of a sovereign country that seems to have no obvious easy resolution (in 2023 at least). Lies dominate all our lives, and it seems control all our destinies. I want to understand the psychology of lies, the processes of lying, and I want to analyse the people who tell them. If we all tell lies, that is if we are all liars, I want to know why, and I want to consider whether that is significant and what its consequences might be. But my guess is that certain types of lies connect to certain types of people and I want to consider the traits of these individuals. I want to consider big lies and small lies, lies with obvious consequences and seemingly inconsequential lies, lies that 'help' others, and lies that only help ourselves. Indeed, I want to ask whether it's easy to distinguish between 'other-oriented' and 'self-oriented' lies as some psychologists have maintained in influential papers. I want to ask whether some lies are acceptable, necessary even, and in what contexts and for what reasons. I'm interested in how lies and lying are justified and rationalised by those who use them because this might be a critical element in their use. I'm interested in why we fall for lies and why we seem so poor at identifying lies. Is there a reason behind this? Do we sometimes want to be fooled by lies for our own personal reasons? Some lies after all may make us feel good and many (or some?) everyday lies may have this particular orientation. But lies also shape our world and perhaps ultimately, they will determine all our destinies. They end the careers of British Prime Ministers (this is 2023, so Boris Johnson has gone), are used by Presidents (and ex-Presidents) of the United States to offer alternative facts about climate change and build seemingly parallel paranoid worlds. They are employed by a President of Russia to justify war and the invasion of a country through a 'special military operation' to rid it of 'Nazism', and lies have led this President into a corner where nuclear war in now threatened. 'The U.K. will be like a Martian landscape,' says one of his approved commentators, but hopefully this too will turn out to be a bluff, a lie.

However, psychological research tells us that lies are not just the bread and butter of politicians, they are the stuff of everyday life. Children learn to lie very early on, and brighter children lie more and at younger ages – sometimes for positive and empathetic reasons, but sometimes not. Some lies are much more significant and damaging, with consequences for both the recipient and the liar. We should never underestimate the destructive power of some lies. I explore some of these themes in the opening chapters of the book.

There is so much that we don't know about lying and if we are to understand lying, we need to view lies and lying in their natural social contexts. That is what is different about the approach I will be taking. Lies are social acts that need to be observed and analysed *in situ*. We need to understand the social structures of lies and how they connect to the people who use them. My initial research has been focusing on historical and political autobiographies and biographies, philosophical texts, and the core psychological literature, including sociobiological perspectives. I have background empirical research material (both observations and interviews) with individuals who live their lives though lies – conmen, 'ten-bob' millionaires, cheats, and adulterers. I will explore the views (and sometimes the personal experiences of lying) of a wide range of scholars including Aristotle, Quintilian, Al-Ghazali, Machiavelli, Michel de Montaigne, Jean Jacques Rousseau, and others.

I am interested in the psychology of the liar, strategies of deceit, remorse or lack of it, emotion and rationalisations, pathological liars, the development of lying, lying and narcissism, functional and effective lies, big lies like those of Putin and how these are maintained, the consequences of lying, and lie detection. There is an element of personal reflection throughout the book. 'I remember the first time my mother lied to me' is the opening sentence of the next chapter, moving towards the end of that chapter onto research in psychology on lies in everyday life, and why psychology (in my view) has drawn the wrong conclusions from this research. My underlying assumption is that lying can only properly be understood in the context of individual lives, including my own.

Perhaps, psychology as a discipline neglects the situation in which natural actions (like lying) occur a little too much, instead of far too often inviting people into the unnatural and artificial laboratory and instructing them to lie, so that they can study it. That is simply not how lies work and any science based exclusively on this approach and method is going to be not just limited but fundamentally flawed. Research in neuroscience now tells us that real spontaneous natural lies and instructed lies use different neural pathways (Yin et al. 2016). Spontaneous lying is associated with higher levels of activity in the subgenual anterior cingulate cortex compared to spontaneously telling the truth; instructed lying shows higher levels of activity in the right inferior frontal gyrus, left supplementary motor area, anterior cingulate cortex, inferior parietal lobule, and superior frontal gyrus (Yin et al. 2016). In other words, in terms of basic brain mechanisms, they are quite different. Delgado-Herrera and colleagues (2021) reviewed the literature on the neuroscience of deception and concluded that experimental studies of deception using functional brain imaging have low ecological validity, that is, any results obtained in this research would not generalise easily to the real world. They summarise the five most frequent weaknesses found in laboratory-based deception studies, namely (1) the use of instructed lies, (2) lies in the laboratory generate little or no sanction, (3) low fear of failure, (4) low motivation experienced by participants, and (5) limited social interaction. They finish with a plea for more research in this area with greater ecological validity, that is, there should be more research on real natural lies, lies that people are motivated to make and with some stake attached to them – the lies that occur out there in the society. Lies are not just utterances that we generate when instructed; they are social acts occasioned by social situations and we will consider some of these social situations in detail.

I am also reminded of what the philosopher Karl Popper once wrote:

Our actions are to a very large extent explicable in terms of the situation in which they occur. Of course, they are never fully explicable in terms of the situation alone; an explanation of the way in which a man, when crossing a street, dodges the cars which move on it may go beyond the situation, and may refer to his motives, to an 'instinct' of self-preservation, or to his wish to avoid pain, etc. But this 'psychological' part of the explanation is very often trivial, as compared with the detailed determination of his action by what we may call the *logic of the situation*; and besides, it is impossible to include all psychological factors in the description of the situation. The analysis of situations, the situational logic, play a very important part in social life.

Karl Popper (1945/1983: 353) *The Autonomy of Sociology*

In this book, we will find ourselves in many diverse situations, from a mill house in Belfast in the late 1960s to the Constantine Palace in the Kremlin on the eve of the invasion of Ukraine, from Crookes in Sheffield after the miners' strike to Charles Darwin's Georgian manor (Down House) in Kent in the mid-nineteenth century, from Samuel Pepys's dowdy London to Donald Trump's shiny Mar-a-Lago estate, with the bathroom crammed with confidential and top-secret government documents (it turns out). But, of course, we should never forget that when it comes to lying, the *social* situation (rather than the physical situation) is the most important thing and social situations have social acts and structures, and they have actors with their own particular needs, beliefs, attitudes, fears, goals, personalities, and experiences. That's what makes a psychological exploration of lies, lying, and liars so challenging, and so very exciting.

2 Lies in Everyday Life

The pre-eminence of truth over falsehood... truth is as a gentle fountain breathing from forth its air-let into the snow piled over and around it, which it turns into its own substance, and flows with greater murmur; and though it be again arrested, still it is but for a time; – it awaits only the change of the wind, to awake and roll onwards its ever increasing stream.

But falsehood is fire in stubble; it likewise turns all the light stuff around it into its own substance for a moment, one crackling blazing moment, – and then dies; and all its converts are scattered in the wind, without place or evidence of their existence, as viewless as the wind which scatters them.

Samuel Taylor Coleridge (1812: 210) *Table Talk*

Please Release Me

I remember the first time my mother lied to me. My father had died a few months before. I was thirteen years old. I hated going to bed. Her sobbing would start almost immediately. She'd be calling out his name. It was so loud that I'm sure that the neighbours could hear through the paper-thin walls of our mill house in that little grey terraced street in North Belfast.

The 'turn-of-the-road,' they called the area, where the Upper Crumlin Road twists round towards the linen mills in Ligoniel, all owned by the Ewarts family. My mother worked in the spinning mill up in Ligoniel. She idolised the owner Sir William Ewart – she would see him on his annual visit. 'He looked like a film star,' she would say.

He wore an eye patch; he had lost his left eye in the war. He was a war hero – very dashing, a bit like David Niven. All the girls would come out to see him, he'd give us all a wee wave. He had lovely overcoats – they must have been made of wool or cashmere or something like that. We'd never seen anything like it.

There was a big sign outside the mill, 'EWARTS,' the sign said. But all I remember now is that later the 'E' fell off some time during the Troubles when nobody cared any longer about things like that. The sign just spelt out 'WARTS,' I laughed every time I passed it. When I told my mother about this,

DOI: 10.4324/9781003394563-2

she looked at me as if I had desecrated it myself. That's where she had spent her working life.

You could hear everything in that house of ours from outside and in. The shooting and the bombs during the Troubles ('they're at it again, not far away tonight,' my mother would say nonchalantly, she was never a nervous woman), and the crying over my father from the front room after his death. There was no privacy or escape in that little house.

'Billy,' my mother would cry over and over again. It went on for month after month. I wanted that noise to stop. I would push my fingers deep into my ears and lie there in the dark, praying for it to cease. I never confessed to her that I ever heard it. It was unbearable. She must have thought that I was asleep. That was my lie. That was what I let her think.

There were only two of us in the house most of the time – my brother was usually away climbing mountains far from here – the Mournes, the Alps, the Rockies, the Hindu Kush, finally the Himalayas, but that was his last adventure. So, there was only me there to comfort her, but I had no idea how.

After my father's death, as the months passed, my mother started meeting her friends for a drink in town on a Saturday afternoon, usually in Corn Market right in the centre of Belfast, and she would sometimes socialise into the early evening, it was the only time she got out, and she'd come back about seven or eight, sometimes with the grocery shopping still in her bag. I remember that she sat on the bag once and fell asleep. I tried to pull it from under her without waking her so that I could have some dinner. She was having trouble coping; I could see that. But I was too shy, too nervous, too ill-prepared to try to get her to open up to me. All I heard about her grief, all she ever communicated to me about her pain, was the sobbing, which came from the front bedroom into the back room, even with the door tightly shut. Sharp, sobbing sentences, sometimes without a pause. The same sentences repeated and repeated, the same theme. 'Why did you leave me?'

My father had gone into the Royal Victoria Hospital for some tests. He wasn't going to tell us. My Uncle Terence let this slip on the night before; he whispered to my father that he had bought the pyjamas for him, and he'd hidden them down the back of the settee so my mother wouldn't see them. My mother overheard the two of them whispering away. We were all shocked, my mother started crying, my father said that he didn't want to worry us, it was just routine tests, he assured us, nothing more. We saw him in his new pyjamas the next night, sitting up in his hospital bed, his glasses loose and hanging off his nose. He was looking forward to getting it sorted out. Whatever it was. My mother was the last to leave. She was holding his hand to the last minute. I watched them. That was the last time I saw him alive.

Something must have happened in the operation, it was always more than a test, nobody in my family was sure what, and he never regained consciousness. They never really explained much to a mill worker like my mother. He lay in a coma for a week and died the following Sunday. They just told my mother that he'd have been a vegetable if he'd survived, presumably to try to cheer her up, so that she might agree that his death was the less painful option.

I had examinations at my school, Belfast Royal Academy, the week he was in the coma and every day on the way home when the bus passed the bottom of Barginnis Street I'd look up to our house in Legmore Street to see if the blinds had been pulled down. My heart would be in my mouth. The blinds stayed up all week, which meant there was hope. His body wasn't ready to be laid out in the front room just yet.

I prayed for him every night. I would promise God *anything* He might want, anything I could think of, if He would just make him better. I memorised new prayers, maybe that would make the difference. I would run through ten or eleven Sunday school prayers, memorised to perfection, punishing myself if I made a slip, that slip might be important, it might suggest that I wasn't caring enough, that I wasn't dedicated enough to my father's survival, before I got onto my special direct pleading with Him, God the Father, God the Almighty, that most merciful God.

I wasn't allowed to see my father in that sleeping state of his ('he'll wake up soon,' my mother said), my brother was allowed in, and my mother stayed with him all the time. 'He was always twiddling with my wedding ring when I was holding his hand,' my mother would say, 'he knew I was there – right until the end he knew I was there, I couldn't leave him on his own. I couldn't go home without him.'

'But' she added, 'he never came back to me.'

He died on a wet Sunday night, the Lord's Day, we still call it in Northern Ireland, a night with lashing rain, lashing your face, and freezing cold in February. I heard the news in the car park of the Royal Victoria Hospital. My Aunt Agnes and I were on the way to the hospital, my Uncle Terence was supposed to have picked us up in his Ford Anglia. But he hadn't come; my Aunt Agnes was angry at him – we'd got the bus, she was swearing. We met Big Terry in the car park coming towards us, tears streaming down that big round Irish face of his. The 'Big Fella,' they all called him. I had never seen him cry before. He was a man's man, a hard worker, a good drinker, he could stand up for himself, and he did. Everybody in those mill streets of ours respected him, he'd been a very good amateur boxer. He would roll up his sleeves when he had to, no sneaky first punch, plenty of forewarning, he'd ask them to step outside, 'not in front of the women and children,' he'd say. My mother always said that there was an awful lot of second thoughts when Big Terry started to roll his sleeves up, an awful lot of fear.

One of the best amateur boxers to come out of Ligoniel,' Isaac the barber would say about him when he came down to cut our hair, 'nobody would take him on.' And Isaac, this dapper little man with round glasses, was so old that he knew a thing or two about the history of Ligoniel and its boxers, probably an encyclopaedic knowledge, so that's why his comments about my Uncle Terence mattered. I remember Isaac's barber's shop from when I was a child with the black-and-white photos of boxers around the walls, and the mirrors, and the big brush by the door for sweeping up the hair. It's an almost sensory memory of the clippers taking off the hair at the back, it's like an itch, and I find myself shivering now as I remember him tucking the gown in. Isaac didn't do neck shaves; you had to go to a more modern hairdresser at the bottom of Oakley Street for one of those. He only did short back and sides, and you could either go to his shop or he came to your house. He came to our house once a month on a Thursday night and cut our hair in front of the fire, me, Bill, and then my father, always in that order. 'Who's going first?' he would say, as if there was some room for negotiation. My mother would say, 'Our Geoffrey will go first, Isaac,' the same every month.

Isaac knew a lot about the people of Ligoniel and the boxing but, in my view, he never knew that much about stylish barbering. 'Neck shave? What's that?' he'd say. My brother and I would hide when he came to the house to cut our hair. This was the sixties and a new fashion in hair. But Isaac never cared much for fashion; he was old-fashioned, and he liked Big Terry, who was old-fashioned too in the way he conducted himself, the embodiment of traditional manly values up in Ligoniel.

Isaac always liked to tell my mother and father that he remembered going down with his best friend Edward McMurray to see the shipyard's biggest ship being launched. 'The Titanic was an awful big ship, awful big,' he said, 'with four massive funnels. They said it was unsinkable, but I remember that I wasn't surprised when it went down. There was a lot of talk about it in the barber's shop for weeks afterwards.' On other visits, he would talk about the First World War and how he had tried to enlist with his best friend Edward McMurray in the 36th Ulster Division in 1914. Edward was passed as medically fit, but they wouldn't accept Isaac because he had a weakness in one leg. 'I damaged it playing football,' he would say.

> I argued with them about it, I begged them to let me join up. I told them that you don't pull a trigger with your leg. But it was no good. I had to stay at home while Edward went off to war.

His friend Edward was a runner – he carried the messages in the 15th Battalion of the Ulster Volunteer Force, the 36th Ulster Division. 'Nearly all the Ligoniel men, both Protestant and Catholic, joined the 15th Battalion,' said Isaac.

> Edward fought at the Somme. He came back without one of his legs and with half a hand missing. He was in a sorry state; I can tell you. He talked about the war a lot, but the funny thing was he never talked about the Somme. He never seemed to want to discuss the Somme itself. He used to sit in his front room, picking bits of shrapnel and bits of dirt out of his good leg when he was reminiscing. The problem with his good leg was that because there were so many little wounds in it, all the dirt of the day seemed to get caught in it. I used to look after it for him.

Of course, it wasn't just Edward McMurray who was silent. It seems that few of those who came back from the Somme ever talked about what they had experienced or showed their emotion. Some were literally mute and the Canadian-born therapist Dr, Lewis Yealland (1918) back in the United Kingdom was pioneering new techniques to cure the mutism associated with shell shock, brought on by a new type of warfare, trench warfare, where neither fight nor flight was possible. Yealland would prop the mouths of these young working-class soldiers open by means of a tongue depressor and apply 'a strong faradic current to the posterior wall of the pharynx,' giving them an electric shock to cure their mutism – to get some noise out of them, even a whispered 'ah.' His goal, he explained, was to get them to say 'thank you' at the end of the 'therapy' session – not mouth it, but to say it properly, like a man should.

My grandfather had been in the army, he didn't talk too much about what he had experienced, my mother never seemed to know exactly where he'd served, 'abroad somewhere,' she'd say. She at least knew that he'd served in South Africa and India. Anywhere else? I'd ask. 'The Somme?'

'How would I know,' she'd reply tetchily. 'He didn't like to talk about it. None of them did, even when they'd had a drink, they still wouldn't talk about those things.'

Isaac knew a thing or two about manly values and the history of those wee mill streets. You just get on with things and do what's required, don't let yourself down or make a song and dance of it, never let it all out, say nothing, take your punishment. Even if it's some bloody doctor putting electrodes into your mouth to punish you a bit more. You still say nothing, out of spite.

And he admired Big Terry, he was always a man in control of himself. But Big Terry cried that night in the car park, I'm sure of that, even though I heard him later tell my Aunt Agnes that it was just the rain running down his face, not bloody salty women's tears. And then he cried on the day of the funeral itself, but he hid away up in our back bedroom for that. I caught him up there. I walked right in on it. My mother was wondering where he was, she sent me up the stairs to look for him. He looked embarrassed, ashamed even when I walked in on him; he turned away and covered his face. And he told me that he'd be down in a minute.

I thought that crying twice in a lifetime wasn't really that bad for a man's man like the Big Fella. But I know that he felt ashamed of letting himself down like that.

My Uncle Terence was my father's brother-in-law and his best friend. He loved my father. But they were from either side of that great religious divide in Northern Ireland, that religious divide that has been responsible for so much misery. My Uncle Terence was the Fenian in the family, and we all loved him. But he hadn't been allowed to come to our house to take my Aunt Agnes out until after my grandfather had died. He wasn't allowed into his other brother-in-law's house for nearly forty years. My Uncle Jack, married to my mother's other sister May, was in the Black (the Royal Black Institution, which dates from 1797, two years after the formation of the Orange Order). The Black must have frowned on mixed marriages, although frowned hardly does justice to this level of social exclusion. The Big Fella wasn't allowed in their house; he was never out of ours. My grandfather himself had been an Orangeman, a notch down from the Black; my grandfather's wee Orange Order sash still lay in the top drawer of the dresser in our front room, that big booming sound of the Lambeg drum, that most Protestant of musical instruments, woven into its very fabric. But quelled at last. The sash just lay there quietly in that drawer, smelling of moth balls. My father wasn't interested in joining the Orange Order, even though he was from the Shankill, the Protestant heartland of Belfast, and neither was my brother nor I. We couldn't hate Fenians with Big Terry in the family.

But they, at least, were the days of family. Now there was none. My Aunt Agnes and Uncle Terence moved across the water to England just after my father's death because Big Terry said that he was being discriminated against in his work in the naval stores in Sydenham because of his religion; he said that he was always turned down for promotion in the Protestant Civil Service. Then my brother set off to climb mountains far away, far from our street. Now, there was just the two of us in that house, waiting for those one-sided conversations of grief to start. Every night, lying there waiting for it to start all over again.

I could hear my mother seeming to wait for an answer to those calls of grief of hers, and that was the most unbearable part of all for me to listen to. I had to live with *her* expectation and disappointment. She wanted to hear his voice again. Just the once. That's what grief does. It forces you to cling onto desperate ideas – clinging onto hope where there is none, wanting him back, wanting him to answer.

But then the noise at night in our house stopped. I didn't notice it at first. Not immediately. I was always waiting for it to begin. But it seemed to have passed, like a summer storm. Quieter, in the distance, fading, almost imperceptibly.

I noticed that my mother was coming back from town slightly later now. She was wearing make-up, lipstick. I'd never seen her with lipstick before, except in black-and-white photographs when I was in the pram with my brother standing beside it with a beach ball under his arm, and my father with his jacket and his open-necked shirt looking so proud of his family and his good-looking wife. Everyone told him he was a very lucky man. 'The best-looking girl in Ligoniel,' everybody told him.

She was wearing red lipstick now; I don't know what colour lipstick she was wearing in the black-and-white photographs.

I dreamt about my father most nights at that time. He was a motor mechanic for Belfast Corporation, he worked on the buses in their Falls Road depot, but he knew that I wasn't interested in cars and engines or those kinds of mechanical things. He never tried to persuade me. My brother was more practical in all those sorts of ways, he had served his time as an electrician and even his rock-climbing and mountaineering had, it seems, endless technical activities and devices like the carabineer, the crampon, and the belay to mess about with and fix. My brother would watch what my father did when he tinkered with parts of the seized-up engines of our neighbours lying there on our scullery floor. I would just play or read, the grammar schoolboy indifferent to this practical world of objects and things, oily, messy, dirty things.

'You'll never have to get your hands dirty in work,' my mother would say, and my father would look proudly at me, proud to have had such a clever son. 'The first child from Ligoniel to pass the Eleven-Plus in a generation,' my mother would remind me. 'You could be a wee clerk or something like that. We have clerks in the mill, and they have lovely clean hands, not like the rest of the workers.'

My father would come home from work every night in his oily overalls and then help with the neighbour's cars out on the street. His oily overalls never seemed to come off. But he would never take any money for the work. The Big Fella said that he was too soft; my mother always agreed. He lay below those cars in all weathers on wet sodden newspapers that stuck to the road, and he would smile up at me as if to say, you'll never have to do this for a living. Keep those studies going. My mother always said that she had never seen a father and a son who were so close.

So, in my dreams, my father would be working away on an oily stripped engine sitting on a sheet of newspaper in our scullery, and I would be sitting beside him with my toy soldiers on the linoleum floor, like in real life, but when I talked to him in my dream, he would ignore me, then I would realise that he couldn't hear me. I'd shake him and shake him. Until I realised, I was shaking nothing. Just an oily rag or a dirty bit of blanket.

One night the shaking dream woke me up. I lay there in the dark in our back bedroom, up against the damp wall. The bed only had three good legs – the leg at the top of the bed by the wall had broken years ago and there was nobody there to fix it, so you would inevitably end up against the damp wall. Sometimes, you almost felt trapped there. I lay there listening carefully but there was no sobbing from my mother's bedroom. She must be asleep, I thought to myself, at last. I was relieved. I felt drowsy and about to fall back into a deep sleep, trying to reconnect with my father in my ongoing dream. And then I heard my mother talk and then a man's voice from downstairs. Quiet, whispering but still unmistakable and then some music started playing. It was Engelbert Humperdinck; I'll never forget that. The song was 'Please Release Me.' There were long silences, and then more quiet talk. I listened for a while but couldn't make out any of the words from the man. The same song was played again and then again.

I went to the top of the stairs and listened. I could still hear the quiet voices, whispering away. I shouted down the stairs. 'Mammy, is there somebody in the house with you?' She came to the bottom of the stairs. Our small front room was filled with the smell of alcohol, perfume, and cigarette smoke. It was an overpowering sort of smell, like a creeping smog that advanced up the stairs. My mother smoked occasionally some nights, but that night it was thicker, more pungent, it made me cough.

'There's nobody down here, son. Go back to sleep.'

'But I heard a man's voice, mammy.'

'There's nobody here, son. You must be dreaming.'

But I knew what my dream had been about. There was no man talking in my dream. My father had stopped saying anything in my dreams. He was silent.

I went back to bed and listened. She put the record back on, that same song again, a forty-five played on our little Dansette record player, but I could still hear them whispering away. Eventually, I must have fallen asleep. I don't know what time the man left, but I knew that somebody had been there.

In the morning I never mentioned it. It would have been too embarrassing, too painful for me. We both pretended it had never happened, just like the sobbing, and the desperate conversations with a husband who couldn't answer back. Just one more secret to be buried.

But then I started questioning myself about this. What if grief can do this to you? I could see what it was doing to my mother. What might it be doing to me? Was it making me imagine things?

But the following Saturday night it happened all over again. I recognised that same tune, that long 'P-l-e-a-s-e' at the start and it pulled me out of my sleep. This song still gives me a visceral and very unpleasant feeling. Nauseous, even. I smelt the perfume and the alcohol, and the cigarettes, and I listened and listened, and sure enough there was a man's voice and my mother's whispering again. It wasn't loud enough to allow me to form an image of him, but loud enough for me to know that it was not my imagination. I lay there. I knew she had been lying.

A couple of days later, she was making dinner in the scullery. I lay down on the floor in the front room and pretended that I was dead. I left the TV on. She came in with the plates (we always ate in the front room in front of the TV with our dinners on our lap; the backroom was too damp) and she just stepped right over me. She sat down heavily on the settee; the air made a whooshing sound – I wanted to laugh but didn't.

'Get up, you stupid wee bugger,' she said. I lay there face down, it was better that she couldn't see my face in case I gave the game away, not moving. She put my plate on the pouffe beside me. I was watching her through the thinnest slits of my eyes.

'It's getting cold,' she prodded me with her foot. 'I've gone to all that trouble to make it, and you're just lying there, playing the bloody fool.' She shook me, 'Get up!' I lay there motionless. There was no discernible breathing. She was getting much angrier; I could tell from the tone of her voice; I was listening out for every little change in her pitch.

'If you don't get up, I'll put that bloody dinner in the bin.' There was no response from me; you could just hear the clock on the mantelpiece ticking away below the sound of the TV. She got up and turned the TV off to get my attention. At first, I had been trying not to laugh, and that had been difficult, but now it had become more serious. It was like a contest – a test of wills. It was easier to stay face down and dead. She picked up the plate with some force so that some bits of potato landed on my back, walked out into our back yard, and threw the food, plate, and all into the bin. I noticed later bits of liver and onions around the top of the bin for days afterwards, picked over by stray cats and rats.

I was still lying there, motionless, serious, determined, apparently not breathing. She went into the scullery and then rushed back out in frustration and grabbed me by the shoulders and forcibly lifted me up and started to shake me. She was screaming into the back of my head. I thought she might be about to cry.

I burst out laughing; she let me drop to the floor, bumping my head but I was still laughing.

She wasn't amused by this little 'performance' of mine and sulked for days. She said that she thought that I might need to see someone. 'There's something the matter with you,' she said. She threatened to take me to the doctor.

I've often thought about this incident of feigning death (which was repeated but never with the same force as the first time) and wondered how it might have connected with her lie; indeed, whether it did connect with it. If it did, I suppose one might suggest that it was a strategy for me to regain some control, to show her that I had some power in this relationship, and perhaps it was even a signal that I too could deceive.

The two things – the play-acting and the lie, however, were never connected in *her* mind, I suppose, because she never realised then that I knew she had been lying. Of course, it was just a joke on my part, but at another level, it was a silent and cruel act, given that the person she loved most had been lying quite still in that same little room a few months before. We always bring our dead home so that friends and neighbours can pay their respects, but because we're Protestant, it is never much of a wake. Perhaps, me playing dead at that time had greater psychological significance for me too – I loved my father more than anybody, so perhaps, I just wanted to punish her for her lying (but that's a thought that only came after years of reflection).

We still didn't talk about that song or the smoking on a Saturday night or the whispering. They were still taboo. And then it all happened again. The song started up, always that same bloody song, I felt a little bolder now, perhaps because of my power-play, feigning death, my silent empowerment. Communicating without words.

I went down the stairs quietly, sneakily. My mother spotted me before I could see into the living room, but I was close enough to sense him.

'What are you doing?' She was angry, I could tell that. All I remember thinking was that her anger revealed some guilt about something. Why should she be angry if I just couldn't sleep?

'I told you before, there's nobody here. Do you think I'd bring somebody back, so soon after your father's death? Go back up those stairs. You're just imagining things.'

But I knew that I wasn't imagining things. I didn't want to walk in on it. Whatever it was. I would hear those words of 'Please Release me' and feel physically sick (and oddly, I still do today). A song associated with heavy perfume, the smell of a drink-soaked carpet and lies. But I knew I had to.

I climbed back up the stairs and sat for a few minutes on the top stair out of view and then went back down the stairs and straight into the smog, I felt bold, emboldened by a search for the truth, and there *he* sat on the settee by the TV. Bald and chubby, a bit nondescript, not at all like my father. My father and mother looked like film stars, that's what everybody told me. He threw me a nervous and embarrassed smile. He glanced at my mother. 'Your mother talks a lot about you and your brother, you know,' he said, presumably to reassure me and engage with me. But I didn't want to engage with him, I just nodded and said that I needed the toilet which was out in our yard. I was wondering if he lived in a house like ours. A yard full of broken bricks and a toilet with the corrugated iron roof lifted by the wind and no electric light. I wasn't surprised that later I found out he didn't. He had found a good-looking widow woman who worked in the mill. Poor and desperate.

'Wee millies,' my mother would always complain in those days, 'that's what they call us girls from the mill.' It was always a disparaging comment in the Belfast of the 1960s and 1970s, full of connotations not just about social class and position, but about behaviour and morality, about low sexual mores.

'They think we're "good things" my mother always said, '"easy things." I never tell anyone I'm a millie when I meet them.'

She didn't ask me what I thought of Andy, and she told me very little about him. I knew the area where he lived, where all the houses had wee tidy gardens and inside toilets. He wouldn't have been used to having to go to the toilet in the backyard in the pitch black. But at least Andy coming round stopped the sobbing at nights. It was only many years later I found out that he was married.

With my father gone, I had to toughen up – that's what everybody told me. 'You're not a wee boy anymore, you're thirteen,' relatives would say helpfully. 'You and your brother have to look after your mother, there's no man in the house now.' So, did this toughening up and looking after my mother apply to dealing with these blatant lies? Was this what leaving childhood was all about? You must hear lies and pretend that you haven't? Is that what becoming an adult was all about – putting up with lying?

Of course, I understood what occasioned them, I could see that she was probably trying to protect me, as well as herself perhaps, covering her guilt. It is interesting that when psychologists analyse lies and lying, they often try to maintain this distinction between other-centred lies – lies to make the other person feel better, and self or ego-centred lies – lies to advantage the teller of the lie. But it seems in everyday life the distinction might be a little bit more complex than that. Her lie was doing both simultaneously. And had she thought about the implications of telling her son that amid all this grief that he was starting to imagine things. What psychological harm could that have caused? Psychologists and other social scientists want to consider potential harm as one of the fundamental dimensions when discussing and analysing lies but what degree of anticipation of harm goes into the planning of lies? How empathetic do you have to be to imagine the harm? And what about the effects on the behaviour of the recipient of the lie?

And there are other big questions? Do we all learn to lie as a consequence of what we are exposed to when we are young? Do we find lying adaptive when we've seen how those close to us use them? Did this help shape how I have got through life – indeed how I have lived my life?

But this incident helped me understand that lies can be critically important to relationships and to life. I've never underestimated their power, including their destructive power. Sometimes when I read the psychological studies on lies in everyday life, I don't see this power in operation, they all seem such benign lies, such inconsequential lies, and I therefore need to consider the psychological literature on this topic very carefully. Sometimes, it seems to me that we need the emotional filter of everyday lived experience to properly appraise the more 'objective' science behind ordinary behaviour including lying.

And this incident taught me something else. Lies are embedded in the patterns of everyday life, into social structures, starting with the original lie and the response, which in my case was feigning death (coincidentally, everyone whom I've told this story to seem quite horrified by my 'disturbed' action), but the structures build from there – like growing a crystal from a few specs of magnesium sulphate, where the structure of the crystal eventually becomes solidified and rigid. I ended up telling a lot of lies to my mother, about where I was going into the night in the Belfast of the Troubles. All teenagers do lie but maybe some of my lies were a bit more serious and a bit darker. We were in a gang, after all, the 'turn-of-the-road gang' in that part of North Belfast called 'Murder Triangle' by the media during the Troubles and some of my friends did very serious things in the conflict. So serious in fact that I read about them on the front pages of newspapers when I was safely across the water studying at university (and, of course, my mother never forgave me for leaving her alone in Belfast, even if it was to better myself). Maybe I didn't want to worry her on those dark nights out on the street in North Belfast.

But maybe they were all for my benefit – to keep me out of trouble, to protect myself, lies as defence. You never know. You hear about mothers grassing on their kids for the children's sake. That's what the mothers always say – 'It's for your own good.' Some of my mates warned me about not trusting my mother or anybody else.

But maybe my lies to her did both – I didn't want to worry her, and I wanted our actions, whatever they were, to stay secret. I didn't want the police or the army calling to the house.

And maybe I felt less guilty about lying to my mother because of how all the lying started. Academic psychology doesn't really seem to have considered the ontogenesis of lies in the family or in relationships in this way, or the fact that the emotional response to lying may depend on their pattern of use, or the structures into which they are embedded, or the justifications we use for telling them. Psychology seems to assume that lies are one-off cognitive events with some emotional pay-off and classifiable as other-oriented or self-oriented. I think that sometimes psychology can be very naïve.

In this book, I will take a different approach. I want to see lying from both the victim's and the perpetrator's point of view, and I'm trying to use the term 'perpetrator' in as neutral a way as possible. Sometimes, chance throws things your way, and I want to focus on one such event. An old friend with some secrets contacted me. An old friend with some secrets and many lies. The other side of the lie equation. A perpetrator.

I couldn't talk to my mother, I never did, but I could talk to him, and I could try to understand. But before this, I want to reflect on the psychology of the victim. How can you rationally respond to lies within our most important relationships?

How Lies Can Make You Behave Irrationally

I admit that this is a sad little example of a lie but one that has stuck with me. My mother was only trying to protect me with that lie. Surely? There's nothing more to it than that. But lies do have two sides, depending on whether you're the sender or the receiver, the perpetrator or the victim. 'Harmless' lies can be very destructive, etched on the memory, capable of producing change. Lies can be contradictions, contradicted by what we know to be true, the evidence of our own eyes. So how do individuals cope with such contradictions of this sort? Or does this tell us more about the sensitivity (or perhaps the oversensitivity) of the recipient?

I'm sure that my mother felt guilty about that lie and I'm sure that she was doing her best to control her emotions and her behaviour, for both our sakes. Paul Ekman who really is the pioneer of the scientific studies of lying (studying them for over fifty years) reminds us that there are no tell-tale signs of lying, but there are signs of the thinking that is required to tell a lie, as we construct a false version of events, and there are signs of emotion. Both the thinking and the emotion may provide us with cues to deception.

The thinking behind a lie is often reflected in an increase in the frequency and duration of pauses and hesitations in speech – including *unfilled pauses*, which are periods of silences usually less than half a second in duration, *filled pauses*, where the speaker fills the silence usually after a small but sometimes perceptible delay with an 'um' or an 'ah' (Beattie 1977), and filled hesitations like repetitions of a word or syllable, as they respond to the lengthening silence. Everyday spontaneous speech, even when people are telling the truth, is full of these unfilled pauses and hesitations, the vast majority of which go unnoticed. They seem to be connected to cognitive planning in speech – the more planning, the more frequent they become, but the individual pauses still tend to be very brief (Goldman-Eisler 1968; Beattie 1983). There are regular phases of cognitive planning in speech as speakers plan the semantic content (that is the meaning of the utterance), and these periods are characterised by higher levels of pausing (Butterworth 1975; Beattie 1978, 1979). There is some evidence that because falsification lies involve more cognitive planning, pausing in speech increases (Vrij 2000), although, of course, some lies don't require much planning (or imagination), and many lies are prepared and planned in advance, which makes this a little bit more complicated.

Lies for most people (but as we shall see, there are exceptions) are often associated with a range of negative emotions – fear of being caught, anxiety around detection, guilt, shame, embarrassment, and remorse afterwards. Remorse can be a particularly enduring and damaging emotion. In the *Confessions*, the philosopher Jean Jacques Rousseau confesses to a crime that he committed as a young man whilst he was working as a servant for a family in Geneva, and the terrible remorse he subsequently suffered, having blamed somebody else for the crime. He stole a pink and silver ribbon, and when confronted, he blamed a young cook from the household. She was summoned by the master of the house. Rousseau describes her behaviour as follows: 'she did not get indignant. She merely turned to me and begged me to remember myself and not disgrace an innocent girl who had never done me any harm.' Rousseau repeated his accusation. The master of the house could not decide on this issue and dismissed them both but said that 'the guilty one's conscience would amply revenge the innocent.' Rousseau later wrote somewhat ruefully 'Not a day passes on which it is not fulfilled.'

Remorse for some can be a terrible punishment, but others seem to suffer from no remorse, or even understand what it might feel like. I once interviewed a terrorist responsible for many deaths in the Troubles in Northern Ireland, terrible, heinous crimes, and I asked him if he ever felt any remorse for what he had done, any of those murders he had committed, close-up and personal. He looked at me blankly. He told me that he could *say* that he felt sorry for his actions if I wanted him to, but the truth was that he just felt that 'it was all necessary in the circumstances – I had no sleepless nights about it.' He added that he noticed that other people, including some of his paramilitary pals, did express remorse for what they'd done but that 'they were just doing a bit of acting, to make themselves look good.' He also said that he had never felt remorse about anything; 'in fact, he added, 'if I'm honest, I don't really understand what it is.' He said that it was just something that people make up – a fiction, a lie to make out they're better than they are. Later in this book, we will consider how personality connects with lying and the emotions we feel. Some feel only positive emotions when it comes to lying – duping delight, excitement, pride, feelings of superiority having got one over on someone else, a buzz. Some positive emotions can occur during the lie itself for certain people, some, like smug contentment, only afterwards.

The range of planning that goes into constructing a lie and the diversity of emotions felt makes lie detection particularly difficult but Ekman has attempted to outline some generalities. He writes:

> The stronger the emotion, the more likely it is that some sign of it will leak despite the liar's best attempt to conceal it. Putting on another emotion, one that is not felt, can help disguise the felt emotion being

concealed. Falsifying an emotion can cover the leakage of a concealed emotion.

(Ekman 1985: 31–32)

I remember those nights at home that my mother sounded angry at me for suggesting that there was someone in the house, followed by a weak 'reassuring' smile. That would make perfect sense according to Ekman, it stops her real emotion, presumably the anxiety associated with detection apprehension, from leaking out. It is necessary to control your facial expression. Covering your face, or turning away from the other person, only draws attention to the face, so a false emotion is a more effective mask. In Ekman's words

> It not only misleads, but it is the best camouflage. It is terribly hard to keep the face impassive or the hands inactive when an emotion is felt strongly. Looking unemotional, cool, or neutral is the hardest appearance to maintain when emotions are felt.
>
> (Ekman 1985: 33)

In terms of choice of a mask, Ekman says that although any emotion can be falsified to conceal any other emotion, the most frequently chosen is the smile.

> It serves as the opposite of all the negative emotions – fear, anger, distress, disgust and so on. It is selected often because some variation on happiness is the message required to pull off many deceits.
>
> (Ekman 1985: 35)

But there are other reasons why the smile is used so frequently to conceal the negative emotions of lying. It is the easiest of the facial expressions of emotions to make voluntarily. Ekman reminds us that before the age of one, infants can smile voluntarily. But using smiles as a mask comes with dangers. It is often hard to get the timing right, they can leave the face too quickly, showing a fragment of the real emotion underneath (Ekman and Friesen 1982). Psychologists call these fleeting facial expressions micro-expressions, less than a quarter of a second in duration. Some people notice these micro-expressions in their everyday interactions; some do not. But I saw something that night in my mother's face, maybe I was looking for it, or maybe I've always been wary.

There are layers of human communication and part of finding cues to deception involves a sensitivity to behaviours at different levels and knowing where to look and *when* to look. When a masking smile fades, this may be one of the best times to look at facial expression, given that for most the face is a confusing source of information because although there are many different and quick facial expressions indicative of a range of emotions, we spend a lot of time and effort trying to control our facial expressions, often quite successfully, except for these very brief micro-expressions. Ekman himself has commented on the confusing nature of facial expressions for identifying lying:

> Liars usually monitor and try to control their words and face – what they know other focus upon – more than their voice and body. They will have more success with their words than with their face...Facial expressions are a dual system – voluntary and involuntary, lying and telling the truth, often at the same time. That is why facial expressions can be so complex, confusing, and fascinating.
>
> (Ekman 1985: 83–84)

This confusing nature means that you have to identity the processes of concealment and disguise. You need to learn to identify in real time the fake emotion to cover up the real emotion – fake anger on that night in Belfast rather than fear, anxiety, or guilt and the fake smile to communicate that everything is okay. Some people do learn to do this without much formal tuition.

But why was this little 'altruistic' lie such a big deal in the first place? This is a tougher question. I think that some lies put the recipient in a very difficult position, perhaps an impossible position. What is the correct response to such a lie? Should you accept the lie and disbelieve the evidence of your own senses, or should you confront the sender (your own mother), and call them a liar straight out?

The anthropologist Gregory Bateson suggested in his work on communication and cybernetics in the 1950s that contradictory communications can potentially be very damaging for the recipient, especially in certain circumstances. He suggests that the relationship between the two people (the sender and the recipient/the perpetrator and the victim) is critical. The extent of the 'damage' may well depend upon psychological dependency, imbalances of power, and an enclosed social space where no escape is possible. If you agree with Bateson's argument, then lies within a family may be particularly damaging, particularly those from a parent to a child in the small, family home. It's hard in a family just to ignore something, to just walk away. And much harder for the weaker member to challenge the lie.

Bateson identified certain types of contradictions, which he called 'double binds' that may be relevant here to this personal recollection. It is interesting how family narratives develop. My performance of pretending to be dead at this time was sometimes recalled by my mother ('very odd') but never recalled in a fuller context with the correct antecedents (in my view). That was my response to the lie. Perhaps, she never identified what preceded it, the situational logic so to speak. As Karl Popper warned us in *The Autonomy of Sociology*: 'The analysis of situations, the situational logic, play a very important part in social life' (1945/1983: 353). Perhaps, the association existed more firmly in my mind than in hers. In classic attributional terms, at least in terms of attributional biases (Ross 1977), we have two distinct perspectives on the *idiosyncratic* behaviour in question (Malle 2006) with semi-automatic reasoning about causality (Kahneman 2011). I had an *external* explanation for my behaviour (that is to say, something outside me – the lie), she had an *internal* explanation (something inside me, indeed something the matter with me, prompting her to say 'I'll need to take you to the doctor'). Lies contradicted by other physical evidence puts the recipient in a difficult *conflicted* position where any more typical, expected, and rational response might be difficult, particularly if there is a power imbalance, as in a mother–son relationship. Pretending to be dead was more than just idiosyncratic – it was genuinely odd.

In his classic volume *'Steps to an Ecology of Mind'* (1972/2000), Bateson identified a double bind as a conflicting communication where it is difficult or impossible for the recipient of the communication to respond appropriately and rationally. Indeed, Bateson attempted to explain how certain family members propagate *irrational* behaviour in others through their use of these double binds. Somewhat provocatively, Bateson suggested that double bind communications may even play a major role in the ontogenesis of schizophrenia, which was an enormous step and way beyond the empirical or clinical data he presented (Beattie 2018a; Berger 1965; Ciotola 1961; Hartwell 1996; Potash 1965; Ringuette and Kennedy 1966; Schuham 1967), although he himself does acknowledge this: 'This hypothesis has not been statistically tested; it selects and emphasises a rather simple set of interactional phenomena and does not attempt to describe comprehensively the extraordinary complexity of a family relationships' (Bateson 1972/2000: 212). But what he did present were some extremely insightful ideas about how communication can work, and the importance of understanding communication and communicational signals as critical components of everyday life for thinking, behaviour, and mental well-being. Below we have one of Bateson's best-known examples of a double bind in action. It involves a young man hospitalised with the disorder, Bateson reports this observation, on the assumption that the interaction sequence described was a recurring feature in the life of this relationship and therefore could have played a role in the aetiology of the disorder itself:

> A young man [a diagnosed schizophrenic] who had fairly well recovered …was visited in the hospital by his mother. He was glad to see her and impulsively put his arm around her shoulders, whereupon she stiffened. He withdrew his arm and she asked, "Don't you love my anymore? He then blushed, and she said, "Dear, you must not be so easily embarrassed and afraid of your feelings." The patient was able to stay with her only a few minutes more and following her departure he assaulted an orderly and was put in the tubs.
>
> (Bateson 1972/2000: 217)

According to Bateson, there is no way that the son can respond without being 'punished.' If he keeps his arm around her shoulders, he is punished with her nonverbal response (stiffening up); if he withdraws his arm, he is punished with her verbal response (her comment 'Don't you love me anymore?'). He is too weak or 'psychologically dependent' to challenge what is going on. That is why power in the relationship vis-a-vis his mother is so important.

Bateson also comments that 'The mother's reaction of not accepting her son's affectionate gesture is masterfully covered up by her condemnation of him for withdrawing, and the patient denies his perception of the situation by accepting her condemnation' (Bateson 1972/2000: 217). So, it's not just that the son has no clear and obvious way out of the situation, he has to deny his very perception of the situation and accept her version of what has just happened. The interactional sequence augments the existing power dynamic between the two of them.

My mother's lie to me about whether there was a man in the house has certain similarities to this kind of double bind, in that hearing her in conversation and outright denial of the presence of others clearly contradict one another. They are conflicting communications, and I was too weak or 'psychologically dependent' to challenge what was going on. But there's more than just conflicting communications here, there's an explanation offered by my mother as to why I must have 'misheard,' 'imagined,' or experienced this auditory hallucination – I was in the middle of a dream. This was reminiscent of the maternal soothing of a much younger child who might wake up frightened in the middle of the night, having imagined scary monsters.

'Mammy, is there somebody in the house with you?'

'There's nobody down here, son. Go back to sleep.'

'But I heard a man's voice, mammy.'

'There's nobody here, son. You must be dreaming.'

So how should the recipient of such a communication behave? Should they accept that they're mistaken and that they've dreamt it, despite all the evidence to the contrary, and accept that they're subject to imaginings and can't tell the difference between being awake from dreaming? Bateson himself wrote:

> We all have some difficulty in deciding sometimes whether a dream was a dream or not and it would not be very easy for most of us to say how we know that a piece of our own fantasy is fantasy, and not experience. The ability to place an experience in time is one of the important cues and referring it to a sense organ is another.
>
> (Bateson 1972/2000: 197)

So there often can be some jeopardy with regard to one's thinking about whether you are dreaming or not, but sometimes you just know. And that night I just knew. Or do you accuse your own mother of lying to her face? This might not be that easy for some people, as Bateson himself highlighted in his example:

> Obviously, this result could have been avoided if the young man had been able to say, "Mother, it is obvious that you become uncomfortable when I put my arm around you, and that you have difficulty in accepting a gesture of affection from me." However, the schizophrenic patient

doesn't have this possibility open to him. His intense dependency and training prevent him from communicating upon his mother's communicative behaviour, though she comments on his and forces him to accept and to attempt to deal with the complicated sequence.

(Bateson 1972/2000: 217)

But, as Bateson himself accepts, it may not just be the schizophrenic patients (with his or her 'intense dependency and training'), who is unable to comment on the nature of a contradictory utterance from a mother (for example, a lie contradicted by other evidence) but any child with such 'intense dependency' (like, for example, a child who really loves his mother, or a recently orphaned child who has only now got this one caretaker). And Bateson does comment on the power imbalance between the mother and the child when he writes that although the son can't comment on what is going on – 'she comments on his and forces him to accept and to attempt to deal with the complicated sequence.'

So, in the personal case I outlined, we might gloss it like

you are wrong in what you believe, you must be dreaming, even though you don't realise it; therefore, you can't tell real life from dreams, this may be due to the trauma of losing your father, you are losing your grip on reality.

It might look very harsh and unkind when it is expanded and written out in this way, but sometimes everyday utterances have powerful and deep consequences.

Bateson attempted to specify in detail what features constitute double bind communications. He said that 'the necessary ingredients' are as follows: it must involve two or more people, usually (and controversially) the mother. I say 'controversially' because there did not seem to be any a priori theoretical reason why this should be the case. Bateson added a qualification of sorts 'We do not assume that the double bind is inflicted by the mother alone, but that it may be done either by mother alone or by some combination of mother, father and/or siblings' (Bateson 1972/2000: 206). In other words, the role of the mother either acting on her own or in combination with other members of the family seems clear and unambiguous in his thinking on the dynamics of families. And interestingly, all of the clinical examples he cited in support of his theory involved the mother. This idea had its roots in the work of Sullivan (1927), Levy (1931), Kasanin et al. (1934), Fromm-Reichman (1948), and others, but this particular focus has come in for severe criticism from some quarters (see Hartwell 1996).

Secondly, it must be recurrent rather than a one-off, 'Our hypothesis does not invoke a single traumatic experience, but such repeated experience that the double bind structure comes to be a habitual expectation' (Bateson 1972/2000: 206). Thirdly, it must have a primary negative injunction issued by one member of an intense relationship to another. This may have the form of 'Do not do so and so, or I will punish you' or 'If you do not do so and so,

I will punish you.' Bateson assumed that punishment 'may be either the with-drawal of love or the expression of hate or anger, or most devastating the kind of abandonment that results from the parent's expression of extreme helpless-ness.' Fourthly, there must be a secondary injunction, a more 'abstract' com-munication that conflicts with the first and again 'enforced by punishments or signal which threaten survival.' He wrote that 'This secondary injunction is commonly communicated to the child by nonverbal means. Posture, ges-ture, tone of voice, meaningful action and the implications concealed in verbal comment may all be used to convey this more abstract message' (Bateson 1972/2000: 207). Bateson also made the point that 'the secondary injunction may impinge upon any element of the primary prohibition.' If one were to translate the secondary injunction into words, then it would translate as 'Do not see this as punishment,' 'Do not see me as the punishing agent,' 'Do not submit to me prohibitions,' 'Do not think of what you must not do,' 'Do not question my love of which the primary prohibition is (or is not) and example.' The fifth feature is that there must be 'A tertiary negative injunction prohibit-ing the victim from escaping the field' (Bateson 1972/2000: 207). Bateson wrote 'The mother's reaction of not accepting her son's affectionate gesture is masterfully covered up by her condemnation of him for withdrawing, and the patient denies his perception of the situation by accepting her condemnation' (Bateson 1972/2000: 217).

So, it is clear that the double bind is not just about two mutually contradic-tory communications; it is in Bateson's example about the son accepting the condemnation of his mother and thus agreeing to her version of reality. In other words, Bateson maintains that double binds are about control and not just control of the course of the interaction, or the interpretation and mean-ing of the acts that constitute the interaction, but about the very nature of the situation itself. They control the 'reality' of the situation.

The lie about the man present in our house wasn't being presented as just a denial, it was an attempt to falsely reassure ('you're dreaming') based on an untruth (I wasn't dreaming in the first place). This was the construction of the reality of the situation, a home life with a caring mother despite her own diffi-culties in coping with the loss of her husband. So why did I pretend to be dead?

Bateson himself hypothesised about the psychological and behavioural ef-fects of these double bind communications (and he was particularly interested in the more extreme reactions found in schizophrenia). Some people, accord-ing to Bateson, get confused about what is called the metacommunicative system of communication, which involves communication about communica-tion. For example, if someone says something and then says that it is a lie or a joke, or indicates this in the accompanying nonverbal behaviour, then you don't represent it as the truth. This is metacommunication in action. But if you are subject to a history of double binds, then according to Bateson, you end up not being able to use this system accurately.

If a person said to him, "What would you like to do today?" he would be unable to judge accurately by the context or by the tone of voice or gesture whether he was being condemned for what he did yesterday, or being offered a sexual invitation, or just what was meant.

(Bateson 1972/2000: 211)

But that is just one type of response. Bateson says that others become concerned about the hidden meanings behind every utterance (and become paranoid). Some accept literally what is said regardless of whether it is contradicted by 'tone or gesture or context' and laugh off these metacommunicative signs (and develop into hebephrenic schizophrenics). Others choose to ignore all utterances and 'detach their interest from the external world and concentrate on their own internal processes' (catatonic schizophrenics). Again, these hypotheses are way beyond the data that Bateson presents, and, of course, extremely difficult to empirically test, requiring detailed longitudinal and ethnographic research. Bateson does hypothesise that 'What the patient is up against today – and was up against in childhood is the false interpretation of his messages,' but he is always working backwards with patients after their diagnosis. But his work does highlight the importance of certain features of communication for the thinking and behaviour of the recipients of the communication.

Perhaps, me playing dead was just one way of coping with this conflicted communication, of ostentatiously signalling that I was going to 'ignore all utterances and detach [my] interest from the external world.' It wasn't being catatonic; I was signalling that I was worse than catatonic to get a response. I was deceiving to produce a perceptible emotional response in my mother. Of course, I could have laughed off everything my mother told me, and not taken anything she said seriously (as I may have done in later years). Or I could have become more paranoid, thinking that it was hard to believe anything she said, and that there's something hidden and darker behind everything. But no, I just lay there until she got upset. I turned the tables. And that made me feel better because it is clear that a major aspect of lying is that it is about power and control, and I was perhaps attempting to usurp that power, to get some power back.

Bateson later refined his theory and argued that all of the five original features are no longer necessary when the victim has learned to perceive his universe in double bind patterns. 'Almost any part of a double bind sequence may then be sufficient to precipitate panic or rage' (Bateson 1972/2000: 207). He said that the general characteristics of a double bind are:

1 When the individual is involved in an intense relationship; that is, a relationship in which he feels it is vitally important that he discriminate accurately what sort of message is being communicated so that he may respond appropriately.
2 And the individual is caught in a situation in which the other person is expressing two orders of a message and one of these denies the other.

3 And the individual is unable to comment on the messages being expressed
to correct his discrimination of what order to respond to, i.e., he cannot
make a metacommunicative statement (1972/2000: 208).

The criteria now are clearer and more easily applied to that house back in
Belfast – an intense relationship, conflicted messages, one denying the other
(and all locked in that claustrophobic little mill house), where the recipient is 'unable to comment on the messages...to correct his discrimination.'
I wouldn't have dared to call her a liar to her face because of the emotional
consequences. Again, Bateson wrote:

> The only way the child can really escape from the situation is to com-
> ment on the contradictory position his mother has put him in. However,
> if he did so, the mother would take this as an accusation that she is
> unloving, and both punish him and insist that his perception of the situ-
> ation is distorted. By preventing the child from talking about the situa-
> tion, the mother forbids him using the metacommunicative level – the
> level we use to correct our perception of communicative behaviour. ...
> In any normal relationship, there is a constant interchange of metacom-
> municative messages such as 'What do you mean?' or 'Why did you do
> that?' or 'Are you kidding me?' and so on. To discriminate accurately
> what people are really expressing, we must be able to comment directly
> or indirectly on that expression.
>
> (Bateson 1972/2000: 215–216)

So, I went quiet, not just quiet, I was dead, a metaphorical extension of just
not responding, but for a few moments, it may present as the literal truth. This
shift into a metaphorical mode of communication may not be that uncommon; it offers protection. Bateson had commented that:

> As an answer to the double bind situation, a shift to a metaphorical state-
> ment brings safety. However, it also prevents the patient from making
> the accusation he wants to make....It is not only safer for the victim of a
> double bind to shift to a metaphorical order of message, but in an impos-
> sible situation it is better to shift and become somebody else or shift and
> insist that he is somewhere else. Then the double bind cannot work on
> the victim because it isn't he and besides he is in a different place.
>
> (Bateson 1972/2000: 210)

There is one obvious conclusion from all of this, when we think about lies, we
need to think carefully about the recipients, the victims of the lies, and what
options they really have. Bateson sketched out some of the irrational options,
I discovered one of these for myself, we will see others throughout the course
of this book. We also need to think about power imbalances and control; these

would seem to be bound up with the use of lies, even in the poorest house-holds where power and control are often constructed and displayed in the language itself, including the lies we tell. I never mentioned my feigning of death to anyone for a very long time, except perhaps in the past year or so, or what may have given rise to it, the lies, and the obvious contradictions with what I knew to be true. The death of my father was critical. 'The absence of anyone in the family, such as a strong and insightful father, who can intervene in the relationship between the mother and child and support the child in the face of the contradictions involved' (Bateson 1972/2000: 213). Some are shocked by my account of my play-acting, but others tell me that it is not uncommon in children, that they knew someone just like me who liked to play dead like this, until I describe how long it went on, and the point at which I would stop. This, they say, makes it a little bit more unusual. I mentioned it recently (as I was thinking about this book) to one comparative psychologist I know whose research focuses on other species, and he burst out laughing. He referred me to the work of the esteemed sociobiologist Robert Trivers who has written about the feigning of death in animals. He writes:

> It has long been known in predator/prey relations that deception can work anywhere from first detection until final consumption. Consider two examples near the time of death itself. The feigning of death typically occurs after the prey is caught and is thought to inhibit the final death-dealing strike. The bird acts dead, lifeless, but remains conscious and alert so that often the only sign of life is its open eyes. Chickens run at the first opportunity, typically when the predator lets go, but a duck threatened by a fox often remains immobile for some time after release, especially if other foxes appear to be present.
>
> (Trivers 2011: 41)

I laughed when I read this. It turns out that I have something in common with chickens. Lying there on our floor, trying 'to inhibit the final death-dealing strike,' waiting to run at the first opportunity, all metaphorically speaking of course, just trying to prevent the *death* of a mother–child relationship.

The Packed Lunch

I'd known him since we were undergraduates but that had been many years ago. We had never been that close, but he had once said that he had found me to be a great help. I had once talked to him when he was high and a little scared by this feeling of being totally out of control on an acid trip. I think that it's called talking him down. He was trembling, his long black hair hanging in ringlets over his shoulder shook a little, as if he was sitting on a moving train that was going a little too fast. He looked frightened.

He had written some poetry on his acid trip before the fear kicked in. I just remember the opening line. 'Turtles are lentils in my soup.' I had no idea what it meant. Funnily enough, neither did he. He said that he saw the writing in the sky, and he was trying to interpret it. He knew it was a message from God. He showed me his shaky writing. It was just gibberish, although God did mention LSD a few times in his or her message, which I thought was indicative of a God with a little too much time on his (or her) hands. And when we graduated, there were years of the inevitable silence – careers, families, social mobility, change, that sort of thing. So, I was surprised to hear from him just like that, out of the blue. A call from a voice I didn't immediately recognise. He had to say his name and then with a bit of effort I matched this voice, oddly hesitant and not quite how I remember it, to a name and a face. It turned out we were now living in the same city. He had read about me in the local newspaper; it was not a very interesting article about some psychological research of mine on hand gestures. 'The hands don't lie claims professor,' was the headline. So, he thought we might catch up. He said, I hope you're still a good listener. I thought he might be thinking of someone else. It had only been that once really. Maybe it was more significant to him than me. Maybe the lentils in his soup had come back to haunt him.

I pulled up outside a house in a nice part of the city. Middle class, comfortable, a road for families, kids playing in the street, secure in that lower middle-class way. Highly desirable, that's what they would call the area. The house was painted white at the front over the brickwork. A spacious family home, bay windows, the original-coloured glass in the door, probably Edwardian. He came to the door. He hadn't changed *that* much. Certainly recognisable. His face with that same laughing smile, lively twinkling eyes. But he looked a bit older and sadder, especially when he relaxed after the initial formalities. A worry line across his forehead, quite a deep groove I noticed and a very pronounced fleck of grey hair. But he was still charming and still witty. Perhaps too charming. I think that was his problem. He was always very popular. His three children played in the back garden of his semi-detached house.

His wife was 'out,' he said, and he left it at that. When he rang me, I had suggested meeting up in a trendy university coffee shop nearby, but he had suggested me coming to his home. 'Because I'm babysitting.' His children were ten, seven, and five. They kept running in from the back garden, excited to see the visitor and even more excited to get the attention of their father, begging him to come out and play. They were playing badminton with pink plastic bats. The scores were already in the hundreds. They kept asking how long we'd be.

He asked me about my job but didn't seem particularly interested in what I was saying. He didn't seem that interested in me at all. I asked him if everything was okay. He looked out through the bay window at this settled suburban street.

'Not really,' he said. But he told me that he thought that I might understand.

He explained that he had done something silly. I smiled kindly at him, 'haven't we all,' I said. I thought that he might have dabbled in some illegal substances again, after all this time, the confessions of a middle-aged drug user, and that was why he had called me. That was why he had thought of me. That was the link. I hoped that he hadn't been reading messages in the sky again.

'I cheated,' he said, although he immediately tried to correct himself, by saying that he this was not really the correct word for it. He worked in a university. He was a lecturer in social sciences, she was a student, such a bloody cliché, he laughed at the idea. The older male lecturer exploiting the young innocent female, an abuse of power.

'Really?' he added after a pause, as if to flatter me, as if to say you can see beyond clichés, or you could at one time. You know things are never that simple.

'Where should I start?' he said, he looked at me again – it was a sort of unnerving eye contact.

'Maybe with first impressions,' he said answering his own question, and glanced at me again. 'That's where you expect me to start, that's where everything starts, that's where confessions start. All physical, all superficial, all culpable,' he chuckled again with feigned embarrassment, he smiled at the cliché in that superior academic way of his.

Long silky dark hair, beautiful brown eyes, a beautiful smile. I noticed her immediately, she had a certain walk – not too confident, not too shy. She saw me looking at her walking along and smiled at me. The smile lingered. I was taken aback. She was with a group of friends – I'm sure they must have noticed.

I wasn't sure what role he wanted me to play. Did he just have some secrets he wanted to get off his chest? And had he found a ready listener in some psychology professor who hardly knew him and who, it seems, would come out with ridiculous overblown quotes about hand movements for the local paper for some cheap publicity. Someone who shamelessly courted publicity and thus could hardly look down on a serious academic like himself. He always saw himself as a very serious thinker, a scholar of thought, not really belonging in the mid-tier university in which he found himself. Better than that.

He was looking away as if wondering what to say, wondering how delicate he should be.

'That might have been that,' he continued, 'but she was assigned to my seminar group for her final year. She sat right in front of me. It seemed deliberate. I was flattered by the attention to be honest. I don't really get on with my colleagues.'

He coughed, it seemed to be a bit of a nervous cough, as if he had just revealed too much in mentioning his relationship with his colleagues. Was that at the centre of all this? I asked myself. Was he just kicking out in protest at his position, like a naughty child?

'We were discussing male-female differences in conversation,' he continued,

you know the old clichéd stuff on the micro-politics of interaction – male dominance and interruption strategies. Men interrupt women all the time by butting-in to control the conversation. I mentioned my wife at that point in the discussion and the way she "interrupts" – all very gentle with a slight overlap at exactly the right points in the other person's talk but without any warning,

he explained,

I nodded – but he probably didn't need that encouragement.

'But *you* know that they're really subtle *control* devices,' he emphasised 'you' and then 'control.' He was flattering me, explaining that I was there for a reason. You may like to hawk your theories around the local papers but, at least, you know something about human behaviour – a little, at least, surely.

'But nobody ever sees them like that – that's why overlaps are so effective.' He waited for me to nod this time to make sure that I was on the same page.

The student just smiled at me as if to say – why is that relevant to any-thing? You must be a bit nervous of me to have to mention that you're married. The other students were all nudging each other, I don't know why, they obviously found something funny. I don't know if it was her or me. Probably her.

'Maybe both of you,' I suggested. 'That's the point about interaction, there's always more than one person involved, but we often only see it from one point of view.'

He didn't look that pleased. That frown opened up again. Like a wound across his forehead. I was just trying to be helpful.

One day after a lecture she came to me for advice about a *friend* who was stressed by a possessive boyfriend. I listened; the truth is I enjoyed talking to her. She wore this loose summer clothing, it was still warm at the start of term, exposing her black bra. I couldn't help noticing that. She said that she wanted to do her dissertation with me. But she'd no idea what on. "Why don't you suggest something," she had said. So, I did. It was a standard sort of list. And she smiled pleasantly at each of my suggestions but said they didn't really work for her. What about sexist relationships? she said eventually. This bore no relationship to what I'd been suggesting, or indeed, what I'm knowledgeable about. "I'm inter-ested in sexist relationships", she explained.

My friend explained that he had misheard this, he said that at first, he thought that she had said 'sexual.' He felt embarrassed, he blushed slightly, he was nervous. He asked what she meant. 'Men and women feel relationships dif-ferently,' she explained – 'they stereotype the others' views. I'm interested in the difference between men and women. This great gulf. I want to understand that gulf. Not little trivial things like interruptions in talk.'

He asked her whether her interest was based on personal experience. And then felt embarrassed immediately by his question. It was wrong to ask students about such personal issues. She said that she had finished with men, and then corrected herself, *boys*. That's what students are 'immature boys.'

'They don't understand girls or women or me, they just don't get it, they're weak.'

The two of them talked for maybe an hour or more, perhaps a little too long for a preliminary dissertation chat, some of it was academic some a bit more personal. Perhaps, dangerously personal at times.

Later that day, he said, she called again unexpectedly to say that she had an idea. He thought that it would be about her dissertation topic, but she asked if they could go out for lunch 'to talk properly' about the work, away from the distractions of the university. 'Students are always knocking on your door,' she had said, 'that way we wouldn't be interrupted.'

He explained that the university doesn't really approve of that kind of thing. And she said, 'but who's going to tell them?' So, they both smiled and agreed that the following day, that soon, at lunchtime, they would go for a drive into the country so they could talk uninterrupted.

He drove a small red BMW sports car. His wife always said it was hardly appropriate for a married family man with three children, but he enjoyed the car, and that very brief sense of freedom when he was on his own. A sort of symbolic freedom rather than an actual freedom. The children fitted into their family car much more easily.

The two of them had arranged to meet a few streets away from the university. He said that she wore little make-up but looked stunning and as she got in, she noticed a neat tin foil package sitting in an open Waitrose carrier bag on the backseat.

'It's my lunch,' he explained embarrassed. 'My wife makes it for me every day. She likes me arriving at the university with a packed lunch. She knows how busy I am.'

The dark-haired girl, whom he still hadn't named for me, apparently found this story hilarious. Every aspect of it, it seems.

They drove out to a pub in the country on this warm Indian summer day in early October and after he pulled up, he started to unwrap the tin foil and eat the cheese sandwiches. He explained that he just couldn't leave them untouched.

'She's gone to all the trouble of making them, I can't just throw them away.'

And the dark-haired student just sat there laughing at all this domestic bliss or domestic control, or whatever it was, and all he could think was that she had such white teeth and such delicious minty fresh breath. The old coach house pub overlooked some reservoirs and they both gazed at the view. He never went there with his wife, or very seldom did. He wasn't sure why.

She talked about her life – her successful businessman father, the complications of her own family. She explained that her father had a second family and he had to juggle his time. 'That must be very difficult,' my friend had said, 'very stressful.'

She laughed again. 'I think he likes the excitement. The feeling that everybody needs him.'

'But what about having to eat two dinners every night?' my friend asked. 'How does he cope?'

'Maybe a bit like you today. Two lunches. That's a start,' and again she laughed in a playful way at her own joke. 'We are going to have lunch together, aren't we?' They had lunch and he gazed at her, he said, while she talked about her ordinary student life. Normally, he would have been yawning with a story like this, but this wasn't a normal sort of day.

My friend explained that he didn't see her for a week, she didn't turn up for their next seminar, which worried him, but then she called in to his office quite late in the day and invited him to her flat for some supper.

'We could have a nice quiet meal in total privacy – you looked so nervous in that pub,' she said, 'as if someone was going to walk in and catch us at it – and we weren't even doing anything, except for you gobbling down two lunches.'

He knew that he should have declined. He had never done anything like this before. But, of course, it was innocent enough, surely. His tutors back in Cambridge would invite students to their rooms all the time. Although perhaps they wouldn't go to the student's room. But he was very nervous that night and began the big lie or more accurately the first of several big lies, all necessary and all interconnected. He could not refuse dinner at home because that would be very suspicious. So, he started eating his dinner but said he couldn't finish it because he had stomach-ache. He then said that he had to go to a lecture that a visiting academic was giving at the university. He passed his children at the bottom of the stairs and kissed them goodnight and said that he had to go to work.

Lie upon lie cascading from his tongue. He kissed his wife on the cheek, but that was a lie too, cold, cursory, for effect, a kiss can be a sort of nonverbal lie. A lie of pretence.

As he drove off, he knew that he had to control his thinking that night, suppressing all intrusive thoughts. That's how you must deal with lies. Otherwise, the whole night would just be an unenjoyable waste of time. He'd already told a series of lies even to his children – for what? If he let those thoughts get the better of him and get into his head, then the lies would be for nothing. Surely, he was allowed some relaxation.

When he got there, she had cooked dinner, some chicken and rice. His wife had cooked chicken and potatoes. That was a strange coincidence, although perhaps not that strange. The fact that he thought about it and compared the two seemed to have worried him. He was embarrassed at the thought. He drank wine, too much wine because he was driving, and he told her a bit about his life. She asked what his wife was like, but his descriptions were brief and to the point. It wouldn't have felt right to reveal too much. But then, she asked whether his wife minded him going out on his own socially like this.

'No,' he said, 'she's cool with that.' This was another big lie. He was lying to her as well. Of course, he was. He said they kissed, she had made the first move, and then they made love on a rug on the floor. He had a similar rug in his bedroom; his was from IKEA, hers looked more genuinely ethnic.

This night, he explained, would always stick in his mind because for years afterwards she had a carpet burn on the small of her back, like some sort of a stigmata.

'I'll have to tell my boyfriend that I fell down the stairs tonight,' she had said. This was the first time that she had mentioned her boyfriend and she didn't seem that bothered about having to lie to him.

He had enjoyed the excitement of the night, he said, but it took effort to suppress the guilt and the fear. He knew that none of this should have happened.

As he left, he told her that she couldn't tell anybody about this. 'Of course not,' she replied. 'But I still want to work with you on sexist relationships.'

He told her that this wouldn't be a problem, which was another big lie because it would inevitably be a problem – having to meet up with her for a year, having to grade her work, the shame of having to declare a conflict of interest at the examiners' meeting because of a personal relationship with a student, or to lie and pretend that there was no conflict of interest. He still wasn't sure what 'sexist relationships' meant, which also worried him.

This was clearly now a relationship of sorts and perhaps it was going to be a very intimate relationship, who could tell, but it was also going to be a relationship built on lies. Lies that would filter right through several competing social structures. Lies to his wife, lies to his lover, lies to his employer and his peers, lies to his children. That would be the worst lie of all. He knew that.

He also realised that if he stopped seeing her, she might make it difficult for him. He had already crossed the Rubicon. He was terrified of having to come clean about their chats, or the cheese sandwiches in tin foil in his sports car, or the mundane nature of his everyday life, opening it all up to public scrutiny. And besides he liked her, perhaps more than that?

In what seemed like a very short time, she had finished with her boyfriend. 'He accused me of seeing some tutor,' she told him. My old friend said that he wondered whether it was him or whether she was seeing several tutors at the same time. But when she told him that the boyfriend had mentioned the carpet burn, he felt relieved – at least it was him. My friend hadn't spotted more than one carpet burn on her back.

The wife must not find out about any of this, he emphasised. He stressed that. It was always the wife in the third person, no name, just a role, impersonal, collateral damage.

He sat back on his sofa looking directly at me. 'A right bloody mess, it's all completely traumatic but who I can tell about this?' He looked at me. He had nobody else, just someone from the past with no real knowledge of his present.

I could see the toys sticking out the back of the sofa. That was the scene I was looking at. A bewildered man with all the trappings and responsibilities of family life. The girlfriend got pregnant.

'Christmas Day is almost the worst,' he continued.

How can you leave three children to go out on Christmas Day without any sensible explanation. They would be left at home for a few hours, puzzled and abandoned. My wife would look at me with contempt. "Who the fuck goes out on Christmas morning after the presents have been opened?" she would say. I had never seen that look before directed right at me. "It's a time for families," then she would go off and cry.

'For me,' he explained

it's a day of dread and timekeeping, and having to be two places at once, which as we all know, is impossible. When my girlfriend got pregnant, I knew that was going to be even more impossible to live this life. I couldn't leave my wife – we had shared too much, bonded since we were teenagers, we'd grown up together, so I was stuck. There was one lie after the other until they became routine. I didn't get any better at lying, just more practised but practice doesn't make perfect – I've just got vaguer and vaguer in my replies to be honest.

He glanced at the floor.

My wife finds the vagueness insulting, to be honest. And it wasn't long before my children could see through the whole vague charade. I could see it in their eyes, much worse than just puzzled, but they never confronted me.

He was looking down at the floor the whole time. He looked back up maybe for reassurance from the good listener.
'I was vague for a reason,' he continued.

It was my way of saying that I do care about you all, I do care about my family. I'm not trying to deceive you. I'm sorry about all the things I've done and all the lies. But I don't know if they understood this. I think it just infuriated everyone.

He looked up at the clock. I had said very little. Perhaps, that was what he wanted.
'My wife will be home very soon. I don't want to be rude, but you'd better be gone by then. Or she'll be wondering what we've been talking about.'
There had been a torrent of words, all from him, non-stop, like a dam bursting, confessing his lies, confessing the strain of it all, the trauma, presumably to elicit some sort of sympathy. His children would periodically come in and he would wave them away again. He needed to get all of this off his chest. He needed a virtual stranger. He wanted to see my reactions. I tried not to give anything away, like a priest, but I'm not a Catholic and I don't really know what they say so I was having to make it up – non-committal nods and vague responses in that confessional of his front room. Is that what priests do?

He was looking much sadder than ever. 'I've mentioned you in the past as someone I could open up to when I was young,' he said.

A good listener. My wife wants this secret, whatever that secret is, to stay in the house. She doesn't know exactly what it is, but she probably strongly suspects. If she saw you, she would guess that I've been talking to you about you know what?

I looked around at his house and surroundings, a room that represented security, striving, a good enough career but perhaps not good enough for him (he had been at Cambridge for one year but had failed his exams and then had to go to a Redbrick university; he had always resented it), an arrival, a home, imperfect – a little messy with children's toys and books and papers, and therefore quite perfect in every way. He wanted my attention back.

'But before you go, I do need to ask you something, do you have any advice?' You could see that he was panicking, a visit from a friendly non-committal sort of priest might not have been enough for him. He was starting to sense that.

'You've been very quiet. Can you say anything that might help? You understand the situation, I'm sure. You're a man of the world. You've known me from way back – you know that I'm basically good.'

There was a long pause. I didn't know what to say. Should I share my own history of being lied to? Or tell him about some lies that I've told over the years? Should I try to rebuke him or bond with him? That's the thing about lies, it depends on your starting position.

There was a very long pause if I'm honest, a very long pause. It's rare for me to run through options in my head like this, all the time smiling at him as benevolently as I could. I could have come out with some righteous bourgeois waffle about morality, or I could have tried to frame it in hegemonic terms, he would have appreciated that, and the power imbalance between the lecturer and the student and the obvious implications for them both. He was after all a social scientist interested in the implicit dynamics of society that keep us all locked in position. But he was also a broken man in a way, and he would have found both equally insulting.

Instead, I thought maybe I should try to be the person that he thought I once was, the (stereotypic) happy-go-lucky Irish lad, the carefree student who had found some time for him that night in that hall of residence, lending him an ear because some paranoia was setting in after a little bit of careless drug misuse. Bad acid. I was always witty then (he always described me as superficial and funny), and he had found that gentle humour reassuring that night, stabilising, normalising, grounding him in the everyday. Exactly what he needed at that point in time with the bad trip.

'Time is a great healer,' I suggested, and he smiled gently at me at this platitude. Perhaps, that was all he wanted. Some platitudes. A chance to get things off his chest. A chance to feel better about the whole thing, to dampen the emotional experience of lying to his wife and children. A connection with a man; I guessed that he didn't have many male friends. Careers and families can do that sort of thing – they can isolate.

I stood in the doorway and glanced out into the Autumn night, a slight chill in the air now, families all along the street settling down to their early evening meal, you could see the warm glow from the houses. His own children in the back room watching television waiting for their mummy to come home from yoga. What more could I say?

He wanted understanding, reassurance, maybe even some attempt at bonding. The male perspective. He was trying to elicit all of this with a smile, that charming smile of his but it was wasted on me now. I was remembering things from my own past. Lies and the effects they can have. I wanted him to get down on that floor and shut his eyes and pretend he was dead. I wanted to see that level of remorse. I wanted to see that he understood the effects of his lies on other people. How they felt. Just for one moment.

I hesitated at the doorway – he thought that I was going to leave without saying another word. I half-turned.

'Roll on Christmas,' I said, and winked.

I thought that he might find it humorous. What else do you do or say to someone in a double bind, with no way out? What can you say? It was me who felt trapped. And I swear he shut that door behind me a little too forcefully. And that Edwardian glass door panel, all original features, and shiny yellow and blue and highly desirable, shook, and nearly shattered.

The 'Trauma' of Lying to Your Partner

Some psychologists have suggested that some of the most serious lies of everyday life are lies about extra-marital affairs (DePaulo 2018). Extra-marital affairs, it seems, are not uncommon, but an exact figure is hard to pin down. The number is somewhat elusive and shifts from survey to survey. Some surveys have used large samples of respondents, some much smaller samples; some are conducted face-to-face, some are not. Face-to-face surveys (perhaps not surprisingly) tend to generate lower estimates of infidelity. According to the General Social Survey conducted in the United States in 2020, men were more likely to cheat than women, with 20% of the men and 13% of the women reporting having sex whilst still being married, and this is despite the fact that according to DePaulo the percentage of Americans who say that cheating is *always wrong* appeared to have increased from the 1970s into the 2000s – the figures she quotes are 65% in 1973 to 81% in 2008 (DePaulo 2018: 92), but apparently dropping in the more recent General Social Survey data released in 2021 (now estimated at 74%). Cheating (perhaps counter-intuitively) is higher in the fifty-five to sixty-four-year-olds than in the forty-one to fifty-four or eighteen to forty age groups.

When partners are asked if they were glad that they found out about their partner cheating, their stated reasons include things like 'Because now I know I'm not crazy,' 'Glad it ended early than to find out way down the road,' and 'Knowledge is power.' Most American relationships, it seems, do survive cheating (women are slightly more likely than men to break up with a partner who has cheated: 48%, compared with 43% for men), but the process is often very painful, and has been from time immemorial.

The diarist Samuel Pepys, for example, recorded in his diary on 25 October 1668 how his wife caught him in a sexual act with their maid. He had put his hand up her skirt, and it was thus 'with my main in her cunny,' that his wife came upon the two of them locked in an embrace. He admitted that he had hugged the girl but denied kissing her (or anything else). Pepys recorded in his diary (9–10 November 1668) how he had tried to persuade the maid to lie, with the excuse that he did not want what had happened 'to be the ruin of the girl.' The infidelity made his wife both angry and ill ('mightily troubled again'). She only seems to have forgiven him when she had the chance to get even and tell him about other men, and the 'Temptations she hath refused out of faithfulness to me.' These other men included Lord Sandwich, Captain Ferrer, and Lord Hinchingbrooke. This upset Pepys greatly and he broke down and wept; this was his wife's revenge. He vowed 'to bid the girl be gone and show my dislike to her – which I shall endeavour to perform, but with much trouble.' He was clearly not over the maid, but some sort of truce in his marital relationship had been called. He and his wife both hurt each other, and the marriage did survive, but this is a small reminder that the statistic about most marriages surviving infidelity does not really do justice to the pain and suffering involved.

When David Lloyd George was Chancellor of the Exchequer, he was accused (quite correctly as it turns out) of having an affair with a married woman. He decided to sue the newspaper and he swore on oath that it was not true. He then persuaded his wife to perjure herself in the upcoming court case. According to his son, Earl Lloyd George:

> Father knew that win, or lose, his career was greatly endangered. He had an unerring instinct about the public temper. "You must stand by me, Maggie. Otherwise, it's all over for me." ...I know that my mother, a deeply religious woman, was in torment in giving support to the lie to be sworn on oath. As a woman, she had been mortally hurt by his infidelities. As a wife, she had been gravely wronged.
>
> (Lloyd George 1960)

David Lloyd George won the case and was awarded one thousand pounds in damages (which he gave to charity). The humiliation and torment experienced by his wife is hard to imagine in this 'successful' marriage.

So why are married men unfaithful to their partners? A small (and not particularly compelling) survey carried out by one tabloid newspaper in the United Kingdom identified eight key reasons, including anger, low self-esteem, lack of love, low commitment, need for variety, neglect, sexual desire, and 'circumstance.' Of course, this is the full gamut of possible explanations, and many will co-occur and overlap. DePaulo goes for a simpler explanation. Married men cheat because of the lies they tell themselves, including the biggest lie of all – 'I can get away with this lie.' And this lie to oneself is supported by others – 'No one will ever challenge me – I'll make sure of it' and 'Even if my lie is discovered, I can make it up to the person I deceived. Eventually, we can have just as good a relationship as we had before.' But there are others in the armoury 'I have their best interests in mind' and 'I'm going to confess – later' (DePaulo 2018). DePaulo also warns that:

> Most people who are about to tell a serious lie have no idea just how much work it is to maintain the lie. They have no idea just how much work it is to maintain the lie. They are obsessively preoccupied with escaping detection and insistently tell themselves that if only they can forever avoid detection or will be well. I do not think this is merely self-deception. Rather, would-be liars are often genuinely oblivious to the intensity and the scope of the burdens of concealment. They don't realise how hard it is to protect a serious lie until they've tried.
>
> (DePaulo 2018: 30–31)

She reminds us that even if the lies are never discovered, liars still need to deal with their own guilt and shame and this can have a profound effect on them and on their relationship. My old university friend was clearly suffering in this regard (although I suspect that many will think that no matter how much he was suffering; it was not enough). Keeping secrets, deceiving his wife, deceiving his children, no one to talk to about any of this, except me, an unlikely therapist in the circumstances. But that's how desperate he was.

We know from other areas of psychology that repressing 'traumatic' experiences like this laden with negative emotions (and he used that word himself), in this way is not psychologically or physically healthy. He needed to talk; he needed some release. The American psychologist Jamie Pennebaker posed the question some time ago why it is that 'When people put their emotional upheavals into words, their physical and mental health improved markedly.' Pennebaker's answer was that 'the act of constructing stories appeared to be a natural human process that helped individuals understand their experiences and themselves' (Pennebaker 2000: 3). My old friend needed to understand what he had done and understand more about himself in the process. That's why he had me in his house.

Pennebaker (1982) proposed that if you do not 'confront' emotionally laden, traumatic events, then both your physical and your mental health will suffer (Pennebaker 1997). The principal assumption behind this is that inhibiting thoughts, feelings, and behaviour require considerable effort, and that if you do this over a significant period, it puts considerable stress on both the body and the mind and makes you susceptible to stress-related diseases. Pennebaker, Hughes, and O'Heeron (1987) demonstrated that 'individuals classified as repressors, inhibitors, or suppressors demonstrate higher cancer rates (Kissen 1966), elevated blood pressure levels (Davies 1970; McClelland 1979), and more physical disease in general (Blackburn 1965) than do more expressive individuals' (see Pennebaker, Hughes, and O'Heeron 1987: 782). And so, the argument continues, 'disinhibiting' or disclosing thoughts and feelings relating to past or present traumatic experiences should be associated with an improvement in physical and mental health. There is clear evidence to back this up. Pennebaker and Beall (1986) reported that those subjects who recounted the 'facts' surrounding an emotionally laden, traumatic events in combination with their feelings concerning the event evidenced great health benefits.

But what is it about talking about these sorts of events that leads to health benefits, especially in the absence of a therapist? Pennebaker (1993) argued that 'Through language individuals are able to organise, structure and ultimately assimilate both their emotional experiences and the events that may have provoked the emotions' (Pennebaker 1995: 5). In other words, he believes that disclosure does basically three things. The first is cognitive – talking about negative emotional experiences requires giving these memories a sequential, organised structure (I listened to my friend's sequential, organised story with interest). Secondly, it allows for the recognition, labelling, and the expression of emotions concerning what happened. Thirdly, it allows for the organisation and assimilation of an individual's perceptions and emotions about the event with their understanding of the event itself. This was the story that was delivered, actions, thoughts, interpretations, emotions, all assimilated and interconnected. These are the narratives that we construct about ourselves to others (and what we often tell ourselves). Pennebaker has also stressed that 'translating traumas and their accompanying images and emotions into language demands that all features of the experience be encoded and stored in a more organized, coherent and simplified manner' (Pennebaker, Mayne, and Francis 1997: 864). Therefore, it is also about 'simplifying' the account, and making it more 'coherent.' This will involve dealing with any conflicted aspects of the memory, which would be necessary in any process of simplifying the account.

Others, however, have placed the emphasis elsewhere. Stiles (1995) emphasised that disclosure

> helps relieve the distress — by catharsis and by promoting self-understanding. Thus, the relation of disclosure to psychological distress is analogous to the relation of fever to physical infection: both an indicator of some underlying disturbance and part of a restorative process.
>
> (1995: 82)

Pennebaker would argue that this is only part of the process – his analyses focused on the use of certain words in emotional disclosure, and he observed some interesting effects. Francis and Pennebaker (1993) devised a text analysis program, LIWC (Linguistic Inquiry and Word Count), to analyse individual lexical items in the accounts. LIWC measures the percentage of negative and positive emotion words and the number of words suggesting 'self-reflection' or 'insight.' Using LIWC, Pennebaker and his colleagues considered changes in usage of positive and negative emotion words, insight words, and causal words from one disclosure to the next over consecutive days and found that the most important factor for reliably predicting improved physical health was an increase in both causal and insight words. My friend was trying to understand how and why the affair had happened and why he ended up lying to those who meant the most to him.

Pennebaker has argued throughout that disclosing a traumatic experience does more than just allow for the reduction of inhibitory processes (Pennebaker 1989). He suggests that 'linguistically labelling an event and its emotions forces the experience to be structured. This structure promotes the assimilation and understanding of the event, and reduces the associated emotional arousal' (Pennebaker, Mayne, and Francis 1997: 864). Clark (1993) argued that through talking, an individual

> attempts to communicate a coherent explanation of the situation, along with an account of his/her own reactions to it. The planful, creative nature of conversation may produce coherence, insights, emotional reactions, and a broadening of perspectives that directly enhance problem solving and interpretive coping.
>
> (1993: 49)

Pennebaker believes that verbalisation allows for the integration or cognitive reorganisation of the person's perceptions and feelings about an event. In other words, through verbalisation, the person may discuss many different aspects of the experience and the mere act of putting one's thoughts and feelings into words may increase the person's understanding of the event. Clark stated that whilst expressing one's innermost feelings about a traumatic event can be important, as in catharsis, like Pennebaker, Clark also believes that 'it is also important that the individual have the opportunity to respond to his/her developing understanding of the problem as well' (1993: 37). Clark explained that:

> In the act of creating and producing a communicative act, the speaker has the opportunity to react to the evolving product. In this "product", the speaker's words give a reality to his/her thoughts and understanding beyond that which exists inside the mind. These processes make that particular version of what happened seem more real. It seems plausible that creating an explanation for a listener of some event is also likely to make the speaker feel more confident about this version's "reality"
>
> (Clark 1993: 37–38)

My own research in this area (Lee and Beattie 1998, 2000), which focused on a micro-analysis of the nonverbal behaviour of the narrator as well as what was actually said, goes slightly beyond this. It suggests that effective emotional disclosure is not just about developing a narrative construction which offers insight into why the events occurred (as Pennebaker maintains), or generating a tangible product to make a particular version more 'real' (as Clark would suggest) but critically, the account has to be one that others accept – feedback from the recipient is important. Our analyses revealed that the eye gaze of the narrator to monitor the facial reactions of the recipient is organised around critical periods in the disclosure (see also Beattie and Ellis 2017) to check how the story is being received at these critical junctures (with opportunities for on-line modifications) in an attempt to help ensure social acceptance of the 'truth' of the account (see Beattie 2018a). There was a 'truth' that my friend wanted me to accept. The spider to a fly metaphor underpinned the whole sorry story (hard for Pennebaker's LIWC to pick up things at that level). That poor fly sat right in front of me.

When people open up in this way, they're constantly checking that you accept it, that you believe their version of events, the story of that poor innocent fly (in this case). That's why he was lying to his wife and children, which was obviously causing him some distress). He desperately wanted me to accept this. My irony might not have been what he was looking for.

But there is another important matter here? Will the marriage last? It seems that most marriages do survive infidelity, but of course not all. And there is one feature of this relationship which might be potentially very significant. My old friend described how his wife looked at him with contempt – research by John Gottman and his colleagues from the University of Washington suggest that marriages that end in divorce can be predicted by certain micro-behaviours; one of them is a display of contempt, which does not augur well for that particular marriage.

For the past forty years, Gottman (1994, 1997) has been investigating the behavioural sequences that characterise successful marriages, compared with marriages that end in divorce, and he has written a number of important and influential books on the subject with ominous titles like, '*What Predicts Divorce: The Measures*,' and (perhaps even more frightening) '*The Mathematics of Divorce*.'

Gottman points out that there are many myths about what makes a happy marriage, including the view that anger in a marriage is the kiss of death. He cites Hendrix (1998) who concluded that

> Anger is destructive to a relationship, no matter what its form. When anger is expressed, the person on the receiving end of the attack feels brutalized, whether or not there has been any physical violence; the old brain does not distinguish between choice of weapons.

Another strongly held belief about marriage, according to Gottman, is that the 'act of listening' (as an expression of empathy in a relationship) is one of the single most important factors in underpinning a successful marriage and this, of course, forms the basis for many different types of marital therapies. Couples, and particularly the husband, are taught to listen more. They are taught to 'hear' things like complaints and to paraphrase the complaint in the conversation, 'in a non-defensive way' in order 'to validate the complainant's feelings.'

Gottman, however, started his research with few assumptions about what the key features might be. What he found was that the expression of anger was not necessarily predictive of divorce. He also found that active listening was rare even in the happiest of relationships. He did, however, find certain sequences of behaviour correlated very highly with the success or failure of relationships. The way that Gottman conducted his research was to recruit a sample of newly married couples who filled in various measures of marital satisfaction. In the second phase of the research, 130 couples were invited to the lab and filmed. The mean age of the husbands was, at that time, twenty-seven and the mean age of the wife was twenty-five. Once each year, their marital status and their marital satisfaction were both measured. At the end of the six-year research period, there had been seventeen divorces in his sample. The couples were filmed discussing a chosen problem that was the cause of ongoing disagreement within the marriage and there were also what Gottman called 'recall sessions' in which the couples reviewed the discussion of their disagreement. The couples discussed the topic for fifteen minutes and then they watched video-recordings back, the husband and wife then had to rate their emotions during the discussion both for themselves and for their partner. The emotional expressions for both members of the couples were analysed, focusing on facial expression, tone of voice, and speech content. The five positive emotions focused on were: interest, validation, affection, humour, and joy; the ten negative emotions focused on were: disgust, contempt, belligerence, domineering, anger, fear/tension, defensiveness, whining, sadness, and stonewalling (or listener withdrawal).

The research question was what types of emotional displays were associated with happy and unhappy marriages and what type of emotional displays predicted divorce? The analyses revealed that 'criticism,' 'defensiveness,' '*contempt*,' 'stonewalling,' and 'belligerence' both by the husband and wife, when in a sufficiently high intensity, predicted divorce but did not necessarily differentiate happy and unhappy marriages. In terms of low-intensity emotional displays, 'whining, anger, sadness, domineering, disgust, fear and stonewalling' by the wife also predicted divorce but did not reliably differentiate happy and unhappy marriages. Displays of anger in the relationship, contrary to the previous received wisdom, did not predict divorce and did not discriminate between happy and unhappy marriages.

In other words, if you want a marriage to succeed, you should not be too concerned about expressions of anger, but there are other types of emotional displays that should concern you greatly. There are four of them – criticism, defensiveness, contempt, and stonewalling which Gottman called '*The Four Horsemen of the Apocalypse.*' In Gottman's view, these behaviours characterise some of the most 'destructive patterns' that can occur in a marriage and were all highly predictive of whether the marriage would last or not. On the other hand, 'active listening' which is such an integral component of much of marital therapy, was found by Gottman to be relatively infrequent even in the happiest and most successful of marriages.

Gottman moved on from the identification of individual units of behaviour to a description of interactional sequences that characterise happy and unhappy marriages and that predict divorce. The main sequence that Gottman identified was described by him in the following way

> The pattern predictive of divorce was negative start-up by the wife, refusal of the husband to accept influence from his wife, wife's reciprocation of low intensity negativity in kind, and the absence of de-escalation of low intensity negativity by the husband.

And you can see that this is a pattern that merely ramps up and up – the wife brings up some irritation, the husband blocks the discussion using negative emotional signals, the wife responds in kind to these signals and the whole thing escalates from there. When couples get locked in this kind of pattern, divorce seems often to be a highly probable option.

On the other hand, those marriages that turn out to be happy and stable were those which had a

> softened start-up by the wife, that the husband accepted influence from her, that he de-escalated low-intensity negative affect, that she was likely to use humour to effectively soothe him, and that he was likely to use positive affect and de-escalation to effectively soothe himself.

In other words, in happy and stable relationships, the wife introduces the touchy topic in a less intense way, and she uses some humour to soften the criticism and stop the whole thing getting out of hand and the husband uses the expression of positive emotion to keep his own psychological state in control. One critical finding from Gottman's research is that it is only couples in which the husband accepts influence from their wives that end up both stable and happy because the husband's response to the initial conversational move from the wife seems critical to this research.

But Gottman's analysis of behavioural sequences in marriage does not just predict divorce rate, it also predicts illness within the marriage. Gottman found, for example, that the display of contempt by your partner actually predicted an increase in infectious illness (for women at least, but interestingly not for men). In the case of men, the relationship between conflict and illness was affected by the psychological dimension of loneliness. Gottman's analysis here suggests that men are more likely than women to start to withdraw from a relationship when stressed and it is this withdrawal which mediates the relationship between conflict and illness.

So, what would Gottman's advice be about saving a marriage? The answer would appear to be don't be overly concerned about temper tantrums (certainly unpleasant but not fatal), but do be concerned about criticism, contempt, stonewalling, and belligerence. Contempt appears to be particularly serious because it doesn't just finish your relationship off; it can finish your partner off as well and make them more prone to infectious illness. The secret of a happy, stable relationship is that when the wife introduces some criticism, don't block it with negativity. For the wife, the secret would appear to be to introduce criticism gently and to use humour to soften the criticism (without appearing to be too sarcastic) and don't let *The Four Horsemen of the Apocalypse* (and their fellow rider, belligerence) carry you to a place beyond hope.

Gottman's research has been the focus of much popular discussion over the years (Gladwell 2005). In his initial experiments, he used an observational sample of fifteen minutes to predict the patterns of divorce, subsequently researchers argue that this can be done on the basis of a sample of three minutes. Three minutes, according to some analysts, can tell you all that you need to know about whether a marriage will survive or fail.

But there are clearly shortcomings in the research. It is interesting that the number of divorces in the original sample is not that large, and all of the sample was drawn from the same small part of the United States, so we have to be very careful about drawing general conclusions from such a small sample. However, perhaps the biggest danger with Gottman's work (and similar research) is that there is always the possibility that the behavioural descriptions may merely be the *symptoms* of some deep underlying cause or some underlying issue – some basic incompatibility between the partners that may be realised on a daily basis in these behavioural sequences.

But, of course, there is something else that Gottman fails to consider – lies in the relationship and how, on occasion, we display nothing but contempt for the cheating partner. In other words, contempt may sometimes be a response to lies.

Remember what my friend told me about Christmas Day at home:

> Christmas Day is almost the worst. How can you leave three children to go out on Christmas Day without any sensible explanation? They would be left at home for a few hours, puzzled and abandoned. My wife would look at me with contempt. "Who the fuck goes out on Christmas morning after the presents have been opened? It's a time for families," then she would go off and cry.

We may not want to call our cheating partner out even when it is that obvious, we may not want to make the whole thing explicit, so instead, we display it nonverbally through the silent and implicit language of the body (Argyle 1973; Beattie 2016a), through that one look of contempt that says it all. Gottman's *objective* micro-analysis of nonverbal behaviour in the interaction of married couples only focuses on behaviours, not what may lie behind them. It cannot pick up on lies for his formulation of the mathematics of divorce. But lies undoubtedly will be there and potentially at the centre of so much difficulty.

When my old friend told me that day in his house about how his wife re-acted to him, I knew what that look of contempt meant. What should I have said to that *fly* just sitting there in front of me? Nervously waiting, for some reassurance that I, of course, understood him. A reassurance from one 'man-of-the-world' to another, that things would be okay in the end, that his lies would be forgiven by his family, by his wife, by his children. But I couldn't. That day of all days I didn't want to lie.

Your Muffins Are the Best

The classic psychological research on lies in everyday life was conducted by Bella DePaulo from the University of Virginia and her colleagues and published in a set of (very closely connected) papers in the late 1990s (DePaulo et al. 1996; Kashy and DePaulo 1996; DePaulo and Kashy 1998). These papers are highly cited and are often used as a guide by both psychologists and the public as to how lies operate in everyday life. The conclusion either drawn or extrapolated from these studies have been incredibly broad, as if they tell us definitively about how lies generally are used in everyday life. Kashy and DePaulo (1996) called their paper 'Who Lies?': the answer they provide is that we all do. This answer and their research do, however, require careful scrutiny.

They begin the first of their 1996 papers by outlining their position on lies and deceit. They write

> Perspectives on lying are as diverse as their sources...Pronouncements about deceit are staggeringly varied not only because of the nature of the beast, but also because the debate on deceit has in some important ways proceeded virtually unconstrained by data. Many perspectives on deceit rest on assumptions about patterns of lying in everyday life.
>
> (DePaulo et al. 1996: 979)

They set about gathering the data on how lying operates in everyday life by asking college students (either university undergraduates with a mean age of 18.7, or students from a community college with a mean age of 34.2) to keep lie diaries. There were seventy-seven university undergraduates in the sample and seventy community college students (the same 147 students were used in all three papers), 89.1% of the participants were white; 59.2% were female. The participants were told to record in a notebook all of their social interactions (lasting ten minutes or more) each day for a week and record all of their lies. A lie was defined in the following way 'a lie occurs any time you intentionally try to mislead someone. Both the intent to deceive and the actual deception must occur...Participants were urged to record all lies, no matter how big or small' (DePaulo et al. 1996: 981). If they didn't want to disclose the content of the lie, they could write 'rather not say.' If they remembered the lie the following day, they could include those as well. So, the resulting data was a mixture of real-time observation (presumably after some delay – there's nothing like getting a notebook out to kill a conversation) and memory for lies, with presumably some judicious editing on the part of the participants given that they had a sanctioned category they could use ('rather not say') if it was too embarrassing, painful, serious, or whatever.

The participants also had to rate how 'intimate' the conversation was on a nine-point scale from 'superficial' to 'meaningful' and the 'quality' of the interaction from 'unpleasant' to 'pleasant,' again on a nine-point scale. They also had to briefly describe the lie and the reasons why they told the lie in a free-response format and note the degree of planning (from *completely spontaneous* to *carefully planned* in advance), how important it was not to be caught (*very unimportant* to *very important*), their feelings (from *very comfortable* to *very uncomfortable*), the seriousness of the lie (from *trivial* to *very serious*), and the target's reaction to the lie in terms of whether they were fooled or not (*they didn't believe me at all* to *believed me completely*).

In terms of the results, the researchers found that participants lied about their feelings, opinions, and evaluations ('Told her that her muffins were the best ever'), their achievements, their knowledge, their actions, plans and whereabouts, explanation for their own behaviour, and facts about their objects, people, and possessions ('Told him my father was an ambassador').

The reasons for lying were categorised as either 'self-oriented'

> Lies told to protect or enhance the liars psychologically, or to advantage or protect the liars' interests, lies told to elicit a particular emotional response that the liars desired, lies told to protect the liars from embarrassment, loss of face, or looking bad…lies told to make the liars appear better…personal gain…to protect the liar from loss of status etc.,

or as 'other-oriented' lies, which were

> Lies told to protect or enhance the other person psychologically or to advantage or protect the interests of the other person…to protect their feelings…to make things easier or more pleasant for them… to protect them from loss of position or status.
>
> (DePaulo et al. 1996: 983)

DePaulo found that the male students told more self-oriented lies, boastful lies to make themselves look better, female students, on the other hand, told more other-oriented lies to make the other person feel better. Aristotle in *The Nicomachean Ethics* had this to say about the sorts of lies that the male students told –

> the boaster is regarded as one who pretends to have distinguished qualities which he possesses either not at all or to a lesser degree than he pretends…[even] without an ulterior motive … deceivers are to be censured, particularly the boaster.
>
> (*trans.* Thomson 1953/1976)

The lies in the DePaulo study were also classified as 'outright' (total falsehoods – 'I told my mother that I did not drink beer at college'), 'exaggerations' ('Exaggerated how sorry I was to be late') or 'subtle' where relevant details are omitted ('I told my co-worker on a project that I'd been working hard, I didn't say that it was on our particular project').

The examples provided all seem like fragments of everyday student life as they manoeuvre around relationships and situations, not wanting to hurt the feelings of others, or trying to self-present in a particular way to deal with their insecurities. Aristotle may have been a little harsh. Many seem trivial, stories about how delicious muffins were. When they don't seem trivial, the method and the coding don't allow for greater insight. I wanted to know what happened next when the student told someone (on a date?) that her father was an ambassador. Was this the start of some great pretext that had to be maintained over weeks and months and at great personal cost? Or was this something that was just forgotten the next day? As in 'ha hah ha, you believed me, you fell for it.' Was it a little bit of fun, maybe a little bit of flirting, or something much more serious? When I was a student at Trinity College Cambridge, a fellow student once pointed out to me that I never mentioned my family in any of our conversations. He said to me

> I know another student from Belfast, and he never mentions his family either – his father is a High Court Judge and there are massive security issues around the family and the house. I bet it's something like that in your case.

I just smiled back at him in the dining hall of that college where several Kings of England had been educated, and I said, '*Something* like that.' That's where I left it: DePaulo might classify this as a 'subtle' lie, a lie which allows the target to make certain incorrect inferences. I didn't want to talk about my mother and my father, and the bombs and the bullets, or Ewarts mill missing the letter 'E,' or my friends from the turn-of-the-road gang, and what had become of them in the conflict (including the ones on the front pages of newspapers). But my lie to my fellow student was a lie with real consequences. I had to be careful around him, anticipating where any of his questions might go, I was wary, uncomfortable, it stopped our friendship from developing. It was very stressful. He believed I was from the upper echelons of British society – I didn't want to be accused of being a liar. I didn't want him to discover my real past.

Of course, when it comes to graduation, families do descend on the college. And after my three years were up, I had to hide my mother and my Uncle Terence and Aunt Agnes away when they came to my graduation. When I say hide away, I really mean that this was my goal, but it was impossible. They had been recommended a pub in Cambridge (on the other side of town) so when the time came for me to graduate in the early afternoon, my uncle had by then downed ten or more pints of Guinness. He was hard to shepherd along Trinity Street. I was on edge. I don't think anyone could have mistaken him for a

High Court judge, leaning up against the wall of Heffers bookshop, sweating in his thick wool suit in mid-summer, swearing about where the hell we were going. I was embarrassed and (if the truth be told) I was deeply ashamed of my embarrassment. The 'subtle' lie to my college friend made the embarrassment and the shame so much more intense.

So, what did DePaulo's classic research on lying really reveal? Students lie frequently but 'they did not regard their lies as serious and did not plan them much or worry about being caught' (DePaulo et al. 1996: 979). College students lie twice a day, and they tell more self-centred lies than other-oriented lies. The commonest lies were outright lies and the faking of positive emotions. These after all were students, in the case of the university undergraduate sample, very young first-year students, living away from home probably for the first time and desperately trying to establish new friendships. They probably didn't know their 'targets' well enough to tell them how they really felt inside – probably a bit homesick, a little unsure, nervous with their new acquaintances. This is less a study about the ethnography of lying than a study on the constraints on self-disclosure in new social relationships at university.

In the second paper in the set, Kashy and DePaulo (1996) in answer to the question they pose in the title of their paper 'Who Lies?' tell us with some authority that we all do this, seemingly as a matter of course, although some do it more frequently than others, dependent upon their underlying personality – 'the people who told more lies were more manipulative, more concerned with self-presentation, and more sociable' (Kashy and DePaulo 1996: 1037), which is an interesting set of juxtaposed personality characteristics that we will explore in much more detail in a later chapter. In the third paper on this cohort of students, DePaulo and Kashy (1998) explored the relationship between closeness of relationship and lying in that same sample of 147 college students. They reported more altruistic lies told to friends and best friends and more self-serving lies to acquaintances and strangers. Their participants lied in about one in every three social interactions with their romantic partners, but again, it must be remembered that most of their sample were very young undergraduates desperately trying to impress their new partners. We should be careful about the conclusions we try to draw from this about lying, in everyday life, away from the lecture theatre and the hall of residence.

These three papers, really representing one empirical study, were innovative in some ways, using the well-used diary method to collect data on lying, but they hardly provide any kind of definitive description of how lies are used in everyday life except in a very narrow sample, where a few moment's reflections on the social dynamics of college students should allow us to anticipate the kinds of results observed. Students tell their new acquaintance in college that their muffins are the best that they've ever tasted, and they hide their homesickness from them because they want to be liked and they want to appear mature and sophisticated, and then they lie to their mums about drinking beer so that their mums won't worry about other temptations coming their way. But there is so much to lying than this, and I don't want to trivialise the subject of lying, which is why I started with lies that mattered and to understand why they mattered I had to describe the social context. Lies also operate in social structures, which is part of the social context, starting with what might be called appropriately in this case, the adjacency pair. My 'subtle' lie about my father being a High Court judge was a response to what was for me an intrusive question/challenge about why I never talked about my family. My lie would only have occurred as a second part of this challenge-response adjacency pair, never as the first item, never as a spontaneous lie 'out of the blue.' The DePaulo research treats lies as isolated events, disconnected from social context and social structure. In real life, they are rarely like this.

DePaulo and her colleagues wrote that the liars they studied 'did not regard their lies as serious and did not plan them much or worry about being caught,' but that's not true of all liars, or even most liars. Lies may be very common but they are often very serious. They damage people. Getting caught can be devastating. Getting fooled can be equally devastating. That's what we are exploring in this book. And throughout, we will try to explore the psychological significance of lies in the social contexts in which they naturally occur. This I suspect may be particularly revealing.

3 Learning to Lie

Lying – and in a lesser degree obstinacy – are, in my opinion, the only faults whose birth and progress we should consistently oppose. They grow with a child's growth, and once the tongue has got the knack of lying, it is difficult to imagine how impossible it is to correct it. Whence it happens that we find some otherwise excellent men subject to this fault and enslaved by it.

Michel De Montaigne (1602)

The Innocence of Childhood

Charles Darwin published the first scientific paper on lying in childhood in the journal *Mind* in 1877. The subject was his first child, William Erasmus. This paper was based on observations recorded in his diary which he had kept thirty-seven years previously on the development of his children, but observations on William in particular. 'I had excellent opportunities for close observation, and wrote down at once what was observed,' he wrote (Darwin 1877: 285). He was, of course, interested in the role of instinct versus experience in shaping the development of his child and how nature and nurture interact in the various developmental pathways.

Darwin begins his description of the child's development by describing the behaviour of his infant in the first seven days of life, the instinctive (and un-learnt) reflex actions like sneezing, hiccupping, yawning, stretching, sucking, and screaming, and the instinctive reaction to loud noises:

Once, when he was 66 days old, I happened to sneeze, and he started violently, frowned, looked frightened, and cried rather badly: for an hour afterwards, he was in a state which would be called nervous in an older person, for every slight noise made him start.

(Darwin 1877: 286)

He describes the development of the emotions (fear is probably the first, he notes, at four and a half months), the development of affection (very clear at

DOI: 10.4324/9781003394563-3

five months, he says), 'practical reasoning' (for example, the infant slipping his hand down his father's finger so that he could suck on the finger on the 114th day), the development of curiosity, imitation, and communication (using gestures then his first word at twelve months – the child's first word was 'mum' for food).

He also describes the development of 'moral sense' in the child, appearing clearly at just over two years old. 'When 2 years and 3 months old, he gave his last bit of gingerbread to his little sister, and then cried out with high self-approbation "Oh kind Doddy [his nickname], kind Doddy"' Darwin (1877: 291). Darwin then describes the first instances of his son lying to him. He described how his son then aged 2 years 7½ months ate some sugar in the dining room which he had been told not to do:

> I met him coming out of the dining room with his eyes unnaturally bright, and an odd unnatural or affected manner, so that I went into the room to see who was there, and found that he had been taking pounded sugar, which he had been told not to do. As he had never been in any way punished, his odd manner certainly was not due to fear, and I suppose it was pleasurable excitement struggling with conscience.
>
> (Darwin 1877: 292)

A fortnight later, Darwin describes how his son was looking at his pinafore which he had carefully rolled up, and Darwin notes that his manner was just a little odd. Darwin wanted to see what was within the child's pinafore, but his son *commanded* him to 'go away.' The pinafore, it turns out, was stained with pickle-juice, so Darwin concludes that 'here was carefully planned deceit.'

It's almost as if these actions of his young child have taken Darwin by surprise, having witnessed what he interprets as the *pleasure of lying* in one so young. And Darwin emphasised that this child was being brought up in a household where he had 'never been in any way punished,' so there was no necessity to lie. Furthermore, his son's lies were carefully planned. Darwin does not say so explicitly but he clearly cannot seem to find any *environmental* explanation for the child's behaviour, anything in his upbringing or early childhood experience which it could be attributed to, and on that great seesaw of nature versus nurture, you can see that he's grappling with lying tipping in the opposite direction, towards a non-learned instinctive response to the world. He reassures himself in the paper with the comment about how his child eventually turned out 'As this child was educated solely by working on his good feelings, he soon became as truthful, open and tender, as anyone could desire' (Darwin 1877: 292). In other words, it is as if Darwin is suggesting that the motivation to lie (and the pleasure derived from it) may be more or less instinctual, but with the right moral and emotional training, it can be suppressed.

Following Darwin, developmental psychologists studied how children learn to tell lies, and were often interested in the moral development of the child (see Hartshorne and May 1928; Piaget 1932/1948 for some early attempts). However, lies and lying are also complex cognitive skills, but attempts to uncover the role of cognitive factors in lying came much later. Two cognitive factors have been identified which are thought to play a major role in lying and the ability to lie effectively (see Sai et al. 2021). These are Theory of Mind (ToM) and Executive Function (EF).

ToM refers to the ability to understand and attribute mental states, such as beliefs, desires, intentions, emotions, and knowledge to oneself and other and critically, to recognise that other people have thoughts and feelings that might be different from one's own. This cognitive skill is crucial for social interaction and communication, as it enables individuals to predict and interpret the behaviour of others based on their mental state. Having a ToM allows us to empathise with others, understand their intentions, and make more accurate predictions about their behaviour. It's also critical to lying.

According to Talwar and Lee (2008), a lie is associated with what they call both first-order and second-order ToM understanding. In order to tell a lie, children must represent and differentiate between the mental states of themselves and the recipient of the lie, and then use words (or actions) to instil false beliefs in this other person using the lie (Talwar and Lee 2008). This is first-order ToM understanding, which develops around the age of four to five years old. But Talwar and Lee (2008) also suggest that that the children's ability to tell a follow-up lie that actually works involves second-order ToM understanding (this develops around five to six years old). In order to tell a successful follow-up lie and maintain consistency with the initial lie, children must also be able to infer what false beliefs they have implanted in the mind of the recipient of the lie (Talwar and Lee 2008).

EF, on the other hand, refers to a set of higher-order mental processes and cognitive abilities that are crucial for goal-directed behaviour, decision-making, planning, and self-regulation. It manages and coordinates different cognitive functions to achieve desired outcomes effectively. Some of the key components are *working memory* (the ability to hold and manipulate information in the mind for short periods whilst performing cognitive tasks), *inhibitory control* (the capacity to control impulsive behaviour, resist distractions and suppress irrelevant or inappropriate responses), and *cognitive flexibility* (the capacity to adapt to new situations, think creatively, and adjust one's thinking when circumstances change) (Diamond 2006; Zelazo and Müller 2002). Research suggests that all three of these cognitive abilities are important to lying.

Working memory refers to the ability to hold and manipulate information in one's mind (Diamond and Lee 2011). To lie successfully, children need to be able to hold the truth, and keep it hidden, and to create an alternative in the form of a lie which they must also remember if they are not to give the game away (Alloway et al. 2015). Inhibitory control refers to the ability to override a more automatic response (Williams et al. 1999) – in order to lie successfully, children need to exercise sufficient inhibitory control to suppress the tendency to tell the truth (Evans and Lee 2013). Cognitive flexibility refers to the ability to think creatively and to adjust one's thinking when circumstances change between truth and lie (Christ et al. 2009).

There are clearly good a priori grounds for proposing that both ToM and EF should be critical to the development of lying in children, and research evidence seems to back this up, but the results are not necessarily that consistent. In a recent review of the literature, Sai from Hangzhou University and colleagues (2021) write that:

> Some studies have found ToM to be strongly correlated with children's lying behavior: children with better ToM are more likely to lie and are more able to maintain their lies. However, other studies failed to find any correlation between children's lying and ToM. Thus, the associations between children's lying and ToM, as well as the specific nature of these associations remain unclear. Similarly, the links between children's lying and different EF components, though theoretically plausible, have not been fully elucidated. Various studies have obtained inconsistent or weak associations between EF and children's lying.
>
> (see Sai et al. 2021: 2)

These researchers, therefore, carried out the first meta-analysis of 47 papers consisting of 5099 participants between 2 and 19 years of age to determine what conclusions can be drawn about the relationship between children's lying and both ToM and EF. A meta-analysis of this kind is considered the most effective way to synthesise findings from all existing studies on a specific topic. The research studies on this question used a variety of paradigms and situations, but mainly experimental laboratory-based situations, including hide-and-seek (where a child hides a toy and can mislead an opponent in order to win the toy), the 'temptation resistance paradigm' (where a toy is placed in the room and the child, often naturally inquisitive of course, is asked 'Did you peak at the toy?' when asked not to), or an adult confederate breaks a toy in the laboratory and asks the child to conceal this from the experimenter. Only two of the forty-seven studies covered in the meta-analysis used actual lies in everyday life (these real-life lies were recorded by the mother soon after the incident). This statistic is very telling.

The researchers found that both ToM and EF were positively correlated with frequency of lying, and there was a stronger association between EF and the ability to maintain lies compared to the telling of initial lies. The association between EF and lying was also strongest for self-protective lies (lies to conceal transgressions to avoid negative consequences) and self-benefitting lies (lies to get a strategic advantage) rather than for white lies (prosocial lies in order to be polite) or lies to protect somebody else.

In other words, the brightest children in terms of their ToM and EF abilities lie the most and lie most selfishly. There was no significant relationship between age and EF ability – rather, the researchers concluded that EF plays a consistent role in children's lying regardless of age. So, children with a good working memory, flexible in their thinking and able to stop themselves automatically telling the truth through good inhibitory control, lie the most and maintain their lies more effectively. They seem to recognise their abilities early.

None of this research would surprise the sociobiologist Robert Trivers (2011) who has argued that children learn to deceive at a very young age and that this is evolutionarily adaptive. He says that both scientific research and everyday observation demonstrate that children are capable of deception between two and three years old (like Darwin's son). But if you take a very broad perspective on deception, he says, then there is evidence that children as young as six months show in his words 'clear signs' of deceptive behaviour. He points to fake crying and pretend laughing as some of the earliest signs of deception. You can tell that the crying is fake, he suggests, because very young children often pause to check whether anyone is listening before resuming. Trivers says that this shows that they can moderate the deceptive behaviour according to the victim's (usually the mother's) response. Trivers sketches out a timeline for the development of lying in young children as follows:

> By eight months, infants are capable of concealing forbidden activities and distracting parental attention. By age two, a child can bluff a threat of punishment, for example, by saying, "I don't care", about a proposed punishment, when he or she clearly cares. In one study, two-thirds of children age two and a half practiced deception at least once in a two-hour period. Motives for children's lies seem broadly similar to those of adults. Lies to protect the feelings of others – so called white lies – appear only by age five.
>
> (Trivers 2011: 88–89)

Trivers views the ability to lie as evolutionarily adaptive. He says that 'he has never seen any signs of natural guilt in children when practicing deception' (although this kind of universal generalisation can often be refuted with specific examples) and that 'children seem to regard deception as their first line of defense' but essentially, he is trying to reframe how we think about deception in young children and there is clearly some merit in rethinking how and why it operates in the way it does. He also says that there is clear evidence that the ability to lie connects to cognitive ability (as we have just seen), and given the cognitive resources required to lie effectively, it increases with age:

> As children mature, they become increasingly intelligent and increasingly deceptive. This is not an accident. The very maturing capacity that gives them greater general intelligence also gives them greater ability to suppress behavior and create novel behavior. There is also clear evidence that natural variation in intelligence, corrected for age, is positively correlated with deception. A child is left in a room and told not to look in a box. By the time the experimenter returns, most children

have peeked. Now they are asked whether they peeked. Most say no, and the brighter the children are on simple cognitive tasks, the more likely they are to lie.

(Trivers 2011: 90)

Lying is a skill. Deliberate and successful lying makes demands on our EF. It requires more cognitive effort and more cognitive resources than telling the truth (Vrij et al. 2006, 2011). It's something we must learn to do, but some seem more equipped than others, as we have just seen. Liars must fabricate the lie and to check, whilst delivering it, that it's being believed. The cognitive act of making up a lie and the monitoring and decoding of the nonverbal signals of another person are harder than you might at first imagine. This monitoring impacts on the speaker's pattern of eye gaze and eye contact in interaction (Beattie 1979) because it is very difficult to plan what you're going to say and monitor and decode signals from the other person simultaneously (even when you're not lying), it leads to more dysfluencies (Beattie 1981). So, all speakers (not just liars) have these very brief periods of looking away at certain peaks of cognitive planning. If they don't, there's an increase in dysfluencies – ums and ah's, repetitions, and false starts. But gaze aversion *and* dysfluencies may well be taken as evidence of deceit (Vrij 2000), so liars must plan their lie, often in real time (some effective liars, of course, plan **well** in advance) and attempt to control these behaviours (some of which may not even be connected to the lie), whilst inhibiting or concealing the truth. It is not that surprising that several neuroimaging studies have provided evidence that liars are engaged in a cognitively demanding task with prefrontal brain regions which are involved in cognitive control (i.e., the anterior cingulate, dorsolateral prefrontal, and inferior frontal regions) more active when people are lying compared to when they are telling the truth (Christ et al. 2009).

But, of course, this only tells us about the cognitive skills that support children's early lying and that children with well-developed cognitive abilities are more likely to lie (but with scant data on how these skills relate to lies in everyday life). But what factors influence whether we use these skills or not? This is a critical issue.

In a paper in *Current Opinions in Psychology* in 2022, Victoria Talwar from McGill University and her colleague Angela Crossman argue that:

Whether or not one chooses to lie is a function of more than knowing how to lie. We must also know when to lie' and 'holistic examinations of cognitive, social, environmental, cultural and child factors, interacting over time, is required to understand divergent trajectories of lying and truth-telling across development, particularly at the extremes.'

(Talwar and Crossman 2022: 1)

The authors outline several sources of social–environmental influence, including direct parental influence, which they say is often contradictory and muddled – on the one hand, parents will often tell their young children that lying is never acceptable whilst offering older children more 'nuanced' messages about lying. The authors also argue that how parents respond to children's lies teaches their children about the value of honesty and the authors report that in families where the lies of the children go unchecked, the children are more likely to lie two years later. They also remind us that many parents do encourage their children to lie in specific circumstances ('Don't tell your father that the dog peed on the floor'), or to tell a polite lie to a friend who has given them a disappointing gift. But children also learn about lying more indirectly though modelling. They witness their parents lying to them to get them to behave ('If you don't come with me now, I will leave you here by yourself'), and they copy this behaviour. Siblings, they say are another significant source of influence and there is evidence that children with a younger sibling are better at maintaining lies. They can become practised at lying to their younger sibling – 'I'm going to bed now honestly, just like you' is, I would guess, a regular lie in this context, in a strategic alliance with their parents!

But perhaps what is most interesting about this paper is their summary of what we do not currently know, their appraisal of 'future directions' for research. They write:

> There remains a wide scope for research on the processes that shape honest and dishonest behaviors throughout the lifespan. For example, we do not yet understand how children perceive and react to parental hypocrisy around lying (e.g., trust in their parents: likelihood of lying to their parents), as well as the reciprocal – how children's lie-telling influences the behaviours and reactions of their parents...Beyond the individual and the family, we do not know what roles other social agents might play, such as teachers and peers, in shaping dis (honesty), and we do not fully appreciate all of the contextual factors that influence an individual's lie-telling decisions across situations.
>
> (Talwar and Crossman 2022: 4)

Regarding their first suggestion about future directions, I attempted to sketch out some of the issues about trust and response to a parental lie (including my own highly irrational response) in 'Please Release Me' in Chapter 2. In the next section of the book, I turn to their second suggestion – the role of other social agents, particularly peers in shaping dishonesty and lies. I reflect on my gang at the street corner in Belfast, and that process of socialisation and the learning opportunities of 'disaffected' youths. The gang offered a range of new role models, and new sets of explicit and implicit rules about lying, and many opportunities to practise lying where practice is evidently important. Indeed, Van Bockstaele from Ghent University and his colleagues demonstrated in 2012 that lying becomes easier when experimental participants are trained to lie and becomes more difficult when they are trained to tell the truth. In other words, practice makes…if not perfect…then telling the lie much easier. Many religious figures in the past have warned about the way that lying can become established through practice, beginning even with innocuous lies and lies told in jest (and on the street corner, many lies were told in jest – just to amuse bored teenagers; some were much more serious). Once lying becomes a habit, however, it becomes easier to tell more serious lies. Al-Ghazali, often referred to as the 'Light of Islam' wrote:

> Keep your tongue from lying, whether in earnest or in jest. Do not accustom yourself to lying in jest, for it will lead you to lying in earnest. Lying is one of the sources of the greater sins, and if you come to be known as a liar, your uprightness becomes worthless, your word is not accepted and eyes scorn and despise you.

From a different religious perspective, Cardinal Newman in 1880 warned of a similar fate:

> thus the Apostle admonishes, "Putting aside lying, speak ye truth." For therein is the great danger of lapsing into frequent and more serious lying, and from lies in joke men gain the habit of lying, whence they gain the character of not being truthful.

There is clearly learning involved in lying (although the motivation to lie, as we have seen in Charles Darwin's own family may start very young) and as children mature, and right through the teenage years, they become increasingly intelligent and increasingly deceptive, according to Trivers. Timothy Levine and his colleagues writing in *Communication Research Reports* in 2013 found that high school students told on average 4.1 lies in the previous twenty-four hours, a rate, they tell us, that is 75% higher than that reported by college students and 150% higher than that reported in a nationwide sample of adults. They also found that in their sample, there were some very prolific liars who told a disproportionate number of lies.

But perhaps we need to investigate specific teenage sub-cultures to view and understand this with a clearer focus, to see how increasing intelligence is put to use, to appreciate how lies are used, and what their consequences might be. We can try to understand lies in that major life transition to adulthood, perhaps with the words of Al-Ghazali and Cardinal Newman at the back of our minds, and all the time trying to appreciate the context and how teenagers use these natural cognitive talents, and at what cost. We can then start to consider the role of other 'social agents,' as Talwar and Crossman called them, social agents like corner boys, corner boys like me.

Gangs, Lies, and Belonging

We were the 'turn-of-the-road gang.' That was what we called ourselves, it signalled our patch, our territory, in Belfast that most territorial of cities, with invisible peace lines separating the Protestants and the Catholics. We were the *Protestant* turn-of-the-road gang.

We would stand in a long row, as if on guard, on a little strip outside the chip shop where the Upper Crumlin Road turns into the Ligoniel Road. Greasy Jim's we called the chippie, blasting out its hot, fetid smells. Watching and waiting, but for nothing in particular.

The police would regularly drive past and move us on, but we'd nowhere to go, so we'd go for a wee dander down Primrose Street and over that bit of waste ground by the Pigeon Club, and head back to Greasy Jim's as soon as we could, as soon as it was safe.

We lived in these two-up, two-down mill houses. There was no privacy in those houses, you didn't have a room of your own or your own private space (as we might call it today) so you wouldn't want to go home early if you could help it – you might have to talk or explain yourself. You might have to lie too much about what you'd been up to, and get yourself all tangled up, you couldn't be yourself. Not like at the corner.

I was 'Beats' in the turn-of-the-road gang, not Geoffrey (at home), or Beattie, which is what they called me at school. Just Beats. Two personas really, maybe three. There was never much to observe, just standing there, night after night. Maybe, just the locals making their way to Paddy's for a drink. But there was a strong sense of community, of belonging.

'All right, boys.'

'All right, Mr. Smith.'

'Back again.'

'Yeah, back again'

We watched him walk off. 'He'll be full in a couple of hours,' said Duck. Duck knew how to break the boredom of all that standing and waiting.

'He'll be fucking pishing himself in an hour's time. He won't be able to get his wee man out in time.' Duck was now imitating him, playing with his zip, the zip that had stuck. 'Pish running down his leg.' He zigzagged across the grey, wet pavement as if trying to shake urine out of his trousers.

That was the craic, sometimes not very funny but sometimes, just sometimes hilarious, even about those that we were fond of, like, old Mr Smith, even when it wasn't true.

Duck would imitate how he'd be walking home after ten or eleven pints of Guinness. 'Two steps to the left and then one to the right. That's how people walk when they're full,' He acted it out. 'Everybody knows this.'

All the lads would say that if you wanted to roll somebody, that's what you should look out for – that walk. 'They won't even feel it; they won't know what's hit them.' But I had no intention of ever robbing a drunk man, but I went along with it. This was street corner society that Whyte (1943) wrote about in the South Side of Chicago; this was the social performance of belonging (Goffman 1963), the social construction of acting hard, of knowing the score. We looked up to the hard men from the corner, we loved the way they walked, the way they swung their shoulders, their dander, the arrogance of it all. You would literally step aside as they came towards you.

'Alright, lads?' they'd smile at us.

We were delighted when they gave us a wee nod of approval and tossed it our way. Sometimes, I thought the hard men walked like pigeons, short fast steps, the way a pigeon walks with its head up and its chest out and its shoulders (I mean the bit above its wings) moving in time with its feet. Pigeons always seem in a hurry, always going somewhere important, very territorial, and mean, if you've ever seen them fighting over scraps of bread. But I kept that thought to myself, for obvious reasons.

'Aright, lads?'

'Aright Sammy?'

'Back at Greasy Jim's again?'

'We're back again, Sammy.'

'I wouldn't eat that shite,' he said, gesturing towards the window. 'Just look at that, it turns my stomach.' He was gesturing in at the fryer at the back of the shop, bubbling away. Greasy Jim waved back at him – he must have mistaken his gesture for a wee wave. Greasy Jim was always desperately trying to please Sammy the Hard Man.

'You can see the grease sticking to his dirty fucking windows,' said Sammy.

We all nodded in agreement, although two of the lads had just eaten a fish supper.

'Terrible, Sammy, I know. He should wash those fucking windows,' said Duck. 'Wash that fucking grease off.'

Sammy threw him a look to say, 'shut the fuck up,' the comments about the grease on the windows were his and not to be shared and repeated by the likes of us. We also shouldn't be using the 'f' word in conversation with him, as if we were on a par with him. You don't swear in front of your elders and betters.

Sammy was the hardest man in our neighbourhood. His nephew was an occasional member of our gang. He would show up to boast about Sammy's exploits, and once he took a hammer to a local disco and hit someone with it. It was chaos after that. Sammy hated Fenians (what we called Catholics), the implication being that so should we (the hammer victim was a Fenian, of course). I did struggle with this because of my Uncle Terence, and the fact that my next-door neighbours and the family next to them, the Rocks, were all Catholic. My street was 'mixed,' you see (at least at the start of the Troubles). Many of the streets were not.

Sammy would go into Paddy's bar, and then an hour or two later, we'd still be hanging about, and he'd nip into Greasy Jim's for a fish supper and a couple of extra pasties ('slip a few wee pasties in there, Jim'), despite his apparent misgivings about the quality of the food. It would have been a brave man to point out these apparent inconsistencies. Duck always said that he had never once seen Sammy paying for his supper, and he swears that Greasy Jim always told Sammy that it was 'on the house, as usual.' I didn't know whether it was true, but I could believe it.

Some of the old men who walked past would have stood at the corner like us a generation before. Few ever left that area. That was just the way it was. A couple of bars, a bookie's, couple of chippies, a chemist shop, a greengrocer's, a sweet shop, a draper's, a hardware store, and a bakery. The bakery was full of iced buns. For some reason, we ate a lot of iced buns. That was our one big treat. Poor families like to spoil their children with sweet things.

Buses would snake past the turn of the road, to turn up into Ligoniel village. The Ligoniel bus meant something. It was a marker, a sign, a signifier of religion, of tribe, Protestant or Catholic. One or the other, no grey areas. Protestants at the bottom (with some exceptions like my street), Catholics at the top, anything above St Marks Church was Catholic, a subtle enough peace line. The Ligoniel bus took the Catholics home. It went through our neighbourhood.

You always had to be one thing or the other in Belfast. Names and schools were both dead give-aways. Telling any stranger your name was always tinged with jeopardy, if you had to lie about it, this was a high-stakes lie.

A mate of mine, Jackie, had once been cornered outside the Forum cinema in Ardoyne. Three young hoods walked up this nervous line queuing to get in to see Von Ryan's Express. Ardoyne was very Catholic, and it became famous during the Troubles (one of the infamous Shankill bombers came from Ardoyne). We called it Comanche territory, the Westerns on TV gave us a way of viewing and labelling our world. 'Are you a Protestant or a Catholic?' they asked each boy in turn with a more direct approach. Jackie thought long and hard as they worked their way along the queue before they got to him. 'I'm a Jew,' he replied. He didn't mean it as a joke – it was a way out, a way of evading the question, a way of not giving the wrong answer with all the risks that entailed. He told me later that he was shitting himself, that this reply just (sort of) popped into his head, and he couldn't get it out of his head. It just stuck there. He'd never even met a Jew. The only Jew he could think of by name was Jesus. He was praying that night that they wouldn't ask him his name.

There was a pause when he answered, this was a response that they hadn't expected. 'But are you a Protestant Jew or a Catholic Jew?'

They meant it. Get it wrong and you got a good digging. Not necessarily at that precise moment, it was when you got out of the cinema you had to worry. They had time to kill as well; they were corner boys as well with nothing better to do. He told them that he was a Catholic Jew, after a bit of prompting, and by that, I mean a surreptitious knee in the balls. It was the right guess that night. Protestant youths from the Shankill would sometimes come up to Ardoyne to trouble those waiting to get into the Forum, so the 'correct' answer wasn't necessarily that obvious.

These moments were always very tense. The ability to lie successfully was a necessary skill up our way, and there was no shame in saying that you were a Catholic when you were outnumbered by Catholics in Comanche territory.

On that corner, we'd watch the buses carefully, staring up at the top deck and the top deck would sometimes stare back. Three lads about our age. We glared at them; they glared back. Then the fingers, and the fingers back. I can't recall who did the fingers first. It was always hard to remember who started it.

'Fenian bastards,' Duck would shout. He was quick off the mark, 'very cheeky,' my mother would say. They were mouthing something back, but you could never make out what they were saying; the windows were always closed. Another old man with a very bad limp walked past; I can't remember what his name was. He walked into our little exchange with the figures mouthing away on the bus.

> Look at those dirty wee fucking Fenians giving you all the fingers. Dirty wee bastards. They're always trying to start something. If you see any of them trying to sneak down to St. Gabriel's, you need to give them a good digging. Do you hear me?

'We'll knock the baaaalicks of them, Mr. King,' said Duck. 'Don't you worry about that.'

It seems that we were always saying that we were going to knock the baaaalicks of somebody.

So, what was this exactly? A threat, a promise, a commitment, just our chance to act hard, to rise in the hierarchy of the group. Or was it just a plain lie? In our gang, there were a lot of overblown commitments to action like this. You might not want to call them lies exactly. But, if they were lies, then lying was a device to keep us together. Standing there doing nothing, night after night, just watching, where the most important thing to signal and communicate was the cohesion of the group.

My problem was that I always felt that time was precious and that I had better things to do. I had homework every night measured in twenty-minute intervals in my homework diary. Each piece of homework be it Latin, French, Russian, or physics had to last twenty minutes. No more, no less. My pals, on the other hand, had nothing much to do with their time when they got back from their work as apprentices in the shipyard or Mackies. I only went down to the corner when I'd finished my homework. I was disciplined; I was never there for the whole evening during the week. But my father was now dead. So, who was I going to run to when the boys from that bus cornered me in the park to knock the baaaalicks of me? I'll tell you who – Duck and Moke, and Kingo and Hacksaw and Tampy, that's who, they'd back me up.

We all had nicknames, of course, apart from the Bills, and being good Ulster Protestants there were always quite a few of those in the group, named after King William of Orange, the conqueror of the Catholics (the Fenians) at the Battle of the Boyne in 1690 (in Ireland we have long memories). All the 'Bills' got their first name and surname in order to distinguish them. It sounded quite formal when you referred to them.

There were always plans, lots of them. Sometimes elaborate, sometimes less so, always something to break the boredom. Duck was always coming up with capers. One night, he suggested we should go 'grave-robbing,' and that was his exact expression, although what we were going to 'rob' was less clear. There was an old disused, and somewhat spooky cemetery down by Carlisle Circus. There was a high wall, but you could see the elaborate graves from the top deck of the bus. It would be a bit of a walk down the Crumlin Road but good craic.

'Where are you boys off to?' my mother asked.

'Just down the road, for a wee dander, to get some exercise, Mrs Beattie,' Duck replied. That might be one of the four lies a day that teenagers tell. It would be hard to tell your mother or somebody else's mother that you're going grave-robbing.

I wasn't keen on the grave-robbing idea to be honest. Death and burial were a little too raw for me, after my father's death. I was having nightmares. Our Protestant religion, and this one mission hall that we went to, didn't help with my nightmares. My brother Bill had become a born-again Christian when he was in his teens (and was so at the time of my father's death), so I shared a room and a bed for several years with a born-again Christian, which is not necessarily the easiest type of person to share a room with. He kept a box on the dressing table with hundreds of rolled-up biblical quotes which he would extract with tweezers and read over and over before going to bed. It took him ages to get into the bed that we shared. I would kneel to say my prayers aloud at the side of the bed, as he watched, and I would usually say eight or nine prayers, all word perfect. He studied the Bible, and then he would pray silently; I tended just to memorise bits of it, that's what he said, and I knew a lot of prayers, which I would recite perfectly from memory.

'You have to mean it, you know' he would say, 'not just say the words to show off – if you want to be saved that is – if you don't want to go to hell.' With a born-again Christian in the house, hell was rarely far from our thoughts, and there was no getting away from hell in our street. My friends and I would sometimes go down to the local Elim mission hall on a Tuesday night because they gave out lollipops to children on a Tuesday to entice us in, without our parents. They would walk round with a cardboard box full of lollies, before the preacher started. You were only allowed one lollipop each. And then as you sucked the lolly, the great reward, the preacher would start in his loud, bellowing voice. He was shouting at us.

He would elaborate on the hell that was waiting for every one of us, unless we became born again, reborn in Jesus Christ. We were about nine or ten. My pals just told me to ignore what he was saying and enjoy the sticky lolly that tasted of sugar and nothing else, it wasn't much of a distraction to be honest, but it was hard to ignore hearing about your parents burning in hell, forever. I always laughed to myself to see my friends sucking harder and harder as the pains of hell were spelt out to them in the most graphic detail. At least, we were in this together.

'You'll not recognise your parents in the flames,' the preacher bellowed at us, 'there will be no comfort. Your ma won't be looking after you then, she'll not be running after you to wipe your nose, she'll be screaming in agony.'

My friends tried to act tough, but I could see through them; you could see it in their eyes, that fear, that vivid imagining, when they thought you weren't looking. And they'd dander back home afterwards, with a wee swing in their shoulders, like the hard men from the corner, who we all looked up to, but there was no confidence in that walk at the best of times, none, we were only practising. And certainly not on the way back from the mission hall.

Those words, sentences, and endless threats were etched into my tender childhood brain. 'Each day, you go down one more step towards Hell, one wee child's step but it makes no difference, you're heading right for the flames. Your ma will be burning right in front of you when you get there.'

That formed the basis for many of my nightmares. The lies we were told by grown-up Christian men who should have known better than to tell these sorts of stories to vulnerable children. Even if they had strongly held convictions about the Bible, beliefs about good and evil, and the existence of heaven and hell, their elaborations went beyond what was necessary or permissible.

'How the hell do they know what it's like down there, unless they've already been?' Duck said on the way home one night.

But we all went together the night of the grave-robbing; it was always about the group, groups give you courage, two lads went in over the high stone wall, and came back about ten or fifteen minutes later with something wrapped up in Duck's denim jacket. They jumped back down. Duck tossed his denim jacket over to me. I wasn't sure what might be inside, a gold-plated vase, a silver bowl, something worth stealing at least. They were all watching my face (I do remember that; I must have missed the wink), as I unwrapped it. I nearly dropped the loot. It was a grey, mouldy skull, the discoloured yellow teeth were still in it, staring at me through these two hollows where the eyes had been.

Duck snatched it out of my hands, but he snatched it so forcefully he dropped it by accident, and some of the teeth fell out, and a bit off the side. They were all laughing. I just thought that for all those years that man has been alive and then dead with his whole skull intact and attached to his body, and then we turn up and now it's a fucking mess, with bits falling off.

Duck called the skull (or the deceased) 'Archie,' I wasn't sure whether it was the head or the person. I don't know why that name popped into Duck's head, I thought at first it might have been the name on the tomb, something like Archibald, but the song 'Sugar, Sugar,' by the Archies was popular at the time, and, on reflection, this seemed like a more likely explanation in Duck's case.

I asked Duck what he planned to do with…Archie. I paused before articulating his name, as the thought of 'Sugar, Sugar' came to me. It seemed almost sacrilegious.

Duck said that he wanted to bring it home with him, to frighten people.

'Will it go off?' somebody asked. I wasn't sure who. 'You know, like rotten eggs?'

'How the fuck should I know,' Duck replied with some slight displeasure in his voice. I assumed that he hadn't thought about that. Maybe he thought it would be like a Halloween skull that would just last indefinitely.

He put his denim jacket back on and stuffed the skull up inside the front of it. It didn't look that secure and it fell out several times on the way home, with chunks of skull splitting off. Duck kicked it once or twice when it was on the ground. I thought that was an unnecessary form of desecration, taking it from the graveyards was bad enough. We eventually got to *my* house. It wasn't my idea to go there, but my house was on the way, and they suggested hiding it in my yard.

My mother came out to the front door to see what we were all laughing about. 'What are you boys playing with there?' she enquired.

Duck stuffed it back up his jacket. 'It's just something we found, Mrs Beattie.'

'Give us a wee look,' she said.

He opened his jacket gingerly.

'Oh my God, what the hell is that?'

'Just some wee bones,' Duck answered reassuringly. 'Probably some old sheep that wandered down off the hill and met its unfortunate demise with all the stray dogs around here,' Duck was always quick on his feet. But why he would pick up bits of a massacred sheep was beyond me, and clearly beyond my mother who made that blowing sound she sometimes did, when she didn't believe a word of something.

The woman from next door had come out, to see what all the fuss was about. She'd obviously been listening, peering through the curtains (which she did frequently), with the door surreptitiously opened, ever so slightly, so that she could hear every word. My mother called her a nosey old bitch. She used to throw bricks over the yard wall when we were going to the outside toilet and shout 'whoremaster' at us, but I never knew who the intended target was. I certainly was no 'whoremaster,' I didn't know what one was, I was very shy with girls, but presumably you have to be a 'man' to be a whoremaster, and I was the only man in the house, except for my mother's 'friends.'

'I hope that it wasn't done by that bloody dog Keeper,' said our neighbour. 'That bloody dog that Geoffrey looks after for Mrs Connor down the street. That poor old woman has Parkinson's.' I knew my neighbour would have a go at Keeper, any excuse really.

'That dog looks like a sheep killer to me,' she hadn't finished yet.

It's half Alsatian and half bloody wolf. It nearly took his mother's hand off once. Geoffrey and the dog were playing in the front room, and Geoffrey told her to pretend to be angry with him and go to hit him, and that bloody dog went for her, she told me all about it. She was very upset.

The truth is that my mother had never forgiven me for that particular incident. It was more evidence that I was somewhat 'troubled.'

Duck meanwhile was trying to keep a straight face.

'If it was that dog that did this,' our neighbour paused for effect 'we'll have to get Billy the Coalman to take him up the hill and shoot him dead.' She looked at Duck straight in the eyes for support. She was itching to give Billy the Coalman the word. She was encouraging Duck with her eyes as if to say I'll give Billy the Coalman the word and he'll take you with him, so that you can watch.

I reassured her and my mother that it wasn't the head of a dead sheep killed by Keeper.

'Maybe just some old bones from the butchers,' added Duck helpfully. 'It might not have been a sheep.' Our neighbour went back in, realising her helpful suggestions weren't getting her anywhere. She didn't ask him what he was doing with old bones from the butchers up his coat, perhaps she thought that he had a dog and that was his dinner. My mother left us to it.

I asked Duck what had happened to his first plan, to keep it under his bed to scare people.'

'The skull fucking stinks,' he said, although I couldn't smell anything as I'd been holding my nose since we'd left the cemetery with Archie.

I explained that the only solution was to put it back, at least what remained of it, to let it rest in peace.

'As opposed to resting in pieces,' said Duck, and they all laughed at his great wit.

Only two of them went back with me, and they moaned all the way back down the Crumlin. This time, it was my turn to climb in and find a suitable resting place. I wasn't keen to try to find the original coffin they'd opened (I'd no idea where it was) or open a new one, I just left it quietly beside a large gravestone from around 1870. That's what I think it said in the moonlight. I said a short prayer and apologised to both God and the original owner of the skull.

Of course, the story was retold many times at the corner. 'Soft Beats, soft as fucking shite.' I'd mentioned the prayer to them and that had them in stiches in the retellings. That's how we kept ourselves amused in the corner, that was the craic, picking on some flaw in a member of the gang to verbally abuse them to see how they'd take it – truth, half-truth, or lie, it didn't matter. It was their response that mattered. Did they stand up to it?

We were still standing there in the corner. Kingo's dad was leaving Paddy's early. 'Are you lads scheming again? You need to be ready for when it comes.' That's how they were now talking about things, about getting prepared for what was to come. 'We're always ready,' Duck would say. A little murmur would slowly go round the group, all in agreement. This was also a lie. I didn't think we were ready for anything. Lies can sometimes be just a false commitment to a person, a group, or a cause.

Kingo's dad was enjoying his impressionable audience. 'There's going to be a civil war. This town is going to blow.' He was slurring his words. He had been in Paddy's most of the night. But Hacksaw was getting excited. 'My father tells me that as well. He's going to be a vigilante. There's going to be roadblocks, I'm going to help him out. I'll join up as well. Baseball bats, the works.'

There was no father in my house. There was nobody to tell me what was going to happen or what I should do to get ready.

They started to light up. 'Smokes all round.' I was the only one who didn't smoke. My mother smoked; my father had smoked. I just didn't fancy it.

'Why don't you want a wee puff?' Duck held his wet butt my way. I didn't answer. 'He likes his running,' said Chunky. 'Leave him alone. My dad says anyway that fags will kill you. Beats' mother thinks that all that running, and all that sweating, can kill you. Either way, we're all goners. We're all fucked in the end.'

The conversation then turned to who they would like to have sex with. This was another part of the nightly routine. There was an old, crippled woman with polio who lived in the next street to me. There was a lot of argument about who would and who wouldn't have sex with her. They all agreed that I wouldn't. I wasn't experienced enough. They explained that sex is all about concentration and attention.

'You can do anybody if you know how to concentrate,' said Duck. 'After all. You don't have to look at the clock on the mantelpiece when you're stoking the fire.' And they all laughed, I'd heard that a hundred times. They never tired of this little maxim; I hated it.

Duck would go on, 'You just need to be able to concentrate. If she's a cripple, you just have to forget that she's got a gammy leg or a calliper. You must focus on other things.'

They all agreed that my mind was inclined to wander. I was full of ideas about academic things, and I might not be the best candidate as a serial shagger of women with polio.

'Have you actually done it yet?' Kingo asked me. I smiled and said that I had. That was a lie, and they knew it.

'Like fuck yeah. He's too fucking shy. He thinks too much. He'd spend all night talking to them.'

Suddenly, they spotted somebody going into the sweet shop opposite. It was a girl that we all knew originally from primary school with very large breasts and her mother who had even larger breasts and a very tight sweater. It was the mother that generated the most interest, probably for that reason. Three of the lads made loud sucking-in noises, certainly loud enough for them both to hear us from across the street. The mother gave us that look, as if flattered by the attention. The daughter looked disgusted by all this attention – especially because it was obviously directed at her mother. I made no sound; I was just embarrassed by the way she looked at us all. My mates shouted over, demanding they join us for a fag. The daughter swore back at them, and me too, I suppose, as I was one of them. The mother still looked quite pleased by all this adolescent attention. I noticed that. They walked off; the mother glanced back. That made our night.

Duck said that he had done the mother; I didn't believe it. He was just using her glance back to give this lie a little credibility. This was what you might call an opportunistic lie. There were a lot of those at the corner.

Eventually, I did ask a girl out. I knew her from the church badminton club, and after a very long time, I plucked up the courage to ask her out on a date. I was delighted when she said yes. I was never very forward with girls, indeed even my mother said that I was a bit 'backward' in this regard. I never liked the connotations of this term. 'You'll never get very far in life being like that,' she said. Carol had beautiful big grey eyes and a dark fringe. I took her for a Wimpy in the town centre, away from the safety, and the prying eyes, of our patch. We got the Silverstream bus into town. We went for a walk around the City Hall and then went for a couple of Wimpy burgers and Cokes to take out. Two lads walked towards us that night as we strolled along Royal Avenue in the city centre eating our hamburgers. Carol and I were getting on well, I could talk to her, I was laughing. Perhaps, my laughter attracted their attention. I was very happy; I couldn't help it. I remember nothing about them physically. They were just a couple of strangers, a few years older than me. I paid them very little attention to be honest. They stopped us quite suddenly, and one said that he recognised me. 'Hey boy,' he said, 'you're from Silverstream, aren't you?' I had no idea who they were, I must have looked puzzled, just some sixteen-year-old with a girl with large grey surprised eyes. There was no real pause for me to answer because just out of nowhere, one punched me in the face, a right hook from the side, I never saw it coming, and my cheeseburger fell from my hand and rolled across the wet pavement. I stumbled slightly backwards and was kicked in the head by the other one, but just the once. He had a metal tip in his shoe, so it left a dent on my forehead. 'They told me to take that back to Silverstream with me.' They were obviously Catholics from Ligoniel. They'd probably spotted me from the top of a bus some time in the past.

I wasn't from Silverstream itself, but some of my friends from the turn of the road were so I suppose that it was close enough for them. They just walked off laughing at me. I stood there in the drizzle, looking at Carol, in an intense state of embarrassment. I didn't say anything. My cheeseburger had rolled onto the road and Carol went over and picked it up and tried to rub some of the oily dirt of it. 'If you're still hungry, it's not that bad,' she said, 'the dirt's only on the one side.'

To save the embarrassment of talking about what had just happened, I turned the cheeseburger around and bit into the clean side. It was hard to chew because the inside of my mouth was starting to throb. I wanted to act nonchalant, as if to say that this sort of thing happens all the time, if you're part of the 'turn-of-the-road' gang. I was hoping that she hadn't seen the dent, which I could feel swelling on my forehead. We walked to the bus stop in silence. I think that she had lost her appetite as well. I knew I would have to lie to my friends about what had happened. The fact that I had got a digging would have been obvious to anyone. The fact that I hadn't got a punch in was what needed to be concealed. I would have been the butt of all their jokes.

When I next saw them and they pointed out the dent on my head, I told them that I had thrown a punch but that I wasn't sure if it connected – to make it less of a lie. This was an attempt at face-saving. They asked me how I'd managed to throw a punch if I was on the way down from this sudden right hook. I said that I'd rather not go into it.

The Troubles were now raging, and you could hear the shooting at nights from somewhere out there in the dark and the rain, and sometimes a bomb that would make the windows shake. 'Jesus, that one was close,' my mother would say, and then she'd apologise for taking the Lord's name in vain. When she still cared that is, before it all got so much worse.

'All the women around here are on nerve tablets,' she'd say, 'many of the men just drink – that's their way of coping with it.'

The gunfire was like a conversation, or an argument, the taking of turns, you might say, if you were a psychologist interested in those sorts of things, you'd hear one gunshot and wait for the reply, trying to work out who's voice it was, an angry and staccato opening, and the return fire, sometimes much louder than the one before, an amplification of intensity and purpose. That never sounded good in this dyadic exchange.

Sometimes, I'd be upstairs in the back bedroom doing my homework when the shooting would start. I'd go downstairs to see what was going on. My mother would be sitting in front of the TV, the TV that had never worked, ever since she'd bought it secondhand from a neighbour, a TV *engineer* she said, but it was just a local OAP with such bad eyesight that he was nearly blind. 'Joe 90,' they called him because of the thickness of his glasses. I always thought that his occupation was slightly improbable.

You could see the grey streets of Ardoyne on the screen, just down the road from us, where the Forum cinema stood, with some serious-looking journalist in a raincoat and some bullet holes in front of a house, which he pointed out one by one, in a painstaking and slightly bored way, and then on the news there was another story and yet another atrocity and an image of some wee country road (I wasn't sure where, I missed that bit, they all look the same) with a tree with no leaves and glistening scraps of butchered animals caught in the forks of the tree, and the debris of a car, and a dead person covered in a blanket stained with seeping blood, and a hole in the road from the blast. Just a two or three second scan of rural life in our province and a story that was already becoming old and familiar. I wasn't sure whether they were horses or cows in that tree, the camera didn't linger, it just hinted at what was happening to this quiet wee country of ours, full of hedgerows and farm animals and unspeakable acts, and then the tree with the bits in it was edited out of the later bulletins. The stained blanket with the shape underneath was left in.

Seamus Heaney (1975/1992) wrote 'the voice of sanity is getting hoarse' and it certainly was around here.

The TV was still on the blink. 'Hit that a wee skite for me on the way past to get it working,' she said, 'I've been up and down four times.' She needed some distraction. The windowpane shook again.

I walked over to the TV and slapped it hard on the side, almost knocking it off its stand. 'Jesus you've hit that too bloody hard, now the picture's gone off completely. You're so bloody careless.'

I sat for a few minutes in front of the television now with no picture. 'They're at it again,' she said, motioning into the dark and the distant gunfire. She got up and turned the TV down, so she could hear better, now there was no picture and no sound, just some wavy hypnotic lines.

'That's the army firing back,' she said, she'd become an expert on the sounds of gunfire, or so she liked to think. 'You wouldn't know who'd started it tonight. It was one or the other.' There was another loud bang. Jesus, it's getting closer. Did you hear that one? That's not far away now.' We sat there in silence, if sporadic gunfire in the far or near distance could be considered silence.

I had heard that somebody had chalked 'Is there life before death?' up on a gable wall just off the Falls Road, and somebody had tried to write the same message up our way, but it had been washed off almost immediately, doused by water. 'Making fun of the Bible,' my mother said, by way of explanation. 'What do you expect?'

I glanced down at my watch and told her that I had to get back to my homework. 'That's right, you leave me sitting here on my own. They'll be firing through the window next, and you'll be up those stairs reading those big books, oblivious to what's going on down here.'

She hated being on her own. Life a few years earlier had been so different in that same little house. 'You father was one in a million,' she'd say. 'We were inseparable.' There was always life in that house and singing and dancing on a Saturday night when the pubs had closed, and the men came back with fish and chips for us all, from Greasy Jim's.

And now it was just this. Me upstairs doing my homework and her sitting there on her own waiting for the next round of gunfire, and maybe Andy or Ernie or whoever would turn up. The men now had names.

I told her that I had lots of homework to finish for the morning. 'Some of your friends will be out on the street as we speak trying to protect this area. There's going to be roadblocks and all sorts. So, what's so important for you to do tonight?'

'I have to do some Russian,' I said. 'You know that it doesn't fit into my timetable anymore, I must work on it myself. I'm translating some Russian literature tonight.'

'Well, that's going to be very useful, if the Russians ever land up by the mill dam, you can direct them to all the best joints in town,' she said, 'a lot of bloody use that's ever going to be. When are you going to Russia?'

She was alone and angry, I understood that, and anxious, undoubtedly, everybody was. She was trapped in that house. The Troubles now meant that nobody went out after dark, and the shooting was getting worse – more frequent and ever closer. Nobody ever visited, even the Minister had stopped calling. Bill was always away, and we looked forward to his visits home with his bottles of absinthe, and cocktails that they might drink in ski lodges in Chamonix. It was like a holiday when he turned up, with his stories about a glamorous life beyond these streets, but I had work to do up those stairs every night with that thick, intoxicating smell of paraffin that made my head light.

Sometimes, I would try to work at the yellow card table in the front room to keep my mother company, but if I did, it looked like I was just sitting there, gazing out of the window of the front room. But that wasn't right, I was working – I was thinking – that's work, but it didn't look that way. At school, it would have been hard to explain how bad things were getting around here, around Ligoniel way, around the turn-of-the-road. They would have thought that I was exaggerating or making excuses. That would have been the worst thing. I wanted to get the work done without excuses. I hate excuses; I always have.

Life was changing all around me – roadblocks, bomb scares, random shootings, I saw the change in my friends, boys I had known for years from church and Sunday school, the lads from the corner. It was a slight change in their characters, as they got sucked into the conflict, slowly at first, but faster now. They were getting more serious somehow. There were more fights. 'Skirmishes,' we always called the fights. We were always being picked on when we left our patch, or that's how it felt, and we had to leave our territory to find something to do – going down the Crumlin to the cinema, going into the city centre, going up the Hightown, making yourself vulnerable, always wary, always watching and waiting, ready to run, ready to fight. The gang wasn't designed to be aggressive to others, it was designed to protect you from the violence all around you.

But there was always a line that wasn't crossed in these skirmishes. I have a very small, almost imperceptible scar on the middle finger of my left hand when a fight broke out at a party somewhere near the Shore Road. I was seventeen. The fight continued onto the street outside, miles from the turn of the road – Comanche territory in this most territorial of cities. We started for home and suddenly from nowhere – we never saw it coming or expected this – a car drew up beside us and some man, for he was indeed a grown adult man, jumped out and pushed me to the ground and tried to push a broken bottle into my face. I protected myself with my hands. I was beaten and lay pinned on the ground, he was a heavy, broad-shouldered man, but he never got the bottle into my face, and I pushed him off with the sort of strength that comes from terror and ran off. I'd had some drink, a few pints of lager, so the pain was bearable. A mile away, I collapsed on the pavement somewhere on this side of the Antrim Road and oddly and surprisingly a friend from my grammar school, passing in a car with his father, saw me lying there, they carried me to their car and brought me back to their house, and his father plucked the slithers of glass out of my neck and hand with tweezers, as I thanked them over and over again for their kindness. That was just the drink talking though. I'm normally not so effusive.

This scar is a small, embodied memory that reminds me of small wounds that have grown with me over the years.

That was all on the right side of the line, just, but suddenly that line seemed to be disappearing altogether.

I was always studying now. That's what my mother would say, when the lads from the corner came around to see me. 'He's up in that wee room, studying again for A levels. I've told him that he'll be wearing glasses before too long.' I'd come down and chat with them in the hall, three foot by three foot, about nothing in particular, and they would go off laughing, and that would happen a few nights a week until Friday night when I'd wander down to Greasy Jim's, and stand by the hot air vent with the rest of them, as the police patrols drove by aimlessly, and we stood there aimlessly, and I'd catch up with what I'd missed. It was never anything much.

But one Friday, Duck arrived, talking with great excitement about what was happening down the road, just off the Shankill. We couldn't miss it; we couldn't miss out. So, we walked down the Woodvale and then down the Shankill, through the streets of terraced houses between the Shankill and the Falls, streets and houses just like ours, until we got to the invisible line between the two communities – the houses on each side were the same as each other, no difference between the Protestant and the Catholic houses, no difference at all between those condemned mill houses. We could hear the crackle as we approached. There was a fire raging and a crowd in front of the flames cheering, a Protestant crowd, we were amongst our own, and there were these punctuated howls from women somewhere in the dark behind the flames, perhaps from the houses themselves, perhaps from the yards at the back of the houses, or perhaps even from the street behind – you couldn't tell. It was like a disembodied emotional commentary on the whole thing, part fear, part anger, part desperation. This odd, disturbing noise that would rise and fall unpredictably, with strange pauses, and you wondered whether it had suddenly finished and whether it was all over, whatever it was. And then it would restart, reminding us that this was not the sectarianism we knew, that we had grown up with – the bonfires on the 11th Night, menacing perhaps to the other side, but purely symbolic – Lundy or the Pope on the top, only in effigy form.

The noise of the flames and the cheers and the howls of the women, wherever or whoever they were, filled the air and I felt sick to my stomach. My friends weren't enjoying it either, I could tell by their faces, this wasn't the excitement that any of us were looking for.

And then I heard a whoosh behind me, and I turned to see a man, balding and grey, in the middle of the crowd with a catapult of all things firing at the houses at some dark wavering shapes somewhere behind the flames. It could have just been shadows; I couldn't tell. That's what I remember most vividly about that night – this grown man, somebody's father, with this big shiny metal catapult glinting in the dark with thick rubber cords. Perhaps, it was a Christmas present (from a few Christmases ago) for one of his sons to fire at shoe boxes, or at rats in the street, now being used to fire marbles at the burning houses. He had brought a big bag of marbles with him; his friend was holding them for him. 'Pass us another one of those wee marbles, try to avoid the wee beauties (the intricately coloured marbles prized by all of us) – my boy loves those – he'd feel terrible if I lost them,' the man said.

He was standing just behind me, to my right; I remember so vividly after all these years, just behind my right shoulder, and I turned round and looked him in the face but he didn't once return my gaze, so intent was he on trying to keep any remaining residents in the burning houses by firing marbles at the windows, before the flames flicked up to lick them seductively at first and then harder and harder with this ferocious passion. The residents of these small mill houses were probably neighbours of his for years, good neighbours, that's what I didn't understand.

I prayed that everybody had got out hours ago – there were just flames and shadows and wood crackling and burning, and this little act of his which I hoped was just a symbolic act, as the crowd roared their approval at him, and the flames roared through the wood and plaster work.

I prayed like I meant it – I wasn't just saying the words.

'Burning them out,' that's what they called it then, in the years before ethnic cleansing was a recognisable expression in any part of the world. Each side was now burning the other out. The Protestants had been burned out, now it was their turn or vice versa, nobody knew who started it. A lot of lies were being told to fuel the flames.

'We'll do it to them, only harder,' was the philosophy, the motto, the justification. I heard it dozens of times.

We were just spectators that night, young lads, I was seventeen, inquisitive, excited, fearful – then CS gas was fired, and we were stumbling back blindly with the old women coming out of those same wee houses as ours with the wet-soaked cloths for our eyes, with the gas still in the air, and I remember how kind and affectionate that felt, almost loving.

'There you are son; press down hard. The pain will go; it'll only sting for a few minutes. Those RUC bastards, whose side are they on anyway?'

Burning them out, gassing your own, being on one side, being on the other, being a member of your community, becoming a staunch member (no more IRA on the gable walls meaning 'I ran away'), becoming a Protestant Defender. It was a time of perceptible change; we could all feel it.

And I had to lie about it all, about what was happening to the turn of the road again. My mother would find out eventually. Like everyone else she read about my friends on the front pages of the newspapers. One of the lads from the Protestant paramilitary organisation, the Ulster Volunteer Force, got eight life sentences for his part in six murders and two attempted murders. He had asked Carol out the same night as I had. 'He was such a quiet wee boy,' my mother would say, 'you would never have imagined that he'd do a thing like that. They say that he's killed more people than Billy the Kid.' Always the Westerns in our mind, the Westerns and the Forum cinema, and stories of us and them, cowboys and the Comanches.

I went to visit this friend with his father in the Maze prison, years later. We travelled on the paramilitary minibus. His father couldn't believe what he'd done – he had a good job and he'd grown up with Catholics, he said. My old friend would have had to keep a lot to himself and tell many lies. But his lies must have worked because they had left his family heartbroken. But I knew a little of the context in which those lies and lying had been nurtured. We were after all the turn-of-the-road gang, and we had to lie. We became good at it, sometimes in jest, sometimes not. But we had lots and lots of practice on those nights standing there with nothing to do and no way out.

Lies, Cognitive Dissonance, and Change

I've no idea what happened to Sammy the Hard Man in the end, or why exactly he was such a potent role model for us all. I don't know if he was killed in the Troubles, imprisoned, or just disappeared. The last time I saw him, it was the summer, and he was walking along by the dam at the back of the park, with his shirt off and his Alsatian dog beside him. He didn't see me. He was still swinging his shoulders just in case there were any on-lookers like me, I suppose.

But respect, however obtained, was such an important feature of the community and we all looked up to Sammy the Hardman (Beattie 1992). My mother warned me about this and about keeping bad company, because we have always known that in the words of Robert Vargas from Northwestern University that 'lower status adolescents are likely to adopt the behaviours of high status adolescents…By status, I am referring to one's standing in a social hierarchy as determined by respect or deference' (Vargas 2011: 310) and Sammy had very high standing, which came with all those privileges. Nobody had ever seen him paying for his fish suppers, that's what they said, although I had seen him paying, but I kept that to myself.

Psychologists often talk about conformity (Asch 1951) and peer involvement (Brown and Theobald 1999) when it comes to gangs, but Vargas makes the important point that 'While the literature has shown the importance of peers, studies rarely identify the mechanisms behind their effects. By mechanisms, I refer to modes of influence, or ways by which peer influence is likely to manifest during interactions' (Vargas 2011: 312). Brown et al. (2008) identified four possible mechanisms by which peers can influence each other. The first was *peer pressure*, defined as direct attempts to influence certain attitudes or behaviours (always present in the turn-of-the-road gang). The second was *modelling* or *behavioural display* (just think of Sammy). The third was *antagonistic behaviour* – teasing or ridicule that maintained group status hierarchies (Adler and Adler 1995), which happened every night on the corner. The fourth was *structuring opportunities* – where an adolescent was invited to a situation that 'facilitated a behaviour' without imposing it (the corner itself).

All four of these mechanisms operated at the turn of the road, of course. But I think that lies are an important, indeed critical, part of the mechanisms of peer pressure, lies about who we were ('wee hard men with a reputation we had to live up to,' always a lie, think of me with my cheeseburger) and what Catholics were and what we thought of them ('we hate them all,' even my Uncle Terence?), lies about what we would do when we got hold of them ('kick the baaaalicks of them,' but our skirmishes were never like that). All lies in those early days but perhaps lies that became the truth for some, through some awful self-fulfilling prophecy. The thing about our gang, and I suspect most gangs, was that talk was central. There was always the craic and teasing each other endlessly in those prolonged routines of insults and counter-insults that lasted not just a night, but weeks and months on end. Those social scientists who have tried to comprehend 'street corner society' or delinquent gangs or the underclass would do well to start with these verbal routines, rule-governed and orderly in their own way. Perhaps, not quite as orderly as the verbal duelling, the 'sounding,' of the black gangs in Harlem studied by the sociolinguist William Labov (1972), where every insult ('Your momma drink pee') has a prescribed set of permissible responses ('Your father eat shit'), matching in form and content and not too personal (never too personal), but nevertheless with room for elaboration and invention ('Your father eat dog yummies'). But there were rules in the ritual insults at the turn of the road, rules about content, structure, and timing:

'I saw your ma going into chapel' (both a lie and an insult)

'Only for a fucking pish in the Holy Water'

'Your ma has gone out with a Taig?' (again, a lie and an insult)

'Yeah, your fucking da!'

And rules about the display of emotion just as when black gangs engaged in 'sounding.' The first rule was that you mustn't take it too personally; the second was that you must come back strongly with a good thematically relevant response; the third was that you must never show your emotion and get upset. You can't break down; you must toughen up. If you ever cried (and I never saw that happen no matter how insulting it ever got), you would have to go home, and stay there – for the rest of your life.

That was part of the lessons learned at the turn of the road. Lies can make you stronger when they're directed at you, they are social acts, performed for your own good. If you want to stay part of the gang, if you want to survive, that is.

Then, there were those endless threats, again woven into the social discourses about us and them, about the enemy (Beattie 2013). 'We'll knock the baaaalicks of them, Mr. King. Don't you worry about that.' Just young lads talking, showing off, trying to be hard, mimicking some of the talk they'd heard. But nobody was forcing them to say these things. One might therefore wonder if this *social* act can become the *personal* thought and the personal attitude. I am reminded of Leon Festinger's work on cognitive dissonance. Could cognitive dissonance operate here because of the gulf between what we said and how we really felt? Festinger's theory of cognitive dissonance was an attempt to explain what happens when one's *cognitions* (opinions and beliefs) and actions conflict with each other (Festinger, Riecken and Schachter 1956: 25). Festinger wrote that this dissonance produces discomfort and pressure arises to reduce or eliminate the dissonance by, for example, changing the beliefs or opinions involved in the dissonance, or by acquiring new information that will help reduce the dissonance. The best-known studies reported in Festinger's classic 1957 book are the studies of *forced compliance*, where 'forced compliance' means 'public compliance without private acceptance' (Festinger 1957: 87), perhaps like saying that you hate all Fenians (public compliance) without really believing it (private acceptance).

The context of Festinger's research is important. His research began in 1951 during the Korean War (1950–1953) and was funded by the Ford Foundation. Festinger says that he was approached directly by Bernard Berelson, the Director of the Behavioral Sciences Division and asked whether he would produce a substantive summary of research on 'communication and social influence.' There was major concern in the United States at that time about the behaviour of American prisoners of war captured by the Chinese in Korea. There were few escape attempts by the prisoners, and little or no camp organisation and resistance; some prisoners of war had even started broadcasting propaganda for the enemy, as 'guests of the Chinese People's Volunteer Army.' There was this fear that the Chinese had found, and were beginning to exploit, weaknesses in the American character which they were now using to control them.

A good example of the moral panic that was setting in can be seen in the film '*The Ultimate Weapon,*' narrated by Ronald Reagan, where the ultimate weapon in the title is not nuclear bombs but the human mind. The film suggested that the Chinese had perfected the 'brainwashing' of these prisoners of war, effective brainwashing without apparent brutality, hypnosis, drugs, or even coercion. This was the ultimate weapon turning captured American soldiers into communists.

Prisoners in Korea were asked to write down a few pro-communist statements ('Communism is wonderful'; 'Communism is the way of the future'). According to Wiseman (2012), many of the prisoners were happy to oblige 'because the request seemed trivial' in and off itself in the endless months of captivity. Later, they were asked to read the statements aloud, and then to read them to the other prisoners for discussion. To encourage them to do this, they were reinforced with small rewards – small portions of extra rice, sweets, and subtle praise. Rewards, not great enough to be obvious determinants of behaviour – rewards not great enough to blame. They were themselves saying that 'Communism is the way of the future' without any threat or punishment and without being enticed with any great reward. And then, they were discussing the idea with their fellow American prisoners, arguing about it, defending the idea, criticising fellow prisoners, and then encouraged to engage in public self-criticism. They started informing the guards of the bad attitudes of other prisoners, thus shattering the social bonds between the men. The men ended up no longer trusting one another and became isolated and vulnerable.

The death rate amongst the American prisoners of war in Korea was very high, 30% by some estimates, but according to Ronald Reagan's narration, this was principally down to 'giveupitis,' where the prisoners just gave up the will to live rather than the brutal and inhumane conditions (although William Shadish's book *When Hell Froze Over* gives a fuller picture of the physical conditions and the illnesses). The cause of this high incidence of mortality was psychological rather than physical, the film maintains, and the American government needed to fight this, to make the American prisoner stronger, to halt this moral decline in the American character. The U.S. government also needed to understand the implications of these methods for the future security of the United States. After all significant numbers of prisoners of war were returning to the United States after three years of captivity. How would this 'forced compliance' of these prisoners by their Chinese guards, with only minimal reward and encouragement, impact on their underlying attitudes, opinions, and beliefs? Would these ex-prisoners of war turn out to be Communist sympathisers because of their experiences in the camps of North Korea, as many obviously feared at the time?

This is the geopolitical background to Festinger's experimental research, although interestingly and tellingly the Korean War, and the experience of the prisoners, is not mentioned in the book, even though the book was completed in March 1956, when these concerns were being widely voiced in the media, films, and newspapers.

Festinger's original experiments were very simple both in terms of theory and execution. If you are offered a large reward (say a million dollars), or a large punishment ('I will shoot you') for saying something that you do not believe ('I like comic books'; 'I hate Fenians'), then little cognitive dissonance will be produced. You are likely to do it, of course, but there will be no effect on your underlying attitude about comic books (or Fenians). Festinger wrote:

> There is some slight dissonance, to be sure. You said you liked comic books, and you really do not. But there are some very important elements that are consonant with having uttered this public statement, namely, the knowledge of the money now in your pocket. Relative to this, the dissonance is negligible.
>
> (Festinger 1957: 91)

And similarly, with the threat of the bullet to the head. If you threaten to shoot someone for not saying 'Communism is the way of the future' (or 'I hate Fenians'), there is no cognitive dissonance and no attitude change. Festinger reasoned that:

> As the promised reward, or threatened punishment, becomes smaller in importance, the dissonance resulting from compliance increases. The maximum possible dissonance would be created if the reward, or

punishment, was just barely enough to elicit the desired overt behaviour or expression.

(Festinger 1957: 91)

It is clear why this is so redolent of the experience of the prisoners of war in Korea – it was the effects of very small encouragements that produced the change, that was the most frightening aspect of this new form of brainwashing. At the turn of the road, it was the small encouragements from your friends that were behind you saying these anti-Catholic sentiments.

This theory of cognitive dissonance is considered by some to be one of the greatest achievements of social psychology although it has not been without its critics (Bem 1967; Tedeschi et al. 1971; Greenwald and Ronis 1978). Festinger's theory was developed to explain 'brainwashing' in the Korean War. But sometimes, I wonder if it applies to the turn of the road and all those specific threats about what we were going to do when we encountered Catholics and all the public statements without necessarily private acceptance statements ('I hate all Fenians.' Really? My Uncle Terence was a Fenian; our friend Moke was a Fenian). These public statements said endlessly at the corner may have been part of a mechanism of change. They're not just the outpourings of wee corner boys trying to act hard. They may be more significant than that; they were lies and lies that were central to both the group and perhaps our private cognitions. In *some* individuals (perhaps not all), they may have set up a state of cognitive dissonance which may be resolved by the individual bringing their underlying attitudes more in line with their statements (public compliance encouraged by small signs of approval from the group), and then they may seek more information to help reduce this dissonance (as Festinger suggested) by selective attention to bad information about the Catholics and what they were 'guilty' of. In any civil conflict, like the Troubles in Northern Ireland, there is a lot of first-hand information that you can use to do this – to see how heartless members of Catholic paramilitary organisations like the IRA and the INLA were in the Troubles (see Beattie 2004; Beattie and Doherty 1995). You pay little or no attention to the crimes and atrocities of your own side. This new, and heavily biased, information helps reduce the cognitive dissonance as your underlying anti-Catholic attitude changes and hardens (and, of course, vice versa for the other side in the conflict). This might suggest that these public statements, essentially lies at the outset, play some role in this process of change through the mechanism of cognitive dissonance.

It was obvious in the end that my friends did change in significant ways. We can blame bad company, adolescent peer groups, social deprivation, poverty, or poor moral standards but perhaps the lies we tell each other to gain social acceptability (and through the process of cognitive dissonance) played some role in this.

But one of the most important caveats of this theory that is rarely mentioned is who might, or might not, suffer from the sort of dissonance that has to be resolved when encouraged to say something at odds with their underlying beliefs. Festinger raises this issue in the final chapter of his book, when he writes 'For some people dissonance is an extremely painful and intolerable thing, while there are others who seem to be able to tolerate a large amount of dissonance' (Festinger 1957: 266–267). In other words, he says that for some individuals, they may say things that they don't actually believe and there is no painful dissonance to deal with and therefore no behaviour changes, but this was not really elaborated. But his theory as stated satisfied one audience – the American public in the 1950s. The prisoners of war *had been brainwashed* by subtly being persuaded to make pro-Communist statements. You can see why individual differences in reactions to 'dissonance' might not have been at the forefront of Festinger's research. The prisoners of war were all subject to the same brainwashing techniques and they all succumbed, or would have, when it is done properly. They were all tortured heroes. That as an idea that the American public could live with. That and the idea that, of course, there was no merit in the Communist philosophy, and that was the philosophy itself was not the real reason for the change in attitudes. Why forced compliance even works when its applied to people making statements about comic books. Isn't that what Festinger's research had demonstrated? Communism, comic books, it's all the same really.

But what about Protestants and Catholics in the ghettos of Belfast, and the senseless killing of near neighbours throughout the Troubles based on what? The lies we tell each other. What role did they play? It's easy to dismiss the talk of teenagers as just young lads trying to act hard to cover their insecurities, but we learned to lie at the turn of the road and some of the lies had particular themes and content which may have played some role in ultimately changing how we thought and acted, in all sorts of important ways. Not all of us, perhaps, but some of us – the more vulnerable amongst us.

Many in authority (politicians, religious leaders, important members of the community, paramilitary leaders, the godfathers) lied to us, and members of my gang acted on these lies. The lines between truth and lies from those in authority were often very blurred. Very, very blurred.

Cloaking the Past

My three years at the University of Cambridge were, for me, years of extreme pride, immense gratitude, and pretence. There's a weight you feel, the weight of expectation, of tradition, of standards. You read about the history of the college and the university, and who has preceded you. That old, stooped man nearly bent double threading his way to High Table at Trinity College, had discovered how neurons work. Lord Adrian had been awarded the Nobel Prize in Physiology or Medicine for that work, shared with Sir Charles Sherrington, back in 1932, and there he was. Moving slowly to High Table. You couldn't help feeling the weight of what was required, Bertrand Russell had sat at that table, Wittgenstein, Lord Byron, his tame bear no doubt tethered outside. Isaac Newton lived in Neville's Court, and changed our understanding of the nature of light, vision and colour using the shutter of his college window – 'having darkened my chamber, and made a small hole in my window-shuts...' (Newton 1672: 3077). Newton discovered that colour is an intrinsic property of light and doesn't arise from passing through a medium. I would walk around Neville's Court every day in those first few days in Cambridge in the bright light of an Indian summer, that bright white light full of colour, according to the Master alchemist, Isaac Newton himself. You must act the part when you're at Cambridge, at least I did, but that's not the same as lying. It's about control. It's about editing your words, monitoring your manners, longer pauses than normal, don't say the first thing that comes into your head. When you really think about it, it's quite similar to lying in so many ways, but not quite the same.

The irony is that's exactly what I was studying for my PhD at Cambridge – how short periods of silence in speech called 'unfilled pauses,' filled pauses like um's and ah's, and filled hesitations like repetitions and false starts might allow some insight into how thoughts, deep and hidden, work their way to the surface in speech itself (Beattie 1983). My supervisor, Brian Butterworth, called our research 'the science of silence.' But then, I noticed something early on in my research that these pauses are often associated with changes in bodily movement (Beattie 1983; Butterworth and Beattie 1978). It is as if the voice and the body are jointly trying to articulate thoughts and ideas to another person. We needed to find a new term to include the body, our term this time wasn't so elegant or poetic, we called them 'speech-focussed movements,' we could see that speech influences the actions of the body – the hand movements, the gestural movements, the movements of the eye, towards or away from another person, as a person plans what they're going to say. It's hard, after all, to think creatively when you look directly into the eyes of another person. It's just too distracting. So adaptively, we must look away, we called that 'gaze aversion,' a clunky type of language to describe the fine-grained actions of everyday life and the realisation that speech and nonverbal behaviour are intimately connected.

Human communication is embodied. Good actors intuitively know that and so we set up our recording equipment in the Psychological Laboratory at the University of Cambridge to record everyday university talk on video, tutorials, seminars, that sort of thing, dissecting them all to get to a level of detail that may miss even the best actors. My PhD supervisor was getting excited, as was his old supervisor from University College London, Professor Frieda Goldman-Eisler. She had begun her professional career as a psychoanalyst but had moved on to pauses and spontaneous speech. Her work had guided my undergraduate research. She was then just some great distinguished name, another Jewish intellectual escaping from Nazi Germany, now she was reading the preliminary academic research of a boy from Belfast with great interest.

But it never felt real if I'm honest. I was still that boy from Legmore Street, now pausing long enough to stop myself saying certain things, to stop myself qualifying every utterance with a 'fuck' or a 'shite' (Beattie 2021). Never say baaaalicks. Never say baaaalicks. The proper word is bollocks if you must refer to that part of the male body at all. Not once did I let it slip, or maybe just the once – I got drunk at the Trinity College Field Club dinner, I was newly elected Field Club Captain, I lost the college badminton singles cup which I'd been presented with that night. It was a prank, I suppose, a sort of upper-class student prank – a theft without the usual consequences for posh and privileged people. I was terrified that I'd lost something valuable and important that had been in the college for decades, maybe longer. I swore at my badminton doubles partner (he wasn't remotely responsible) and I'm sure that he thought that I was talking some foreign language, something harsh, something guttural, Eastern European perhaps, he told me afterwards that he didn't understand a word of it. He couldn't work out what was going on. This wasn't just me talking with an accent. These were foreign words that he didn't know or understand, that he had never heard before. Baaaalicks, you can stretch this word as long as you like. He told me to go to bed. You'll feel better in the morning, he said. You will be back to your old self. The cup of course, was returned the next day, and I was back in control. He asked me whether I was play-acting the previous night. I said, 'sort of.'

I have my Trinity College matriculation photograph in front of me. I suspect that you would find it hard to pick me out from the other freshmen (at least at first sight), neat, a sober tie, a grey jumper under my suit, this odd smile on my face. I look slightly condescending like some middle-class grammar schoolboy who aspires to greater things. Some of the students look happy, some look gloomy, I seem to be smirking in that misleading snapshot. Perhaps, it was a trick that I had learned. A disguise. The names are missing so I can't identify the Lords and young men with the title 'the Right Honourable' scattered across the benches in front of the Wren Library in Neville's Court. I'm standing and I seem smaller than the rest, which might be a tell-tale sign. The poor diet of the less privileged, which always seems to inhibit upward growth. I'm certainly one of the smaller ones. The rich and privileged are head and shoulders above me, I suppose quite literally.

I never spoke about my background when I was at the University of Cambridge. As I've already mentioned, over dinner in Hall one night a fellow student commented that he had a friend from Belfast who never talked about his family either. His father, my friend explained, was a High Court judge. 'Far too dangerous to mention this given the security situation over in Northern Ireland. I bet it's something similar with you.' I never corrected him. There was a massive embarrassed and ashamed lie in that silence.

I thought back to Legmore Street and my bedroom overlooking the entry, the bed with three legs, one had broken off years ago, the damp walls, the cobwebs hanging from the ceiling, washing in the kitchen sink whilst standing in a basin on the scullery floor. The tin bath rusted over years ago, rusted and stuck to the yard wall. That's why we stood in that basin on the floor to wash.

I never sketched out my home life for them. What would they think of me? This all might not have been an appropriate topic of conversation in the Great Hall of Trinity College Cambridge as the Archbishop of Canterbury gossiped away on High Table, a few yards away from where I was sitting, whilst other students reflected longingly on their childhood days in Ascot or Harrow or wherever they were from, in their days before university. I was already isolated enough socially.

But my lies at Cambridge were those of omission, non-articulated lies about my childhood friends, as if I had none, and non-lies about family, as if it didn't exist. I thought of my mother sitting in her front room of our wee mill house with nothing to do all day, staring down Barginnis Street, with the long nights drawing in, the second-hand TV in the corner that never worked properly, blinking away at her, and the shooting just down the road in Ardoyne, and then later in the shops at the bottom of Barginnis Street. Always creeping closer and closer, the way murder does. Murder in the chip shop, the bookie's, the video shop, the fruit shop, the dry cleaners, the public bar, then both local bars burned to the ground…. I couldn't have explained this to my fellow students at Cambridge; I wouldn't have known where to start.

My friends back in Belfast were now setting up roadblocks and walking around life 'the fella in the big picture,' in my mother's words (she was always very fond of the old Hollywood films). She was always going on about the Protestant paramilitary organisations being set up to defend the neighbourhood.

> All your pals have their balaclavas on, and they shout over at me. "How's your Geoffrey, Mrs Beattie? Is he still reading them big books of his? Send him my regards." You wouldn't know who anybody was any longer. I can't tell your friends apart when they've got their balaclavas on.

My mother was, however, more forthcoming about her predicament and her loneliness, and her days filled with nothingness. Years later at an awards ceremony in Belfast (one of my books *We Are the People: Journeys through the Heart of Protestant Ulster* was shortlisted for the Ewart-Biggs Literary Prize), she met Brian Keenan, the Norther Irish lecturer kidnapped by Islamic Jihad in Beirut in 1986 and kept as a hostage for over four years. My mother had no idea who he was. I heard him explain to her that he had been blindfolded and chained to a radiator for months on end. I heard my mother say to him 'I know what it's like Brian, I never get out either. I'm locked in that bloody house night after night, with nowhere to go.'

She kept telling him to speak up. 'I can hardly hear you, Brian' she was saying. 'Could you talk a bit louder, please.'

Brian explained to her that they were beaten if they were heard talking whilst in captivity. 'That's terrible Brian,' she said, 'you shouldn't be beaten for that, maybe for some things, but definitely not for that.'

When he went up for his prize, she told me that she and Brian had a lot in common. 'He's spent a lot of time on his own as well. He knows what it's like.

You're too busy gallivanting over in England to worry about me. You're only interested in number one and chasing women around.'

She glanced his way. 'Maybe if he's ever up near Ligoniel, he'll take me out for a wee drink,' she said to me. 'Perhaps, you should give him a wee hint about this.'

She had once been the best-looking girl in Ligoniel, she was desperate for that attention again. That need stays with you.

I stayed silent when I was in Cambridge about all of this. Nobody there really knew me. That was the way it had to be. My academic gown was my disguise, and that slight smirk of a smile in that fresher's photo, the matriculation photo of Trinity College Cambridge, that makes me uncomfortable to look at now. A mask no less, The Lone Ranger, the fella in the small picture. It was a different sort of lie. I'm sure that some of my fellow students may have suspected something, but I never gave the game away, entirely.

Bring on the Chicken

I have enjoyed reading about the lives of some notorious conmen and liars like 'Yellow Kid' Weil. What a character! And the movies, who doesn't love that 1973 classic '*The Sting*,' starring Paul Newman and Robert Redford (and winner of seven Oscars). The wit and audacity of those two handsome conmen in the Chicago of the Great Depression. I smile just thinking about that film – a film about lies and deception.

The real conman 'Yellow Kid' Weil also operated in Chicago but in 1929 in the decade leading up to the Great Depression. He has been described, probably quite rightly, as the greatest con artist of all time. His autobiography (Weil 1948) describes how he 'cooked up endless ingenious schemes to extract money from wealthy people who were out for a quick and dirty buck.' He puts it this way – 'They wanted something for nothing. I gave them nothing for something.' We laugh at his cleverness and gumption, and howl with laughter at the poor suckers who fell for it all.

In one of his cons, he pretended to be a Dr Reuel who would give a demonstration of his latest invention, a device that would roast a chicken in thirty seconds. 'Bring on the chicken!' he would shout to the audience. His assistant would hold up the chicken so everyone could see it, and then he'd pop it into the 'electric roaster' (a case without any electric wiring). Thirty seconds later, he would pull out a freshly roasted chicken. The appliance of science! Not really. He explains how a man under the platform would remove the chicken from the roaster and substitute one that was freshly roasted. He was amazed that he got away with it. 'Any but the most gullible should have realised what was going on,' he writes. He was approached by a University of Chicago professor who was in the audience and urged him to bring it to market. The professor wanted to invest his own money in the company that would manufacture it. 'No other incident in my entire career so convinced me of the gullibility of man,' Weil writes. The world seems to be full of suckers. It wasn't his fault that he was taking advantage of them. It's sometimes easy to turn the emotional connotations of a lie around with a little bit of disparagement of the victims. It's especially easy if you've got colleagues or accomplices that can help you in this, a shared consensus of the fools out there, but this again is part of learning to lie – the building of these representations. I have watched this in action but perhaps it wasn't quite as funny as the life of 'Yellow Kid' Weil.

It was a little jeweller's shop in the suburbs of Sheffield, it looked cosy inside, it was just up the hill from the university. I would pass it when I was working in the university there in the years after I left Cambridge. It was on the way home. The shop is something else now. They were tough times in the Sheffield I knew in the decade after the miners' strike. It was the owner of the shop who invited me in (Beattie 1990).

Inside the shop – the nerve centre of the operation – you could hear the laughter out the back. Behind the jewellery, behind the glass cases, behind the gold and silver. Somebody was telling a funny story. The laughter dampened down. Then it erupted again. Great guffaws of laughter. Bodies curled up in spasms of mirth, behind those four walls. Behind the thick, blue velvet curtain. I edged closer. The voice had a Black Country accent. 'I've sold vacuum cleaners to people without a carpet in the house.' The laughter started again slower this time but quickening. The pitch rose in volume. 'I sold a woman two ironing boards – one for upstairs. She only had a hundred-pound credit limit, so she couldn't have the iron.' This time the laughter sounded harsher; it came out like 'tak, tak, tak.'

You have to learn to be this cruel, to be this unkind, to lie this amount without much care. This reminds us of the social dimension to lying, and the fact that development, including the development of lying, doesn't stop in adolescence. Neither does the importance of the social group.

'I've sold a woman velvet windows for every window in the house including the toilet.'

This time there was no response. 'Velvet windows?'

'Velvet curtains, I mean.' He had fluffed his lines, and the laughter never came. I could see in now. The man with the Black Country accent had a ruddy complexion. Too much time out in the biting wind, knocking on doors, canvassing – as they put it. His partner sat in a leather chair. Balding with a paunch, wearing a brightly coloured shirt. A large Rolex glinted on his arm, thick gold rings on two fingers of each hand. Two women were doing the accounts in an adjoining room. Brian, the owner of the shop, watched as the fifty-pound notes changed hands. He listened intently to the tales from the field. His employees had been out there and survived.

It was his turn in the round of stories.

I remember Ron telling us about having to go back to this customer who had complained about his carpet, which had a hole worn in it. He went into the house and said "What have you been doing here, then? It's not for walking on this, you know." The punter said, "Oh, I'm sorry."

So, Ron said, "You've worn it out because you're supposed to pick your feet up when you walk. You're not supposed to shuffle along it."

The laughter crackled as Brian shuffled along his imitation of the gait of the hapless punter.

You lie and then you denigrate the victim to your mates.

In the background, you could hear the quiet but confident tapping of the calculators as the figures were being totalled. 'A very good week,' said Brian. 'A very, very good week,' said the bald man with the Rolex in a parody of the AA advertisement that was current at the time.

We were in the back room of the shop. The jeweller's car, all fifty grand of it (big money in those days), sat outside the shop, looking just slightly incongruous in front of a shop that size. The shop, despite its tasteful jewellery, didn't look capable of sustaining a car of that sort. And it didn't. It was the back room that paid for the car, the back room with the little charts on the wall and the rows of noughts after each figure.

This little room was the centre of a highly successful company selling jewellery in what it called a 'direct sales operation.' In the past, they had sold other items in a similar fashion – duvets, ironing boards, sheets, Hi-Fi's, carpets, vacuum cleaners, even frying pans. But now they were concentrating on jewellery. Brian explained how it all worked. The company worked hand in glove with a credit collection company. The idea was simple and very neat. Agents from the credit company would go out on a weekly basis to collect outstanding debts from clients. They obviously got to know their clients very well. A representative of the jewellery company would then accompany the agents to certain targeted customers – customers who were paying off their outstanding credit. 'But only to the very good payers, or to the "crème-de-la-menthe" [sic] of the good payers, as we put it,' explained Brian. The jewellery would then be offered to the customer on the never-never. They showed me an attaché case containing all the gleaming, glittering merchandise. Roes of gold horseshoes and coats of arms, and rings inlaid with semi-precious stones ('*Semi-precious* covers a lot of bloody things,' explained one of Brian's salesmen helpfully; 'it's better than saying the stones aren't real'). All this temptation to clients already in debt.

'We're doing a social service to the public,' continued Brian. 'We sell directly to some disabled customers who can't get out to the shops. We bring a jeweller's shop right to their own doorstep in some of these high-rise flats they live in.'

And don't forget that ninety-nine per cent of our customers couldn't go out and borrow a tanner from anybody else. And if a customer decides not to pay, there's not a lot you can do about it. If a guy's unemployed and you take him to court, the court won't have a lot of sympathy for the guys who've got him into debt. The court will end up telling him that he'll have to pay you off at fifty pence a week. We're in a business where we have to take a lot of risks. You can't go in with a hard edge because they're your customers.

Brian blew on his coffee.

And believe me there are some right evil bastards out there, who just want to screw you for what they can get. They'll borrow money, they'll take your jewellery, they'll take anything that's going with no intention of paying any of it back. Then when the credit company says that they must pay up, they'll try to return the goods. We had one of our agents ring up and say that his customer wasn't going to pay because she was dissatisfied with the ring we'd sold her – the stone must have been loose or something because the bloody thing had fallen out. So, we got the agent to send the ring back in. The stone was still there, but the ring was so dirty that you couldn't see the stone. It was all misshapen as well. We've had rings returned when the punters have obviously punched somebody with the ring on their fingers. These are the kinds of people that we have to deal with.

Two more salesmen arrived back. A case of jewellery lay open on the table. One of the salesmen stood well away from the attaché case, as if it might contain a hidden, unexploded bomb. 'I hope that's not the case that the dog tiddled on last week,' he said.

Perhaps you should sniff it and see. How did you let things like that happen? The worst thing that ever happened to me with a dog was when this little Jack Russell ate one of my rings. I put the dog's name down on the voucher. My boss at the time went mad. But what else could you do? Anyway, we got the ring back after a week, although the label had disintegrated.

They all laughed. These were people on a high. You could see that everyone here was a winner. The jewellery company had a group of customers targeted for it, plus the introduction from someone who was almost a friend of the family, and the credit company got its customers to continue to borrow. The jeweller got his money directly from the credit company, which in turn took a hefty commission. The credit company had, however, to collect the debt, but this was their business. Sweet. Very sweet. Everyone was a winner.

Except, perhaps, the customer.

A customer buying a 300-pound ring over 120 weeks would pay 204 pounds on top of that for credit, and this is an individual on a low income and already in debt. 'But the customers themselves care little about the interest rate being charged. All they're interested in is how much per week the ring or gold chain or whatever will cost them,' explained Brian.

This one-hundred-pound ring will cost them £1.60 a week over two years. We always say in this game that we leave all the multiplication up to the customer. It's not our problem, after all. But you couldn't walk into a High Street shop anywhere in the world and get a ring like this for a fiver a week.

I looked at the ring with the horse's head on it. 'It's Red Rum, I think,' said Brian.

You see, many of our customers are unemployed. But we always say that the unemployed are often better managers of money than those in work. They know exactly how much is coming in. They might be paying between ten and thirty quid a week to the credit company, for all sorts of things – household goods, car repairs, plus, of course, to clear previous debts – but they know they have to meet the repayments, because they've nowhere else to go for credit.

'We're basically salesmen, we're not their financial consultants,' explained one of his salesmen.

Our customers often tend to be at the very bottom of the heap. You should see some of the houses that our men have to go into. I've been in a house in Winsford in Cheshire where the mother was selecting a £300 diamond ring and the six kids were sitting around having dinner out of a jumbo tin of processed peas. I've been to houses where you can see piles of disposable nappies chucked out the back and left to dissolve in the rain.

'I've been to houses where I wouldn't crap in the bog,' said Brian, not wishing to be left out of all this. This notion that the customers are somehow different from themselves, somehow alien, is very important to maintaining the spirit of the team. 'It's a different planet out there,' added Brian unselfconsciously.

I left that cosy little office with Brian for a look. It was a bitterly cold night on the other side of the town. Brian parked his jeep at the end of the street. Some teenagers on the corner eyed us suspiciously. This was a regular call. Brian was on his own tonight. He poked his head in through the broken window between the kitchen and living room. The house may have been poor, but still it had a coloured TV, a video-recorder, and a library of videotapes, including, incongruously, *Jane Fonda's Workout*. Brian was welcomed into the house like an old friend of the family, which he undoubtedly was. Angela's husband was not about. 'He's off again,' said Angela. Brian told her not to worry. 'You've got some new curtains since I was last here…I've got some goodies here for you to look at.' Angela's father sat beside her. Things, you could say, were not going too well for the family. 'I was married forty-nine years, eleven and a half months. If she'd just lived another two weeks, we would have made our golden wedding anniversary,' said the father. Brian was settling in – 'It's like coming home, you know, coming here. When I sit down on this settee, I don't want to get up again.'

'I always have a right good laugh when Brian comes round,' said Angela. 'It's one of the few good laughs I ever have.'

Angela's son woke up at this point. He ate some ice cream out of a plastic bowl. A pile of coins had fallen into the bowl; the coins remained there as he ate the ice cream. Angela said she wasn't interested in any jewellery, until the case was opened. The rings sparkled brilliantly in those surroundings.

'Ooooooh, come here, let's have a look, then.'

'Try it on,' said Brian.

Now let me tell you how much that would be a week if you were to buy it. That would be a week if you were to buy it. That would be four pounds eight pence a week. Very reasonable, eh?

Brian turned to Angela's father. 'We've got some nice men's tackle here if you're interested.' He unfurled the gold chains in their velvet case with a practised flourish. The old man sat up straight for the first time. 'Try it on,' said Brian. The old man fingered the chains as Angela started pouring her heart out to Brian, mainly about financial worries.

'I'm more like a social worker sometimes,' said Brian as he climbed back into his jeep. 'Some of our customers are really decent people in hard times, and it's all very sad, but what can you do?'

If Brian was the social worker, Billy was the clinician. 'You can't afford to get involved,' he said. His technique was quite different. 'I'm a master at this game. It's all done as a series of moves. Watch me.'

The frost was worse the following night. The punter looked as if he had just been roused from a deep sleep. He looked like the sort of man you wouldn't like to upset. Probably early forties but could in real time be younger. 'What are you trying to sell me this time? Not more bloody rubbish, I hope.' This was Billy's cue. Mention 'rubbish' and Billy is right in there.

'Not rubbish, sir. Certainly not rubbish.' Billy had explained to me previously that selling works on objections. 'I've got some smashing jewellery for you today, sir, and a little bit special it is.' Billy was now ushering the punter, the agent, and myself all into the front room of the little house. This house was a good deal more orderly than the previous one. Billy was in charge, and we could feel it already. The wife emerged from the kitchen. Billy had told me that the first thing you must do when selling is to assess the situation – see what priorities the customer has got. The wife had obviously just finished washing up, so there were no problems there. The telly was blaring in the background, but they'd obviously only been half watching it. The situation was 'ripe,' as Billy liked to say.

As the agent sorted out the financial transaction, which was ostensibly the real purpose of the visit, Billy started to open his attaché case. All that glittering gold. He had their attention, their undivided attention – well, almost. 'Is anyone watching that?' said Billy, pointing at the television, and then without waiting for an answer he nipped across and switched it off. There was a stunned silence for a moment. The television probably acted as a backdrop to every conversation that had ever taken place in that front room, at least since the time when someone like Billy had last visited.

'Now, madam,' said Billy, 'if I said to you that you could have whatever you wanted from this box free of charge, what would you have?' There was another slightly stunned silence as everyone in the room tried to work out whether this was a genuine offer or some elaborate ploy. 'I'd have one of those rings. I love rings and so does Frank there.' Frank nodded enthusiastically. If there were any rings going free, he wanted to be in there as a potential re-cipient of any largesse. So, Billy now knew that it was a ring they were both after, and he knew exactly what they could afford. 'Ripe,' I thought I heard him muttering, but he may just have said 'Right.' Billy guided them through the rings. Rings were no longer 180 pounds or 220 pounds; they were just a couple of pounds a week over 2 years.

It was now just a case of selecting the items. 'What job do you do, Frank? Lorry driver? Right, then. You don't want anything with a stone in it, that's for sure. It'll make your finger go black.' Frank nodded and his gaze shifted to the solid gold horseshoe rings.

Billy started to chuckle.

You know, I once said the very same thing to a blackie. It took me a few seconds before I realised what I'd just said. I apologised and told him that it was just a figure of speech. "No offence taken, mate," he said. You can't be too careful, though, can you, Frank? You have to watch what you say to them. Now, what about this smashing ring here with the horse's head on it? Are you a gambling man yourself, Frank? I like a bit of a flutter. I'm sure that's Arkle. Just think – you could be wearing a racing legend on your finger for years. It could be a family heirloom. Leave it to your kids, Frank, there's a little bit of history on that ring. And don't forget the price can only go up, especially with inflation. That ring's only one pound eighty a week.

You could see that Frank was far from prepared to carry out the necessary mental arithmetic that would tell him exactly how much this nag's head ring at £1.80 a week over 2 years would eventually cost him. He didn't care. One look around the house told you that here was a family very short of heir-looms. Ripe.

It was now Alison's turn. 'I would have thought something with one of these ruby or emerald stones would be right up your street, madam,' said Billy. 'They are real, aren't they?' asked Alison nervously. 'A friend of mine bought a ring with fake stones in it a while ago. She'd been taken in, but I'd never fall for that.' Billy adopted a tone of some seriousness. He wanted to sound sincere, scholarly. 'They're what you call semi-precious, love. They keep their value very well, do semi-precious stones. They're a really good investment.' But it was time to get off that track double-quick.

> Here, let me try to guess your ring size, love. "P", I reckon. Is that pretty close? Now try this one. Didn't I tell you? A perfect fit. That one's only one pound twenty. What do you think of it, Frank?

Before we had made the call, Billy had drawn me a graph of the whole procedure from going through the door in the first place to finding the egress double-quick at the end. Even I recognised where we were now on the graph. We were, at that very moment, sliding down the hill, on the other side from the sale. Billy had now only to do the paperwork and then we were out. His rule was to talk about anything other than the sale at this stage. A little bit difficult with two customers still mulling over the concept of *semi-precious* on the same settee as him. 'Aren't you going to put the kettle on, then, love? We're all parched in here, and I'm sure that Frank could do with a cuppa. Isn't that right, Frank?'

Friday was the day when all the salesmen came back from the field with their tales of survival out there with the punters. They swapped stories and compared sales. 'Now, Bob, are you going to explain to us all how you managed to lose an eighty-six-pound gold chain? I wouldn't have thought that a salesman with thirty-three years in the business would have fallen for something like that?' The rest of the salesmen laughed.

'Well, it was like this,' said Bob. 'I went to this jewellery party at this house, where there were fourteen scantily clad women. Now, you can't sell to all fourteen in one go, especially because they were all new to credit. So I had them in three at a time in the kitchen. I'd already sold a grand's worth of stuff when this eighty-six-quid gold chain suddenly went missing. One of the birds had obviously tried it on and then let it drop down her bra. What could I do? I couldn't very well line them all up for a strip search, now, could I? Even if I'd wanted to. I've always believed, by the way, that you should never get involved with customers like that – even when I used to sell sheets and bedding. Business comes first, you have to remember that. Some of the reps I've known haven't been as disciplined as me. There was one rep I used to work with who had five kids in five different houses on the same estate. Straight up. But I've always put the sale first. My old boss used to say, "Never get your fishing tackle out when you're trying to make a sale," and I think that's a good philosophy of life. So, I wasn't interested in any strip search at this jewellery party. So, I played on their sympathies instead.

'I told them that it was a hundred-quid chain, and that the money would be coming out of my commission. Then I watched their reactions. One bird asked if it really was worth as much as that. You see that gives you a clue – she must have seen the price on the ticket by that stage. Then the same bird asked, "Aren't you insured?" That gives you another bloody clue. So, I say, "For the whole case, madam, not for a single item. So, who wants to hit me on the head and take the whole bloody lot?" You see, I'm still working on their sympathies.

And it worked. One of the husbands, who had turned up by this stage, then ordered a three-hundred-quid chain. So, I'm in profit, even if I have lost a chain.'

> But this is small-time thieving. It's a dangerous game walking around some of these places with thirty-six grand's worth of stuff in an attaché case. I can tell you. I've had a few near misses over the years. I was in this block of flats in Birmingham one time, and I was the only white face to be seen. My heart's pounding, and I'm gripping my case. There are these four big black guys in the lift with me, and I'm already thinking that I've been set up. There had been a single order, you see, from one of the flats on the top floor. So this big black guy turns to me and says, "Which floor are you going to, Doctor?" You see, I was wearing a pinstriped suit, a collar and tie, and was carrying this attaché case. So, I played along with it.

A close friend of Bob's, however, who also worked for the same company, was not so lucky. He had been mugged in Moss Side in Manchester. As he emerged from one house, he was hit over the head with an iron bar and knocked unconscious. He was off work for a fortnight. 'And the worst thing about it,' said Bob,

> was that he was treated like a bloody criminal by the police for a fortnight. The police always seem to assume that it's an inside job, even if you're lying in the gutter with your brains smashed in. They think that you were involved in it somehow or other. My pal's carried all his jewellery in a sports holdall rather than an attaché case since the mugging.

Bob had a theory about the violence that goes along with such robbery. 'The problem with muggings is that the people who do them always get so hyped up beforehand. They think that they're going to have to do you, so even if you offer to hand over the case of jewellery, they end up doing you just the same. If anyone tried to mug me, I'd hurt them, for the simple reason that I know they'd end up doing me anyway, so I might as well leave my mark on them. That way, they'd have to go to hospital sooner or later, and you stand at least some chance of getting your gear back. If you end up losing your gear, then you know that you're going to be the number-one suspect and that's not very pleasant, believe me.' That's the negative side of the business, but on the plus side, there's the thrill of selling, although you have to have a sense of humour for this job.

> I've got a joke for every occasion. OK, try this one: What do ostriches, pelicans and poll tax collectors have in common?... They can all shove their bills up their ass. I've been using this joke on some of the estates where the poll tax isn't too popular. Or did you hear the one about this fellow who went to the ticket office at the train station, and said, "Two

tickets to Nottingham, please" (in that very nasal, blocked-up voice from a current TV advert). So, the guy from the ticket office says, "What you need is some Tunes." And the other guy says, "Why, do they cure cerebral palsy?" I use this joke all over the place. You need a good sense of humour in this business.

Bob has spent a lifetime in direct selling and telling jokes; it has not always been jewellery, although he reckons jewellery is easy.

The basic argument with jewellery is that you have it for ever. It will give you years of pleasure, even after you've forgotten what you've paid for it. You buy it now and you even get two years to pay it off, so it's cheaper than it would be in two years' time. You get a new jacket, on the other hand, and the same time next year it's out of fashion. I've sold everything. I used to sell Calor gas heaters. They produced so much condensation that one woman rang the water board because she thought she'd got a leak. Then it was fitted suits. You should have seen the state of some of those suits – hanging right off the poor bastards who ordered them. One salesman couldn't fill in the forms correctly with all the details. I put it to him, "Have you ever seen someone with a fifty-six-inch waist, and a forty-inch chest?" Then it was safety rings for children to wear in the water, which came in the shape of ducks. With these particular rings, when the kids went into the water the ring turned over. There were all these complaints from parents that their children had been nearly drowned with them. Then it was the furniture, now it's jewellery. It's all the same to me, to be honest. But the truth is with jewellery we get a lot of respect from the police for carrying this much jewellery around with us. I was in an accident last year when my car went down a ditch. You should have seen this copper's face when I told him what was in my attaché case. He climbed down and got it for me. When I told him where I'd been with the gear, he told me I deserved a medal. Well, it's all a service to the public, I told him. Somebody has to be prepared to do it.

4 Expert Liars

Men are so simple, and so much creatures of circumstance, that the deceiver will always find someone ready to be deceived.

Niccolo Machiavelli (1513) *The Prince*

What about a Job as a Dog Walker?

After I left Cambridge, I was appointed lecturer in psychology at the University of Sheffield, a city world-famous for 'Sheffield Steel,' but now in sharp decline. I wrote about this Sheffield for *The Guardian* and then in books (Beattie 1986, 1987, 1998). These were the years of Margaret Thatcher and her aftermath, the miners' strike, the steel works closing, the battle of Orgreave, the war on the miners and their communities, unemployment rocketing in the city, and throughout South Yorkshire (Thatcher 2012). In 1981, the proud but now unemployed workers of Sheffield were advised by Norman Tebbit, the then Employment Secretary, to get on their bike to find work – 'get on your bike' became the political advice/slogan of the Conservatives (he didn't actually tell them this directly, instead he explained that in the 1930s, his unemployed father 'got on his bike and looked for work, and he kept looking till he found it,' the implication being that they should do the same thing). This was the Sheffield that I would come to know, massive unemployment with all the psychological pressures that brings and enormous political resentment against the lying and deceitful government ('no such thing as society.' What does it even mean? I would be asked).

The psychology department at the University of Sheffield was a contemporary building full of sharp corners on the outside. It looked almost pink sometimes with the sun glinting off it. It had a modern shape with narrow corridors and doors painted in bright, primary colours. Reds, blues, greens. It was a world away from the Victorian torpor of the academic department at Cambridge. The porter sat behind a glass partition. He had a thin moustache and a stammer. He liked to tell me all about his life in the steel mills before he was made redundant and ended up here.

DOI: 10.4324/9781003394563-4

'Here' is all he ever called it. Here. Not the university, not this great seat of learning. Just here. The place where he ended up. 'Better than the scrap heap, I suppose. I can keep an eye on you lot for a start.'

He seemed to resent the whole thing, the students, the staff, the flexible hours we all worked, the lack of real graft, and he would often display his contempt for other members of staff quite openly to me, and his contempt for me, no doubt, behind my back. I was twenty-four when I started at Sheffield University. In the early eighties, Carol and I moved to a little terraced house in Netherfield Road in Crookes with our daughter Zoe whose first days of life were spent in an old coach house, owned by the university, just off Fulwood Road, with the rats clawing at the ceiling on her bedroom (after they were poisoned by pest control, they made an even bigger racket – the poison apparently makes them extremely dehydrated).

I remember that first summer in our new home, this new beginning of ours. It was a bright sunny, terraced street, full of steelworkers, most now unemployed. They may have been made redundant they still had to *be* somebody, that was obvious, hard graft in the steel mills had made them who they were. They might have been slaves of the factory clock as Engels might have called them, but they got enormous respect for that work. 'Sheffield Steel' was known throughout the world. They still needed to be respected; it was as if the clock was still ticking. They worked on their kitchens or bathrooms and took regular breaks and sat outside with the dirt on their faces so that their neighbours could see them, grafters still, even without paid work. It wasn't exactly deceit, but it wasn't completely necessary either. They could have had a tea break out the back or in their front room. The sociologist Erving Goffman (1976) might have described it as a social performance of sorts, part of the theatre of everyday life, acting the part. The audience was their friends and neighbours. They had to dramatise the hidden work in their homes for this audience; they had to leave the dirt on their faces, to make the work visible – to make it real. And they were creatures of habit – they were used to coming home with the grime on their faces and their hands. This social performance was critical to their perception of self. This was that summer.

Summer had to come to 'Brick Street' some time and the mist eventually did lift from the Rivelin Valley so that you could see the grey slab flats of Stannington (they turned out to be brown and white, but they had looked grey all year). Swallows appeared overhead, dipping for flies. Boys with fishing nets set forth. Funny, I thought that sticklebacks had gone for ever, but they obviously knew different. Old familiar smells – hot tarmac, rain on warm pavements – returned to haunt the memory and tease the imagination. Steel City was heating up after a year of wind and rain. Cold Steel City to chill the bone and dampen the spirit, but now the chill had gone.

But Brick Street was different that summer. The noises were different. The feeling was different. People were getting up later. There was no bustle. It was now a street of people who didn't work. Some were retired, some hadn't got jobs yet; but most had been made redundant. Work was never really discussed. People were bitter. Casual enquiries about work or job prospects could hurl you into an endless spiral of accusation and complaint. 'Thatcher.' 'Foreign steel.' 'Bloody recession.' Most people only fall down this well once. Some things are better left unsaid; everybody knows that everybody else knows who's to blame and that's all that matters. And anyway, there were more important things to talk about – the decorating, the price of houses, the weather. This summer, especially the weather.

The women seemed to rise first. Two old, retired dears brought their milk in first. They lived side by side and hated each other. Both were in their seventies; both were widows and both natives of Sheffield. One had a son; one hadn't got anyone. Mrs Hill's son came to visit her once a week in his S-registration Polo. He would sit for an hour in her house on a Sunday, then leave. If it was a good day, they would drive for an hour. But one Sunday, he had his two corgis with him. He was supposed to be taking his mother to Chatsworth for the day but, Mrs Hill says, 'There was no room with the dogs in the back. I don't mind. It would have been too cramped. It's a good day for just sitting out anyway,' and then she went off to the Bingo. Her luck was in – she won a tenner. 'It pays me to go,' she said.

Mrs Hill's neighbour, whom she always referred to as Mrs What's-her-name (even though she had an excellent memory), was new to the street. She had bought the terraced house after her husband had died – it was a step down for her from lower-middle to upper-working. She had lived in Sheffield all her life, but not in this street. Mrs Hill didn't like her – she didn't like strangers. Mrs Hill left her living-room curtains undrawn well into the night and watched the comings and goings. Mrs Hill patrolled up and down her living room pretending to tidy it but really, she was just watching the street. Her black and white television was always on (Errol Flynn in the afternoon, Magnum at night). Mrs What's-her-name also watched the street, but from behind drawn living-room curtains and after she had gone to bed, she liked to watch from behind the bedroom curtains (Mrs What's-her-name was from a higher social class). You didn't have to page the oracle in our street; you just asked Mrs Hill. She knew who was moving and why; she was good on the price of houses; she was top on adultery and divorce. She told Mrs What's-her-name the spicier bits, but they were both a bit deaf, so they shouted. It was strange to hear yourself talked about in this way, but of course they thought they were whispering – it would have been too embarrassing to tell them. Mrs Hill went to the shops at 10 am and 3 pm. Mrs What's-her-name went at 11 am and 4.30 pm. Mrs What's-her-name also went somewhere at 7 pm, although no one knew where. Mrs Hill had tried to wheedle it out of her but Mrs What's-her-name's lips were sealed. Mrs Hill suspected that she took a drink.

Mr Smith and Mr Forrest were another unlikely pair. Both were steel workers, both redundant for two years. Both bitter. Mr Smith was in his forties. His wife was a clerk; his daughter had just left school but hadn't got a job yet. Fred Smith had been decorating his home all year. Now he had reached the outside, he was replacing the window frames and varnishing the door. He started at about 9 am and took breaks every few hours out in the sun. He didn't sit out in the sun before he started, but only after he had worked for a couple of hours and at the end of the day. At the end of the day, he didn't wash immediately, he liked to feel he had been grafting. He could then sit and enjoy the sun for a bit – he'd earned it. He liked this stage of the decorating, its hard work, plenty of graft: all the poncey bits done. He didn't know what he'd do when the decorating was finished, though.

Mr Forrest, the other former steelworker, was fifty-seven, and lived at the bottom of the street. In a street overlooking the Bole Hills and the Rivelin Valley – a street which was really exposed – Mr Forrest had the most exposed house of all. The wind tore at his house, he was constantly replacing his tiles and his guttering. He had been made redundant just over two years earlier. He didn't mind much at the time – his wife was very ill with kidney failure. This summer, she wasted and died. He always referred to her as Mrs Forrest. 'Mrs Forrest is in a better place now,' he said. But he didn't let her death get him down. He was constantly on the move, constantly busy. He ran everywhere with his dog Suki. 'I could be out dancing every night,' he said, 'if I'd got the brass.' He was always up ladders replacing people's guttering, unblocking their drains, digging their gardens – he needed any money people could afford to give him. He'd worked for a day for a couple of quid. He got business by worrying people.

'The next time we have a good storm that drainpipe is going to come right off.'

'Oh,' said Mrs What's-her-name.

'I could do it for you tomorrow.'

'Oh, all right then.'

And off he went, whistling his happy tune. He talked in the same kind of shout as the old people because he was deaf from the years in the noisy steel mill. The whole street shouted their private messages at each other. There was little privacy here.

It was a funny, old-fashioned street. There was no graffiti, little vandalism. There were too many people watching what was going on for these to occur. Everybody knew everybody else's business. And yet the houses themselves with their neat little gardens were very private. No posh houses, mind. They were just stone-terraced houses or fifty-year-old unfashionable red-brick ter-raced houses. Privately owned houses for the working class with the discipline and the thrift, once a way station for the economically mobile steelworkers reared in council houses. And houses for the retired folk when they found themselves a bit of money.

But now things were different. Instead of standing on the parapets and plan-ning their advance into new unconquered territories, these people were in a state of siege. Constantly reworking their decorations, their fortifications, con-stantly mending their guttering, varnishing their doors, constantly polishing their J-registration cars. These people wouldn't be leaving their castles and they knew it. They also wouldn't have to retreat, thanks to redundancy payments.

So this summer, the sun was shining and the temperature rose but they were not tempted out. These were the working class, reared on discipline and hard work; sitting in the sun was redolent of idleness and waste. Sitting in the sun was skiving. And these were the people who didn't skive, who had timetables fixed and immutably etched on their brains, the people who thrived on overtime. But now the overtime had gone, as had the work. So they were poorer and a bit disillusioned. Some of them had lost all their aspirations and yet the little foremen in their heads still made them feel guilty for enjoying the hot summer sun.

And the sun was shining and the grey slab flats of Stannington across the valley seemed even closer. And the three-bedroom semis of middle-class Sheffield seemed a million miles away.

I became interested in how a community can cope with this sort of seismic economic and social change, so-called 'negative industrialisation' and how people can cope psychologically. In the summer of 1985, there were over 3 million unemployed, 13.4% of the working population. Nearly 1.5 million had been unemployed for more than a year. The rate of unemployment had doubled since 1980. In South Yorkshire (covering Barnsley, Doncaster, Rotherham, and Sheffield) in 1985, unemployment was 17.3% (see Beattie 1986, 1998).

I could, of course, see it all around me. But this wasn't just an economic blow, this was a psychic blow. Brian was one of the 'luckier' ones that I met at that time. He was forty-six then. In November 1983, the men in his engineering works were told that the firm would close in six months. Brian got a bit of a reprieve; he got an extra five months in the firm where he had worked for twenty-five years. He told me that the Department of Employment sent a team of redundancy 'counsellors' to give them a series of lectures to ease this rite of passage. Brian said that he found the lady from the Department of Employment somewhat disconcerting when she told them that the rules and regulations about unemployment benefit were so complicated that nobody really knew what anybody was entitled to. The redundancy counsellors gave a lecture on finding a job. All that Brian remembered was that they suggested dog-walking, pet-sitting, and fish-feeding for neighbours as real possibilities. They also gave lectures on interview technique, with the advice to dress reasonably and not to squirm or fidget. Brian didn't squirm or fidget anyway. So, equipped with this knowledge (and £6500 redundancy money) Brian joined the army of the unemployed in August 1984, with strict orders to sign on and search for jobs and trudge the streets for the long, long, empty hours. We talked in a McDonalds, where he spent a significant part of most days.

He had tried to cheer himself up – at least he had some interests outside work, he told himself. He was a keen marathon runner and he thought that if he was unemployed for a while, this would give him some more time to train. But things didn't turn out that well. On his very first day on the dole he went out for a run with his wife. She had just taken up running and he was going to be her mentor. He says he was quite relaxed about redundancy, but that day, that critical day when it finally materialised, he found that he just couldn't keep up with her. He tried going out with his old running club and the same thing happened – they left him behind. He had never had asthma in his life but suddenly here he was puffing and panting and gasping for breath. The other runners couldn't understand it. It got so bad that he couldn't even walk home from the Jobcentre without continually stopping. He read somewhere that nerves could bring on asthmatic symptoms, but he refused to believe that was what was happening with him. He thought perhaps it was his house-cleaning, which he did while his wife went to work, or the fact that there was a lot of dust in the factory for the last few weeks before the closure. He was looking for some physical cause, something that he could put his finger on and say, 'That's it,' something tangible. He didn't want to believe that it was something psychological, that it was all in his mind.

The psychological effects of this negative de-industrialisation,' this failure to support the industrial North were enormous. Brian and hundreds of thousands like him were the victims, victims of government policy, victims of Thatcher's government's desire to smash the Unions and in particular the miners. Most took small measures to regain some control (like the endless DIY in the houses in Brick Street) and to actively avoid embarrassment (like only going into local supermarkets for the family shopping in the afternoon to avoid ex-work colleagues). Some, however, took bigger steps, steps based on explicit lies and deceit; I discovered this quite by accident.

Shadow Lives

There was one nightclub right in the centre of Sheffield, which was always packed, even during this economic collapse. The club was called Josephine's. 'Sheffield's Ultimate Nitespot,' it said on the ticket. 'Dress to impress,' it warned at the door. The doormen enforced the rule vigorously – no long-hairs, no jeans, no casual jackets, shirts must have buttons all the way down the front. In the club, men had to always keep their jackets on. Plush carpets, crushed velvet padded toilet doors, mirrored walls, mirrored ceiling, flashing lights, scented loos with aftershave sitting out to be used, and an attendant to keep everything clean and to pursue the select clientele when they tried to disappear with the aftershave. Loud disco music with a smooth very short-statured DJ talking over it. They called him 'Nick Nack' after the character in the James Bond film *'The Man with the Golden Gun.'*

'Does any girl know what car James Bond drives in his latest film?' he would ask. 'A bottle of champagne if you know the answer!' (the champagne was sparkling plonk).

'What's the most expensive perfume in the world?'

'A bottle of champagne for the most gorgeous girl in the club' (more sparkling plonk, always sparkling plonk).

'A bottle of champagne for the first woman to dance on stage!'

'Two bottles if she strips!' (She does).

Waitresses in leotards, go-go dancers in suspenders. 'A little bit of Vegas in Sheffield,' said the owner Dave Allen to me, entrepreneur, and pigeon fancier. He drove a Jaguar rather than a Rolls Royce because he explained 'I'd look bloody ridiculous getting the pigeons of out the back of a Roller.'

This one club taught me a great deal about how changing economic conditions can change people. I found this place by accident, but it taught me so much about lies and deception and how important these can be (Beattie 1986, 1987).

It was 12.15 am, the nightclub right in the centre of the city was already full. He made his entrance. A vision in black and gold – black silk shirt unbuttoned almost to the waist, black trousers, black shoes, and gold – everywhere. Three gold medallions dangling on his chest, two gold rings on the same hand, he was about forty, his hair was cropped short, he was smoking a cigar. He walked slowly in a cool, confident manner, scanning the faces. He greeted the bouncers, they greeted him. Don Corleone was back. He walked to the wine bar and greeted the owner of the club. The owner ordered champagne. Don Corleone kept watching, he kept scanning the faces. Strangers to the club stared back at this small dark man. But Don Corleone was not what he seemed. He was just an Italian waiter from a restaurant in a northern industrial town. He hadn't any money; he hadn't even got a car. He got the bus into town with all that jewellery hanging around him. He knew the nightclub owner from way back and he'd got a free pass to the club. If he hadn't, he couldn't afford to go in. But here he was – six nights a week, laden with gold, almost certainly fake. But in the dim light of the club, all that glistened was surely gold and people assumed that he was somebody. When he was standing at the bus stop during the day, with a bag of washing for the laundrette, he would jump into hiding if he spotted anybody he recognised. He lived alone in a bedsitter. Luigi, the waiter, by day – Don Corleone, the somebody, by night.

Another character strode in. He was also small, but he'd gone for the sailing look. Blue double-breasted jacket with a silk handkerchief in the pocket, his tie had a crest on it. He was getting on a bit and was balding. His hair was in the Bobby Charlton style and the long strands were weaved around his bald patch. But in here there were no cruel winds to give the game away; he could relax. He walked about as if his Rolls Royce was ready and waiting to take some lucky lady off to his yacht on a moonlit Bay. But there was no yacht and no Roller, just drizzle and a J-registration Hillman Minx. There was a flat of sorts – a little terraced house full of unwashed pots and pans (he lived alone and hadn't time to do them before he went out) and after shave. By day he was a bus conductor; by night, well, he was a randy, old, rich seadog, four hours a night, six nights a week. He'd also got a free pass. He knew the club owner from the time when the club owner still used the bus service.

Anyone who had seen Don Corleone on a bus or Lone Yachtsman in his Hillman Minx could not take them too seriously, but John was different. He was thirty-six, tanned, fit, his hair – streaked blond. He looked the part in a way that Don Corleone or the Lone Yachtsman didn't. They had become submerged in images from the past; his was more contemporary (it was remember the 1980s). John (not his real name) got to the club at about 11:30 pm in his brown Silver Shadow. He parked it in the underground car park just by the club. The car park is used by many of the club's customers. As he was parking it, he noticed that he was being watched by a gaggle of girls emerging from a white Mini.

'Did you see that car?' a tall blonde girl with buck teeth said to her friends. John pretended not to hear and turned around and walked to the exit. He walked slowly to give them a chance to identify his features. When he had left, the girls went over and looked at the car. They peered inside; one touched the paintwork, her sweaty palm leaving a thumbprint on the door. 'He must be bloody well loaded. Imagine going home in that tonight.'

John went into the club and ordered a gin and tonic. He stood by the bar. The four girls, now arranged in two sets of two (a strategic configuration for picking up men), passed him at the bar. The girl with buck teeth gave him a quick smile, as did her friend (the one who had been admiring the paintwork). They thought he might buy them a drink, but he just smiled back. They ordered four Bacardi and Cokes. It came to four pounds eighty. John looked nonchalant. A male acquaintance came over. 'Not much in tonight,' he said.

'No, not much talent tonight,' John replied.

It was Buck Teeth's round. She glanced over at John again. He was still sipping his gin and tonic. Buck Teeth forked out another four eighty. John was making his gin and tonic last. He went to the toilet; he took his drink with him and filled it up from a quarter bottle of gin he'd been keeping in his inside pocket. He came back to the bar with his glass full. Buck Teeth assumed he'd been to the other bar. He quite fancied Buck Teeth's friend and he started chatting her up. Buck Teeth hung about until her friend started touching John's arm. At this point, she felt really excluded and went in search of her other two friends. 'Joanne's got off with that filthy rich man in the Rolls,' she said, 'Lucky bastard,' they replied in unison.

Joanne had finished her Bacardi. 'Would you like a drink?' she said to John and they both laughed at the suggestion and the situation. Joanne had just told John that she was unemployed (she borrowed a tenner from her mother for the evening). John had just told her that he owned a company. One of them was telling fibs. John said, 'Oh, go on then.' Joanne didn't think he was mean; she just wanted to show him that she was not after his money, which she was. John accepted the drink and made this one last as well. The manager went past and said to one of the bouncers, 'I see John's got one on.'

The evening progressed. John went to the toilet and met a friend who bought him a drink. Joanne bought herself a double while he was away. John had told her that there might be a job in his company for her. Joanne had been unemployed for three months – she was over the moon and nearly under the table. They danced to the slow music at the end. John asked her if she'd like a lift home. 'Oh, have you got a car then?' she said innocently. 'Yes, a Rolls-Royce,' he said. 'You're kidding.' 'No, I'm not come and see.' They left together. The manager said, 'Goodnight, sir; goodnight, madam.'

The Rolls gleamed in the artificial light. The thumb print was still there. John let her play with the electric windows. 'Can we drive round past the front of the club so that my friends can see me?' she said. They did, but her friends had gone. 'Oh, it's a real pity,' she said. John asked her where she lived. 'Upperthorpe,' she said. John knew it was five miles out and not in his direction.

He gulped but didn't say anything. All the way there, at every set of traffic lights, she looked around into all the taxis, hoping to see someone she knew.

They got home at a quarter to three. She insisted on waking her mother up to show her the car. Her mother came downstairs in curlers and stared out through the curtains. 'It's a real beauty,' she said. 'Yes,' said John. The mother made tea. It wasn't exactly what John had had in mind. After he'd gone, the mother said, 'What a nice lad, success hasn't spoiled him at all. He's very down-to-earth.'

He had promised Joanne he'd ring the following Tuesday, but he didn't. Joanne went round to Buck Teeth's house. 'I'm not going back to that club, it's full of rich flash bastards who treat you like shit.'

But John hadn't meant to let her down or hurt her. It was just that she lived too far out. He simply couldn't afford the petrol to Upperthorpe. If she'd lived closer, he would have taken her out. John didn't own a company; he was a van driver when I first met him, married with two adolescent boys. Most of his salary went on running the car. His wife worked – she paid reluctantly for the running of their council house. He had friends in the motor trade, and he had got the car at a good price about four years earlier when he'd made some money selling another car. He only used the car at night. He couldn't afford the petrol to take it to work. He ran instead – five miles there and five back. One of the new sets of marathon men, but out of necessity rather than choice. And it saved him going to a trendy and expensive fitness club.

But sometimes he did score. He had a two-year relationship with a girl called Debbie who worked in the make-up section of a large department store. Her make-up was always immaculate – a perfect mask. John's mask was subtler. She was blonde and always wore white – tight white jeans or white dresses. Men always gawped at her, and John loved the attention. They would drive out to pubs in the country and leave the car in the front car park. The customers would stare. 'It's all right for bloody some,' they would say. John saw Debbie every night from 10 pm to 2 am. They were a lovely couple. People in the club would enquire when they were going to get married. At weekends, Debbie said, they would go and look at £80,000 pound houses (that was a lot in the early 1980s, especially in Sheffield). 'We'd drive up in the car, and I'd get really made up. I used to have to loan John the money for petrol.' During this time, John had his electricity cut off for non-payment of bills. John used one set of pubs for his wife and one set for Debbie. Everyone thought that Debbie and he were the perfect couple. 'We even went looking for an engagement ring,' said Debbie,

> a £500 job, but he hadn't a bean; it was all a bit stupid. I didn't even see his wife until after we'd split up. She was all right, a bit rough, but even she's too good for him. She looked at me as if I was a real tart, but he always told me the marriage was finished anyway.

John was on his own now. He still missed Debbie, but her absence didn't prompt him to take his wife out instead. 'People would wonder who she was,' he said, 'And I couldn't afford it anyway.' Instead, he had one or two male friends. One of his friends had got a yellow Rolls Royce with a TV in it. 'He's really cracked it,' said John.

> He'll pick up a girl on Saturday night and instead of taking her to the pictures on Sunday – that would be four quid at least – or for a drink – nearer eight quid – they just sit in the Roller and watch TV. All he has to pay for is the petrol and sometimes he can get the girl to pay for that.

John only ever went to one club. And one might imagine that after a short period, everyone would know that he was a van driver rather than a company director. But no, that kind of news seems to travel slow. It was almost as if people wanted to believe his story, despite evidence to the contrary. For, after all, the club was founded on fantasy for the Martini set and John came as close to the image (at least in terms of appearance) in this northern town as anyone. If he wasn't what he seemed, then who was? And he could always update his story to keep just ahead of the news hounds and the bloodhounds of gossip. 'Oh yes, I used to be a van driver when I went out with Debbie, but that was before I opened my own company, and have you seen my Rolls-Royce, by the way?'

I got to know John a little better over the next few years, but it was always difficult. He wasn't particularly forthcoming. His lies and deceit were primarily visual rather than carefully crafted stories. His Rolls Royce was always parked underneath the club; it was a regular fixture and that was the message, with just a gallon or so of petrol in the tank. If he pulled a girl, he always had to work out exactly how many miles away she lived, to see if he could get there and back without running out of gas. That was his word. Gas. He said that it sounded more American, more glamorous. He knew all the districts in Sheffield and whether he could make it there or not on the couple of gallons of gas he had in the tank. He told any attractive girl that he met that he was looking for an au pair for his children. The fact that his children were both teenagers was never mentioned. But John looked the part.

'The man with the five-octane smile,' is how he described himself. White flashing teeth that he liked to expose. He would bring a little phial of water with him and brush his teeth in the underground car park just before entering the nightclub. Great slabs of newly polished ivory glinting in the dark of the club. VIP's who knew him called him 'the man with the five-octane breath.' He told me that he was really an entrepreneur. He had started trading cars from home – Vauxhall to Ford back to Vauxhall to Nissan to old BMW to Old Merc to old Roller. He wasn't making any money, but he was getting some cheap thrills through his business dealings. He was addicted to business. That's how he described it.

Sometimes John lost money. He took his family on holiday to Skegness and came back in a hearse. He traded his Vauxhall Carlton for the hearse. 'The art of the deal,' he called it. He tried to sell the hearse to a sandwich shop outside

Barnsley. He suggested the advertising slogan – 'People are dying for our beef sandwiches.' They didn't go for it. So, he tried a local butcher's instead, and a new slogan. 'People are dying for our Barnsley chop.' They bought the idea and the hearse, and his career was launched. He really was an entrepreneur now.

He kept the Roller to give him an edge in business, that was his explanation. 'I want people to know who they are dealing with,' he said. '"It doesn't matter who you are, or where you come from". That's what Mrs. Thatcher said. There's no law against us Northerners doing well.' He had just spent the last four months collecting pig meal bags for profit. His brother who kept pigs had suggested this to him. 'Some of the best entrepreneurial ideas come second hand,' he had told me. 'It doesn't matter where you get the idea from, as long as it's a little gem, a little corker.'

He used the same language to describe women. Little gem, little corker, and at the end of the evening he would be out there looking for any wee bargains left. Wee bargains or cheap goods. Anything when he was desperate. No matter how damaged or soiled.

In the four months after he had become the self-declared pig bag king of South Yorkshire, he had collected two thousand pig meal bags. 'Half a ton – a mountain of bags in a field at the bottom of my garden,' he said.

> I used to sit in my kitchen and look at all that money I was accumulating. The neighbours were all ringing the council to complain, but I think that they were just jealous of my success. I was thinking about what I was going to spend all my money on.

The mountain of pig meal bags was growing; he would watch this organic process from his kitchen. 'It was almost too easy,' he had said. 'Capitalism is as natural as farming,' he would say. That day he had sold the pig meal bags. He got sixty quid for the lot. 'Less than four pounds a week for all of my effort.' He was drinking tonic water in the club that night. He said that he had a queasy tummy.

But John was still a millionaire in here, in the club with little lights on the carpet like those on an aircraft floor to guide you to safety in the event of an emergency. Lights to follow when the power goes, lights to follow in the dark. The Roller was underneath the club. John lied for years. He was still a budding, thrusting entrepreneur. In there, at least.

'Mrs. Thatcher knows that it's all to do with luck,' he would say. 'You don't necessarily need brains. I know lots of millionaires and none of them are brain surgeons.' He used the word 'brain' a lot. 'You've got brains,' he said, 'I've got a little savvy.' He always wanted me to say that he had got brains as well, but I never did. I was trying to be honest even in that club, which was full of lies and liars. But I understood the lies, perhaps I even empathised with their predicament. I couldn't talk to John without thinking about Brian and the rest, the men who could hardly walk from a to b without a shortage of breath. John positively glowed.

But I've been lied to, I know how it feels and I'm sure that a lot of people were hurt by John's deceptions. In fact, I know they were because I met several of them who had dreamt of a new future with him. They asked me if I'd seen him recently. He had gone, temporarily at least 'on the missing list,' as they liked to say in Josephine's. These girls were dreaming of a life away from Manor Top or Upperthorpe, life in the fast lane, Las Vegas all the time, and a new house on Millionaire's Row. They were still looking for the man with the five-octane smile and the Roller. That modest man who didn't have to show off by splashing the cash to impress them, or by boasting about how much money he had. Modest and loaded, that's how he liked to portray himself, always the best combination in Sheffield's top nightclub.

He rang me a short while ago.

'Alright?' he asked.

Always brief, always vague.

'And how's it going with you?' I replied.

'Ah, still the same. A bit up and down,' and we both laughed; the expression no doubt from some 1970s sitcom. A brief pointer to forgotten times. But these were modern times and he'd obviously checked me out on the internet because he seemed to know already where I was working. He never enquired; it was always what John didn't say or ask that was more informative.

There was a long pause. 'I've got a new car,' John finally said. 'A convertible Bentley,' he was warming up, his tone had become more jovial. He always liked mentioning his cars but was always silent about how he afforded them. There was another pause.

'I'll come and pick you up in Oxford, if you like, and we'll have a drive around in it. I'm sure there are some nice posh birds down there who like a bit of style.'

The VIP

I first saw 'Cockney,' no, let's start again. I first heard 'Cockney' in Josephine's in the section reserved for VIPs. He was loud, brash, and very verbal (as I believe they say south of Watford). He was introducing someone to his 'very best pal' Terry Curran, the ex-Everton and ex-Sheffield Wednesday and ex-Sheffield United Football (and arguably one of the best-known footballers in Sheffield at that time). Cockney was drinking 'a little shampoo.' Cockney had a silk suit and a Cartier watch, a diamond earring, and a pair of handcrafted shoes. Terry had some of those things as well, but not all. They made a formidable couple, with Terry's fame and Cockney's loud voice.

Someone asked Terry for his autograph. Terry signed.

'That's the thing about Terry Curran,' said one watchful bystander. 'He may be the Sheffield George Best, but he's always a gentleman, even on his night out.'

Terry passed the signed napkin back and the eager autograph hunter passed
it to Cockney. He smiled and signed 'Cockney Richard,' the eager autograph
hunter wasn't quite sure whose signature she'd managed to acquire – she knew
he was definitely a somebody, she just wasn't sure exactly which one. Cockney
went back to the 'shampoo.'

'I think I'll get another bottle,' said Cockney, 'or what about another two?
I feel like a right good drink.'

He turned to a hanger-on.

This is nothing, what I'm getting through tonight. Last week me and a
few mates got through nine bottles of champagne, and a while ago I was
in Stringfellows with some lads and one of them ordered eight butterfly
cocktails – they're one hundred guineas each – there are two bottles of
champagne in each one, and they're meant to be for eight people. But
my mate ordered one for everyone in his company. The barmaid said,
"Excuse me, sir. Are you sure you haven't made a mistake here?" And he
said, "You're quite right, luv – I have made a mistake – I forgot to you –
make it nine." Nine hundred guineas for a round of drinks – that's style.
Mind you, he got barred a week later for running up and down the bar
with his trousers down. He was a scrap dealer, by the way, and he looked
a bit ridiculous when he dropped them. Even though you buy all that
drink you can still get barred. You have to have genuine style as well. It's
not enough to be a big spender, you've got to have class.

Some of the younger Sheffield Wednesday players arrived. One had just been
given a transfer. His large doleful eyes were like basins full of dishwater, slightly
discoloured. He looked a bit like a Disneyfied fawn gone a bit wrong. It was
obviously an emotional moment, and he certainly wasn't over the moon about
the whole thing.

How much are you getting again? … Bloody hell, is that all? … What
about a car? I don't care whether you've got one or not, ask for a car. You
never get anything unless you ask … Do you know how much Terry got
when he went from Wednesday to United? … and all you're getting is
that … I was down at the PFA dinner last week as a guest of the Everton
lads and Andy Gray was telling me … You don't want to be taken for a
mug, do you? …

The fawn was beginning to resemble a parrot. He had gone a bit green, and
he was only able to repeat back the odd word that Cockney was firing at him.

The slightly surprising thing about all this is that this particular fawn was
a well-known footballer, difficult to imagine in his role as victim. But in the
concrete jungle, Cockney was the ultimate survivor and he'd got proof. He

pulled out a wad of photographs. 'Here's a photo of me and Freddie Laker on his yacht in Palma and here's a picture of me and the Everton lads at the PFA dinner in London.' He was keen on Everton (after all they did win the First Division) and Fred, before the collapse. His verbals started again.

> See, Everton and Liverpool, they're in a different class from other football clubs. They don't even bother training – they run around the pitch five times and that's their lot. Sheffield Wednesday had to run ten miles on a Monday, never mind the rest of the week. And Sheffield Wednesday have to stay in early all week – the only time an Everton or Liverpool player doesn't drink is the day before the game. But I'll always support Wednesday. Wednesday and I go back a long way. When I was eleven, I broke my arm playing football and I wrote to three England players, and only one wrote back to me – Ron Springer from Wednesday. He sent me a load of autographs, so I started supporting them. I only moved to Sheffield because it was cheaper to get to the games. It caused the breakup of my first marriage though. My wife said to me, "You prefer Sheffield Wednesday to me," and I said, "I prefer bloody Sheffield United to you." She was a millionaire's daughter, you know. I met her on 11 July, we got married on 11 August – Sheffield Wednesday played Swindon away and got beaten 4–0. She first left me on 11 January, Sheffield Wednesday were playing Portsmouth away. The second time she left me – when she gave me the ultimatum, Sheffield Wednesday, or her – it was the 11th again – they were playing Portsmouth again – at home – this time Wednesday won. I love this club. I'll always support them.

Cockneys magnanimity was clearly impressing his audience.

Cockney noticed my Irish accent. 'What poets the Irish are,' Cockney said, and launched into Oscar Wilde's *The Ballad of Reading Goal*.

'He did not wear his scarlet coat,
For blood and wine or red…'

He got to the fifth verse before he was stopped. The audience was clearly impressed by his literary knowledge. His offer to recite 'the first three verses' from any Shakespeare play was, however, graciously refused. What scholarship! What adaptability! What verbals! From extravagant consumerism to football mastermind to English scholar – all in the space of one large swig of 'shampoo.' A lord of the concrete jungle who could change his spots.

In a city of moderate public behaviour and moderate, if not downright dour, talk, Cockney's colourful and adaptable hyperbole, like a well-known brand of toothpaste, got him noticed. 'I'm the most famous man in Sheffield,' he said.

But what exactly did Cockney do? My question met with a stony silence, then evasiveness. 'Let's just say I'm a man with no visible means of support. I get by but don't worry, when I'm out with the lads, I buy more champagne than they do.' How did he get promotion into the first division of champagne cocktails, famous personages, and public recognition?

> Let's just say I know everybody who's worth knowing. I've introduced Terry to quite a few of my famous mates. Sheffield's just small time. As to what the celebrities around here think of me – maybe they just wonder how I can get out every night of the week drinking champagne.

How did he get to know Freddie Laker?

> I saw Freddie in Palma – I'd never met him before – I just went up to him and said, "Hello, Fred, long time no see." He said, "It's a long time please forgive me, but I seem to have forgotten your name." A friend and I were with a couple of birds he wanted to meet so we got invited out to his yacht that way. I've been out with loads of famous people. What's that guy from the Who called? I'd go up to anybody. I've been out with some right upper-class birds. But I haven't met old Prince Charles yet.

But who financed the old shampoo? What were the invisible means of support? He agreed to explain. We met back at his small flat – 'my little palace,' bursting with all the expensive ephemera of the consumer age. A video with a screen that wouldn't shame a cinema, silver cutlery, expensive carpet.

'It's handy living here,' he said, 'right in the centre of town, since I got done for drink driving in my XJS.' He'd been on the dole for the past two years. 'I get sixty quid a fortnight. But I can spend that on a Friday night. Who could live on that?' And he showed me his wardrobe with its seven silk suits and twenty-odd pairs of expensive shoes. He looked at my clothes. 'You're a right scruff bag, you know. You can always tell a man by his shoes and look at yours – they're a bloody disgrace.' I had to agree. His weren't. So how come, in the style wars, he was a fighter ace, and I was trudging around like a refugee?

'Well, the first thing to know is that I've been in trouble a few times. But who hasn't? Scratch any rich man and you'll find a thief. I was a thief since I was fourteen until last year when I was thirty-two, but I've come to the conclusion that it's just not worth it. I've had six custodial sentences, but I've been nicked thirty-seven times in all. I've been out of prison for nearly a year. Nothing heavy, mind. I got into trouble for the first time when I was at school for stealing by finding a motorbike. But the first time I got sent away was for stealing from a dwelling house (they didn't call it burglary). I nicked some cufflinks from a house in which my girlfriend was baby-sitting. I got five quid for them and then ten weeks in a detention centre. Ten weeks of marching up and down. When I got out, I started hanging about with some lads who had never worked. We used to buy something small in a Marks and Spencer's and as the girl opened the till, we'd grab some money out and run. I don't mind talking about these things – I've been done for all of them. The lads I knocked about with then got into armed robbery, but I never got into anything too heavy. I got into deception, you know, buying stolen chequebooks for four quid a page and passing the cheque.

> The person who nicks the chequebook never tries to pass the cheques off himself. He sells it. People always wonder how you copy the name so well – you don't. You take the original name off in a solution of warm water, brake fluid, washing-up liquid with a little bleach and you just sign the name yourself. I've had Sheffield police puzzled as to how I did it. In fact, I even explained it to them. They're making it more difficult now by having a pattern strip where you sign the name. My wife and I got done for passing off these cheques. We used to go to DIY shops because they cash cheques there, so you don't have to queue at the till. They were easier than banks. I used to do a lot of this in London as well – at one time I was making ten grand a month. I got my wife involved – I think she was just doing it to impress me.

His wife interrupted. 'Tell him where you got your Cartier watch though.' He declined. 'I came back one day, and he'd sold my Mini. I paid 600 quid for it,' she said. 'He bought himself a Cartier watch.'

'What are you complaining about?' he said. 'I bought you a gold sovereign from the sale.' Cockney clearly bought his worldly ways home with him.

> Look, I admit I've been a thief and a con man, but who isn't bent. I'm making a bit of cash now through some people I know who worked for the council. You can get anything fixed, you know, if you know the right people. Housing lists, anything.

He winked.

> I hate this bloody council as well, by the way – talk about the blind leading the blind. I'm Margaret Thatcher's biggest supporter. Anybody who wants to earn a living can earn a living. I'm on the dole through choice. I'm taking a break from work, that's all. I do keep myself busy – I use my contacts. I know all the big jewellers in Sheffield, and I'll sell things for them. See this gold chain – it's worth nearly 500. I paid one and a half for it and I'll get two and a half. I know the kinds of people who would want a chain like this. I also sell tickets – I know all the famous ticket touts down in London – Stan Flashman, David Brown. I was selling fifteen quid Bruce Springsteen tickets recently for thirty and twenty-five. Live Aid tickets for fifty quid.

Didn't he have any reservation about making money out of the latter venture? He looked at me as if I was some kind of idiot. 'Nobody, nobody does anything for nothing. Those bloody groups got an audience of millions – a good free plug. Do you think they'd have done it if it wasn't for that? Cockney was proselytising now – the doctrine of the free-market economy and the sanctity of the entrepreneurial spirit, unhampered by common morality or civil law.

'I also do a lot of cup final tickets. I give the players who get them five times their market value – that's thirty quid. I get fifty quid for them. Just a bit of bobbing and weaving. That's all I do now. But, as you know, I'm well in with the footballers – I also sell them clothes, for example snide [false] Lacoste shirts, even suits. I once sold a load of suits at fifty quid each to the Hillsborough players. It's all right, they weren't nicked or anything. It's all down to who you know and what you know. I'm not ashamed of what I've done. Why should I be? The world is full of bent people – in any section of society, just look at the judges and the police. How come the police can afford to go out to nightclubs every night? You just have to have the cheek to get by. I had my eyes done recently by one of the top cosmetic surgeons in Britain – the bill was six hundred quid, but I didn't pay – they weren't quite right. So why should I?'

And then he returns to his second favourite subject (his first is naturally himself). 'I learned Wilde's *The Ballot of Reading Gaol* when I was in prison. It was Oscar Wilde who said, "There's only one thing in the world worse than being talked about, and that is not being talked about at all." That man had real style; he didn't have any money, just plenty of style. If I don't have any money, I'll just get things on account – meals, champagne, anything. I've even had bets on account at a racecourse, believe it or not.'

> They made a scapegoat of Wilde; he wasn't really a queer – he just had syphilis and he didn't want to give it to his wife. Half the bloody aristocrats and half the judges in this country are bent anyway. They just wanted to victimise him. All great Irishmen are sent to prison – look at George Best. Only Barry McGuigan has got to go. God help him if he gets into trouble. When you're in the public eye you have to expect trouble of this sort, especially if you're Irish, like you. My grandmother's Irish so I'm watching out.

As I left, Cockney was just fixing up the use of a friend's apartment in Marbella for his holidays. He then requested a fee for the interview. 'Five hundred pounds will do nicely,' he said. 'Well, you don't do it for nothing, do you?' But, as I left, he looked at my shoes once again, with the look that said, they can't be paying you very much anyway.

The Disguise

I was now 'undercover' in my work in the Sheffield at that time, hanging about in nightclubs, going for a job interview as a bouncer (I didn't get the job, I didn't want it, I just wanted to see what the interview would be like, a bouncer friend was supposed to join me but he never turned up), training in a gym in Wincobank, 'the "professional" stranger' in ethnographic jargon, trying to make sense of my new world and how some of it sometimes rested on a bedrock of lies and deceit. I took up boxing to see how young men were trying to survive in the ring (Beattie 1996, 2002). After my first sparring session, somebody asked me whether I'd been in a road accident, I had so many bruises on my chest and on my back.

I was trying to blend in, friends with the big hitters whom I needed to take me sufficiently seriously that they would talk to me in the first place. Cockney hounded me for months for his payment for an article I wrote about him. I explained that *The Guardian* didn't pay for interviews. It was a point of principle. He said, 'they'll pay me. Get it sorted.' Eventually, I gave him half of what he thought I'd been paid. He was not impressed with the fee (mine or his).

'Not a bit of wonder you dress like that,' he said. I felt that I had to adapt, especially in the top nitespot. The first thing that you would see was the queue for Josephine's, back then. It would stretch from the front door down towards the steps and right along the glass office block. The queue would start early. It was long that particular night. Just the way VIPs with their gold cards liked it. They would say that it felt marvellous to walk right up past them – the respectable citizens of this fine old town – all queuing in the frigging rain. Soaked to the bloody skin. I just found it a little embarrassing, trying to jump the queue. You could feel all these eyes on your back. That night, the door staff had got everything in hand. They had managed to get the ordinary punter right up against the wall, leaving a little space to the right. This space was important. It gave the doormen a chance to see past the ordinary punter. They could then watch you as you arrive and nudge the ordinary punter even closer to the wall. Just enough room to squeeze in, in front of the paying customer – the mugs standing freezing in the rain. Sometimes the queue would get a little sensitive and the gap would close. The doormen would peer over their heads looking out for the likes of me. Then you would need a little deception. 'Er, Mr. Beattie, there's a call for you inside,' said one doorman. I hurried in, winking at him as I passed. I could hear a female voice behind me, still waiting in the rain. 'Hey, is he a famous footballer or somebody like that?'

It's the 'somebody' that you can grow to like. They knew that you must be a somebody, if you can skip the queue like that, even if you do it somewhat reluctantly. It may all seem a little pathetic, but it's still better than being a nobody.

That night, the club was packed. The ordinary punter would walk in and get hit with all these bodies, all this noise, all this disarray. I would just see order. I walked slowly to the hallowed ground – the wine bar, but it was more than just a wine bar. There was an invisible line on the floor, which ordinary punter felt unable to pass, and three critical steps. There was a doorman at the top of these steps. He was a pal. He shook my hand as I passed. He was there to spot any trouble in the club and to stop any punter passing with a pint mug in his hand, but his presence was symbolic. One observant manager of the club once told me that it took me three years to make it up those steps. And probably another three before I could order a drink. But that was then, when I was still an ordinary punter, when I was still a mug.

On a good night, you would know everyone in this Northern nightclub. That night, Big Alex was in his favourite spot, just to the right of the edge of the top bar. I got my Tag Heuer watch from him. Nineteen quid it cost. Of course, it wasn't real. But it looked the part in there, in the dim light. You could only tell that it was snide when you took it off. If you took it off, that is. It was as light as a feather. But I never took it off, except in bed.

You didn't have to have money to have style. That's what they said around there. It was just as well. You got to know all the other VIPs – the big hitters and the rest. Bernard was by the pillar; he was big in fire insulation for factories. He was talking to Brian. Brian owned his own hairdressers, or he did once. I heard that he was currently unemployed. But he could get in the club for nothing, and he could make half a lager last a very long time indeed. Some other VIP would always buy him a drink. Perhaps things were a little vague sometimes. But in this club, we were all superstars. For a while.

I was standing there enjoying the ambience. The ordinary punters were running around desperate for their three hours away from the wife or the husband. Their three hours of freedom. I was taking it nice and steady. Mick came up to me. Mick 'The Bomb,' Mick the bouncer, or the security consultant as he liked to put it those days. He was wearing a sort of startled expression, as if he had just seen something truly awful. He asked me to turn around. I thought for a second that somebody had been sick over my back. 'Do you know that you've got creases all down the back of your jacket?' he said. 'Never,' I said, without any reflection. 'I know exactly what you need,' said Mick, taking hold of my arm. 'Some upmarket clobber. Some top notch gear. Do you know I could get you a Yves St Laurent for a hundred quid, or a Louis Feraud for one hundred and fifty?'

I might have been a VIP, but I had never heard of Louis Feraud. I thought it might be because of how he was saying it. He became a little defensive. 'You've never heard of Louis Feraud? You'll be telling me next that you've never heard of Bruno Kirches, or Van Kollem? What about Armani, have you heard of that?' I said that I had heard of Armani. 'Thank God for that. I thought you might be into Man at C&A for a moment there.' He started smoothing the creases in my suit. The creases which, I must confess, only he seemed able to detect.

'Look, you can sleep in the back of your car with the quality of suit I'm offering you. Wake up, give it a shake, and there won't be a crease in it. Not like that crap you're wearing.' He pulled my jacket open a shade aggressively and peered at the label. 'Principles? Fucking Principles. What's a VIP like you shopping doing shopping in Principles? How much did that cost you? One hundred and twenty quid? You were fucking well robbed. Feel the material of this jacket.' And he lifted my hand and placed it on the arm of his suit. I didn't know whether to stroke the material or squeeze the muscle bulging right through the suit that never creases.

'Marvellous,' is all I could think of to say.

'Where are the suits?' I asked, my voice descending into a whisper.

'They're in the toilet,' replied Mick at full volume. 'Just tell Tom that Mick sent you.'

I pushed my way past the ordinary punters, now swaying gently in their alcohol-induced haze, and headed towards the toilet. Tom, the toilet attendant was looking harassed, as the ordinary punters tried to spray themselves with the aftershave sitting out for them without paying the customary twenty pence.

'Come on, lads, it's twenty pence a shot. I've got plenty of change,' he said, as aftershave dispensers fired off indiscriminately into the surrounding ether.

'I'm here to have a look at the suits,' I whispered conspiratorially in Tom's ear. I didn't want the ordinary punter to get a hint of what was going on between the men in the know. I stood there wondering if Tom was going to direct me into one of the cubicles. Instead, he told me to stay where I was. He nipped out for a second and came back with three suits in a bin liner. He unpacked them in front of everybody. Another VIP came into the toilet. 'Are you getting into the dry-cleaning business?' he asked helpfully. And then winked. He knew the score.

'Try them on,' Tom suggested. Unfortunately, you could have fitted two of me into the Louis Feraud. 'The arms need taking up a little,' said Tom. By now there was more than a little interest being shown by the passing trade of the ordinary punter in the toilet.

'Have you got it in a forty-four?' asked one punter, slurring every syllable as he did so. Tom told him that these suits were way out of his league.

'You can try on the trousers as well if you like,' suggested Tom, as one pair of trousers landed on the floor of the toilet.

When he picked them up, there was a wet stain on one leg. I didn't fancy being blamed for causing the stain, so I declined the offer. 'The trousers might be a bit long, but you can always have them taken up,' added Tom, continuing his sales pitch. Tom's prices seem to be a little different from those mentioned earlier, the Louis Feraud had risen inexplicably to two hundred pounds. I pointed this discrepancy out to him. He told me to go back and check the prices with Mick. I then confessed that I didn't even have a hundred on me in cash. He assured me that the money would do tomorrow night. 'If we can't trust a VIP like you, who can we trust? After all, you are a regular.'

I went back out to look for Mick to query the price. Mick explained that Tom had given me the price of the Louis Feraud for the ordinary punter.

'Not that I'd ever tried to sell to the ordinary punter you understand. I'm offering you the suit at cost price.'

My body language must have been leaking a slight reluctance. So Mick called over two other VIPs from the wine bar, Phil and Mark. Both were wearing immaculate suits. Mick asked them to do at twirl for me. Phil, the taller of the two, told me that the waist tended to be a bit big on these cut-price suits, but all I needed was a good trendy belt to pull in the waist. He told me that Mick might even throw one in for nothing.

'He can get you a shirt to go with the suit as well if you like for a tenner. All designer gear.'

Phil stood right in front of me modelling the suit, running his hands up and down the lapels like some gentleman tailor. He even offered his own sales pitch.

'Do you know that you can sleep in the back of your car with this quality of suit, wake up, give it a shake and there won't be a crease in it.'

The only problem with this spiel was that it did not sound very original. I started seriously to consider whether everyone in the club was working on a commission basis.

After a while, I started to wonder how many of these VIPs habitually had to sleep in their cars at the end of an average night. When Mick went off to tour the club to do some security consultancy, I asked Phil where he thought Mick might get the suits from. I wanted to know how hot they really were. Phil had a slightly different understanding from myself of the provenance.

'Working in a place like this you're bound to get to know people. And a lot of people remember Mick from his boxing days,' he said. 'He probably gets them at cost from the factory. All I know is that they're top notch and they're cheap. I don't ask anything else.'

It might have been my imagination, but the question seemed to have irritated Phil, dressed from head to toe in his top-notch clothes, which came from God knows where. He stood incessantly sipping his half of lager, gazing out into the great unknown of the ordinary punter. Finally, he turned to me.

Look, if you want to pay full price for your gear, go ahead. The next thing you will be saying is that you want to queue in the rain to get in here with the rest of the mugs. I'm sure Mick could arrange that for you, if I asked if you ask him.

It was a long night. I eventually started to leave the club with my new Louis Feraud clutched tightly under my arm. It was wrapped in half a bin liner. Mick shook my hand as I departed.

'You'll look like a proper VIP in that suit,' he said, 'even if you do have to sleep in the back of your car tonight.'

He laughed as he glanced at his watch. It was now four o'clock in the morning and the birds were starting to sing.

Perhaps, I was learning.

The Good Samaritan

We skip forward in time now, but some things like lying do not change.

The hill was a dense rich green, no paths or tracks anywhere. It tumbled down to the pool. It was tree covered – an even sort of green. Some firs, some conifers, all crammed together, not an inch not covered. It looked tropical with a line of manicured palm trees on the fringes of the pool. The hill looked like a giant crashing wave coming in fast, reminding you of adventure, or a fluffy cauliflower, or perhaps most like a poster in an office wall to fill all those moments of a long-drawn-out office day, just daydreaming. You lie back in your sunbed and sigh heavily at the beauty of nature. This was a dream setting in summer 2022, post-Covid.

But then, as your attention drifts towards the pool, you can hear the chatter. Men with bald heads, reading paperbacks about the Rat Pack or the Krays with little random asides.

> Reggie was a right character, but I'd love to have met Mad Frankie Fraser. But you wouldn't like to upset him. He wasn't called "Mad Frankie" because he was angry mad, you know, he was called that because he was criminally insane. Imagine living next door to him.

Their wives in turquoise and white dotted bikinis but with large pants to cover years of abuse or neglect. One or the other, or both.

A group of six, evidently three couples, were gathered in the pool bobbing up and down, evenly spaced, in an oblong shape. All it must be said were a little obese, the women, all blondes had their hair in a bob, they were reflecting loudly on holidays of the past.

> There was this fella in this little market stall in Marmaris in Turkey, he had five hats on his head, all different colours. You could take pictures of him, there was no pressure. But once you left him, all these Turks jumped out on you and were grabbing you by the arm to come and see their leather bags or their tea pots. My son bought five Lacoste tee shirts off one of them for a tenner. "Hundred per cent genuine. No way fakes," the Turkish fella told him. When my son got home, his best friend told him they were one hundred per cent fake, and terrible fakes at that.

The women and the men and shook their heads in unison at the brass-necked lies of the traders of Marmaris.

Her husband joined in, 'I prefer Benidorm – Blackpool by the Sea. No hassle with the Turks there.' A cock was crowing in the background in bursts of three. He seemed to be competing with the noise from the pool.

My partner worked happily away blissfully unaware of all of this. She had taken in the view and then relaxed, her headphones shut out the chatter that would rise and fall between gulps of loud laughter with the heads tilted back. I perched on my sunbed and pulled my left leg back bent at the knee to stretch my IT band. I'm a runner, this is a common problem. I held it there locked in position, really painful. I could see him watching me from the edge of the pool. He had a large tattoo across the left-hand side of his chest onto his left arm and bicep. The tattoo was coloured blue and orange. He was heavily built, about thirty, on his own. He pulled himself up out of the pool and walked towards us. He smiled at my partner and then at me, with a slight gap in between.

'You're doing that all wrong,' he said. 'Let me show you.' He sat on the edge of my sunbed and took hold of my ankle. He pulled it towards him and pushed the left side of my upper leg across my body. I grimaced. My partner suddenly took notice. She removed her headphones just in time to hear me making low groaning noises. She looked over; the tattooed stranger smiled back at her.

'I'm just showing him how to do this exercise properly,' he said. 'I'm a trained physio and I do some weights – as you will probably have noticed.' He flexed his muscles. 'I can make my pectorals on my left side move independently if you want to see that. I'm really quite talented. I can even get them to spell out a message when they're moving.'

'What's the message?' she asked with some disbelief in her voice.

'You will have to wait and see,' he replied. I didn't like how he was smiling at her. He took hold of my leg again more forcefully this time and pulled it back.

'Your fella here doesn't like pain,' he said, smiling at her again. 'That's pretty obvious. And I know it's a bit of a cliché, but no pain, no gain in anything. Sport, work...sex.' There was a pause before sex, a dramatic pause you might say. My partner looked at me a little puzzled. A little incredulous. He didn't release my leg. I lay there crumpled on the sunbed with this total stranger putting me through agony. My partner was now embarrassed for me and said that she was nipping up to the room for some suntan lotion. She left us there to talk. He watched her walk away, a little too intently for my liking. I went back to my hamstring. 'It feels like I'm running with a handbrake on,' I suggested. He was looking slightly bored now.

'Well, just take the handbrake off,' he said. 'Run free. That's what you runners say.'

'That's easier said than done,' I replied. A tall dark-haired girl walked past, possibly Italian, certainly not English. His eyes tracked her. I was now fighting for his attention.

'Are you on your own?' I enquired.

'No, my girlfriend's up in the room,' he replied. 'She's sleeping it off.' I wasn't sure what 'it' was here – a good night out, jet lag, painful sex. Whatever that was. I didn't like to ask.

'I'm off the leash,' he said, interrupting my thoughts. 'For an hour or so at least. That's the point about a guy like me. We need let off the chain occasionally.' He continued to track the tall Italian like a slobbering muscly Rottweiler that's just slipped its chain.

'Where did you train?' I asked. He looked surprised by my question, as if I had just asked him something a bit too personal, impossibly personal.

'Where *do I* train?' he replied. 'Do you mean what gym?'

This seemed like a deliberate misinterpretation, an evasive sort of response. I was sure he hadn't misunderstood.

'I mean, where did you do your physio training?'

Oh, I didn't really. I just picked a few bits and pieces up in the gym. None of those physios are trained properly anyway. It's all just a bit of pushing and pulling and getting through the client through pain barrier. But I know something about you – when you get anywhere near the pain barrier, you put the brakes on. That's what you said, isn't it? My motto is no pain, no gain. You have to say it repeatedly to yourself. You don't think that I've got muscles like this without a bit of pain, do you?

He looked at me for affirmation for what a psychologist might call narcissistic reassurance. A reopening of the pipeline of narcissistic flow in these oil-starved times. I didn't oblige.

'Or tattoos,' I said. 'I bet they're painful.' I thought that he would like this comment.

What are you on about? I thought we were talking about my bodybuilding. You don't really like to keep to the point, do you? Any muppet can get a tattoo if he's pissed enough. Body sculpture, on the other hand, needs dedication, hard work, pain.

'So, what do you do?' he asked, feigning some interest in somebody other than himself. I told him that I was a psychologist.

'A bloody psychologist. I've had dealings with you lot before.' He was angry.

I had to see one when I was a kid. He was a bloody toss-pot, no offence, but it wasn't a waste of time – I discovered something, I discovered that I was smarter than him. And I bet I'm smarter than you…

I didn't reply.

So, what are you looking into at the moment? What do you want to ask me? Have I ever dreamt of having sex with my mother … or my dog? Ask me whatever you like. I have no secrets. I'm happy to talk about my dreams. As long as you can tell me something interesting about myself.

'Do you ever tell lies,' I asked. He laughed loudly and forcefully. His eyes did not look happy.

'What sort of lies? Do you mean big porkies like the politicians tell all the time, or the little ones like when you say to your girlfriend "your ass doesn't look big in those jeans – you fat bitch"?'

I didn't say anything.

'For example, if I said to you now, you could have a body like mine – that would put your mind at rest. But you know it would be a lie.'

There was a long pause.

'Just in case you didn't get the point. That's a lie, of course,' he said.

You don't like pain. We've already established that. Of course, you can tell yourself that your IT band is fucked, or your hamstring's fucked but everybody's hamstring is the same. You're lying to yourself. You're walking around with a semi-limp saying "Oh, my hamstring" but really, it's because you're weak.

I felt like walking away, but he was still sitting on my sunbed deliberately violating my personal space.

'So, what do you want to know about lies?' he asked, trying to humour me.

The school sent me to see a psychologist because they said I was stealing from the other children and lying about it. But this is what really annoyed me – I had to see the psychologist because they said I was too good at lying. The teachers threatened me, but I never showed any fear or guilt. What was there to feel guilty about? I had the bottle to take their lunch money, I felt great about it.

'So,' I asked, 'what do you think makes a good liar because you're obviously a good liar.'

'Do you mean what makes me good at everything?' he replied. 'I'll tell you what. I'm not frightened of authority figures or tosspots or psychologists. I don't give a fuck to be honest. So, you can't intimidate me.'

I changed tact. 'But what makes a good lie?'

'That's a very silly question if you don't mind me saying,' he replied. 'There's no such thing as a good lie. They don't exist in isolation. I like to make a good impression and once I've started to do that, all the words, all the sentences, all the bullshit flows naturally. Like today. I was interested in talking to you, not you exactly you rather your partner, although she pissed off and left us. So, I created a situation – the Good Samaritan, the man here to help the injured, the man who may show you that you may need a bit of self-awareness to get over this self-pitying sports injury crap. I'm never just going to tell a lie for the sake of it. I look out for situations, opportunities, moments, then I jump in, and everything else just flows.'

'But you lied about being a trained physio,' I pointed out.

'What did you want me to say? I'd got hold of your leg at that moment. I was just reassuring you. I was just trying to help.'

I asked him how he spotted opportunities. 'What did he look for?'

'Opportunities is what life is all about? I'm on holiday. My mind is only on one thing as you may well realise, Mr. Psychologist.'

We were then distracted by the tall brunette woman chasing a pink and green lilo in the shape of a crocodile, which had been lifted by the wind and carried out of the paddling pool. Her child of about four or five, and as pretty as the mother, had begun crying. He smirked at me and jumped up. 'You just see a little bit of everyday family distress at this point, I see an enormous opportunity.'

He ran after the lilo and just managed to catch it before it went over the fence. He walked back slowly dragging it behind him, to hand it over to the lady with the child. She smiled at him and said what sounded like 'gracias.' My new 'friend' clearly spoke no Italian or Spanish or Greek, so he spoke a dialect all of his own, semi-English, semi something else. 'No problemo …I'm a fireman.'

He mimicked holding a hose in front of him and waving it about in the direction of embers. 'I'm used to saving children and helping damsels in distress.' She smiled at his brave attempt to communicate. A handsome tall Italian man walked over drawn by the sound of his child crying and the commotion. He had been sleeping. He stood beside his wife, glaring at my new friend – the heroic fireman.

He walked back over to me. 'That's one for later,' he said.

You never just dive in. That's what the muppets always get wrong. I'm just dipping my toe in the pool at this point. I'll come back later. We know each other now. Oh, and I know your bird as well. That makes two. Not bad for twenty minutes by the pool.

'So, are you a fireman?' I asked.

'Of course not,' he replied, 'but one of the kids from my school is, the one whose lunch money I used to pinch. He was always a bit of a mug. Now he risks his life daily for other people.'

'So, what do you actually do?' I enquired.

I'm currently trying to get into property. When the time's right or when I've got a bit of capital behind me. At the moment, I'm just enjoying life. My girlfriend paid for this holiday. She can afford it; she works in an office, no idea what she does, her parents have some cash. I make her feel good. I'm a therapist really – a bit like you. But you're probably useless at that – too tied up with yourself, too worried about where your next pain is going to come from.

I'm a little bit more confident. I'm a little bit more use to other people.

'But you're a bit of a liar,' I said, as he finally got up.

I have never seen a more malevolent smile.

'I make the world a better place,' he said. 'Unlike most people…even those with big fancy titles who pretend to.'

He turned as he walked away. 'Are you and your bird coming down tonight? I think me and her would have something in common. Let's leave it at that.'

Advice from Quintilian

One of the most basic features of the lies of expert liars in the real world, like John and his Rolls Royce, Cockney and his gear (and hence my great desire to get hold of such gear) is that many lies rely on 'evidence' from other sources. In Ancient Rome, studies of rhetoric highlighted this important feature of successful lies. Those who were skilled in rhetoric and the arts of persuasion needed to bear this feature in mind and they certainly concerned the Roman orator Marcus Fabius Quintilianus, or Quintilian as he is known to us (born in Calagurris in Hispania in A.D. 35). Quintilian was sent to Rome by his father to study rhetoric early in the reign of Nero. He is the author of a famous twelve-volume textbook on rhetoric entitled *Institutio Oratoria* (the *Institutes of Oratory*). The books cover not just the theory and practice of rhetoric, but they are also concerned with the education and development of the orator himself. For Quintilian, the perfect orator is first and foremost a good man and after that he is a good speaker. Indeed, his very definition of rhetoric aligns with that of Cato the Elder's *vir bonus, dicendi peritus* or 'the good man skilled at speaking.'

So how should falsehoods be used by a good speaker (and presumably a good man)? Quintilian says that there are two distinct categories of falsehood: the first depends on external support but Quintilian warns that we must pick our external support carefully. It needs to be secure and effective – it should not be contradicted by the available evidence, or better still even easily checked. External support can be invaluable in the transmission of a lie. The second type of falsehood does not rely on external support in this way but is constructed solely in the speech itself, relying exclusively and on nothing more than the speaker's 'native talent.' One obvious aspect of such native talent is the ability to remember what one has already said. As Quintilian points out, there is much wisdom in the old aphorism that we are apt to forget our falsehoods. A liar needs a good memory or needs to learn when to reach for external support to make their lie convincing. Quintilian writes:

> Sometimes, too, we get a false statement of fact; these, as far as actual pleading is concerned, fall into two classes. In the first case the statement depends on external support...The other has to be supported by the speaker's native talent...Whichever of these two forms we employ, we must take care, first that our fiction is within the bounds of possibility, secondly that it is consistent with the persons, dates, and places involved, and thirdly that it presents a character and sequence that are not beyond belief: if possible, it should be connected with something that is admittedly true and should be supported by some arguments that forms part of the actual case. For if we draw our fictions entirely from circumstances lying outside the case, the liberty which we have taken in resorting to falsehood will stand revealed. Above all we must see that we do not contradict ourselves, a slip which is far from rare on the part of spinners of fiction: for some things may put a most favourable complexion on portions of our case, and yet fail to agree as a whole. Further, what we say must not be at variance with the admitted truth...the orator should bear clearly in mind throughout his whole speech what the fiction is to which he has committed himself, since we are apt to forget our falsehoods, and there is no doubt about the truth of the proverb that a liar should have

a good memory …But we must remember only to invent such things as cannot be checked by evidence.

Quintilian (100/1902)

Some of our most important lies are the lies that we tell about who we are, lies about our identity, our place in the world, our profession, our true values and interests, our personality, and our wealth. And Quintilian was right with his basic but important distinction regarding types of lies and both types are employed when it comes to lies about the self. Some of these lies about identity rely on external sources – objects, luxury goods, status symbols, styles of dress, important or celebrity friends who may send an immediate and visual message that may misinform, disguise, or conceal information about the self – an academic gown, an expensive car, those friends and associates that we mix with, the very suit we wear. They become part of the lie and because they are such a routine aspect of our everyday life, after all, our clothes, friends, and modes of transport, are everywhere, we don't question them as much as we might, we take them for granted, we don't check. They communicate often without much awareness, and they can influence us accordingly. Sometimes they are a core part of the lie, and they may be particularly important when it comes to lies about identity, about who we really are (even though we aren't really that at all).

5   Natural Liars and Personality

The devil can cite Scripture for his purpose.
An evil soul producing holy witness
Is like a villain with a smiling cheek,
A goodly apple rotten at the heart.
Oh, what a goodly outside falsehood hath
                    Shakespeare (1598) *The Merchant of Venice*, Act 1, Scene iii

The Outsider

Tampy was an outsider to our gang. The turn-of-the-road gang was always a hard group to join. The rest of us had grown up together in those mill streets and the newer houses of Silverstream. We had all gone to the same church and Sunday school, and as we got older, we joked our way through the Sunday services and the Church Lads Brigade. Silverstream always had a beautiful ring about it – a tinkling mountain stream coming off the hills that surround Belfast, the reality was different. Tampy's family had moved up from the Shankill to Glencairn. He had a charisma about him, handsome (although I have no photographs of him to check), meticulous in his style of dress, but slightly unsettling and slightly dangerous. He liked to be the centre of attention, he liked an audience, that was obvious. We noticed that from the start.

He arrived one night with a friend who was called Chuck and after a little bit of chat, they started play-fighting, right in front of us. There was nothing new and surprising about that. We often pretended to fight just to ease the boredom. The first time I got a broken nose, Craigy kicked me square on right in the face whilst play-fighting. He always said that he had intended to miss, he just wanted to show me how high he could kick someone in the face just by stepping back slightly in a face-to-face confrontation, and then doing a little jump and then two kicks, one with each foot, right smack in the face. He was very athletic, and he wore special shoes with metal tips to make it more effective. I saw Craigy doing this in real fights, it always surprised the other person. That night he was very apologetic. My mother was very angry at him.

DOI: 10.4324/9781003394563-5

She said that my nose would never go back to its normal size. But Tampy's play-fighting was different, we could all see that.

Tampy instigated the fight, he took affront at nothing really. Chuck had commented that the new Glencairn estate looked a little 'unfinished.' It was just a pretext, Tampy hated Glencairn. After a few minutes, Tampy grabbed Chuck by the neck and put him in a headlock and trailed him around the greasy pavement. Not for a few seconds but minutes, that's what was different about this. If he just wanted to display his strength or skill, he didn't need to do it for that length of time. You could see the distress in Chuck's face, he looked anxious, fearful even, as if he wasn't sure what was happening. This was his best friend. What was going on? Chuck's shoes were at an angle, skimming the pavement, he was trying to regain some balance, one shoe came off and ended up in the middle of the road.

The whole thing was performed for us the audience, just standing there watching. This was Tampy's audition, his best friend Chuck was incidental, as if he didn't really matter. Tampy smiled at us in the middle of the performance, impervious to Chuck's evident distress, squeezing his neck and pushing him down but taking the time to smile back at us. Nobody intervened, not because my mates were frightened of him but because Tampy and Chuck were just 'playing.' But it never looked like playing to me. Years later, when I read Gregory Bateson, I saw the merit in his point that 'this leads us to recognition of a more complex form of play; the game which is constructed not upon the premise "This is play" but rather around the question "Is this play?"' (Bateson 1972/2000: 182). Bateson wrote:

> In the Andaman Islands, peace is concluded after each side has been given ceremonial freedom to strike the other. This example, however, also illustrates the labile nature of the frame. 'This is play,' or 'this is ritual.' The discrimination between map and territory is always liable to break down, and the ritual blows of peace-making are always liable to be mistaken for the 'real' blows of combat. In this event, the peace-making ceremony becomes a battle (Radcliffe Brown 1922).
>
> (Bateson 1972/2000: 182)

And he reminds us that:

> Even among the lower mammals, there appears to be an exchange of signals which identify certain meaningful behavior as play.
>
> (Bateson 1972/2000: 203)

This wasn't play. All of the little meta-signals from Chuck were being consciously ignored. 'I surrender,' 'I give up,' 'get the fuck off me,' 'leave me alone.' There was no 'exchange of signals,' no shared agreement.

Eventually, Tampy pushed him to the ground and smiled broadly. Chuck cleaned himself up, he was bleeding and filthy from the dirty pavement, and said he was going home on his own. He went into the road to get his shoe. Tampy just shrugged. From that night on Tampy was with us. Chuck never came back.

I lived just by the turn-of-the-road and Tampy would turn up at my house always unannounced. He had heard that I went to a good school, so he turned up with some old friends from the Shankill and made me tell them all how many O levels I'd got. 'I've fucking never heard of anybody with twelve O levels before,' was his comment. That statement etched in my brain. His friends smiled at him rather than me, as if it was his achievement. 'Tell them how you got into that school,' he nudged my elbow. I explained that when I went to Belfast Royal Academy for the interview at eleven years old, the headmaster had asked me what was the last novel I'd read. I'd never read a novel, but I had seen the film *Gulliver's Travels*, well not the whole film, we'd been ejected just after the interval for throwing marbles from the balcony into the stall down below (we ended up barred from every cinema for this), so I described the 'novel' in great cinematic detail up to the point where we were ejected and asked whether he wanted me to continue. The headmaster said that he was content with what he had heard. This lie and Belfast Royal Academy changed my life (and for this I am eternally grateful).

Tampy befriended me after that. I don't know why. I think it was because the O levels would make him look good, he had a smart friend, and maybe one who could lie, if he had to. That might come in handy.

Tampy loved lying; I realised this early on. He was a prolific liar, a natural; it was a game for him, a challenge; the more outrageous, the better. He would take me for a Wimpy in town. We'd have double cheeseburgers and chips and he'd fill in the little bill that the waitresses used and change the figures on it (he'd stolen one of their bill pads), so we'd only ever pay for two cokes. But he'd insist on sitting near the cashier, who would often query what we'd actually had. He liked the jeopardy, the excitement. When the cashier questioned us, his answer was always the same. 'I wouldn't eat the shite in here, if you paid me,' and he'd burst out laughing in the street. They never stopped us leaving.

He dropped a lit cigarette into the pocket of a boy from my school who had come to my house for some help with his homework, whilst he sat in our front room with my mother and Craigy. None of us saw anything. The blazer went on fire on the boy's way back home, and his angry father arrived with the burnt-out blazer. Tampy denied stone-cold that it wasn't anybody in that room that did it. He offered an alternative explanation; he said that the boy must have been a secret smoker and that he'd had a wee puff on the way home. 'He was keeping the cigarette butt for later and hadn't put it out properly.' He had this very slight smile whilst he said it. I can remember that look to this day. That little unexpected smirk. I nearly believed his story myself until I saw that smile. He and I knew that this schoolboy had never smoked but my mother was convinced by his statement. The father left even more angry. My mother said that it was terrible that he was trying to blame my friends on this. 'Some people need to take responsibility for their children and bring them up better.'

There was a fight at the disco in our local church hall. This was an attempt to bring the two sides together, Protestant and Catholic, in the Troubles. Our minister told my mother on one of his regular visits to our house that he didn't know who had started it. 'It had all turned really nasty,' he explained. One of my friends was stabbed in the knee and had to hijack a bus to take him to the hospital (the knife was still in the kneecap, which led to much joking at his expense). But our minister described the boy at the centre of everything – he had cornered a terrified Catholic lad down by the lower church gate. My mother said that it sounded awfully like my friend. And when he next came to the house, she asked him whether he'd been there and whether he'd seen what had happened. He told her with a completely straight face that he hadn't gone, that his aunt had been sick and that he'd gone to visit her instead. My mother was completely taken in. She said afterwards, 'What a lovely boy, he looks after his aunt, better than you look after me.' She liked him more than my other friends and said that she wished I could be more like him.

My brother had moved on now, climbing now in Scotland, and making a living from his hobby; he was sick of Belfast and the Troubles, so I had the back bedroom to myself. I made it my own like any teenager would. My mother refused to clean it, or even go into it, because of all the 'shite' I put on the walls. The shite was just black-and-white images ripped out of *NME* or *Melody Maker*, *Taste, Cream, Jimi Hendrix*, just scraggly bits of newsprint that hung untidily off the walls. Nothing would stick to the walls; they were too damp. I'd started pinning these photos from music papers to the ceiling so they could hang down without having to touch the walls. It was less embarrassing somehow. They hung down with the cobwebs that had been growing over the months since my mother refused to go into the room. I wasn't going to clean it. I had a red bulb to disguise the damp ugliness of the room, to make it look cosy. My mother said it looked like a whorehouse. I would tell the lads at the corner all about the room to make them laugh. I brought my first girlfriend Carol into that room (she pretended that she had forgotten about the incident with the cheeseburger). She looked alarmed in that bedroom. It was hard to get her to relax, I gave up eventually.

So, my gang would ask me to 'mind' things for them in the one drawer of the chest of drawers that worked, or under the bed. I didn't ask where they'd come from, it was no big deal.

One night, Tampy arrived at my house and pulled a small solid looking object wrapped in an oily cloth from under his denim jacket and handed it to me. This wasn't a pair of brand-new jeans ripped off a hanger in some trendy shop in town, or neat polythene-wrapped boxes with pristine tablets inside. Most of these tablets that were lifted were for random ailments (but they were still 'drugs' to us, you never know), but occasionally we hit the jackpot with slimming tablets, Durophet 200 mg, 'Black Bombers,' or Durophet 125 mg, 'Black-and-White Minstrels' – we all knew what they looked like. We'd had a lecture in our youth club about the danger of drugs, and they very helpfully showed us some pictures. I recognised them immediately – my mother had a big bottle of Black Bombers which she kept in our scullery next to the sink to help her lose weight. She was always trying to lose weight. That was our gang's first somewhat nervy high. We guessed that the chemists must have been full of them (unfortunately Carol's mother worked in the chemists which was one reason that I never went in with them after dark. That was my great excuse).

Tampy told me to put this small oily object with the other gear – the jeans lifted in a city centre store on a Saturday afternoon, the random drugs from the local chemists, a chain, a skittle which somebody had filled with moist sand ('it's like a cosh now,' the friend said, 'it might come in handy; you never know. Hang onto it, just in case') and schoolbooks piled high on top. That was my room and my life.

I told Tampy that I wanted to know what was inside that cloth. He said, 'you don't need to know,' trying to give his answer that kind of conspiratorial tone that hardened criminals use in films. I always thought that he watched a lot of gangster films. He had a bit of a practised aura about him. I told him that I wanted to know what it was. I was insistent, as insistent as I'd ever been with him. Usually, I just went along with things; it was easier that way. He was surprised at my defiance. He might have called it a 'stand-off.'

He snatched it back off me and slowly started to unwrap it. It lay there in his open hands; I have that image in my head now, as he looked at me like it was some sort of offering. He looked proud of himself, 'like the fella in the big picture,' is how my mother would have described his look. The lead actor in the Westerns – your man who played Jesse James or Billy the Kid, big John Wayne, the star of the show.

I'd never seen a handgun close before. I didn't want to examine it or touch it. We just stood there on the street with that damp fog hanging over the bottom of Barginnis Street, with this thing just sitting there in the palm of his hands, on open view. He didn't try to hide it. For a second, I thought he might threaten me with it. He could be a little unpredictable sometimes.

There was no explanation for why he wanted it hid in my bedroom, other than he couldn't look after it himself because *his* mother might find it. There was no history of the object or where it had come from, nothing about what it might be used for, if anything. It was an object with no past and no future beyond a planned rest in my chest of drawers next to the useless cosh and the chain.

It didn't feel like the execution of a crime, a conspiracy, or one of our usual capers. It was just a favour amongst friends, nothing more, nothing less. Just the give and take for us lads from the corner, the 'turn-of-the-road' gang, who depended on each other for these sorts of things. We couldn't have got by without doing favours for one another, without backing each other up when trouble started. But this never felt right from that very first moment; I knew that I had to lie. I'd never lied to him before, but I lied to him that night and it was as serious as you can get. I told him that I couldn't hide the gun for him because my mother now cleaned my room. 'Nearly every day,' I said. 'She's always in that bloody room now, rubbing away at all the dirt.'

He just looked at me and then made this little 'hhhhh' noise, which sounded like a cross between a blow and a hiss, as if he was clearing his throat of some unpleasant blockage. He repeated it, but it came out the second time sounding like 'huh' with this little laugh in his voice, and this look which said you can't kid a kidder, you must know that, and I'm one of the best. Don't forget my reputation, and Tampy did have that reputation for violent unpredictability. Many of the lads from the turn-of-the-road could fight but Tampy's outbursts were always more sudden. He had been *angry* at me only once before. He had turned up at my house in a stolen car one night and wanted me to go for a ride with him, up the Horseshoe Road, 'over the hill,' as we liked to say, as if it was a location on a map. He couldn't drive properly. I knew there were army road-blocks up past the Horseshoe Road. They sometimes fired at joyriders; one or two of them had been killed. They called the joyriders who sat in the back 'sandbaggers'; they were there to stop the bullets from hitting the driver. Of course, nobody is going to deliberately shoot teenage joyriders, but these were just fast dark cars approaching a roadblock in North Belfast in the Troubles. 'Murder Triangle,' they called our neighbourhood then, just fast cars all over the road, and then swerving away from the roadblock in the opposite direction at the last minute. Anybody could be a terrorist out there dark.

I told him that night that I had too much homework to do (which was the truth). He tried to blackmail me, and I still laugh about it to this day. He said that if I didn't go with him, he would tell my mother that I used to put on two bars of our little electric fire when she was out. The electric fire was the only source of heat in our house; you were only allowed one bar, that was the rule, a rule that could never be broken, and the source of many bitter and very long arguments in our wee house. His blackmail worked – that's how sensitive the issue of money and heating was in our house. I acquiesced and went with him. The drive was trouble-free; we didn't see any army patrols which was just as well because his driving was dangerously erratic. Only when he was dumping the car did I notice that he was wearing gloves, I wasn't. I'm no car thief, it's not something I would think about in advance or even notice, until it's too late. I wanted to clean the handles of the car, but he told me to get a move on and get out. We dumped it down the side of Paddy's bar. He even parked it badly, that's how bad a driver he was.

But that night with the gun I put my foot down. Defiance personified. I didn't say that, of course, but I felt it. It was a very working-class Protestant sort of thing to feel. He was shocked.

'Don't fucking lie to me, Beats,' he wasn't threatening me, at least I don't think he was, it was more just annoyance on his part.

'Show me the fucking room, Beats.'

So, I took him upstairs as my mother sat in the front room watching TV, with the one bar of the electric fire on.

'Where are you boys going,' she said. 'I hope you're not up to no good.'

He just stood there at the door of my bedroom, open-mouthed, not enter-ing, gazing in at the shards of newspaper hanging off the damp walls and from the ceiling, the cobwebs, the dirt on the mirror and the windows, the strag-gly curtains, the clothes and books all over the place, mathematics, physics, and chemistry textbooks, Russian literature, dog-eared copies of Dostoevsky,

Pushkin, Tolstoy, with sheets of paper sticking out of them, as if they had been kicked out of the way by someone leaving in a hurry. It all looked like some filthy crime scene.

He ran his finger along the wall nearest the door and glanced at the dirt on his fingers and then at me. He vibrated his hand, his fingers splayed, in front of his face, and half turned it towards me to gaze with him at the long trail of sooty dirt all along his three middle fingers. His fingers stopped moving, so that we would both peruse it. There was the evidence. He was Colombo himself; he was the ace detective.

'You're telling me,' he began, 'that she regularly cleans this shite hole?' He looked around the room one more time.

I told him that she did. I was shaking my head, I remember that. 'She does'; perhaps I should have nodded instead. I thought that it might be more endearing to shake it.

He clearly didn't believe me. There was a long silence. I got nervous.

He just waited for me to say something more, to dig a hole for myself. He was staring right at me. I had to stare back otherwise he might have thought that I was lying (which, of course, I was).

'My mother's got very bad eyesight,' I said eventually, I know that I was stammering. 'She does her best,' I said, 'she tries.' There was another long pause.

'Holy Jesus,' he said eventually. He was shaking his head. I think that my response was so implausible that perhaps he thought it must be true.

We went back downstairs. Tampy glanced sideways at my mother with a little bit of pity in his eyes. I'd never thought of him as being terribly empathetic.

'Goodnight Mrs Beattie,' he said, and then he glanced back at her as he got to the door.

> I hope you don't mind me saying something, but I think you need glasses very badly. Now don't put off going down to that optician on the Shankill, those eyes of yours will only just get worse if you leave them,

and he went off into the night with the gun still in his jacket. I stood in my doorway and watched him walk away. My heart was beating so loud that I thought he must surely have heard it.

My mother asked me what he was going on about and whether he'd been drinking, or worse, whether he was on the drugs.

Our gang was close but that was a necessary lie maybe an existential lie. I hated telling that lie but I had to. That felt like my emotional break with the turn-of-the-road gang. I would be going off to university in the next academic year and I decided there and then to go across the water, as they say in Northern Ireland, rather than to the local university Queens. I was always very nervous when the gun was mentioned in those last few months and felt that Tampy could see right through me. But he had taught me that when it comes to lying, there are significant differences in the emotions we feel. For years,

I felt real guilt about that lie, but I suspect that he felt differently about the lies that he told and some of them, I guess, were very much worse. But I never understood why at that time.

Lies Are Easier without Empathy

Tampy was a *natural liar*. Paul Ekman uses the term 'natural liar' to describe some of the participants that took part in his first (and now classic) lab-based research on lying in the early 1970s. Lying is always very difficult to study in the laboratory; some might say impossible. Lies in the laboratory are usually nothing like the real thing; they are surrogates at best (an attempt to capture some of the underlying process in action without much of the cognitive or emotional complexity of real lies). Lies are part of our everyday social fabric, told for social purposes, sometimes carefully thought out, couched in emotions, with penalties if you're found out. In the laboratory, you have to request that people lie, and you need to 'motivate' them so that they at least try a bit to do this successfully (psychologists sometimes tell participants that the ability to lie successfully correlates with intelligence as an incentive), and then you need to try to generate some of the emotions we feel about lying or getting caught, fear, guilt, shame, embarrassment, and remorse, if you're interested in possible cues to deception. It is a considerable challenge.

Paul Ekman's attempt at a solution in his first experimental study was to use student nurses as his participants because he argued they must be able to conceal negative emotions when they see 'surgical or other bloody scenes' in their everyday work, and therefore, he suggested, they would be more motivated than most to try to succeed. They wanted, after all, to be good and successful nurses.

In his experiment, he showed them a film of some of the most gruesome scenes that they might have to encounter as nurses (a burns victim with an amputation) and they had to try to convince the interviewer that they were watching a pleasant film ('like pretty flowers in Golden Gate Park'). He found wide variation in the student nurses' ability to lie; some could conceal their true feelings at seeing the film; some were very poor at this. Some suffered from severe detection apprehension, with a great fear of being caught lying. But others lied easily and with great success. Ekman described these participants in the following terms:

> *Natural liars* know about their ability, and so do those who know them well. They have been getting away with things since childhood, fooling their parents, teachers, and friends when they wanted to. They feel no detection apprehension. Just the opposite. They are confident in their ability to deceive. Such confidence, not feeling much detection apprehension when lying, is one of the hallmarks of the psychopathic personality.
>
> (Ekman 1985: 56–57)

It was obviously important for him to empathise that not all natural liars are psychopaths (none of us would want a ward full of psychopathic nurses, after all). He said that using a variety of objective tests that he could find 'nothing anti-social in their make-up' and that 'Unlike psychopaths, they did not use their ability to lie to harm others' (Ekman 1985: 57). But this latter statement about the harming of others is a bold claim. How could he know this on the basis of his short time he spent with his experimental participants? He says that they had been practising lying since childhood – so what were they lying about and with what consequences? What constitutes harm in Ekman's view? Did these natural liars just use their gift for 'altruistic' lies out there in the world? Did he ask them? And remember all sorts of lies can cause harm, even 'well-intentioned' lies, like lies about whether there was a stranger in the house to protect a child who has just lost his father. And when they told lies out there in the real world – did they not feel any shame or guilt, alongside not feeling much by way of detection apprehension? Getting nurses to attempt to conceal their feelings in an experimental setting and then extrapolating from it to an understanding of lying in everyday interaction, might be more problematic than Ekman seems to assume here.

But *psychopaths* are always likely to be a special case, always more extreme. 'Pathological lying' is one of the criteria used to identify psychopathy, although exactly how 'pathological lying' differs from the frequent use of lies across multiple targets told without fear of being caught, as in Ekman's *natural liars*, might need some careful consideration. Psychopaths are a subset of natural liars; like them they lie easily; they do not suffer from shame, guilt, or the fear of detection apprehension, and, importantly, they have low levels of affect generally (things that get the rest of us excited have less of an effect on them; things that scare the rest of us scare them less). Psychopaths are prone to boredom and lie to give themselves a little bit more excitement; they need that buzz. They can be charming, and they use lies to be even more charming – to present themselves in particular ways without the truth getting in the way. They have a grandiose sense of self-worth and lies are used to maintain this. They are conning and manipulative, and they lie to con and manipulate people out of money or into relationships. They are callous and don't care about the feelings of the other person, the person that they're lying to. They just don't feel the other person's suffering in the normal way. They have low levels of empathy; this makes lying very easy. They tend to be cruel to animals (Beattie 2019).

Psychopathy is diagnosed using the Psychopathy Checklist (Hare 1991). This is the principal diagnostic tool based on twenty individual criteria – pathological lying is one of the core criteria, lack of remorse or guilt is another. Each item on the checklist is rated on a three-point scale, 0 = item doesn't apply; 1 = item applies somewhat; 2 = item definitely applies, based on a clinical interview and other evidence. Scores can thus range from zero to forty, with a cut-off greater than thirty reflecting a prototypical psychopath. The incidence of psychopathy in the general population is thought to be 1 in 100. The test has apparently good psychometric properties and a stable factor structure. It measures two factors: Factor 1 focuses on interpersonal and affective traits; Factor 2 reflects the behavioural components of psychopathy. The number after each of the items reflects the factor (1 or 2):

- Glibness/superficial charm (1)
- Grandiose sense of self-worth (1)
- Need for stimulation/proneness to boredom (2)
- Pathological lying (1)
- Conning/manipulative (1)
- Lack of remorse or guilt (1)
- Shallow affect (1)
- Callous/lack of sympathy (1)
- Parasitic lifestyle (2)
- Poor behavioural controls (2)
- Promiscuous sexual behaviour (1)
- Early behavioural problems (2)
- Lack of realistic long-term goals (2)
- Impulsivity (2)
- Irresponsibility (2)
- Failure to accept responsibility (1)
- Many short-term marital relationships (1)
- Juvenile delinquency (2)
- Revocation of conditional release (2)
- Criminal versatility (2)

Psychopathy is considered a developmental disorder which continues through-out the lifespan, but usually showing the first signs by early childhood (eight years of age) and labelled at that point as *Conduct Disorder* and later as *Antisocial Personality Disorder*. It is important to emphasise that psychopathy is not an officially accepted clinical diagnosis in the *Diagnostic and Statistical Manual, DSM-5*. Some have suggested that this is because it is too stigmatis-ing a label (it makes us think of Hannibal Lecter or similar *psychos* in film and literature); others argue that some of the criteria are somewhat vague and hard to assess (e.g., 'callousness'). But psychopaths are a subset (25%) of individuals who meet criteria for the psychiatric classifications of *Conduct Disorder* and *Antisocial Personality Disorder* (ASPD) and considered a 'specifier' of clinical ASPD.

Conduct disorder, which is identified in children and teenagers, is char-acterised by not caring about social norms, ignoring the rights and feelings of others, enjoying causing harm, lying or manipulating people, committing physical or sexual violence, hurting animals, extreme bullying, and physically or emotionally abusing others. ASPD in older teenagers and adults is charac-terised by persistent antisocial behaviour, impulsive, irresponsible, aggressive, and often criminal behaviour, being manipulative, deceitful, and reckless, a disregard for the harm or distress caused to other people, not caring for the feelings of others and an inability to maintain long-term social and personal relationships). Lying and deceit are common to each of these disorders.

ASPD is typically not diagnosed until eighteen years old (with usually evidence of Conduct Disorder before age fifteen) with psychopaths having a severe form of ASPD. The developmental pathway (at least in terms of identification and diagnosis) is Conduct Disorder, then ASPD, then psychopathy. There would appear to be an underlying biological cause for psychopathy. Areas of the brain involved in emotion processing, empathising, and decision-making (such as the amygdala, the insula, and the ventromedial prefrontal cortex) show reduced activity in psychopaths when they see other people in distress. This impaired emotional functioning affects their ability to form associations between stimuli and consequences such as hurting people and the fear and distress that others display as a consequence. You can see why this might encourage lying, it doesn't matter if you're found out or that others suffer, it means nothing to you. It also impairs their ability to form associations between them making a poor choice and receiving a punishment. For that reason, they are very hard to change as punishment does not work and we cannot cure psychopathy.

Of course, this is all a somewhat reductionist perspective on the disorder. We may lose sight of the individual and how they live their lives with all these separate components in place. I have always been interested in how the various components interact to allow the individuals themselves to form a coherent view of the world and themselves. Perhaps, this is why I try to explore lives in more detail than is typical in much of psychology (using more ethnographic and naturalistic approaches including memoir and direct observation), including lives that stand out from the group. Psychopaths are often smart and charming; they can influence people; they have a high sense of self-worth, but when they are prone to boredom, they need excitement. So, what are the consequences of this pattern of behaviours? How do they view partners, relationships, work colleagues? How do factors 1 (the interpersonal and affective) and 2 (the behavioural) connect? What comes first – the shallow affect or lack of guilt and then do the poor treatment of others, or is it the other way round? Have they learned something about interpersonal relations that influences dampening of affect? Have they learned how to disparage people so that they don't have to take them seriously? How do they cognitively deal with any 'problems' of shallow affect? Is nothing, no matter how upsetting for others, no big deal for them?

How will we ever find out unless we try a different approach beyond the clinical interview? Remember, they are charming and manipulative, sometimes, their deeds speak louder than their words. Tampy stood out from the rest of us in terms of behaviour, and don't forget that we had a finely balanced representation in our own minds of the norms of antisocial behaviour of our group. We lived by them every day. I suspect that most or all members of our gang could have been diagnosed as possessing ASPD (persistent antisocial behaviour; impulsive, irresponsible, aggressive, and often criminal behaviour....).

Why it's almost a definition of a teenage gang like ours. These were the norms for the behaviour of our social group that were encouraged (and sometimes enforced). But Tampy stood out from that set of norms – I remember Chuck that night on the pavement outside Greasy Jim's. That's what always sticks in my mind, and in the minds of my friends. That's what was different. That was his best friend who was in distress. Perhaps, we need psychology to be out there on the street where the action is.

Tampy did have a personality that set him apart from the other lads; we all knew that. We were wary of him; we didn't know what it meant at the time. Some of us just thought that's how you had to be if you wanted to end up like Sammy the Hard Man. Perhaps, it was a positive thing. It was the degree of callousness and lack of empathy that was different.

Empathy is a broad concept these days in psychology and cognitive neuroscience. Blair (2005) argues that it is not a unitary concept but 'a loose collection of partially dissociable neurocognitive systems.' The three main divisions are *cognitive empathy* or Theory of Mind (the ability to represent the mental states of others to explain and predict their behaviour), *motor empathy* (the tendency to automatically mimic and synchronise facial expressions, postures, and movements with those of another person), and *emotional empathy* (the ability to recognise and respond appropriately to the display of emotions in others). Psychopaths have a problem with emotional empathy, and not Theory of Mind (Richell et al. 2003). Children with psychopathic tendencies have an impairment in the recognition of sad expressions (Stevens et al. 2001) and fearful expressions (Blair et al. 2005); adults with psychopathy and children with psychopathic tendencies show reduced autonomic responses to the sad expressions of others (Blair 1999), but they show no impairment in the processing of happy expressions (Stevens et al. 2001).

In other words, the problems in emotional empathy shown by individuals with psychopathy appear relatively selective and seem to involve some dysfunction in the amygdala, that part of the brain central for the processing of these sorts of emotions. The behavioural implications of this dysfunction should be clear. If you cannot recognise when someone is sad or fearful, and have a reduced autonomic response to these emotions, then there are few brakes on your own behaviour. Others might stop when they see that someone is frightened or sad; the psychopath does not. Chucky being dragged around that greasy pavement without his shoe didn't have a chance. The effects of lying to victims and seeing their distress, similarly, may have little effect; if you can't interpret their negative emotions, or feel their pain, you can lie to your heart's content.

But psychopathy tends to be associated with other personality characteristics, specifically *narcissism* and *Machiavellianism* (Furnham et al. 2013), and psychologists refer to these as the 'Dark Triad' of personality characteristics. These other personality characteristics are also associated with frequent lying. Narcissists have a grandiose sense of self and crave positive attention – they will lie in order to gain attention; Machiavellians manipulate social situations and will use lies instrumentally to do this; psychopaths are callous and lack empathy and they will be oblivious to the consequences of the lies (Meere and Egan 2017).

Research tells us that self-reported Dark Triad ratings are correlated with several antisocial behaviours, including higher levels of delinquency and aggression in children, as well as risky and sensation-seeking activities (Crysel, Crosier and Webster 2013), and I say that in the context of all the delinquent and aggressive behaviours of our gang. According to Peter Jonason from the University of Western Australia and his colleagues, the traits characteristic of the Dark Triad are thought to be associated with a 'compromised' or 'dysfunctional morality' (Campbell et al. 2009), in that they 'value "self" over "other" in a way that violates implicit communal sentiments in people' (Jonason and Webster 2012).

Tampy was certainly high on narcissism, everything about his appearance, his clothes (all stolen), and his manner suggested that. This is a personality trait 'associated with an inflated, grandiose self-concept and a lack of intimacy in interpersonal relationships' (Campbell et al. 2009). Narcissists are thought to suffer from 'extreme selfishness, with a grandiose view of their own talents.' In other words, people who are high on narcissism think that they are better than others in terms of many dimensions, including their looks, their intelligence, their creativity, and what they do, but as Twenge and Campbell (2009) have said – they are not.

> Measured objectively, narcissists are just like everyone else. Nevertheless, narcissists see themselves as fundamentally superior – they are special, entitled, and unique. Narcissists also lack emotionally warm, caring, and loving relationships with other people. This is a main difference between a narcissist and someone merely high in self-esteem: the high self-esteem person who's not narcissistic values relationships, but the narcissist does not. The result is a fundamentally imbalanced self – a grandiose, inflated self-image and a lack of deep connections to others.
>
> (Twenge and Campbell 2009: 19)

Of course, therein lies the psychological rub – if you see yourself as superior to others but are not actually superior on more objective indicators, then how do you maintain this inflated level of self-esteem? The answer is that you must engage in a variety of strategies to maintain and develop your self-image. For example, narcissists have a need to talk about any achievements or accomplishments in their lives to seek affirmation, indeed, wherever possible they need to broadcast them, to seek the maximum amount of affirmation. They will focus on their physical appearance (amongst other things) and value material goods especially designer goods that can display and communicate *instantly* their social status relative to everyone else. In social interaction, they will try to make sure that conversations centre on them, and attempt to elicit compliments – changing appearance, clothes, etc. are a necessary part of this, or play fight in the street in a way to elicit attention, interest, and (with a somewhat warped thinking) affirmation. In social relationships, narcissists will seek out trophy partners that make them look good (and even clever friends). And then again, given that they seem to lack warm and caring relationships, they will often manipulate and exploit other individuals to ensure that they continue to look good, relative to others.

Narcissism is usually measured using the Narcissistic Personality Infantry (NPI) developed by Robert Raskin and Howard Terry at the Institute of Personality Assessment and Research at the University of California at Berkeley in 1988 which uses pairs of forty statements. In each case, one answer reflects narcissistic tendencies, the other does not. So, for example:

A I prefer to blend in with the crowd.
B I like to be the center of attention.
C I can live my life any way I want to.
D People can't always live their lives in terms of what they want.
E I will never be satisfied until I get all that I deserve.
F I will take my satisfactions as they come.
G I am no better or no worse than most people.
H I think I am a special person.
I I try not to be a show-off.
J I will usually show off if I get the chance.
K I am much like everybody else.
L I am an extraordinary person.

It is quite clear from this list here that showing off ('I like to be the center of attention'), standing out from the crowd and being the focus of attention were core elements of his life. A sense of entitlement ('I can live my life any way I want to'), to feel entitled to do whatever you want to in order to achieve this is also key. In their book *The Narcissism Epidemic*, Twenge and Campbell (2009) have discussed some of the common misunderstandings that abound about narcissism. One common misunderstanding is that narcissists are really just people with high self-esteem. They point out that narcissists do indeed have high self-esteem (and the danger is that techniques used to increase self-esteem can lead to an increase in narcissism), but they argue that 'narcissism and self-esteem differ in an important way. Narcissists think that they are smarter, better looking, and more important than others, but not necessarily more moral, more caring, or more compassionate' (2009: 24). In other words, they are only interested in being better than others in certain 'key' aspects of life rather all aspects of life. Another common myth is that narcissists are fundamentally insecure individuals with low self-esteem (and, therefore, that we should pity or help them). Some psychologists have suggested that narcissists are just wearing a 'mask' to conceal this low self-worth. Again, Twenge and Campbell argue that that is unlikely to be the case based on research measuring the self-esteem of narcissists using the Implicit Association Test (IAT). The IAT measures underlying (and unconscious) associations between concepts, in this case, the strength of the associations between the concepts 'me' or 'not me' with positive or negative words. The results suggest that narcissists are faster at responding when 'me' is paired with 'good,' 'wonderful,' 'great' and 'right,' and slower when 'me' is paired with 'bad,' 'awful,' 'terrible,' and 'wrong.' In other words, they unconsciously associate the word 'me' with more positive attributes than do non-narcissists. In Twenge and Campbell's words, 'it turns out that deep down inside, narcissists think they're *awesome*' (2009: 27). Using the IAT, the evidence suggests that narcissists have higher unconscious self-esteem than non-narcissists on items like 'assertive,' 'active,' 'energetic,' 'outspoken,' 'dominant,' and 'enthusiastic' (versus items like 'quiet,' 'reserved,' 'silent,' 'withdrawn,' and 'inhibited'). However, narcissists score much more average on words like 'kind,' 'friendly,' 'generous,' 'cooperative,' 'pleasant,' and affectionate (versus 'mean,' 'rude,' 'stingy,' 'quarrelsome,' 'grouchy,' and 'cruel'). Twenge and Campbell sum up this pattern of results in the following way – 'narcissists have very similar views of themselves on the inside *and* the outside – they are secure and positive that they are winners but believe that caring about others isn't all that important' (2009: 27).

Another technique that psychologists have used to measure self-esteem is what is called the 'name-letter task' in which you ask people to rate the letters in the alphabet according to how 'beautiful' or 'likeable' they are. Rating the letters in your own name, especially the first letter, as more 'likeable' or more 'beautiful' is identified as a powerful indicator of inner self-esteem (because it's not tapping into conscious or deliberative processes). Again, the results suggest that narcissists think that the letters in their name are 'powerful' and 'assertive,' a little more 'beautiful,' but not more 'kind' and 'nurturing.' In other words, narcissists love many aspects of themselves even the letters in their own name.

Twenge and Campbell also consider whether narcissists really are, in fact, better looking than the rest of us. When you show people photographs of narcissists and non-narcissists and ask them to rate them, it turns out that narcissists are not actually more attractive. However, narcissists are more careful to pick out flattering pictures of themselves to post on social media, and to take enough pictures to ensure that some are flattering.

Narcissism is a major issue for society because it is increasing dramatically (and certainly since the days of our gang). Indeed, the title of Twenge and Campbell's book is *The Narcissism Epidemic*. They point out that almost every trait related to narcissism rose between the 1950s and 1990s, including assertiveness, dominance, extroversion, self-esteem, and individual focus. They point out that two-thirds of high school students in the United States now say that they expect to be in the top 20% of performers in their jobs. They also say that

> In a recent study, 39% of American eighth graders were confident of their math skills, compared to only 6% of Korean eighth graders. The Koreans, however, far exceeded the U.S. students' actual performance on math tests. We're not number one, but we're number one in *thinking* we are number one.
>
> (2009: 48)

Additionally, within the United States, 'the ethnic group with the lowest self-esteem, Asian-Americans, achieves the *highest* academic performance' (2009: 48).

The authors argue that one significant reason for this change in level of narcissism is to do with major sociocultural changes in society. At one point, there were clear social taboos on being overconfident, or loving yourself too much, with the oft-repeated retort of 'who do you think you are?' Children were warned about feelings of entitlement or being a show-off. These days, people are encouraged not just to love themselves, but to tell others about it (wearing tee shirts with 'Diva' or 'Number One'); they are taught to aim for the sky, 'be the best you can,' 'you can be number one.' Twenge and Campbell argue that changes in parenting practice is one major factor here, but they also identify the role of what they call 'super spreaders' which is the role of celebrity and the media in the rise of narcissism. Television, and, in particular, reality television, presents a major opportunity for narcissists to harvest acclaim, and for narcissism to be normalised. The authors write that

> Narcissists are masters at staying in the spotlight; they love attention and will do almost anything to get it. This is also one of the few realms where narcissism is helpful – narcissists thrive on public performance. Unlike many people who find it extremely anxiety-provoking to be in front of a crowd, narcissists love it. With the advent of reality TV, nonstop celebrity coverage, and instant fame, more and more narcissistic people are spreading their disease far and wide.
>
> (2009: 91)

One side effect of all of this is that there is an increase of desire for fame, and they cite the study carried out in 2006 which reported that '51% of 18–25 year-olds said that "becoming famous" was an important goal of their generation – nearly five times as many as named "becoming more spiritual" as an important goal' (2009: 93). A similar poll in the United Kingdom at that time asked children what was 'the very best thing in the world' – the most popular answer was 'being a celebrity.' For those who don't quite make it to TV or even reality television shows, there is always social media where you can be a celebrity in your own social group and increase (and anxiously measure) your narcissistic flow by the number of likes on social media. Social media is all about presenting yourself in particular ways using whatever props are necessary. Blogs, YouTube, Facebook, etc. allow you to construct an image of yourself which is designed to get you the kind of admiration that you want.

The forensic psychiatrist John MacDonald in a well-known article in 1963 in the *American Journal of Psychiatry* identified a connection between violence and the three dimensions of personality that constitute the Dark Triad, namely Machiavellianism (a manipulative personality, which gets its name from Machiavelli's original book on this topic, see Christie and Geis [1970]), subclinical or 'normal' narcissism (with feelings of grandiosity, entitlement, dominance, and superiority as we have seen), and subclinical or 'normal' psychopathy (with characteristics such as high impulsivity and thrill-seeking, combined with low empathy and anxiety, see Hare [1985]). Paulhus and Williams (2002) analysed the relationship between these three personality dimensions in a non-forensic, non-pathological, high-achievement population (a sample of university students). They point out that all three dimensions share a number of important features – 'To varying degrees, all three entail a socially malevolent character with behaviour tendencies toward self-promotion, emotional coldness, duplicity, and aggressiveness' (Paulhus and Williams 2002: 557). They also say that in the *clinical* literature, the connections between the dimensions had been known for some time (Hart and Hare 1998), but newer research was now demonstrating strong degrees of overlap in *non-clinical* samples as well – particularly between Machiavellianism and psychopathy (Fehr, Samson and Paulhus 1992), narcissism and psychopathy (Gustafson and Ritzer 1995), and Machiavellianism and narcissism (McHoskey 1995). Paulhus and Williams (2002) tested the inter-relationships of these three personality dimensions in their sample and also tested their connections with other variables (other measures of personality, intelligence, and over-confidence on various cognitive tasks).

They found that all three dimensions were correlated (with the strongest correlation between narcissism and non-clinical psychopathy), and that although the dimensions were related, they were not equivalent. The one commonality across the triad was 'low agreeableness.' There were also significant differences between them – only psychopaths (but not narcissists nor Machiavellians) were low on anxiety, which is consistent with the general clinical view that psychopaths are very low on anxiety (and resistant to punishment). They also found that narcissists and (to a lesser extent) psychopaths exhibited the most self-enhancement in various cognitive tests, whereas Machiavellians showed little sign of this. Machiavellians are, the researchers concluded, more 'reality-based' in their sense of self. Narcissists exhibited a strong self-deceptive component (with low insight) to their personality and Paulhus and Williams point out that the grandiosity and poor insight found in narcissists have also been noted in clinical psychopaths (Hart and Hare 1998). They also found that the measure of non-clinical psychopathy was the best predictor of self-report and behavioural measures of antisocial behaviour. Paulhus and Williams concluded that the Dark Triad of personalities are 'overlapping but distinct' constructs, each dimension in the triad presenting with its own particular problems.

Jonason et al. (2013) have suggested that 'empathy,' or rather lack of empathy, is another significant feature linking these three dimensions. Empathy plays a major role in the identification of psychopathy; indeed, it is one of the two core dimensions. It also feeds into Machiavellianism, but it has a more complex relationship with narcissism. Jonason et al. argue that a core route for women when it comes to the Dark Triad might be narcissism rather than psychopathy or Machiavellianism. Indeed, using a complex pictorial analysis of the data, they came up with a conclusion which is 'Moderation tests suggest the link between the Dark Triad and limited empathy might primarily be through narcissism in women but psychopathy in men' (2013: 574). They say that 'men who are high on psychopathy and thus have limited empathy may enact a risky lifestyle whereas women who are high on narcissism may enact parasitic relationship styles' (Jonason and Schmitt 2012).

It seems that callousness, lack of emotional empathy and entitlement are the key attributes underpinning the Dark Triad. All three dimensions connect to the frequent and expert use of lies. Lies to make them look good, lies to manipulate, and lies without consequence where they don't react to emotions like the fear and the sadness they cause in others, in the normal way. They don't feel the suffering of any victims; they don't care.

Postscript

I saw some of these behaviours close up. But Tampy could be charming and charismatic, and he made my life back in Legmore Street very exciting, for a time. I must admit that. But excitement is a double-edged sword. When I went off to university, I heard that Tampy had been caught with a gun and sent to prison. I don't know if it was the same gun or a different gun that he had asked me to look after for him in my back bedroom. He was, it seems, by then, according to what the newspapers say, a member of a Protestant paramilitary group. Many of my old friends had joined various paramilitary organisations. I was losing touch with all of them.

When I was in my first year at Cambridge, I learned that Tampy, just a few years after his release from prison, was murdered by members of the Ulster Volunteer Force, a Protestant paramilitary group (that is his own side in that senseless tit-for-tat killing of the Troubles). His mutilated body was dumped in an entry in south Belfast.

I, on the other hand, had moved on, and in this relationship I was the liar.

6 Lie Detection

> Truth is always consistent with itself, and needs nothing to help it out; it is always near at hand, and sits upon our lips, and is ready to drop out before we are aware; whereas a lie is troublesome, and sets a man's invention upon the rack, and one trick needs a great many more to make it good. It is like building upon a false foundation, which continually stands in need of props to shore it up.
>
> Sir Richard Steele (1712) in *The Spectator*

Why We're Bad at Detecting Lies

Psychology suggests that human lie detection is weak and inherently flawed. We are subject to a number of cognitive biases when we make judgements about lying, and we seem to focus on the wrong behaviours that can be easily manipulated by skilful liars. We assume that liars can't look us in the face when they're lying, but they can and they do, except for the very bad ones that is.

In psychological experiments, it has been consistently shown that humans are poor lie detectors. In one *meta-analysis* in 2006, for example, the social psychologists Charles Bond and Bella DePaulo synthesised all the relevant psychological research from 206 studies (involving 24,483 participants), where people were attempting to discriminate truth and lies in real time (with no special aids or training). They found that overall people got 54% of their judgements correct, correctly identifying 47% of lies and 61% of true utterances (chance probability if you were simply guessing would be 50%). As Brianna Verigin and colleagues have commented 'Despite the importance of being able to detect deception, research has consistently found that people are unable to do so. In fact, the accuracy rates vary around chance level' (Verigin et al. 2019: 1).

Bond and DePaulo (2008) also carried out a meta-analysis of individual differences in detecting deception and found that differences in such ability were 'minute.' People seem to have a 'truth' bias, and are more inclined to judge deceptive messages as truthful than truthful messages as deceptive. We assume that most people tell the truth most of the time and make judgements accordingly. This truth bias is often reversed when people have been arrested for a

DOI: 10.4324/9781003394563-6

crime and are subsequently being interviewed, here there is a lie bias, where most people will be assumed to be liars (see Frank and Feeley 2003). Both forms of bias can be equally damaging and lead to serious errors.

There are a number of reasons why human lie detection might be flawed. Firstly, lying is a complex behaviour that involves a combination of verbal and nonverbal cues, cognitive processes, and emotional regulation, some or all of which the liar attempts to suppress. It is challenging for people to accurately interpret and integrate all of these different aspects simultaneously (without more accurate guidance about where and when to look), leading to errors in lie detection. Indeed, it is difficult for the ordinary person to know what to concentrate on in the first place given that there are many stereotypic and false beliefs about the behaviours associated with lying, the so-called 'tell-tale signs of deceit'. Zuckerman and his colleagues (1981), for example, found that American participants associated deception with a range of different behaviours, including averting eye gaze, showing more self-adaptors (self-comforting movements), moving their feet and legs more, shifting posture more, shrugging and speaking more quickly, in other words more 'nervous' activity. Avoiding eye contact (or gaze aversion), tends to come top of the list, but research suggests that avoiding eye contact has little actual association with lying (DePaulo et al. 2003). There is a stereotype that the liar just can't look you in the eye based on the premise that liars will experience anxiety, fear, shame, and guilt like most of us (all negative emotions), and have cognitive difficulties in generating the lie. This *should* lead to significant gaze aversion but doesn't because liars fight to control it.

This stereotypic belief would seem to be global. The *Global Deception Research Team* carried out a study of the stereotypes that people hold about liars in seventy-five different countries (and forty-three different languages) and found that the belief that liars avoid eye contact was found in every single one of the seventy-five countries. The world as a whole seems to believe that 'liars cannot look you in the eye.' That's what people look out for first and foremost when they are trying to make a judgement about deceit. So, it's easy for the liar (particularly the experienced liar) to counteract that by deliberately attempting to control where they look, dealing with any negative emotion through justification or rationalisation (or, of course, having the right kind of personality not to experience these particular negative emotions in the first place, as we have seen in Chapter 5). We know that gaze aversion is also affected by the cognitive planning underlying speech, not just for lies but for all speech, both in terms of what is called the broader semantic planning as we plan the overall content of what we are going to say (Butterworth 1975; Beattie 1983) but also in terms of word finding, which psychologists refer to as lexical access – searching the mental lexicon for the right word in the right slot. This semantic planning often happens quickly and unconsciously but is reflected, nevertheless, in the patterning of micro-pauses in speech, periods of silence over about 200 milliseconds, and these sorts of micro-pauses are also associated with both semantic planning and word finding (Beattie and Ellis 2017; Beattie and Butterworth 1979). People avert their gaze from another person when they are planning what they are going to say; if they don't, there are often dysfluencies in their speech, including repetitions and false starts because of interference between these two tasks, planning speech, and interpreting nonverbal signals from the person you are speaking to (Beattie 1978, 1981). So, speakers may avert their eye gaze when they're talking to you, not because they are lying but because they are trying to give you an accurate account of what actually happened and are putting more effort into it, including finding exactly the right words. Some psychologists have argued that lies require *more* cognitive effort because lies have to be made up rather than just accessed from memory (Vrij 2000), but the experienced liar will plan their story in advance using fragments of the truth as the basic building blocks of their lies to lessen the cognitive load (Verigen et al. 2019). It seems that many of us are fooled by the liar who maintains steadfast eye contact whatever their individual strategy.

The second reason why lie detection might be weak is that people are prone to specific cognitive biases that can influence their judgement and decision-making. *Confirmation bias*, for example, leads individuals to interpret information in a way that confirms their pre-existing beliefs. This bias can make people more susceptible to believing lies that align with their own perspectives and political affiliations, or even their initial perception of an individual based on how they look. It turns out that we make very quick judgements about people, especially (and extraordinarily) about their trustworthiness based on appearance. Willis and Todorov (2006) found that even after an exposure of one-tenth of a second to a picture of a human face, judgements of personality traits were made which were very similar to judgements made when individuals had significantly longer to look at the face. This is instant and unconscious, and can potentially influence what behavioural clues we subsequently pick up about them through this confirmation bias. Once we've 'decided' that someone looks trustworthy, we may be less inclined to find tell-tale signs of deceit. We may also be more prone to notice small clues to deceit in those who disagree with us and fail to notice them in those we agree with. Again, all part of confirmation bias.

We know that *optimism bias* (a bias where people overestimate the probability of good things happening to them in their lives) can also operate. To see optimism bias in operation, just ask a married friend what their probability of getting a divorce will be and then tell them the actual probability and watch their response – they may well suffer from an optimism bias. They think that *they* will have a happy and successful marriage despite the statistics which might suggest otherwise! But optimism bias sits on a platform of perceiving and interpreting the world. It is supported and maintained by biased patterns of eye gaze, with fewer and shorter gaze fixations on sources of negative information ('bad news'), in a number of different domains (see Beattie et al. 2017). To maintain our sense of optimism and level of happiness, we may not attend to any *bad* news and this occurs quite unconsciously (Beattie 2018b), and we may well miss the behavioural clues that might indicate that our partner, our child, our parent, our boss, etc. might be a liar. We want to see the world through rose-tinted glasses, we do not want to think that we are surrounded by liars, and sometimes, we do not see what is in front of us.

The third reason why lie detection might be weak is that there are important contextual factors involved in lying and judging a lie. This book is all about these contextual factors, the social situations in which real lies occur. Just consider, for example, high-stakes situations, such as interrogations or job interviews – these can increase the pressure and stress on both the liar and the lie detector, making it more difficult to accurately assess truthfulness. The suspected liar may well be nervous and anxious *throughout* the encounter, and even more anxious in the case of an interrogation because they have been detained. This is going to dampen down any difference in emotional response between telling the truth and telling a lie because they are feeling strong negative emotion throughout, making it more difficult for the lie detector. When the lie detector is under stress, they may be less accurate in their judgements.

But there is another very important point to be made here about contextual factors. The vast majority of the existing psychological research on lying (unfortunately) focuses on just one particular social context – the highly artificial psychological laboratory (Beattie 1982), where students (and it is almost always students, see Sears 1986) are invited in, to act as experimental participants and *instructed to lie* (different in terms of underlying brain mechanism to spontaneous natural lies, as I discussed in Chapter 1). The strategic overuse of this particular context limits the conclusions we can draw about the behaviour of liars, in my view, and thus judgements of lie detection. I have argued throughout the book that lies are social acts embedded within our natural patterns of social interaction with multiple social functions – lies bond people together, they are used to attack others (who may have lied to us), they act as provocations, as a means of self-defence, they are used to protect our ego, etc. They can have very high stakes attached to them – getting way with the lie might be the most important thing in one's life (see Chapter 2 'The packed lunch'). They are part of our being. How do we bring these embedded communications into the laboratory? Lies are not just individual cognitive events available on request. And how do we generate a psychological stake for the teller of the lie, who has been asked to lie at the request of the experimenter? The answer is with enormous difficulty. Frank and Feeley (2003) criticise the relevance of these types of experimental situations to real-life lie detection; they say that it is simply not possible to generate the kinds of stakes associated with being caught lying that we find in the real world in the lab. Laboratory studies may be able to illustrate certain things, but only as *simulations* of what goes on in the world beyond the laboratory to answer preliminary questions (indeed I will use this approach later in the chapter). That is why the conclusions that people are *so* bad at detecting detection, almost at chance level, and that there is minimal difference between individuals in their ability, do always need careful consideration. These claims are based on an overview of psychological research which has focused primarily on laboratory situations with low or minimal stake in the telling of the lie, and therefore with few real emotional consequences.

How good are ordinary people out there on the street when the stakes are very high? I would suggest that they are probably not at chance level, and that there are significant differences between people in their ability to both lie and to judge a lie, but how good remains to be determined. People also need a baseline of behaviour to judge any deviations from it. Many experimental studies do not even provide that. To understand the psychology of the lie, we need to go beyond the psychological laboratory. To accurately appraise the lie detection abilities of ordinary people, we need to study these in that same real world.

The fourth reason why human lie detection might be weak is that skilled liars are adept at manipulating the cues and behaviours typically associated with deception in the minds of ordinary people. They may intentionally display false cues or mask their true emotions, making it difficult for human lie detectors to accurately assess their truthfulness. They also have a series of verbal strategies for lying including embedding their lies into truthful information, which can reduce pausing for cognitive planning (Verigin et al. 2019).

But there may be another cause of the apparent poor lie detection ability of ordinary people, which I fear psychology has contributed to. The focus of psychology has been an attempt to isolate *individual* behavioural clues to deception, where 'A deception clue answers the question of whether or not the person is lying, although it does not reveal what is being concealed' (Ekman 1985: 40), be they *verbal* (clarity of response, vague content), *paralinguistic* (higher pitch, more pausing), or *nonverbal* (eye contact, gesture, facial expression etc.), and individual aspects of nonverbal leakage, which is 'when the liar mistakenly reveal the truth' (Ekman 1985: 40).

Paul Ekman himself originated this approach following his reading of Darwin (1872), as we shall see in the next section. This led to a burgeoning psychological literature which have followed the same basic approach, and a very large popular psychology literature with many best-selling books making the same promises about what *individual* nonverbal behaviours to look for. But I want to suggest a slightly different approach to this whole issue, a move away from a focus on individual nonverbal (or verbal) behaviours, where verbal and nonverbal behaviours are considered separate channels of communication entirely, to one that considers how they connect in everyday communication when we talk, and, of course, when we lie. This is very much in line with the reconceptualisation of human communication developed by the American psychologist and psycholinguist David McNeill from the University of Chicago (McNeill 1985, 1992), which is transforming much of psychology with a new focus on what is called *multimodal communication*. I want to suggest that the approach that many psychologists have taken thus far has not helped in improving the accuracy of lie detection, indeed it may even have hindered it. It has given rise to *more confident* judgements about one's ability to detect lies without any concomitant rise in accuracy (this is certainly what has been found with professional lie detectors, see Frank and Feeley [2003]). But first, we need a little background.

Darwin (1872) did not give undue emphasis to deception or lying in his seminal work on nonverbal behaviour *The Expression of Emotions in Man and Animals*. But what he did note that such nonverbal behaviours 'reveal the thoughts and intentions of others more truly than do words, which may be falsified' (1872: 359). He starts with the 'common sense' view that words (verbal) are different and separate from behaviours (nonverbal). We can all make up a story about what we've been doing when we are telling a lie, but what do our nonverbal actions reveal? Darwin also wrote that

> when movements, associated through habit with certain states of the mind, are partially repressed by the will, the strictly involuntary muscles, as well as those which are least under the separate control of the will, are liable still to act; and their action is often highly expressive.
>
> (1872: 54)

In other words, people will try to repress or inhibit certain expressive movements when they are lying, but they will not always be successful. Some forms of behaviour, Darwin argued, are much harder to inhibit than others, and these will be the most 'expressive' in this regard. So, some forms of nonverbal behaviour might be more revealing than others when it comes to lying. But the emphasis is now firmly on nonverbal behaviour as opposed to language, and certainly not on the connections between the verbal and nonverbal channels.

Ekman (2003) refers to this general hypothesis of Darwin's as the *inhibition hypothesis* – 'if you cannot make an action voluntarily, then you will not be able to prevent it when involuntary processes such as emotion instigate it' (2003: 206). Therefore, it follows that certain emotional expressions that cannot easily be inhibited may be powerful indicators of felt emotion. Ekman (2003) calls this phenomenon 'nonverbal leakage'.

But Darwin, of course, is also implying that other movements *can* and *will* be inhibited during deception (those that are under volitional control, like hand movements and gesture, for example). Their form and morphology may not be so revealing of the real underlying emotional state, but, of course, *the attempted inhibition itself may be highly revealing*.

Ekman adds one further consideration to this argument, namely that although hand or foot movements 'would be easy to inhibit…most people do not bother to censor their body actions. Because most of us do not get much feedback from others about what our body movements are revealing, we do not learn the need to monitor these actions; and so, we hypothesised, when people lie, they usually do not fine-tune their body actions' (2003: 208). In other words, he says that although hand gestures could be inhibited, they often are not and that therefore 'the body will be a good source of deception cues – exactly the opposite of what Darwin predicted' (Ekman 2003: 208). Elsewhere, Ekman has explicitly criticised Darwin because he 'failed to note the existence of gestural slips (Ekman 1985), which leak concealed feelings and intentions, and other forms of body movement that can betray a lie' (Ekman 2009: 3451). He views gestural slips, where the gesture reveals the real 'true' underlying psychological state as one type of deception clue.

Therefore, if we consider the arguments of these two pioneers in the field of nonverbal communication (separated by a century or more, of course) and try to combine their ideas, we end up with a number of specific hypotheses. Firstly, in deception, there may well be an attempt on the part of individuals to suppress or inhibit certain behaviours that are potentially highly expressive of underlying cognitive or emotional state, and that a decrease in frequency of certain behaviours may itself be one potential indicator of deception. Secondly, because our awareness of certain bodily actions is shaped in part by the conventions and constraints of everyday talk governing talking and looking, etc., then we may have less awareness of some behaviours that can be volitionally controlled (like hand movements) than others (like facial expression). Movements, like gesture could potentially be highly revealing. Both of these hypotheses have interesting implications for research on gesture and deception. However, now that we know from eye-tracking research that interlocutors do monitor hand movements but still much less than facial expression (see Beattie, Webster and Ross 2010), this may have implications for the existence of gestural inhibition in lying (contrary to Ekman's view), although how widespread and generalised this might be, is quite another matter.

The research into people's beliefs about lying compared to their actual behaviour suggests that people generally think that many behaviours increase when people are telling lies, whereas meta-analyses of the data reveal that only a small number of behaviours reliably change during deception, and these behaviours tend to *decrease* when lying is a function of behavioural inhibition. Sporer and Schwandt (2007) conducted a meta-analysis of the published literature on deception and found that only three forms of behaviour were reliably associated with lying and they were 'nodding,' 'foot and leg movements,' and 'hand movements.' All three seem to *decrease* in frequency. It is perhaps worth remembering at that in their classic 1969 paper on '*Nonverbal Leakage and Clues to Deception*,' Ekman and Friesen predicted that because people are generally unaware of the behaviour of their feet and legs, that they should be 'a good source for leakage and deception cues.' They predicted more movements in the feet and legs during deception (things like 'abortive restless flight movements...frequent shift of leg posture, and in restless or repetitive leg and foot acts,' Ekman and Friesen 1969). This prediction has been proven wrong in the vast majority of studies (including in Ekman's own research, see Ekman 2003: 211). People do seem to inhibit their behaviour during deception, even the feet and legs. They also inhibit their hand movements and gestures.

Now, I will argue presently (following McNeill 1992) that human gestural movements are particularly interesting when it comes to lying for a number of very important reasons, namely they are very hard to fake (although some have tried, including Donald Trump, as we shall see in Chapter 7). I will argue that it is very difficult to deliberately fake the form of what are called *iconic gestures* (where the form of the gesture matches the content of the speech) when you are lying, firstly because of the essentially non-conscious nature of gestural communication and secondly because of the complex division of meaning between the two channels of communication, speech, and gesture (which is at the heart of McNeill's argument). It would be very complicated to split meaning into the verbal and gestural channels in a way that might look natural or normal. You would have to get the division of meaning between the two channels just right, as well as the precise iconic form of the gesture and the right degree of anticipation of the associated part of the verbal message by the preparation phase of the gesture because what is interesting is that the gestural movement starts in advance of the associated word or phrase (Butterworth and Beattie 1978).

It is interesting that the evidence suggests that people do not attempt this when they are lying, opting instead for an easier strategy. Generally speaking, people inhibit their hand movements when they are lying, and, consequently, gesture frequency decreases in deception (Cody and O'Hair [1983]; Davis and Hadiks [1995]; Ekman [1988]; Ekman and Friesen [1972]; Ekman et al. [1976]; Ekman et al. [1991]; Greene et al. [1985]; Vrij et al. [1999]; but see Bond et al. [1985]; de Turck and Miller [1985]). Indeed, a decrease in gestural frequency would seem to be one of the more reliable indicators of deception. It suggests perhaps that at some unconscious level, liars do not want to risk giving the game away through revealing hand movements. Therefore, they try to inhibit this form of behaviour by clasping their hands or using similar kinds of strategy. Aldert Vrij (2000) has a useful summary of this research in his book *Detecting Lies and Deceit*. He also summarises the empirical evidence that most people believe that gesture frequency actually increases during deception, which shows that most people have a false belief here, as in so many other areas when it comes to deception.

To understand better why psychology went down a particular route with respect to its search for individual nonverbal clues to deception and nonverbal leakage, I decided to return to Paul Ekman's first and classic study in this field (Ekman and Friesen 1969).

Nonverbal Leakage

Both Darwin (1872/1955) and Freud (1922) may have held disparate views on lying and deception, its motivating factors and functions, but their theories had one thing in common. The process of lying is all about control, and some modalities of communication are easier to control than others. You just must learn to look for the right things. Darwin in *The Expression of the Emotions in Man and Animals* had identified control and repression as central to understanding and reading of accurate emotional displays when it comes to deception, as we have seen. He had written:

> Some actions ordinarily associated through habit with certain states of mind may be partially repressed through the will, and in such cases the muscles which are least under the separate control of the will are the most liable still to act, causing movements which we recognise as expressive. In certain other cases the checking of one habitual movement requires other slight movements; and these are likewise expressive.
>
> (Darwin 1872/1955: 48–49)

But Darwin had been vague about which movements are susceptible to 'control of the will.' Freud (1922) wrote that 'He that has eyes to see and ears to hear may convince himself that no mortal can keep a secret. If his lips are silent, he chatters with his fingertips; betrayal oozes out of him at every pore.' But there was no data or really any degree of specificity to back this up. So, for many contemporary psychologists, the *experimental science* of lie detection really began in 1969. It was then that an associate professor of medical psychology at the University of California Medical School in San Francisco carried out an experiment to see if there were any bodily movements or facial expressions which escape efforts to deceive and emerge as cues to deception. This is the foundation of a voluminous body of research in this area. Critically, it has influenced everyday understandings of what we should look for through popular media, including films and television series. If the science is weak or misleading in any way, this may well have made matters worse. For these reasons, we need to consider the original research very carefully.

The first pioneering study by Ekman and his colleague Wallace Friesen (Ekman and Friesen 1969) asked a simple question – which part or parts of the body are most revealing when it comes to lying? And you can see how this question set the agenda for the next fifty years of research in this area of lying and lie detection. It assumes that verbal and nonverbal behaviours are separate and the focus is on the nonverbal rather than on the verbal, and not on the connections between the two channels.

So, we have the question posed. But what about the answer? Is it the face? The face is, after all, highly visible and capable of sending out many different expressions, often very quickly (we call these very fast expressions – micro expressions). In other words, the face has a very high *sending capacity*, in Ekman's jargon. But the argument goes we are often aware of our facial expression (what the researchers call *internal feedback*) and we know that people focus on and sometimes comment on our facial expression ('wipe that smile of your face,' 'stop looking so pleased with yourself'), so we are all aware that we must try to control our face in certain situations, including when we are attempting to lie. Or is the body more revealing when it comes to detecting lies? What about the hands and the feet, the focus of much less visual attention in everyday social interaction, and with slower movements compared with facial expressions? Each hand gesture or foot movement is comparatively slow compared to brief and fleeting facial expressions, and with fewer discernible different configurations. But, on the other hand, we seem to pay less attention to what our hands and feet are doing, and people rarely comment on these movements and what they might be saying. 'Why are you making that circular movements with your hands?' would seem to be a very odd social comment. 'Why did you just movement your foot up and down here times?' might seem an even odder one.

In the case of the human face, the sending capacity is high but both internal and external feedback is also high, so Ekman and Friesen theorised that the face is likely to be a confusing source of information when it comes to reading genuine emotions when people are trying to deceive – with fast signals concealed, interrupted, or squelched, often with masks, including the commonest mask of them all – the smile. The body, they argued, should be more revealing – lower sending capacity, of course, but given that both internal and external feedback are low, there should be fewer attempts to control the behaviour, and certainly fewer successful attempts. Ekman and Friesen argued that it was all about control and the properties of nonverbal communication that might be responsible for control to be exerted, or not. Darwin had also identified this fight for control as central to understanding and reading accurate emotional displays when it comes to deception. But Darwin had failed to specify which movements are susceptible to control and which are not, as Ekman and Friesen themselves rightly point out. They intended to be more specific on this point particularly with regard to particular modalities of communication (facial expression, hand movement, foot/leg movement).

They devised their classic and well-cited experiment based upon some existing films of brief interviews with a number of female psychiatric inpatients. There were 120 brief interviews in total with forty different patients. From this corpus of material, they selected just *three* examples where they say they could be certain that deception occurred, and they felt confident that they could specify the concealed information. Two of the examples were provided by one individual, Patient A, who had been admitted to the hospital with 'depressed affect, angry outbursts, screaming, threats of suicide.' Ekman and Friesen note that there was some psychiatric disagreement about whether the appropriate diagnosis for this patient was 'agitated depression' or 'schizophrenia.' Patient A was filmed on the first day of hospitalisation, in the middle of her hospitalisation and shortly before her discharge. In the middle of her hospitalisation, Ekman and Friesen said there was evidence that she had tried to deceive an interviewer into believing that she was feeling much better ('simulating optimism, control of affect, and feelings of well-being'). The interviewer and the ward psychiatrist thought that she may be trying to deceive at this point in her hospitalisation, and at the end of the interview she broke down and admitted that she hadn't been feeling better. This was the only example out of the three that involved the attempted deception of another person (the doctor); the other two cases were examples of *self-deception*. For this reason, I focus on this first case as it represents what we normally think of as deception or lies. The research question Ekman and Friesen posed was would an observer just viewing a film of the facial expression and head movement of this patient (at normal speed) miss any concealed information and be misled by her simulation of positive mood. And would those who viewed the body from the neck down be more accurate in their judgement? This was tested in the following way:

> The basic design of the experiments was to show a film of one of the interviews silently to one of two different groups of naïve observers, one group viewing only the face and head, the other viewing the body from the neck down. The observers were not told they were seeing a psychiatric patient; the film was identified as a record of a conversation. After viewing the film, both groups of observers described their impressions by checking words from Gough's Adjective Check List, 300 words descriptive of attitudes, traits, affects, manners. To test hypotheses about the source of leakage of withheld information, the information conveyed by head/face cues was contrasted with information conveyed by body cues.
>
> (Ekman and Friesen 1969: 100)

Eighteen observers viewed the head/face, twenty-eight observed the body from the neck down. A 'head' message was categorised as one that was identified by half or more of the observers who saw the head (and less than half of the observers who saw the body, with a 20% or more difference between the two). A 'body' message was categorised as one that was identified by half or more of the observers who saw the body (and less than half of the observers who saw the head, with a 20% or more difference between the two). A 'head and body' message was checked by more than half of both groups. I have included below the actual percentages for some of the more interesting individual results.

The results do look interesting, but they need some careful consideration. The 'head' messages received were: 'sensitive (83% head, 36% body), friendly, cooperative, self-punishing (50% head, 2% body).' The 'body' messages were: 'tense (44% head, 82% body), excitable, high strung, fearful (33% head, 68% body), hurried, changeable, awkward, complaining, touchy, affected, restless, impulsive, impatient rigid.' The 'head and body' messages were anxious (head 89%, 100% body), emotional, confused, defensive, worrying, dissatisfied, despondent (56% head, 50% body).

These results might, at first sight, seem in agreement with the basic hypotheses. If you focus on the separate list of head and body messages, there would seem to be a significant difference between being perceived as *sensitive* (the top 'head' message) versus *tense* (the top 'body' message), which would seem to support their basic theory about the face being easier to control in deception and therefore more capable of sending disguised messages. But when you consider the 'head and body' messages, the picture starts to look very different. The top 'head and body' message was *anxious*. In other words, the main message that the observers picked up from either the face *or* the body was that Patient A was anxious no matter what she was saying in her speech. Indeed, the associated percentages of 89% for head and 100% for body (in the 'head and body' messages) are the highest observed with Patient A. So, this is clearly not in line with their theory. Despite that they draw the unqualified conclusion that:

> These studies show a difference in the information conveyed by the head as compared to the hands/feet/legs, which is in the direction predicted by our formulation of leakage and deception clues.
>
> (Ekman and Friesen 1969: 103)

I need to point out that here they are referring to the observers' judgements of each of the three examples or extracts as individual studies. The one case of attempted deception of another person clearly didn't show this (the two cases of self-deception are equally problematic which I will discuss presently).

But there is another important issue with this experiment. Patient A was being treated with amitriptyline hydrochloride at the time (Ekman and Friesen 1969: 100), which was a drug commonly used to treat depression. But one of the side effects of this drug is 'mask-like facial expressions,' which is very unfortunate for a study designed to test the hypothesis that observers will be less accurate at reading true underlying emotions in deception from the face! If a patient has mask-like facial expressions because of the drug, their facial expressions may well be hard to read but not for the reasons that they considered. Ekman and Friesen do not comment on whether this side effect was displayed by this patient or indeed comment on any of the side effects of this drug experienced by this patient. They merely mention the medication when they introduce the patient and never discuss it further (Patient B who contributed the third interview extract used in the study was also on medication, fluphenazine hydrochloride, one of the side effects of this drug is tremors, which again is rather unfortunate in a study testing whether bodily movements are more indicative of a negative state. The drug may have been causing the increase in movements!). These critical methodological issues apply to both types of deception studied (other or alter-deception and self-deception) and therefore all three examples.

The possible significance of the medication for any pattern in the results does not seem to have been mentioned in any reviews of this study (to the best of my knowledge). Neither has the absence of a control – a comparable extract from each of the interviews where there was no attempt to conceal or disguise true feelings, in other words, no attempt to deceive. The tremor in bodily movement may have persisted throughout Patient B's interview and may have been interpreted as indicative of a negative emotional state no matter what they were talking about and whether they were trying to deceive or not. Similarly, Patient A's mask-like facial expression might have been present throughout and may have always indicated a neutral, cooperative, and untroubled state. We simply cannot tell because the control wasn't run and the issue of possible side effects from the medication wasn't considered.

But despite these obvious shortcomings, Ekman and Friesen finish this paper in a very optimistic and upbeat way. They write: 'Knowledge of nonverbal leakage and deception clues could also perhaps be utilized in an attempt to develop lie detection procedures which rely upon nonverbal behavior' (Ekman and Friesen 1969: 105). This turned out to be the classic psychological study on the behaviours associated with lying. And Ekman and Friesen were right on one score. A veritable industry was built on this very shaky foundation, with Paul Ekman as the virtual CEO of Lie Detection Inc. His clients included the FBI, many commercial organisations, as well as a change in beliefs in popular culture about lying applied to a whole range of domains (see Ekman 2001). The problem is that much of the ensuing research which retreated into the laboratory proper was as equally flawed as this original study as they used this focus on individual behaviours and they didn't come to terms with real lies, the kinds of lies that we find in everyday life with any kind of meaningful stake ('minimum relevance,' in Frank and Feeley's, 2003, words). I have tried to explore real lies throughout this book, but we need the science of lie detection to use these types of lies as the stimulus material (more possible in the world in which we live where so much of everyday behaviour is now video-recorded).

But next I want to outline an approach to the analysis of the behaviours associated with lying with a focus not on isolated and separated verbal and nonverbal behaviours, but the connections between them. Everyday talk is accompanied by movement, particularly the movements of the hand, and the different modalities are closely integrated. That's the starting point for this research. But let me warn you this study has all of the faults I have been criticising in other experimental studies – artificial context, trivial lies, no real stake in getting ways with it etc., so I view this study as an investigation into the cognitions underlying the generation of false information in an experimental setting. I can't justify it as an analysis of (real) lying, but it's potentially interesting nonetheless. But first some background into David McNeill's theory.

A New Multimodal Approach to Lie Detection

Hand movements, and particularly the spontaneous hand movements that accompany speech (what Ekman and Friesen in 1969 called 'illustrators,' but are nowadays, following McNeill's seminal work called 'iconic gestures,' or if they are most abstract 'metaphoric gestures'), might be particularly interesting when it comes to lying because these movements are unconsciously generated and closely integrated with the speech itself (Butterworth and Beattie 1978: Beattie 2003, 2016a). Certain hand movements like the V for 'peace' sign are conscious, but these stand alone, they do not depend on speech to transmit their meaning, they can be repeated if asked (What gesture did you just make?), they are conscious and deliberative. These are called emblems (Ekman and Friesen 1969). But iconic and metaphoric gestures are not like that; they are qualitatively different. They depend upon speech to give them meaning; they cannot be consciously repeated with any real accuracy; they are generated unconsciously and tied up with the speech stream. That's what makes them potentially important for lie detection.

The focus for clues to deception should perhaps be on the connections between modalities, for example on speech *and* gesture rather than on speech *or* gesture. I will outline a bit more of the underlying theory on how speech and iconic (and metaphoric) gesture connect and are integrated.

Iconic gestures are hand movements whose particular form displays a close relationship to the meaning of the accompanying speech. For example, when describing a scene from a comic book story in which a character bends a tree back to the ground, the speaker appears to grip something and pull it back. This is called an iconic gesture because it refers to the same act mentioned in the speech; the gesture seems to be connected to the words 'and he bends it way back.' This particular example comes from David McNeill's seminal book *Hand and Mind* (1992: 12). I should point out before showing this example that following the conventions introduced by McNeill) the speech actually said is underlined in the text. The boundaries of the meaningful part of the gesture (the so-called 'stroke' phase of the gesture are shown by enclosing the concurrent segments of speech in square brackets, like this [ ]. The gesture accompanying the clause 'and he bends it way back' was as follows; the brackets indicate where the important bit of the gesture occurred:

and he [bends it way back]
   Iconic: hand appears to grip something and pull it from the upper front space back and down near to the shoulder.

This example illustrates the close connection that exists between speech and gesture, the close connection between language and this form of nonverbal communication, which are clearly not separate, as many psychologists have assumed. These iconic gestures only occur during the act of speaking itself. The example shows how what is depicted in the gesture should be incorporated into a complete picture of a person's thought process. The sentence describes the tree being bent 'way back'; the gesture at the same time depicts a bending-back image. The gesture clearly adds meaning here because it shows how the bending back is accomplished and it shows it from the point of view of the agent, the person doing the bending back. The gesture shows that the tree is fastened at one end, which is not made explicit in the accompanying speech.

As David McNeill himself says: 'Speech and gesture refer to the same event and are partially overlapping, but the pictures they present are different. Jointly, speech and gesture give a more complete insight.' Notice also that the gesture is produced at exactly the same time as the speech. It is not that the speaker says the words and then decides to illustrate it with a gesture; the two forms of communication are generated simultaneously by the human brain. Also notice that there is no problem in generating the speech; it is not the case that the speaker is trying to compensate for some defect in the linguistic communication.

What is interesting about this iconic gesture is that not only does it reveal the speaker's mental image about the event in question, but it also reveals the particular point of view that he has taken towards it. The speaker had the choice of depicting the event from the viewpoint of the agent (the person doing the bending) or of the tree itself. In performing this particular gesture, the speaker was clearly 'seeing' the event from the viewpoint of the agent because otherwise, his hand would not have taken the form of a grip. If the speaker had been taking the viewpoint of the tree, the hand would have simply depicted the bend backwards without the grip.

Consider another example of an iconic gesture, also from McNeill (1992: 13):

And she [chases him out again]
   Iconic: hand appears to swing an object through the air.

Again, the speech and gesture refer to the same event and are partially overlapping, but again, the pictures they present are different. The speech conveys the idea of pursuit ('chases') and repetition ('again'), but the speech does not mention what she is chasing him with. The iconic gesture conveys that some form of weapon is being used here because the iconic gesture depicts something being swung through the air. The iconic gesture does not tell us exactly what the object is at this point but we can see quite clearly what kind of object it is. The gesture shows that it is a long object, which can be gripped by a hand, and it is something that can be swung through the air. It is in fact an umbrella. The significant point is that if we were to focus exclusively on the speech, as we do on the telephone, for example, or only on the gesture, then we would have an incomplete picture of the speaker's mental representation of the scene. It is only through a consideration of both forms of communication that we see all of the elements depicted: the agent, the type of action, the repetition of the action, the type of weapon used, and how the weapon was actually being used – swung through the air to frighten the other character.

Below is an example from our own corpus of speech and gestures (Beattie and Shovelton 1999a, 1999b), where we used a similar task to that of McNeill, asking participants to narrate cartoon stories to a listener, without mentioning that the focus of the research was gestures. The advantage of asking people to narrate stories such as cartoons is that we can compare their gesture–speech combinations with what was in the original story to see exactly what was included in their communication and what was left out. Cartoon stories have the additional advantage that depicted in them are a lot of interesting characters doing a wide variety of complex actions.

[she's eating the food]
   Iconic: fingers on left hand are close together, palm is facing body, and thumb is directly behind index finger. Hand moves from waist level towards mouth.

The speech here tells us that the agent is female. It also conveys the nature of the action involved ('eating') and what is being eaten ('the food'), but it does not tell us how this action is being accomplished. There are after all many different ways of eating food. She could be just chewing the food, which is already in her mouth, or using a knife and fork to eat the food from a plate, but she is not. In this cartoon story, she was drawing the food with her left hand up towards her mouth. That is how the action was depicted in the original cartoon and that is how the narrator depicts it in his gesture. The iconic gesture again is critical to communication here because it shows the method of eating – bringing the food to the mouth with the hand. Again, the image depicted was from the point of view of the agent; the hand of the speaker is acting as the hand of the character in the cartoon.

When you consider all of this, it is extraordinary that people have tried to dismiss the movements of the hands and arms which people make when they speak as merely coincidental movements – virtually random flicks and twirls that are merely used for emphasis, merely used to make a point and barely worthy of serious consideration. Alternatively, they are thought of as a relatively minor form of nonverbal communication with a fairly insignificant role in the communication of emotion or interpersonal attitudes. Many psychologists argue that this is the main point of nonverbal communication, and quite inferior to the more obvious forms of nonverbal communication such as bodily posture, facial expression or eye gaze, which are clearly more important in this regard.

But these movements are not insignificant, and they are not merely poor forms of communication about emotion or interpersonal attitudes. They are closely integrated with speech and may provide a unique insight into how speakers are actually thinking.

Let's consider the issue of the integration of speech and gesture in a little more detail. A prototypical iconic gesture involves three phases: first, the preparation phase, where the hand rises from its resting place and moves to the front of the body and away from the speaker in preparation to make the gesture; second, there is the main part of the gesture, the so-called 'stroke' phase where the gesture exhibits its meaning; third, there is the retraction phase where the hand moves back to its rest position. Some gestures, however, have just two phases and some possess just a stroke phase. The example below, from McNeill (1992: 25), shows the preparation and the stroke phase of this gesture:

he grabs a big oak tree and he [bends it way back]
   (1)   (2)

(1) Preparation phase: hand rises from armrest of chair and moves up and forward at eye level, assuming a grip shape at the same time.

(2) Stroke phase: hand appears to pull something backwards and downwards, ending up near the shoulder.

Gestures in their preparation phase anticipate that part of the speech which refers to the same event. Indeed, this observation led another pioneer in the gesture area, Brian Butterworth, now Emeritus Professor of Neuropsychology at the University of London, to suggest that we can actually distinguish iconic gestures that are used alongside speech for intentional effect rather than being used spontaneously by the fact that the preparation phase of intentional gestures does not anticipate the speech in this natural manner. An example he was fond of using was archive footage of Harold Macmillan, former U.K. Prime Minister, who sometimes made iconic gestures when he spoke in his early television broadcasts to suggest, presumably, informality and spontaneity, but these gestures did not display the necessary degree of anticipation of the verbal content. In some research I carried out with Brian Butterworth as a student at Cambridge, we found that the average amount of time that spontaneous gestures precede the noun or verb with which they are most closely associated is in the order of 800 milliseconds (see Beattie 1983). Harold Macmillan's gestures did not show this degree of anticipation, or indeed any degree of anticipation. Consequently, they looked false and almost certainly were false, owing more to Quintilian and work on classic rhetoric than the human mind in spontaneous action.

The anticipation of the verbal content by a spontaneous iconic gesture can be seen in the example below (see Beattie and Aboudan [1994] for related examples). Here the narrator is telling a cartoon story about the exploits of 'Headless Harry,' who goes fishing in a river with a rod but has no luck, so the head decides to frighten the fish out of the water. But the head then falls into the water and has to swim along back to the body. This particular gesture has a preparation phase, a stroke phase, and a retraction phase as follows:

the head starts [swimming] along
(1)   (2)   (3)

(1) Preparation phase: index finger of right hand originally touching temple, hand moves forward with fingers opening, palm facing downwards at level of shoulder.

(2) Stroke phase: right hand indicates the way that the head is swimming in the water, focusing on forward motion with splayed fingers representing the head.

(3) Retraction phase: right hand moves back to temple, to exactly the same start point, index finger straightens up.

The preparation phase of this iconic gesture in which the hand takes on the shape to represent a head swimming was 440 milliseconds in duration. The stroke phase during which the hand shows how the head was swimming along was 240 milliseconds long. The retraction phase during which the hand returns to the original start position was the longest phase at 600 milliseconds. In all, there was just over a second's worth of complex hand movement during which the mind unconsciously portrayed how the head of a ghost propelled itself in a river before returning the hand to exactly the same resting position that it had started from just over a second earlier.

The analysis of the phases of gesture and how they relate to speech demonstrate the close integration of these two channels of communication. They are not separate and they are also not separate in terms of their sequence of development in childhood or in terms of how they break down together with the brain damage that produce a type of speech disorder called aphasia. Iconic gestures develop alongside language when children are learning to talk, with iconic gestures developing at the same time as the early phrases in speech are used. As Susan Goldin-Meadow notes:

> At a time in their development when children are limited in what they can say, there is another avenue of expression open to them, one that can extend the range of ideas they are able to express. In addition to speaking, the child can also gesture (Bates 1976; Bates et al. 1979; Petitto 1988).
>
> (Goldin-Meadow 1999: 118)

Children usually begin gesturing at around ten months of age, using pointing gestures (called 'deictics') whose meaning is given by the context rather than by their precise form – the child may point to an object to draw the adult's attention to it. It is only later that children begin to use iconic gestures, which capture aspects of the form of the object or action and are thus less reliant on specific context to give meaning to the particular gesture. Goldin-Meadow argues that the integration of gesture and speech can be identified in the very earliest stages of linguistic development, that is, at the one-word stage:

> Over time, children become proficient users of their spoken language. At the same time, rather than dropping out of children's communicative repertoires, gesture itself continues to develop and play an important role in communication. Older children frequently use hand gestures as they speak (Jancovic, Devoe and Wiener 1975), gesturing, for example, when asked to narrate a story (McNeill 1992) or when asked to explain their reasoning on a series of problems (Church and Goldin-Meadow 1986).
>
> (Goldin-Meadow 1999: 120–1)

This integration continues until adulthood. When communication starts to break down with the brain damage that produces different types of aphasia, the two channels break down in strikingly similar ways. For example, in Wernicke's aphasia, patients produce fluent speech that has little appropriate semantic content; such individuals are also found to use few iconic gestures. In Broca's aphasia, there is appropriate semantic content but little overall structure or fluency and iconic gestures are preserved.

Iconic gestures are not separate from thinking and speech but part of it. Potentially, they allow us an enormous insight into the way people think because they offer an insight into thinking through a completely different medium from that of language: a medium that is imagistic rather than verbal. Such gestures may indeed offer a window into the human mind and how it represents our thinking about events in the world. It may also tell us, through an analysis of the degree of temporal asynchrony of the gesture and accompanying speech, which utterances are really spontaneous and which are being deliberately sent for effect. Politicians who want to be well prepared in terms of the delivery of their message and in total control at all times, and yet at the same time want to look informal and spontaneous, might like to take note at this point.

The second type of gesture is called a *metaphoric* gesture. These are similar to iconic gestures in that they are essentially pictorial, but the content depicted here is an abstract idea rather than a concrete object or event. In the words of David McNeill: 'The gesture presents an image of the invisible – an image of an abstraction.' McNeill (1992: 14) uses the following example to illustrate the concept of a metaphoric gesture:

It [was a Sylves]ter and Tweety cartoon
  Metaphoric: Hands rise up and offer listener an 'object'.

According to McNeill here the speaker makes the genre of the cartoon, which is an abstract concept, concrete in the form of a gestural image of a bounded object supported in the hands and presented to the listener. In

McNeill's words 'the gesture creates and displays this object and places it into an act of offering.' Borrowing the terminology of the late I. A. Richards (1936) on the nature of metaphor, McNeill argues that the *topic* of the metaphor, the abstract concept that the metaphor is presenting, is the genre of the story (a cartoon) and the *vehicle* of the metaphor, the gestural image, is a bounded, supportable, spatially localisable physical object. The *ground* here, the common ground of meaning on which the vehicle and topic are linked, is that genres of story, meaning and knowledge are like physical containers with physical properties (evidence for this is also found in language itself with expressions such as 'a deep understanding,' 'shallow insight,' 'broad knowledge,' etc.).

David McNeill argues that the method by which gestures convey meaning is fundamentally different to the way language does this. Language acts by segmenting meaning so that an instantaneous thought is divided up into its component parts and strung out through time. Consider the following example from my own corpus, which again derives from someone telling a cartoon story:

> the table can be [raised up towards the ceiling]
> *Iconic: hands are resting on knee; hands move upwards, palms pointing down, forming a large gesture, hands continue moving until the hands reach the area just above shoulder level.*

The single event here is being described both by language and by the accompanying iconic gesture. The speech does this in a linear and segmented fashion, first identifying what is being raised ('the table'), then describing the action ('can be raised up'), and then describing the direction of the action ('towards the ceiling'). The linguist de Saussure (1916) argued that this linear-segmented character of language arises because language is essentially one-dimensional whereas meaning is essentially multidimensional. Language can only vary along the single dimension of time with regard to the units out of which it is comprised. As the psychologist Susan Goldin-Meadow and her colleagues note in 1996: 'This restriction forces language to break meaning complexes into segments and to reconstruct multidimensional meanings by combining the segments in time.' But the gestures that accompany language don't convey meaning in a linear and segmented manner; rather, they can convey a number of aspects of meaning at the same time in a single multidimensional gesture. The gesture above depicts the table (and its size), and the movement (and its speed), and the direction of the movement, all simultaneously. The important point is that, as Goldin-Meadow notes, the iconic gestures which accompany speech 'are themselves free to vary on dimensions of space, time, form, trajectory, and so forth and can present meaning complexes without undergoing segmentation or linearization.'

According to David McNeill (1992), gestures are also different from speech in terms of how they convey meaning. Speech relies on 'bottom-up' processing, in that the meanings of the words are combined to create the meaning of the sentence. To understand a sentence, you have to start with the lower-level words (hence 'bottom-up'), whereas in gestures, we start with the overall concept portrayed by the gesture. It is this concept which gives rise to the meaning of the individual parts (hence 'top-down'). McNeill provides the following example:

> The gesture is a symbol in that it represents something other than itself – the hand is not a hand but a character, the movement is not a hand in motion but the character in motion, the space is not the physical space of the narrator but a narrative space, the wiggling fingers are not fingers but running feet. The gesture is thus a symbol, but the symbol is of a fundamentally different type from the symbols of speech. This gesture–symbol is global in that the whole is not composed out of separately meaningful parts. Rather, the parts gain meaning because of the meaning of the whole. The wiggling fingers mean running only because we know that the gesture, as a whole, depicts someone running.
>
> (McNeill 1992: 20)

The important point to remember here is that when produced by this same speaker, this wiggling finger gesture may well have a different meaning (McNeill points out, for example, that it was also used for 'indecision between two alternatives'). In order to argue that gestures are processed like language in a bottom-up fashion, you would need to be able to demonstrate that the three components which comprise the running gesture – the V hand shape, the wiggling motion, and the forward movement – have relatively stable meanings in the person's communicational repertoire, which can be recognised and interpreted wherever they are used. But this is not the case.

Another important difference between speech and gesture is that different gestures do not combine together to form more complex gestures:

> With gestures, each symbol is a complete expression of meaning unto itself. Most of the time gestures are one to a clause but occasionally more than one gesture occurs within a single clause. Even then the several gestures don't combine into a more complex gesture. Each gesture depicts the content from a different angle, bringing out a different aspect or temporal phase, and each is a complete expression of meaning by itself.
>
> (McNeill 1992: 21)

Gestures also convey meaning in a different way because there are no standards of form with gestures. Standards of form are a defining feature of all languages. All linguistic systems have standards of well-formedness to which all utterances that fall within it must conform, or be dismissed as not proper or not grammatical. Gestures have no such standards of form. Thus, different speakers display the same meaning in idiosyncratic but nevertheless recognisable ways. As McNeill (1992: 41) says:

> Lacking standards of form, individuals create their own gesture symbols for the same event, each incorporating a core meaning but adding details that seem salient, and these are different from speaker to speaker.' This non-standardization of form is very important for theoretical reasons: 'Precisely because gestures are not obliged to meet standards of form, they are free to present just those aspects of meaning that are relevant and salient to the speaker and leave out aspects that language may require but are not relevant to the situation'
>
> (McNeill 1992: 22)

Therefore, iconic gestures and speech convey meaning in radically different ways, with speech relying on a lexicon for breaking meaning down into its component parts and a syntax for combining these various elements into meaningful sentences, whereas iconic gestures represent multidimensional meanings simultaneously in one complex image. Each speaker creates the iconic gestures spontaneously without relying on a lexicon with defined standards of form, and even consecutive iconic gestures do not combine into higher-order units. Each gesture is complete in itself, and the overall meaning of what is being portrayed gives the meaning to the individual components. It is also important to emphasise that the meaning in the gesture may, on occasion, never be represented in the speech itself and thus may carry powerful new information about what the speaker is thinking.

The hands that operate alongside speech, therefore, are likely to be particularly interesting in lying for one very important reason, namely they will be very hard to fake. I want to argue that it is very difficult to deliberately fake the form of iconic gestures when you are lying firstly because of the essentially non-conscious nature of gestural communication and secondly because of the complex division of meaning between the two channels of communication, speech, and gesture. It would be very complicated to split meaning into the verbal and gestural channels in a way that might look natural or normal. You would have to get the division of meaning between the two channels just right, as well as the precise iconic form of the gesture and the right degree of anticipation of the associated part of the verbal message by the preparation phase of the gesture. It is interesting that the evidence, as we have already seen, suggests that people do not attempt this when they are lying, opting instead for an easier strategy. Generally speaking, people inhibit their hand movements when they are lying, and consequently gesture frequency decreases in deception.

Below is an interesting case of gestural inhibition recorded in 2005 in the United Kingdom (Beattie 2016a). The speaker is the then Prime Minister, Tony Blair, meeting a group of young mothers in the run up to the General

Election in 2005. This was a core demographic that he was attempting to appeal to. The child on his knee belongs to one of the young mothers. He gestures throughout the conversation except when he says that looking after his children when his wife Cherie was at work was 'It's the toughest thing you ever do.' It is only during this particular utterance that the gestures are inhibited. Given that Tony Blair had invaded Iraq, revised the constitution of the Labour Party in the face of considerable opposition, abandoned the socialist traditions of his Party, won three General Elections etc., looking after the kids for the day might not have actually been 'the toughest thing' he ever had to do. However, I am sure that the sentiment worked very well with his particular audience that day. Gestural inhibition, however, seems to have occurred largely unnoticed (Figure 6.1).

I was completely wiped out

It's the toughest thing you ever do

It's almost as if it's what you've got to do and I think

Figure 6.1 Tony Blair's gestural inhibition.

It would seem a reasonable hypothesis that if the hands are not prevented from gesturing in this way, then the precise form of the gesture, which until recently had not been considered in any great detail in the research on deception, could potentially be highly revealing when people are lying. I have a number of specific examples here to support this idea. The first example comes from a meeting at a public relations company that I attended where one of the executives was talking about the sales of a particular product after their campaign had finished. She said:

> the sales after that campaign [started to soar]
> *Iconic: right hand makes upward trajectory but falls fractionally at the top most part of the trajectory. The slight fall depicted in the gesture corresponding to the word 'soar'.*

The iconic gesture seemed to contradict what she was saying in her speech. I actually interrupted the meeting at this point to query whether sales had indeed soared as she had said or had declined, as I guessed. She hesitated, slightly embarrassed, and admitted that I was in fact correct. Sales had declined immediately after the campaign, 'but they picked up again' she added defensively. I was 'praised,' if that is the right word, for my perceptiveness.

Here is another anecdotal example. A female friend was telling me about her experiences at a party where a close friend's boyfriend had kissed her. Here is what she said:

> and he [kissed me] on the cheek
> *Iconic: fingers of right hand outstretched and close together, thumb curled in towards palm. Hand moves towards mouth and fingertips touch right-hand side of lips.*

Since the person who kissed her was the boyfriend of a very close friend, she did not want to admit that this kiss was in any way intimate. The speech was under strict editorial control; she said exactly what she intended to. The iconic gesture was under much less strict editorial control and indicated the *relative position* of both sets of lips. This was not a kiss on the cheek, no matter what she said. I queried this and she looked astonished to be challenged in this way. 'You weren't there,' she said. 'How do you know?' I pointed out her gesture to her and she said that she did not even realise that she had made a gesture in the first place.

The hypothesis that the precise form of iconic gestures may change when people are trying to deceive formed the basis for a preliminary study in this area. In this experiment, participants were shown a number of cartoons with particular events depicted in them. They had to narrate the story. Then, they had to narrate the story, which was still projected onto a screen in front of them, for a second time. This time, they had to change some of the critical details and attempt to persuade another person that these changed details were actually part of the real story. For example, in one picture, a boy was dribbling a football around an opponent in a circle. In the second, telling the narrator had to recount the story, changing certain critical details, like the fact that the footballer was dribbling the ball around the other player, but doing so in the shape of a square. This was an attempt to mimic some of the cognitive aspects of lying. Reasonably good liars are often found to base their false accounts partly on things that have actually happened to them, while changing certain core details, rather than making up a completely false account from scratch. As Samuel Butler said: 'The best liar is he who makes the smallest amount of lying go the longest way.' The question was whether the form of the iconic gestures would give some hint as to the real nature of the events at these critical points in the story.

In a simple task like this, our participants found it relatively easily to change the details in their speech. The form of their gestures was, however, a different matter. Thus, one participant narrating the story about the boy dribbling the football said:

and he runs around him [in a square]
Iconic: right hand in space in front of body, index finger straight, other fingers curled, makes a series of anti-clockwise circular movements.

The iconic gesture here still depicted the original 'true' circular movement of the boy and the ball, rather than the changed 'false' version. In other words, the truth seeped through. This is exactly what Ekman and Friesen called 'non-verbal leakage' in their classic paper back in 1969.

Simple *stress-timed* beats would, in all probability, be a good deal simpler to fake than iconic gestures. Indeed, there seems to exist good (and well-viewed) documentary evidence that would attest to this very fact. When Bill Clinton was accused of having sex with Monica Lewinsky, his protestations had quite a number of beats contained within them. Thus:

BILL CLINTON: I did [not have sexual relations] with that woman, Miss Lewinsky.
Beat: index finger of right hand pointing away from body, other fingers curled up. Hand makes four sharp, rapid downwards movements. Each downward movement begins at the start of each of the four words accompanied by the gesture.

BILL CLINTON: The allegations (audible swallow) are false (audible swallow)
Beat: fingers on the right hand are straight and apart; hand is positioned vertically to the body. Hand moves downwards twice – first time on the word 'allegations' and second time on the words 'are false'.

However, there is an important point to make here. Clinton always seemed very determined to use quite a precise language in defending himself during these accusations of sexual misconduct. At the Senate Hearings, Clinton was asked a series of quite specific questions about his sexual relationship with Monica Lewinsky. The written statement he had provided was that 'These meetings did not consist of sexual intercourse.' He was then asked a series of highly embarrassing, more detailed questions including: 'If Miss Lewinsky says that while you were in the Oval Office area you touched her genitalia would she be lying? That calls for a "yes", "no", or "revert to your former statement".' President Clinton replied: 'I will revert to my statement on that.' He was quite determined to stick to a certain form of words.

During his verbal answers, there were quite a few beats actually displayed. So does this mean that he was lying or telling the truth? What he actually said in the Senate Hearings and in a number of interviews at the time is very important here because the words he uses habitually are 'sexual relations' or 'sexual intercourse.' It has since been pointed out to me that there is a saying in the Southern States of the United States that 'eatin' ain't cheatin'.' In other words, oral sex does not constitute 'sexual relations.' If Clinton had managed to persuade himself of the truth of this proposition, then it would allow for the presence of the beats in his speech as an index of truth because he only engaged in oral sex with Miss Lewinsky and not actual sexual intercourse. He might have been using beats in his speech because strictly speaking, in his mind at least, he was actually telling the truth.

Alternatively, of course, it could be that Clinton was a well-rehearsed liar who had become an expert in the control of most aspects of his body language, except the odd micro-expression in his face and the odd swallow that did slip out rather noticeably on occasion, and that he included the easy to fake beats rather than the more difficult to fake iconic gestures in his speech for effect.

However, could nonverbal leakage in gestural movements be demonstrated more systematically than in the observations described so far? This formed the basis for a study we conducted a number of years ago (see Beattie 2016a). We wanted to control for a number of things including the mental effort in telling lies (the so-called 'cognitive load'), so we simply *instructed* participants to narrate a story from a comic book both truthfully and deceptively (the order of which were fully counterbalanced) to a confederate. I know what I've said about the artificiality of instructing participants to lie throughout this book, but this experimental study was a first in this area. It needs to be followed up with research on spontaneous lies! In the deception condition, the participants were told that three of the critical details in the story had to be changed, and they were given explicit instructions on how to change them, in an attempt to simulate the cognitive operations that occur during premeditated deception. Although the implemented changes represent relatively minor modifications, they had been selected to incorporate and build on events depicted in the truthful version of the comic strip, as this simulates much that happens in real-life deception. Furthermore, the modifications were chosen for their potential to elicit a range of spontaneous iconic gestures, as they were largely action-based.

Participants were also provided with as much time as they required to learn the modifications to the three changed details and a projector continually displayed the cartoon story on a wall in front of them (in an attempt to mini-mise the cognitive demands placed on the participants).

The study was designed to test a number of basic experimental hypotheses. Firstly, we assumed that in line with previous research, there would be a sig-nificant decrease in the relative frequency of iconic hand gestures when partici-pants were lying versus when they were telling the truth, although we wanted to analyse how broad or narrow any such behavioural inhibition might be. Secondly, following the argument that speakers will probably generate fewer hand movements when lying, because they are (unconsciously) anxious that the form of the gesture may betray them, we predicted that those gestures that do occur during deception will have significantly shorter durations than those produced during truth-telling. Finally, we predicted that any gesture produced in the deception condition, which in its form appears to contradict the ver-bal content, will contain semantic information from the real viewed stimulus, which would constitute evidence of nonverbal leakage.

Our stimulus material consisted of a static cartoon story – (Ivy the Ter-rible comic taken from the Beano). Each of our thirty participants were indi-vidually invited into an observation room and informed that they were taking part in an experiment which investigated 'how well people tell truths and lies in order to further our understanding of how the brain processes and copes with misinformation and deceit.' All the participants were instructed to nar-rate the comic story both honestly and deceptively, with the order of lying versus truth-telling being fully counterbalanced throughout (Cohen, Beattie and Shovelton 2010).

So as not to interfere with their gesture production rate, the comic story was projected onto a wall directly in front of the participants. This ensured that the participants' hands were free to move naturally. In order to obtain as natural a sample of behaviour as possible, participants were filmed by an unobtrusive video camera. In the truthful condition, the participants were simply instructed to narrate the story in their own words 'as clearly and in as much detail as possible' to the experimenter. At the outset of the decep-tion condition, the participants were informed that three critical details of the comic had to be changed and that once these changes had been implemented, they would have to recount the altered version to another participant who had never seen the comic before. In addition, they were told that at the end of the experiment, the participant would have to guess whether or not they were telling the truth or lying, and consequently that they should try to be 'as convincing as possible.' In reality, the participant who was brought into the room during the deception condition was a confederate of the experimenter. The presence of the stooge served as a motivational cue for the 'real' partici-pants, designed both to encourage them to make a conscious attempt to lie effectively, and to validate the non-truth which they were about to tell (e.g., by providing them with an opportunity to purposefully communicate informa-tion which they knew to be false to another individual).

As an additional motivation, all participants were told that if they managed to convince the second participant (i.e., the stooge) that they were telling the truth, they would be rewarded (hardly much by way of stake!). In any event, at the end of the experiment, all participants (irrespective of lying ability) were given a chocolate bar. In order to prevent the stooge from biasing the participants' behaviour in any way, care was taken to ensure that she had restricted verbal interaction with the participants. Therefore, she occupied a passive role, engaging only in formal greetings when entering or leaving the room (e.g. hello and goodbye).

Three elements of the story had to be changed in the deception condition. The third frame of the comic clearly depicted Ivy, the central character in the story pushing the DJ into the boot of the car, whilst her speech revealed her intention to 'lock him in' [it]. In the deception condition, the participants were instructed to lie by claiming that Ivy locks the DJ in the back of the car, by pushing him through the side-door, not the boot. In the seventh frame of the comic, Ivy was shown pouring the contents of a bottle of extra-strong washing up liquid into a bubble machine in an attempt to produce more bubbles. The participants in the deception condition were told to say that she accidentally spills some of the washing up liquid onto the floor, making a horrible and sticky mess. In the final (eleventh) frame of the comic, bubbles were shown emerging from Ivy's mouth. In the deception condition, the participants were told to say that the bubbles came out of her ears.

As there is evidence that producing bodily actions can result in interlocutors increasing their bodily movements accordingly, especially in the context of lie detection (see Akehurst and Vrij 1999), the experimenter did not 'act out' the changes (i.e., did not gesture himself) when describing them to the participant. Instead, the changes were read off a standardised script. After the three changes had been explained, participants were asked to confirm whether they had fully understood them and could remember those parts of the comic that required modification. Once the participants were satisfied that they could accurately perform the task, the stooge who was always waiting directly outside the door of the observation room, was let in by the experimenter. The stooge sat with her back to the projector at all times, and so could not see the comic, which was still projected onto the wall. If the participants did not start to describe the comic spontaneously after the stooge sat down, they were prompted to do so. At the end of their narratives, the stooge always left the room independently and the participants were either thanked for their participation and de-briefed, or if the deception condition came first in the order of counterbalancing were taken straight into the truthful condition, after which time they were de-briefed.

Seventeen of the thirty participants produced spontaneous iconic gestures. This resulted in a total of thirty-four narratives (seventeen speakers times two conditions – truth versus deception). Although iconic gestures are according to McNeill 'typically large complex movements, performed relatively slowly and carefully in the central gesture space' (1985: 359), it is important to point out that occasionally gestures were coded as iconic which were either small or fast, or which operated outside of the central gesture space, but which were nevertheless still in possession of iconic properties. In total, 351 iconic gestures were recorded and analysed. Of the 351 iconic hand movements that were identified across the seventeen narratives, 169 were produced in the truthful condition and 182 in the deception condition. When the data is considered on a subject-by-subject basis, it was clear that there was considerable variation in gesture frequency by participants with no significant overall trend. In other words, gestural frequency in the story *as a whole* was not affected.

However, what about the relative frequency of iconic gestures exclusively in relation to the three *specific* lies? In order for a gesture to be entered into this analysis, it had to satisfy a number of inclusion criteria. Firstly, only gestures that encoded aspects of the three modified details were considered as they each had to represent a *complete* lie. Recall that with reference to the first semantic event participants, depending on condition, would either have to describe a scene in which Ivy locks the DJ in the *boot* of his car (truthful version), or else claim that she locked him in the car, using the *side-door* (deception version). In order to be included in the analysis, participants would have to execute a gesture that depicted Ivy pushing the DJ and *explicitly* state in the verbal dimension of the corresponding clause that he entered the car through either the boot or the side-door respectively. Alternatively, the morphological structure of the gesture would need to discriminate between the act of closing a boot and that of shutting the door of a vehicle. Consider the example below (Figure 6.2), in which a speaker is describing the first critical detail in the deception condition:

so she [locks him in the car]
    Iconic: Both hands rise slightly, palms facing each other and away from speaker, while arms are bent at elbows. During stroke phase elbows rotate slightly and extend forwards pushing out into the gesture space. Palms momentarily flick outwards, before returning to rest.

Here the gesture provides insufficient information to be entered into the analysis, as Ivy pushes the DJ into the car in *both* conditions, and the gesture only signals that an agent is pushing some object, but fails to disambiguate between the two competing possibilities (boot versus side-door). Interestingly, despite an identical clause structure, the form of the gesture in the next example (Figure 6.3) explicitly reveals that the DJ has been locked in the *boot* of the car, and therefore would be coded as a 'truthful gesture.'

so Ivy locks [him in the car]
    Iconic: Right hand rises to above eye-level, palm faces away from speaker and is perpendicular. Entire right hand then descends rapidly, consistent with the act of shutting a boot, using a single hand. Left hand is locked in a post-hold pause from previous gesture.

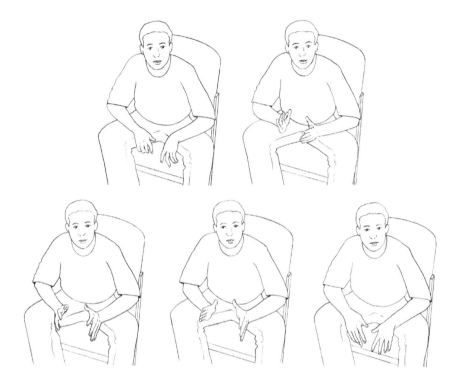

Figure 6.2 A gesture depicting the DJ being locked in the car (deception condition).

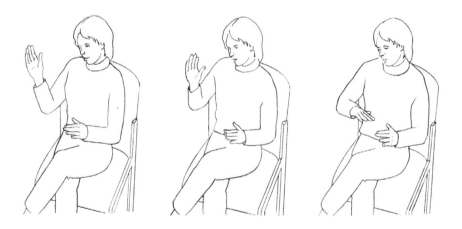

Figure 6.3 A gesture depicting Ivy locking the DJ in the car (truthful condition).

In relation to the second critical change, participants were required either to reference the scene in which Ivy pours washing-up liquid into the bubble machine (truthful version), or to fabricate the event by claiming that Ivy accidentally spills some of the solution making a 'horrible sticky mess' (deception version). Very occasionally, however, participants' descriptions (2/17 speakers) of this event went beyond these instructions, and consequently were not included in the second analysis, even if they did consist of a complete falsification. For instance, one participant produced the following utterance: 'so she gets the bubble mix...mixture and pours it in. Erm but...but there is a ...I think a **[banana skin]** on the floor...and she slips and... anyway it **[spills everywhere making a sticky mess]**.' Here, only the second hand movement was coded as being a 'deception gesture,' as the first gesture represents a confabulation which the participants were not instructed to produce. To incorporate this gesture in the analysis precludes the possibility of making a direct comparison between the truthful and deception narratives, and this lack of equivalence between conditions would bias the data towards an over-estimation of gesture frequency in the deception condition.

The final modified detail required participants to reference a scene in which bubbles contained in some sandwiches that Ivy has unwittingly eaten previously, exit her body through either her mouth (truthful version) or her ears (deception version). One difficulty encountered with this event is that a small number of narrators (3/17) in the truthful condition did not specifically state that bubbles came '*out of* Ivy's mouth,' but rather that the bubbles had contaminated the sandwiches and so they did not 'taste nice.' Again, in order not to violate the equivalence principle, gestures were only included in the second analysis if the participant described the target frame of the comic in speech (e.g., by saying bubbles 'come out of Ivy's mouth'), so that it could be matched across both truthful and deception descriptions. Finally, it should also be noted that in line with McNeill's non-combinatoric approach, participants could be awarded more than one gesture per modified detail. For instance, if a participant produced the following utterance: 'So she **[pushes him into the boot]**, and **[slams it shut]**,' both hand movements would be coded as forming *two* independent gestures that represented the truthful properties of a *single* semantic event.

Out of the 351 iconic gestures that were identified throughout the study, a total of 65 gestures were directly associated with the 3 critical details. Of these 65 gestures, 63.1% occurred in the truthful condition, and 36.9%, in the deception condition. The majority of participants (76.5%) produced *fewer* iconic gestures in the deception than in the truthful condition. The mean gesture rate focusing on just those three critical details revealed that, on average, participants produced nearly twice as many iconic gestures in the truthful condition (2.5) than in the deception (1.4). The level of between-subjects variability across the truthful and deception conditions was comparable. In line with the original predictions, statistical analyses revealed that participants produced significantly more iconic hand gestures when truthfully describing the three critical details, than when recounting the events deceptively. A second gesture-to-word ratio was calculated to account for the unequal word length across conditions. When the gesture-to-word ratio was taken into consideration, the relative frequency of gestures between the conditions remained significant.

The next analysis compared the duration of those gestures that encoded aspects of the three modified details of the story during both truth-telling and deception. However, six of the participants only gestured in one condition and consequently were removed from the analysis, because they were unable to contribute to a direct comparison of gesture duration across conditions. As a result, only fifty-three of the original sixty-five gestures were included in the present analysis (of which thirty-one were executed in the truthful condition, whilst the remaining twenty-two occurred in the deception condition). The duration of each of the fifty-three gesture units (i.e., the *entire* gestures) were individually timed and broken down into their constituent phases. By definition, this included the stroke phase of each gesture, as well as any preparation, pre-stroke, post-stroke, or retraction phases. Occasionally, gestures were coded as having a preparation phase when the hand appeared to be returning to a period of rest, but immediately *before* arriving at the rest position suddenly rose in anticipation of a new stroke phase.

Before presenting the timing data, it is useful at this juncture to consider the *relative frequency* of the different gesture phases for each of the fifty-three target gestures. Whilst most of the fifty-three gestures had both a preparation (94.3%) and a retraction phase (67.9%), the incidence of pre- and post-stroke holds were comparatively small, occurring in 9.4% and 30.2% of cases, respectively. Whilst the relative proportion of preparation, pre-stroke holds and retraction phases were comparable across the conditions (preparation: 96.8% versus 90.9%; pre-stroke hold: 9.7% versus 9.1%; retraction: 67.7% versus 68.2%), post-stoke holds were more than twice as likely to occur in the truthful than in the deception condition (38.7% versus 18.2%). In total, sixteen post-stroke holds were identified across the fifty-three gestures, of which twelve occurred in the truthful condition and four were observed in the deception condition. Ostensibly then the data suggests that liars systematically avoid producing gestures with post-stroke holds. What is particularly interesting here is that the preparation, pre-stroke, and retraction phases can to some extent be considered 'auxiliary' components of the gesture unit, which at best make only a very limited semantic contribution to the speaker's message. Conversely, in both its form and manner of presentation, the post-stroke hold is likely to encode a good deal about the target semantic event. Liars may well avoid producing them as they have the potential to index information that is incompatible with the accompanying speech. Moreover, there is some evidence that post-stroke holds lead to decoder fixation (Gullberg and Holmqvist 2002: 209). Again, consistent with the basic hypothesis is the idea that liars attempt to suppress the frequency of post-stroke holds, because this might well direct listener attention to their gestures, and increase the probability that their deception will be detected. We found that participants were significantly less likely to produce gestures with post-stroke holds when telling the truth, than when lying.

In terms of the duration of the gestures across conditions, we found that the duration of the stroke phases of the gestures were on average 458.2 milliseconds longer when they occurred in the truthful rather than in the deception condition, whilst post-stroke holds were 775.0 milliseconds longer when executed in the truthful condition than during deception. There were no significant differences in the duration of the preparation or retraction phases across conditions was observed. In contrast, it was found that participants produced significantly longer stroke phases when telling the truth than when lying.

Finally, was there any evidence of gesture and speech mismatches in the deception condition. We found three participants' gestures in the deception condition, which in their form appeared to transmit semantic information that was incompatible with the information encoded in the linguistic channel. These participants' iconic gestures seemed to disclose properties of the truthful version of the event, whilst their speech conveyed the non-truths that they had been instructed to communicate to the stooge. Critically, no mismatches between speech and gesture were obtained in the truthful condition.

Consider the following example (Figure 6.4) in which the participant event that Ivy locks the DJ into the back of the car using the side door:

She like pushes the DJ into the side door of the car and like [slams it shut]

Iconic: Left hand is at about shoulder level, with the palm facing outward, away from speaker, fingers outstretched. Suddenly, hand descends rapidly so that the palm faces towards ground.

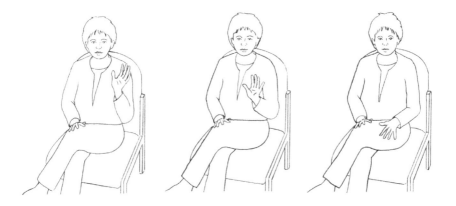

Figure 6.4 Gesture depicting Ivy pushing the DJ into the car and slamming the car door shut (deception condition).

What is interesting about this example is that whilst the speaker claims that the DJ was pushed into the car using the side-door, her iconic gesture reveals that she has accurately retained a truthful mental representation of the event depicted in the comic, in which Ivy pushed the DJ into the *boot* of the car (*hand descends rapidly*). This is very similar to their 'equivalent' gesture in the truthful condition (i.e., when describing the slamming shut of the boot; see example in Figure 6.5 below).

So Ivy like [slams him into the boot of his car]
    Iconic: Left hand is slightly below shoulder level, palm faces away from speaker, fingers outstretched. Hand descends rapidly, until the palm faces towards ground. Right hand is static, and appears to be in a post-hold lock.

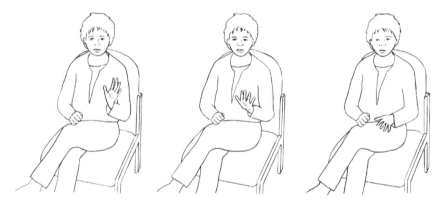

Figure 6.5 Gesture depicting Ivy pushing the DJ into the car and slamming the boot shut (truthful condition).

In both its *form* and *manner of execution*, the gesture that the participant produced when truthfully describing the shutting of the DJ into the boot (Figure 6.5) was almost identical to the gesture she exhibited when falsely describing the locking of the DJ into the side of the car (Figure 6.4). This provides compelling support not only for the idea that the *same* truthful idea was dominant in the speaker's mind during the production of both utterances, but critically that the underlying truthful properties of the event unwittingly found expression through 'gestural leakage.' Furthermore, the gesture made by this participant when describing the opening of the side-door is *markedly different* from those hand movements executed by other participants who gestured on this changed detail. Presented below (Figure 6.6) is a participant's gesture (in the deception condition) made by

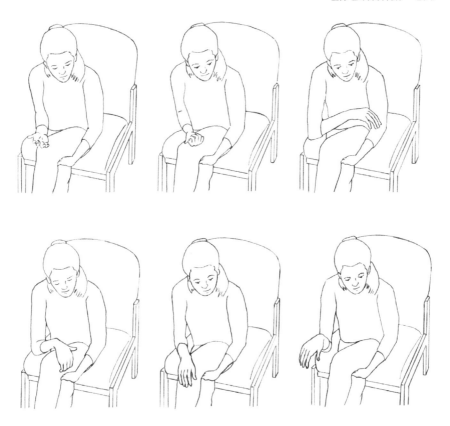

Figure 6.6 Gesture depicting slamming the car door shut (deception condition).

some participants when describing the opening of the side-door. Here there is no gesture-speech mismatch.

shoves him through the [side door and like slams it shut]
    Iconic: Right hand appears to grip a handle (e.g., of a door). Entire arm rapidly swings sideways (from right to left). Action appears consistent with opening a car-door.

No gesture-speech mismatches occurred with the second modified detail of the comic. Nevertheless, two participants demonstrated gesture-speech mismatches in relation to the final changed detail, in which they had to falsely claim that bubbles were coming out of Ivy's ears, as opposed to her mouth. Given their similarity, both gestures are presented together (Figures 6.7 and 6.8):

<u>so then [bubbles start coming out of her ears]</u>

  Iconic: Both hands briefly hover less than an inch from the speaker's mouth. Fingers point inwards towards mouth. Hands then start to move away from each other, and seem to encode the motion-path of the bubbles (i.e., by capturing the idea of dispersion through space). Crucially, the gesture does not occur level with the ears.

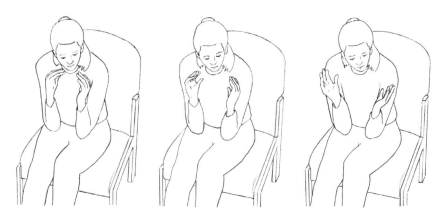

Figure 6.7 Gesture depicting bubbles coming out of Ivy's ears (deception condition).

<u>so in the end all the bubbles [were coming out of her ears]</u>

  Iconic: Right hand rises to immediately below mouth, fingers curled slightly. Fingers begin to uncurl and straighten, before entire hand flicks forward into the gesture space. Again, the gesture occurs close to the speaker's mouth, but away from the ears.

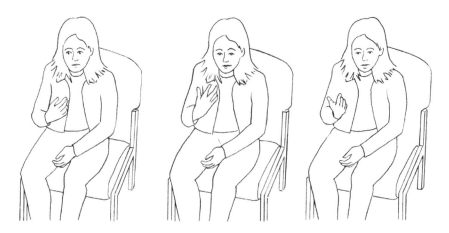

Figure 6.8 Gesture depicting bubbles coming out of Ivy's ears (deception condition).

Once again, it is clear that there is a discrepancy between the participants' speech (*'coming out of her ears'*) and the semantic information communicated by the accompanying iconic gestures (*hands briefly hover less than an inch from the speaker' mouth; Right hand rises to immediately below mouth*). Although subtle differences in gesture morphology were observed for the above speakers across conditions when describing the final frame of the comic, both the truthful and deception gestures *consistently* occurred near to the speakers' mouths. Conversely, an inter-gestural review of the remaining participants who gestured on this event revealed *systematic* differences in where they *located* the gesture by condition. More specifically, when describing the final frame of the comic, the remaining narrators tended to execute their gestures next to the mouth in the truthful condition, or next to the ears in the deception condition.

There were a number of potentially important conclusions from this study. The first finding was that gestures were not inhibited throughout the narratives as a whole, rather the inhibition was more selective than that, operating around the critical changed details. Secondly, gesture stroke duration was significantly shorter in the deception condition, and less likely to include post-stroke holds in the specific lies in the narratives. This provides some experimental support for the central proposition (starting with Darwin 1872) that certain behaviours are 'suppressed by the will' because they 'do not want to risk giving the game away through revealing hand movements' (Beattie 2003: 168). In suppressing the gestural side of communication, speakers subconsciously select a strategy that will reduce the probability that the form of the gesture will signal possible deceit. Ekman (1985, 2003) has argued that liars pay less attention to their body during deception than to their voice, because 'they know that they will be held more accountable for their words than for the sound of their voice, facial expressions or most body movements' (1985/2001: 81). Of course, the hands occupy an unusual status in relation to the human body. After all, because hand gestures are often perceptible in a speaker's visual field, it seems likely that people are at least *partially* aware that these movements perform some function, even though they are almost certainly unaware of precisely what the function is. In turn, this lack of insight into what the hands are doing, together with a peripheral consciousness that they do *something*, might well be the underlying mechanism which makes people anxious that the form of the gesture could potentially reveal information that they are actively attempting to conceal, leading to gesture reduction during deception.

However, why did three speakers produce mismatching gesture–speech compounds, whilst the remaining participants did not? Of course, it is always difficult to resolve individual differences across speakers, especially in the domain of gesture. As Kendon points out '[q]uestions about how gesture usage might vary systematically by age, sex, setting, discourse circumstance and the like, although of great interest and importance, have not been explored' (2004: 110). A detailed re-examination of the data focusing in particular on potential inconsistencies in the performance of the three participants who produced gesture–speech mismatches with the pattern produced by the remaining participants leads to a number of surprising results. Whilst the mean gesture production rate in the deception condition was 1.4, the three participants who produced contradictory iconic gestures had the *highest* gesture rate during deception (with an overall mean gesture rate of 3.7). In other words, when lying, these three participants have a combined gesture rate which is more than two and a half times higher than the mean gesture rate during deception. Of the three speakers who made contradictory gestures, one made the same number of gestures in both conditions (four gestures in each), while the remaining two participants showed a modest reduction in their gesture frequency when lying (both producing four gestures in the truthful and three in the deception conditions). Conversely, almost all of the remaining participants (11/14) reduced their gesture frequency by *at least half* in the deception than the truthful condition.

Additionally, we discovered that both of the participants who made gestures with *longer* stroke phases in the deception condition, and one of the participants who showed little differences across conditions were in fact the *same* speakers who produced the gesture–speech mismatches. It seems therefore that these participants in particular may have only a very limited awareness of their gestural behaviour. Whereas most participants reduced the frequency and duration of their gestures accordingly, these three speakers did not modify their behaviour. By failing to adopt a strategy of inhibition or suppression, these participants appear to have placed themselves 'at risk' of being caught, and indeed went on to generate gesture–speech mismatches. Perhaps these speakers' apparent inability to regulate and constrain their gestural behaviour during deception is the principal factor mediating whether or not they manifest mismatches between speech and gesture.

Overall, then, this study not only corroborates previous research findings regarding the frequency of gestures during the critical phases of deception, but also demonstrates that occasionally gestural morphology may preserve the underlying truthful properties of an event, even when the speaker's verbal output is able to effectively deliver a lie. Studies investigating bodily action during deception should therefore begin to work towards a fuller recognition of, and capitalise on the unique placement of iconic hand movements as an integral component of the linguistic system *per se* (see McNeill 1992). Hand movement and gesture may be much more revealing when it comes to lies and deceit, than even Darwin recognised nearly one hundred and fifty years ago, but critically, it is the relationship with speech that may be crucial. An analysis of *multimodal communication* could potentially be highly illuminating going forward. The connections between the channels of communication might hold the key. But, of course, these are just laboratory lies (which I have criticised throughout this book). We now have to go into the world beyond the laboratory to see how illuminating. The truth, as they say, is out there.

But this research (like most research) must also come with a specific health warning. We cannot conclude that a *single* instance of a gestural slip or a slip of the tongue conclusively demonstrates a lie. That would be folly but one that does occur! We saw this in 2023 with a slip that Joe Biden made. I was asked by *The Conversation* to explain why the world had gone into meltdown over his 'Freudian slip' when he inadvertently said 'Black and Tans' instead of 'All Blacks' when he was visiting Ireland. What did this reveal about his real underlying attitude to Great Britain? Was he repeatedly lying when he said that he was a great friend and supporter of the United Kingdom? Was he anti-British? Was he, in fact, an Irish Republican? This was in danger of causing an international incident with denials having to be issued by the White House. This was my take on this (Beattie 2023b), but there is also a general point. Until we study lies more naturalistically and analyse human communication in terms of multimodality, we should all be cautious about our great abilities as detectors of lies in any domain.

Joe Biden's Freudian Slip?

Joe Biden is proud of his Irish heritage and they say that he has 'the gift of the gaffe,' given how many slips of the tongue he makes (and has been making long before he became president). In various speeches, he has confused presidents Trump and Obama. He also referred to Vice President Kamala Harris as 'the first lady.'

Biden visited Ireland in March 2023. It was, of course, headlines across the world. It was an emotional homecoming for a president fiercely proud of his Irish roots. After a very brief visit to Belfast (and many commented on the brevity and suggested that this told us something about his real attitude to the North of Ireland, the Unionists, and the United Kingdom), he moved onto Dundalk in County Louth where one strand of his family comes from. Home at last and highly emotional – 'I don't know why the hell my ancestors left here. It's beautiful,' he said.

He was giving a speech in a packed Windsor Pub in Dundalk and started to thank his distant cousin Rob Kearney for the shamrock tie he was wearing. Rob had played for Ireland against the All Blacks in Soldier Field in Chicago in 2016. But President Biden's words did not quite come out planned. He said: 'This was given to me by one of these guys, right here.

He was a hell of a rugby player and he beat the hell out of the Black and Tans.' If you get the chance to watch it on YouTube, notice the fist pump just after he says it. This might demonstrate his strong emotional engagement with what psychologists might describe as a repressed message.

He had meant to say 'All Blacks,' of course, instead of 'Black and Tans,' the name of the infamous and brutal British militia used against the Nationalists in the 1920s – this group feared and despised in equal measure. The media pounced on it. There was the danger that a personal lapse could cause a major political storm. The White House had to issue a press statement reiterating that 'President Biden is not anti-British' and that it was 'very clear' what the president was referring to. The slip was 'corrected' to 'All Blacks' in the official White House transcript of the speech.

But was there any deeper significance in the fact that he had substituted 'Black and Tans' for 'All Blacks.' Was this a genuine Freudian slip, where the unconscious somehow leaks into speech, and if so, what does it reveal about his unconscious thinking? Was there a repressed desire to 'beat the hell out of the Black and Tans,' and all other instruments of the cold-hearted and brutal British state?

Joe Biden would after all know all about the Black and Tans. One of the best-known and most stirring Irish Republican songs is Dominic Behan's 'Come out Ye Black and Tans' ('the loving English feet they walked all over us...Come out ye Black and Tans, come out and fight me like a man!'). This particular hatred runs deep in Catholic Ireland. And this is a song that I'm sure Joe Biden could sing word perfect, but not, I suspect, without a tear in his eye. One of his great-great-grandfathers, Patrick Blewitt, had, after all, left Ireland in 1850 during the Potato Famine or 'The Great Hunger' as they call it in Ireland, which left one million dead. Another million left with Patrick for the New World. The immediate cause might have been potato blight, but most Irish people angrily blame the U.K. government (the then government of Ireland as well).

But are slips of the tongue always unconscious repressed thoughts that are finally articulated in speech? Since the first descriptions of slips of the tongue by Rudolph Meringer and Karl Mayer in 1895, there has been significant disagreement about their cause. Wilhelm Wundt, the father of psychology, in 1900, explained them through the 'contact effect of sounds' – similar sounding syllables or words are often exchanged in spontaneous speech ('black' in Biden's example). However, Sigmund Freud would say that slips reveal unconscious and repressed thoughts. Freud collected a corpus of slips of the tongue based on consultations with his patients and said that he could hardly find one example, 'in which I should be obliged to trace the disturbance of speech simply and solely to what Wundt calls "the contact effect of sounds".' Instead, he argued that there was 'invariably a disturbing influence...which comes from something *outside* the intended utterance'; this disturbing element is usually 'a single thought that has remained unconscious, which manifests itself in the slip of the tongue and which can often be brought to consciousness only by means of searching analysis.' In his view, all such slips reveal repressed thoughts.

For example, one of his patients could not remember which part of her body had been 'grasped by a prying and lascivious hand.' Freud wrote:

Immediately afterwards she called on a friend with whom she discussed summer residences. When she was asked where her cottage was situated, she answered: 'on the *Berglende* [hill-thigh] instead of '*Berglehne* [hill-side]'. When I asked another woman patient at the end of the session how her uncle was, she answered: 'I don't know, nowadays I only see him *in flagranti*'.

(Freud 1901/2002)

Next day, she told Freud that she meant to say *en passant*. But Freud then says that she remembered being caught *in flagranti*. Freud's conclusion was that 'The slip of the tongue of the day before had therefore anticipated the memory which at the time had not yet become conscious.'

These are all classic 'Freudian slip,' unconscious and repressed thoughts or wishes appearing in speech, often with a sexual origin. Other psychanalysts whilst accepting the concept of repression believe that Freud had mistakenly emphasised sex. One of Freud's biggest critics was Jung who wrote:

> There was no mistaking the fact that Freud was emotionally involved in his sexual theory to an extraordinary degree. When he spoke of it, his tone became urgent, almost anxious, and all signs of his normally critical and sceptical manner vanished.

(see Beattie 2023a)

Repressed thoughts, it seems, do not have to involve sex.

But what is the more contemporary psychological position on slips of the tongue? Are they mere errors in generating linguistic streams, anticipations, or transpositions on the basis of sound or meaning, or do they have a deeper significance? Research by Garnham and colleagues in a naturalistic corpus of conversational speech suggest that slips of the tongue are much more common that we might have thought, and much more mundane than Freud could have imagined, and full of anticipations and the blending of words with little unconscious symbolism (Garnham et al. 1982). Indeed, it's been suggested by Rosa Ferber that 'Freudian slips' are more often 'slips of the ears' than 'slips of the tongue' in that observers only hear about one-third of the slips that are actually present on a single listen (which would have characterised Freud's method) and about half of these are noted down incorrectly (Ferber 1991).

Freud may also have been particularly sensitive to hearing or mishearing certain types of slips, given his sexual theory. That would be an example of what is now called conformation bias.

But can external factors ever influence slips? One experiment carried out in the 1970s suggest that they can (Motley and Baars 1978). To induce 'Freudian slips' experimentally, speakers were asked to say aloud pairs of words or non-words such as 'darn bore' or 'gad boof' as rapidly as possible. Sometimes, the participants accidentally reversed phonemes when doing this (saying 'barn door' or 'bad goof' for example). To induce 'Freudian slips' word pairs like 'goxi furl' or 'bine foddy' were used and this was run on male speakers either by a male experimenter or by an 'attractive, provocatively attired and seductive' female experimenter! The experimenters found that slips with 'Freudian' outcomes ('foxy girl'; 'fine body') occurred more frequently with the female experimenter than the male, suggesting that factors external to the speech itself can influence the productions of these slips.

But this does not necessarily demonstrate the role of unconscious repressed thoughts, rather it could be simply due to increased activation in the speech output lexicon for context-related words (Beattie and Ellis 2017). In other words, in certain contexts, certain associations are unconsciously primed and become more accessible. This is an example of what the Nobel Laureate Daniel Kahneman calls a System 1 response. The unconscious System 1 then makes suggestions for the conscious and rational System 2, which includes our orderly speech system, but errors can creep in (Kahneman 2011).

And similarly, of course, with Joe Biden. He was in Dundalk that night of the slip, just south of the border, meeting his extended family, childhood memories no doubt stimulated. 'Come out ye Black and Tans.' Words and tunes from childhood and many associations all now unconsciously primed. Just there below consciousness but more accessible now, and ready to slip out and cause an international storm and remind us not to read too much into an individual verbal slip, sometimes indicative of a repressed thought (as we have seen in the previous sub-chapter), but sometimes not.

7   Our Masters' Lying Voices

In watching the course of political events, I was always struck by the active part which propaganda played in them. I saw that it was an instrument which the Marxist Socialists knew how to handle in a masterly way and how to put it to practical uses. Thus, I soon came to realize that the right use of propaganda was an art in itself and that this art was practically unknown to our bourgeois parties.

(Hitler 1925/2022: 167)

Unwelcome Guests

I blame Plato. It was Plato, after all, who introduced the concept of the noble lie. We need political structures, like the city state, he argued, because of the fundamental weakness of man. The noble lie from his perspective is a lie told to preserve the state – a false belief, a fiction, that 'will make them [those who come after us] care more for the city and for one another.' It's as if, he was saying, we need lies in politics.

In 2022 and 2023, when I was working on this book, it was impossible to get away from the lies of politicians. They joined me in my front room, uninvited and unwanted. They glowered in the corner. These were difficult days. The Prime Minister of the United Kingdom, Boris Johnson, was in trouble over Partygate – a political scandal about parties and other social gatherings of government and Conservative Party staff held at 10 Downing Street, its garden, and other government buildings during the COVID-19 pandemic of 2020 and 2021 when public health restrictions explicitly prohibited such gatherings. The Metropolitan Police were investigating. The first report of possible breaches in the law was published in the Daily Mirror on 30 November 2021 of three social gatherings in 10 Downing Street in November and December 2020. At that time, restrictions prohibited indoor gatherings of more than six people, with exceptions for certain work-related activities. Boris Johnson said that rules had been followed and Downing Street denied that a party had taken place. Many said that he was lying (it turns out he was).

Allegra Stratton, the Downing Street Press Secretary appeared in a video of a mock press conference in which she made jokey comments about the 'party.'

DOI: 10.4324/9781003394563-7

It was the nature of her joking as much as the content that seemed to enrage the public. It was seen as patronising and demeaning, as if she was suggesting through her frivolity that the laws did not apply to them. This video was leaked on 7 December 2021. She resigned shortly afterwards. Pressure was building.

At Prime Minister's Questions on the First of December the previous year, Johnson had told the House of Commons 'All guidance was followed completely in Number 10.' On 6 December, embittered former government adviser Dominic Cummings (who subsequently went all out for revenge – see Beattie [2022]) warned in *The Guardian* that it was 'very unwise for No 10 to lie about the events.' At PMQ on 8 December, Johnson was again asked whether there was a party at Number 10, he replied 'No, but I am sure that whatever happened, the guidance was followed, and the rules were followed at all times.' Critics said that he was lying repeatedly.

There was widespread outrage at this notion that somehow the rules did not apply to the toffs who oversaw the country. Some commentators and several opposition MPs, including Sir Keir Starmer, the leader of the Labour Party, contrasted these jovial drunken parties in 10 Downing Street with ordinary people unable to visit their loved ones in hospital or say goodbye at their funerals because of COVID restrictions. The indelible image was of the contract between an old frail woman, a little confused, not sure where she was or what was happening, in some home or other, somewhere from the North of England, maybe Durham, that kind of region, trying to touch their loved ones through tightly closed windows with rain running down the outside of the glass and tears running down her face, and Boris Johnson, wine glass in hand at the 'business meeting' in 10 Downing Street, smiling broadly, addressing the troops. The fact that someone vomited at the 'meeting' because of the amount of alcohol consumed did not help Johnson's cause.

It was these sorts of images that made Partygate what it was. A story of lies and embarrassing attempts to cover them up. The grin of Allegra Stratton in that video, Boris Johnson's repeated denials, that odd smile of his, that old woman behind the glass beseeching with her confused eyes. It was all peculiarly English and peculiarly class-ridden. I was reminded more than anything about what F. Scott Fitzgerald had written about the rich in a different time and in a different country. He wrote:

> Let me tell you about the very rich. They are different from you and me. They possess and enjoy early, and it does something to them, makes them soft where we are hard, and cynical where we are trustful, in a way that, unless you were born rich, it is very difficult to understand.
>
> (Fitzgerald 1925/2010: 289)

They seemed cynical, and we seemed overly trustful. 'We are all in this together,' Boris has assured us, but it seems that we weren't.

Jonathan Swift (1713), that great Irish satirist, has this to say about the political liar, and it seems particularly apposite somehow for Boris Johnson:

> The superiority of his genius consists in nothing else but an inexhaustible fund of political lies, which he plentifully distributes every minute he speaks, and by an unparalleled generosity forgets, and consequently contradicts, the next half-hour. He never yet considered whether any proposition were true or false, but whether it were convenient for the present minute or company to affirm or deny it; so that, if you think fit to refine upon him by interpreting everything he says, as we do dreams, by the contrary, you are still to seek, and will find yourself equally deceived whether you believe or not.
>
> (Jonathan Swift 1713: 153)

But that February, lies became even more central. I was sitting in my front room watching the BBC News. President Putin was giving an address to the Russian people on his 'special military operation' in Ukraine, its goal, he explained solemnly was 'to demilitarise and de-Nazify Ukraine, as well as bring to trial those who perpetrated numerous bloody crimes against civilians.' The term 'special...operation' seemed to imply surgical exactitude (maybe not the dominant meaning of 'operation' but the one that floods through when you hear the term), it suggested something that was precise, limited, and focused. It was for their own good. The next shot on the ten o'clock News was of miles of Russian tanks descending on Kyiv as the invasion began (the precise medical instrument); the war had started. Putin gripped his desk, grim-faced, threatening. He was sticking to his line; it was not a war. You look for some human emotion in that face, you find emotion but not the sorts that binds people together. His address was an attack on the Western bloc, and their 'opportunistic' adventures after the disintegration of the USSR. He reminded everyone threateningly that 'Russia remains one of the most powerful nuclear states.' His 'special military operation' was not attack, it was defence; it was not the beginning of a long war, it was the start of a precise short operation; he was not a liar, they were – 'one can say with good reason and confidence that the whole so-called Western bloc formed by the United States in its own image and likeness is, in its entirety, the very same "empire of lies".'

He was talking directly to the Russian people, urging them to defend themselves '...and to work together with us so as to turn this tragic page.' He also addressed the Ukrainian Armed Forces urging them to rise up against 'the junta,' which, he says, was governing them, 'plundering Ukraine and humiliating the Ukrainian people.' He was telling them to 'lay down their arms and go home.' These were not any realities that the Ukrainian people recognised. These were aberrant constructions; they were lies. The concept of the 'special military operation' was full of logical contradictions – contradicted by the military actions at the start (and the mile upon mile of tank signalling a full-scale invasion), and months of television images as the war with all its horrors unfolded on the Ukrainian people. It seemed to take the partial mobilisation seven months into the war for the Russian public (at least some of the Russian public) to see through this particular lie and to fully appreciate what was being done in their name. The war now involved hundreds of thousands of civilian reservists of all ages. 'Dads' Army,' was how the British press were describing them. The conscripts did not look happy as they were being shipped with minimum training to the front line and told to bring tampons and sanitary pads to use as bandages ('the cheapest pads and the cheapest tampons' warned the female recruiting officer with family economics on her mind) because the army was running out of first-aid supplies ('Do you know what tampons are for? You stick it right into the bullet wound and that's it!' she explained in a video widely shared on social media platform Telegram).

This was all Putin's big lie (or one of his big lies – he is, one must say, a prolific big liar). The phrase 'big lie' was first used by Hitler in *Mein Kampf* (Hitler 1925/2022). It is a gross distortion or misrepresentation of the truth used as a propaganda technique (although, of course, all propaganda is based on lies, but some lies are bigger than others). But big lies require power and not just the power that naturally accrues to a Head of State, even an authoritarian head like Putin who has been in power and president of Russia for eighteen years (in two stints). Power has to be realised, demonstrated, and 'negotiated' in social action, and perhaps power is a dimension that needs to be considered in all types of lies, big and small. But it is a neglected dimension when it comes to lies in everyday life. How do you stop lies being challenged? How do you stop dissent even ridicule?

Putin (like Hitler) has his approach. Months into the war, the images of Putin in the Luzhniki Stadium football stadium surrounded by Russia gymnasts and figure skaters all wearing the now notorious 'Z' symbol, and cheered on by tens of thousands of supporters, chilled me, and I'm sure anyone else who watched it, to the bone. Many Russians, it seems, still supported him and his 'special military operation' to de-Nazify Ukraine, despite the fact that this just sounded ridiculous to outsiders and despite all of the evidence to the contrary. It seemed incomprehensible to many in the West that ordinary Russians could believe this.

Putin clearly believes in the importance of sticking to 'the big lie.' It was Hitler of all people who commented on the psychology of the big lie in Mein Kampf. He wrote:

> It would never come into [the public's] heads to fabricate colossal untruths, and they would not believe others could have the impudence to distort the truth so infamously. Even though the facts which prove this to be so may be brought clearly to their minds, they will still doubt and waver and will continue to think there may be some other explanation. For the grossly impudent lie always leaves traces behind it, even after it has been nailed down, a fact which is known to all expert liars in this world and to all who conspire together in the art of lying.
>
> (Hitler 1925/2022: 213)

Putin has that level of impudence. But why? Does it just derive from all those years in power giving rise to feelings of invincibility, plus his intuitive understanding that big lies can work but that they depend critically on other things. You need to believe in the power and authority of the sender of the message which impacts on credibility and acceptance of the message.

Some forty years ago, the British sociologist Max Atkinson wrote an insightful book about political leadership called *Our Masters' Voices* in which he argued that political 'charisma' is not so much a natural gift or a special type of personality, rather it is a 'method' – ways of influencing the public, eliciting strong and unified responses, ways of repeatedly demonstrating your power, authority, and influence. Atkinson put several charismatic political leaders (both good and bad) under the microscope, including JFK, Martin Luther King, Churchill, and Hitler. His micro-analysis of their public speaking revealed certain common features, with specific types of messages, including strong emotional messages, couched in very specific communicational forms to elicit the right audience response. Mundane features like three-part lists and two-part contrasts have an air of predictability and allow the audience to anticipate end points and respond as one – thus demonstrating the power and charisma of the leader.

But there is more to charismatic authority than public speaking. For years, analysts and commentators have discussed Putin's isolation surrounded by yes men, and the role of Groupthink in leading to dangerous decision-making. But just before the invasion, we got a glimpse, perhaps for the first time, of these processes in action. Here was laid bare the micro-behaviours of Groupthink, the processes of forcing agreement, the role of threat, fear, and humiliation in achieving 'consensus.'

Putin gathered some of his top advisers and intelligence chiefs to a special meeting to seek their approval for the invasion. Sergei Naryshkin Head of Russia's Foreign Intelligence Service was asked to take the stand and asked a series of questions by Putin. This clip will go down in history as a glimpse into the methods and the mind-set of an autocratic dictator.

Naryshkin looks wary but comparatively relaxed at the beginning, but as he starts to say, 'In the worst case, we have to make the decision we're discussing today,' things change. Putin signals his displeasure through slight nonverbal means – he fixes his tie, he drums his fingers, he sighs.

This is the power of the dictator, these small sometimes ambiguous cues (after all, fixing your tie or drumming your fingers can be signs of anxiety and apprehension in the individual concerned) have a clear and unambiguous message here. They are a clear sign of displeasure, a threat, a device for allowing no deviation. Like pulling a chain on a dog. Putin's acolytes in the room shift uncomfortably; they too have read the signs. They are anticipating what will happen next.

Putin then asks, 'What does that mean in the worst case? Are you suggesting we start negotiations?'

Putin's intervention causes Naryshkin to stammer, uncontrollably. Putin interrupts him. Putin has a masking smile, which comes across as quite sinister because it's quite hard to read his emotional state underneath, for a moment or two at least. It could be mild amusement, but when the smile fades, we see the underlying emotion – anger, then fury that Naryshkin is avoiding immediately giving his consent to the invasion in unambiguous terms.

Putin exudes threat through these micro-cues. We talk about 'yes men' in the Kremlin, but this is how yes men are controlled through threat, fear, and humiliation. You can see both Naryshkin and those in the room trying to read Putin's mood state to try to work out what they should or should not say. Commentators on the recording have said that the Head of Russia's Foreign Intelligence Service comes across like a child trying to guess what Putin wants to hear at this point.

Putin needs to assess his power and authority at every level in his communications to force compliance. What kind of leader could threaten and humiliate those close to him in this way? Psychologists talk about lack of empathy, narcissism, failure to take responsibility for actions, willingness to hurt without remorse or guilt as clear evidence of the Dark Triad of personality characteristics – psychopathy, narcissism, and Machiavellianism. But when it comes to Vladimir Putin, we see how these personality characteristics can operate in the social world and impact on other's behaviour, forcing compliance and demonstrating Putin's authority, feeding back into Putin's own concept of self, so that he then has the impudence to use the big lie that would make the rest of us choke with guilt.

And as for the Russian people. We may return to that other commentator on human psychology, Adolf Hitler. Putin's supporters may well cling onto their belief in the great man and think that there is some other explanation for the counterevidence about this 'special military operation.' But, hopefully, not forever.

'Believe Me'

According to Fea (2018), 'Believe me' is the most common phrase in Donald Trump's lexicon. Our everyday intuition would suggest that this phrase is something of a red flag when it comes to detecting lies, and so it might be here. Politicians are not like the rest of us, we expect them to lie, and they rarely disappoint. They confirm all our worse fears.

It was now summer 2023, and we were surrounded by great audacious political liars and Donald Trump was never far from our minds – he was still planning to run for the Presidency in 2024, even if he was behind bars (as many were predicting). Boris Johnson was no longer prime minister, having resigned as an MP and accused by the Privileges Committee of lying to Parliament (he did), and Vladimir Putin, was threatening us all with nuclear war, with his various mouthpieces getting more and more specific (Russian citizens were being told to leave targeted areas in the West, like London), which we all hoped was a baseless threat or a lie.

But if politicians were to be totally candid, I suspect that many would say that lying is an important part of what they must do – they are there to serve the people, but we, the people, need lies for security. We want our side to come out on top, when things are not going well. We want our leaders to be cunning, more cunning than Putin, more duplicitous. 'You want to bomb London, go ahead. See where that gets you.' There is nothing particularly new about this. In the Homeric epic *The Odyssey*, we learn about the siege of Troy, and the brilliance of Odysseus, the King of Ithaca, and his brilliant lie of the Trojan horse – the hollow wooden statue of a horse presented to the besieged city as 'a gift,' but with soldiers concealed inside to take the city after nightfall. As the semiotician Marcel Danesi has commented:

> Homer was obviously intrigued by the persuasive power of artful mendacity describing Odysseus with adjectives such as "the many-sided Odysseus", "resourceful Odysseus", "devious Odysseus" and "subtle Odysseus"
>
> (Danesi 2020: 1)

Danesi reminds us that even today, we take great pleasure in reading about Odysseus' exploits and admiring 'his art of the lie as a manifestation of uncommon intelligence.' When we read about his exploits, we temporarily set aside the concept of the lie as immoral and damaging and focus instead on the positive side – the skills needed to use them effectively. We admire the power of the lie for strategic and military success in that great birthplace of civilisation, and associate it with so many other positive attributes, like intelligence, cunning, bravery, and heroism.

For Homer, admiration of the lie was centred on individual acts of bravery and cunning, it wasn't anything broader than this. This changed with Machiavelli in the sixteenth century who viewed lying as the most effective strategy for acquiring political power, and then clinging onto it – indeed a necessary strategy for political success. Political glory and all it entails justifies such immoral means, in his mind. In *The Prince* (1532), Machiavelli draws on the wisdom of the ancient Greeks (including the allegory of Achilles) and combines this with his own personal experience of the intrigues of political life in Florence in that period. These personal experiences led him to the view that men 'do not keep their word to you,' and so, he argues, one must reciprocate – 'you need not keep your word to them.' He asserts that politicians need a *different* set of skills (including the art of lying – 'one must know how to colour one's actions and to be a great liar and deceiver') and be both fox and lion, cunning like a fox and clever enough to recognise traps, and ferocious like a lion. In *The Prince*, Machiavelli discusses how Achilles was brought up by Chiron, the centaur, so that Chiron might train him his way. Machiavelli writes:

> All the allegory means, in making the teacher half beast and half man, is that a prince must know how to act according to the nature of both, and that he cannot survive otherwise.

> So, as a prince is forced to know how to act like a beast, he should learn from the fox and the lion; because the lion is defenceless against wolves, therefore one must be a fox in order to recognize traps, and a lion to frighten off wolves...If all men were good, this precept would not be good; but because men are wretched creatures who would not keep their word to you, you need not keep your word to them...But one must know how to colour one's actions and to be a great liar and deceiver. Men are so simple, and so much creatures of circumstance, that the deceiver will always find someone ready to be deceived.
>
> (Machiavelli 1513/1977)

Machiavelli drew up his strategy for creating a unity of purpose amongst his 'wretched' followers (to be based on either truth or lies, both may be used, and both are valid and critical), to create a powerful and united political force. This was a new 'theory' of lying, it was to be construed as a device, as an approach, as essential in politics because of the very nature of man. A reactive and pragmatic theory based on observation and learning in the real world. From the Bible onwards, lying had been seen as sinful, destructive, a sign of moral weakness. Machiavelli argued that despite such religious misgivings, one needs to learn to appreciate its effectiveness, its necessity, when the prince or the skilled political leader manages 'to circumvent the intellect of men by craft.'

> Everyone admits how praiseworthy it is in a prince to keep faith, and to live with integrity and not with craft. Nevertheless, our experience has been that those princes who have done great things, have held good faith of little account, and have known how to circumvent the intellect of men by craft, and in the end have overcome those who have relied on their word.
>
> (Machiavelli 1513/1977)

You do not have to look that far to find contemporary politicians in the mould of Machiavelli. Take Donald Trump in 2016 after he had announced his candidacy for the presidency, and in the presidential debates themselves. Here was someone who was going to give the disenchanted, the 'wretched,' a sense of purpose and resolve, he was going to 'drain the swamp,' he would stoke the resentment of his followers against Washington politics, invigorate them. Powerful emotional images. That metaphor of 'draining the swamp' was central to that, and that image was now firmly implanted. He wanted to create resentment against the 'liberal elite' that had taken over America, thwarting its traditional religious and blue-collar values. This elite was the enemy of America supported by the mainstream media, ignoring the values and fears of real ordinary God-fearing Americans. This elite, depraved and unchristian were looking down on them, reading them as uneducated, ignorant, and racist throwbacks, latching on to the simplistic images, words, and phrases of Trump in his 'evangelical' meetings, the myth of the saviour for our times. But as Marcel Danesi has commented 'By repeating such slogans and catchphrases over and over, the mental images they generate become entrenched in many people's minds, suspending their ability to them as metaphors' (Danesi 2020: 13).

Trump's lies have become infamous and have covered a wide range of topics and issues. In his first press conference as President, he claimed that the crowd size at his inauguration was the largest in history, despite photographic evidence and crowd estimates suggesting otherwise. He repeatedly made claims about widespread voter fraud in the 2016 and 2020 elections, without providing any substantial evidence to support these claims. Multiple courts and election officials, including those appointed by Trump, found no evidence to support his claims. Trump tweeted in 2017 that former President Barack Obama had wiretapped his phones during the 2016 election. Again, no evidence was found to support this claim, and it was widely criticised and debunked. Throughout the COVID-19 pandemic, Trump made several misleading or false statements about the severity of the virus, the effectiveness of certain treatments, and the timeline for vaccine development. These statements were contradicted by public health experts and scientific evidence.

But perhaps his lies about climate change were the worst and most pernicious of all (Beattie and McGuire 2018), given their timing – on 20 January 2017, Trump was elected as the 45th President of the United States, and later that year, the Fourth National Climate Assessment Report was published by the U.S. Global Change Research Program: two monumental events for the 'debate' on climate change. Trump said that he would cancel the Paris Climate Agreement within 100 days of taking office; he signed an executive order in March 2017 that reversed the Clean Power Plan that required states to regulate power plants; he described anthropogenic climate change as 'fake news' and 'fictional.'

The Fourth National Climate Assessment Report was yet another report that bolstered the scientific consensus on climate change, but this one was 'the authoritative assessment of the science of climate change,' with a focus on the United States. The fact that the focus was the United States was very important. One major psychological issue with climate change is that it is often perceived to be primarily about *other* places and *other* times, and not of direct concern to us living in the here and now. The belief is that it will impact on more distant locations (sometimes called *spatial bias*) and not our own, and that it will affect future generations rather than this one (this is called *temporal bias*). This is supported by a bias in the processing of climate change messages (Beattie et al. 2017). Indeed, large sections of the population of the United States seems to assume that it will be immune to the whims of climate change (if it exists at all), and Trump, in his election campaign, tapped into these underlying beliefs, reinforced them, and led them (Beattie and McGuire 2015, 2016). They seem to believe that it doesn't really concern them (except perhaps in terms of what they might have to pay, in light of the Paris Climate Agreement). Many, including the new President himself, described it as a 'scam,' and this message played very well in his campaign in those states which had been decimated by the decline of the coal industry. He tweeted on 1 November 2012, 'Let's continue to destroy the competitiveness of our factories & manufacturing so we can fight mythical global warming. China is so happy!' And on 15 February 2015, he tweeted 'Record low temperatures and massive amounts of snow. Where the hell is GLOBAL WARMING?'

'Where the hell is global warming when you need it?' became a recurrent slogan. 'Right here, right now,' was the answer from the Fourth National Climate Assessment Report. Towards the close of the year, things started hotting up. President Trump was on vacation, again, in Mar-a-Lago resort in West Palm Beach, Florida for an eleven-day Christmas break. The sun was shining. On the first morning of his vacation, he was predictably enough back on his own golf course. It seems that this was his 85th day on a golf course since becoming President, according to NBC News. Whilst the rest of the world was worrying about the ongoing nuclear stand-off with North Korea's Kim Jung-un and President Trump's recent boasts about the size of his nuclear button ('I too have a Nuclear Button, but it is a much bigger & more powerful one than his, and my Button works!'), the President reassured us that he would be 'working very hard' on preparing a 2018 agenda that would include both infrastructure plans to 'Make America Great' again and unspecified 'actions' against North Korea. 'I'll be working very hard,' he said again. He seems to like repetition and emphasis, as if talking to a child. We were urged not to worry by this 'stable genius' of a President, as he was soon to describe himself, a stable genius who had everything under control. But consistency, of course, was never his strong point. In October 2014 he had tweeted: 'Can you believe that, with all of the problems and difficulties facing the US, President Obama spent the day playing golf.' Before entering the White House at a campaign rally, he had assured the American people that 'I'm going to be working for you, I'm not going to have time to go play golf.' But that was then. He played three times as much golf as his predecessor Barack Obama, and that other great golfing President George W. Bush who stopped playing altogether in 2003, in response to widespread criticism about his conspicuous leisure time during the Iraq War. President Trump enjoyed golf in the bright sunshine with a few golfing pros and the odd senator. Perfect. The weather did everything that was expected of it that Christmas and New Year. And not just in Florida. A cold snap hit the Northeast Coast of the United States. Dogs froze to death in their kennels. Could life get any better for Donald J. Trump?

> In the East, it could be the COLDEST New Year's Eve on record. Perhaps we could use a little bit of that good old Global Warming that our Country, but not other countries, was going to pay TRILLIONS OF DOLLARS to protect against. Bundle up!

he tweeted gleefully on 28 December. Trump had always been a climate change denier, although 'always' again is a relative term here. In 2009, he was a signatory on an open letter which had been addressed to President Obama and published in the *New York Times* that encouraged positive governmental action on climate change. But his subsequent climate change denial was a big part of his 'Make America Great' campaign. Climate change was a Chinese conspiracy to damage American industry. It was a total hoax, fake news. The message played well to the masses, particularly in those states whose heavy industry had been most affected by foreign competition. In December 2017, the Trump administration dropped climate change from a list of global threats in the new national security strategy that the President unveiled. Then the cold snap occurred. Just look at the news to see what was happening in the northeast states of the Great United States, he was saying.

And then, it just got a whole lot better for Donald Trump. He thought that he had observed something that would support his anti-science views – in the New Year, Florida had its first snowfall in nearly three decades. Frozen iguanas were dropping from the trees. House-owners in the Sunshine State were warned to leave them alone until they defrosted. The most powerful man in the world now had evidence that climate change was a total hoax. That iguana did it for him. You can't fake a frozen iguana. When you must defrost iguanas in Florida, that tells you all you need to know about global warming, was his view. He felt emboldened to make claim after claim, in opposition to all the scientific facts and the truth (Beattie 2010). He spread doubt about global warming and preached an alternative 'fact-based' position on what was happening (Beattie 2023a). He encouraged business as usual when it came to the oil and gas companies. He stopped progress towards Net Zero. In July 2023, the name 'global warming' was changed to 'global boiling.' The U.N. Secretary General Antonio Guterres said, 'The era of global warming has ended and the era of global boiling has arrived.' This was after scientists confirmed that July 2023 was the world's hottest month on record according to the World Meteorological Organisation and the EU's Copernicus Earth observation programme. 'Climate change is here. It is terrifying. And it is just the beginning,' said Guterres. Perhaps, Trump got what he wanted when he tweeted (sarcastically, of course): 'Perhaps we could use a little bit of that good old Global Warming that our Country, but not other countries, was going to pay TRILLIONS OF DOLLARS to protect against. Bundle up!' The United States is certainly getting it now.

The function of Trump's ritualistic language is to identify the enemy (Washington politics, the swamp, the intellectual elite, scientists, the Chinese pulling a fast one in business), to stoke resentment and to bind the group together ('fake news designed to take your jobs away'). Danesi says 'To outsiders, the same words used over and over may appear to be nonsensical, but to insiders, they reinforce a belief system that keeps the group united against perceived enemies' (Danesi 2020: 17).

There are many politicians who might desire to present themselves as saviours – political power of this kind is necessarily about the perception of power and this needs to be constructed. It requires the construction of 'charisma' (Atkinson 1984) and the building of a powerful political persona through behaviour and action – behaviour that is influential, behaviour that affects people, that produces a coordinated and immediate response in meetings and gatherings. So, the construction of the power of the individual is a critical part of the process. Trump always realised that if he was going to present himself as a great leader or a saviour (even a flawed saviour and all too human), then you need a whole series of linguistic, interactional, discursive, and nonverbal strategies which allow you to be perceived as a winner in the first place, never second best, always on top. Politics is often about manipulation as is lying, and some people with the right personality characteristics are better suited to do both (as we saw Chapter 6).

For this reason, it is worth looking quite closely at some of the most significant moments of Trump's developmental pathway to becoming president (and his performative strategies as president) to see how this was done. In other words, the construction of power and charisma is part of the lying process because it influences the acceptance of the lies. It's also, of course, worth considering when we're thinking about lying politicians, that it's not just about what the politician does in the end. Some of the reasons why some politicians' lies are effective is because of us, the audience, society, and the followers at large who want to keep faith, regardless. It might be interesting to reflect back to 2016 and those presidential debates with Hillary Clinton and think about how Trump behaved and what he said as a foretaste for the future. As they ramped up for the third and final televised debate, people were still trying to make sense of what happened at their second one. That was what sticks in the memory (Beattie 2016b).

It was an odd sort of presidential debate, maybe the oddest ever – and it was certainly the ugliest and most tawdry. Mere days after the release of a video in which Trump bragged about using his celebrity status to grab women by their genitals without consent, he was already collapsing in the polls. He responded by parading a number of women who had accused Bill Clinton of inappropriate sexual behaviour in the past, then bringing them along to the debate in an effort to both embarrass him and unsettle Hillary Clinton.

At first, at least, it seemed to work. You didn't need to be a body language expert to see the discomfort on Bill Clinton's face when he was led into the auditorium and seated in the front row. But Trump was seeing his numbers slide into the terminal zone, he was increasingly resorting to the psychological tricks of the pugilistic. All boxers have little games they like to play to unsettle their opponents. They don't see it as cheating; it's just part of the game. That's how Trump seems to think. He also has a penchant for name-calling, something boxers only resort to when they're desperate. He'd called Clinton 'Crooked Hillary' hundreds of times before on Twitter and in speeches to sympathetic crowds, but at the second debate, he went so far as to call her a liar to her face multiple times. Anything for an advantage. Anything to rattle your opponent.

Their latest encounter was debating as street fighting, a metaphor widely used in the run-up to the debate. The idea was so pervasive it turned into a metaphorical frame that affected what we saw and what we noticed, and even how we judged the outcome of this battle. Various commentators summed up Trump's debate performances by speculating that he might have 'stopped the bleeding' from the Republican faithful, despite his comments about how he views and treats women ('locker room talk, folks').

Trump's body language went through several periods of transition in the debate. Having to hold a microphone interfered with the natural two-handed gestures on which he relies heavily. We can all recognise them: arms outstretched, arms pointing downwards, palms forward, characteristically signalling his connection with the common man through the distinctive, demonstrative gestures of New York – gestures that work because they speak straight to the usually unconscious nonverbal system.

Trump is quite expert at using some gestures and sequences of gestures in particular. First comes a barrier signal: arms up, palms out. "Beware," it says. "Danger." Then, he uses a precision hand gesture – a distinctive thumb-and-forefinger position – which alternates with an L-shaped gesture. The danger signal produces an immediate emotional effect, then he reassures the audience with his precision gesture. 'I've got a plan,' he says nonverbally, 'a precise plan. It's time for a change.'

That's what Trump can do, at least when he was not forced to hold a microphone in one hand as he was at the second debate. I was surprised he didn't complain about this, since he complained about everything else: the "bias" of the moderators, "it's three against one," the fact that Clinton got more time – anything, like a child who thinks that the world isn't fair.

Looking tired, he started quietly rocking on his feet as Clinton spoke, a tell-tale sign of negative emotion leaking out nonverbally. Clearly, he wasn't comfortable with the fallout from the leaked tape. He started sniffing when he talked, as he did throughout the first debate. It was a distraction for the audience, not deliberate, and it got noticeably more pronounced when he was on the spot.

He started gesturing demonstratively for the first time when he talked about his wealth. Batonic gestures – stress-timed gestures that have no iconic content, such as the up-and-down beat of a hand – tend to mark out content that's highly significant for the speaker, but when Trump began his personal attacks, the more complex and abstract metaphoric gestures started up in earnest. These were a core part of Trump's implicit message, and they had an immediate effect. Their meaning was processed simultaneously with his speech.

As he went on the attack in the debate, his use of beat gestures duly increased. He chopped, he pointed, he sliced. Trump was now fully armed. He heckled, he interrupted, he glowered as Clinton talked, issuing a nonverbal running commentary on what she was saying.

All in all, this was a bully's performance, a physical attempt to dominate Clinton and manipulate our interpretation of her words. Clinton quoted

Michelle Obama's 'When they go low, we go high,' but with Trump expressing himself as he did – stalking her as she talked, prowling behind her like a big beast of the jungle – the tone of the encounter remained firmly at the lower end of the scale.

The American linguist George Lakoff has commented that Trump 'uses your brain against you.' Much of everyday thought is unconscious, and it's that psychological spot that Trump targets, much as a boxer or street fighter does. The fact that he got us all thinking that only a "knockout" would constitute success for Hillary Clinton was therefore a victory of sorts. He was on the ropes that night, and he knew it; in the end, he bobbed and weaved to fight another day, despite everything, we now know about this most unpresidential of men, but perhaps I, and an awful lot of others, were a little over-optimistic about the way events might turn out. He controlled the narrative using sleights, deception, and lies, and it all, of course, paid off in the end, but at considerable cost.

Trump Lies with his Body Language

Donald Trump has considerable experience of reality television, he understands the power of the image and the power of body language. His gestural movements in that debate with Hillary Clinton had a number of important features. As I explained earlier, it is understood that *iconic gestures* are hand movements that are directly linked to the meaning of the words being spoken, enhancing the clarity and impact of verbal communication. My own research has shown that iconic gestures play a crucial role in communication by providing visual cues that complement and reinforce the spoken message (Beattie 2003). These gestures are not arbitrary or random; instead, they are closely tied to the semantic content of the words being expressed. For example, when someone says 'big,' they might use their arms to make a wide, expansive gesture, visually representing the concept of size and this gesture occurs exactly with the word itself, and thus the preparation phase of the gestural movement starts before the word itself – even before the speaker is consciously aware of being about to use the word (Beattie 2016a; Beattie and Shovelton 2002). These iconic gestures are generated spontaneously by speakers when they're talking without conscious awareness (they will however know that their hands are moving). The form of the gesture will vary often in significant ways from one speaker to the next because there are no standards of form for these, unlike words themselves or so-called emblems (consciously generated gestures with a strict verbal translation, e.g. the V for *peace* sign).

Iconic gestures serve several functions in communication. Firstly, they are core to conveying meaning and clarify the intended message (Beattie and Shovelton 1999a, 1999b). By using gestures that visually represent the content of the words, speakers provide additional visual information that can add core meaning, and aid in comprehension and interpretation. Secondly, iconic gestures can enhance the persuasive power of verbal communication. By using gestures that visually represent key concepts or arguments, speakers can make their message more memorable and engaging (Beattie and Shovelton 2002; 2005). These gestures can capture the attention of the audience and help to convey the speaker's passion and conviction. This research highlights the close relationship between language and gesture – gestures and speech are tightly integrated and are processed by the brain in a coordinated manner. This suggests that gestures are not mere embellishments or add-ons to verbal communication but are an integral part of how we express ourselves and convey meaning. Many studies have shown that iconic gestures can enhance comprehension and memory of verbal information (Beattie and Shovelton 2005). For example, research has found that when children are taught new vocabulary words along with corresponding gestures (Cook et al. 2008), they show improved retention and recall of the words compared to when they are taught words without gestures. These gestural movements are not part of some system of communication completely divorced from speech, some system of 'body language' versus 'verbal language,' as many psychologists of the past seem to have assumed, rather these bodily movements are intimately connected with speaking and with the thinking that underpins it. Iconic (and metaphoric) gestures reflect our thinking, like language itself, but in a completely different manner, using a different sort of system of communication with very different properties, as I've already described.

There are a number of major differences between how the two systems of communication work – there is no dictionary of iconic gesture to draw on (unlike dictionaries of words or even *emblems* – coded gestures which have to be performed in a particular way and have specific verbal equivalents, e.g., a V sign for peace). As McNeill points out, there are clear differences between well-formed and not-well-formed ways of making emblems and they also have culturally determined meanings that can sometimes give rise to significant communication difficulties when cultures interact/meet/collide. These meanings have often been conventionalised for significant periods of our history. Thus, in the first century A.D., the Roman scholar Quintilian describes in his book *Institutio Oratoria* (Book XI, III, 104) how to make the ring gesture: 'If the first finger touches the middle of the right-hand edge of the thumbnail with its extremity, the other fingers being relaxed, we shall have a graceful gesture well suited to express approval.' Morris (1979) made an interesting observation on this description:

> by insisting that the finger-tip touches, not merely the end of the thumb, but "the right-hand edge of the thumbnail", Quintilian ensures that the precision hold is made in such a way that the two digits are more or less forced to adopt a circular posture. It is possible to being the fleshy tips together in such a way that the shape created is a "circle" so squashed as to be hardly circular at all. But the details he gives insist on the ring shape

and leave no doubt that he was writing about exactly the same gesture that we see today.

(Morris 1979: 103)

But in the case of iconic gestures, this is not the case – the individual components of the gesture derive their meaning from the image as a whole rather than vice versa. Language works in a 'bottom up' manner; we understand phrases, clauses, and sentences by first understanding the meanings of the words that comprise them; these iconic gestures work in the opposite way, a 'top down' manner, we know what the gesture as a whole is alluding to and that allows us to interpret the meanings of the individual gestural movements that comprise it. This is how McNeill (2012) described this property:

> The elements of the gesture (the handshape, the location, the direction, the tension) are meaningful only as parts of the whole. They are not meaningful in themselves – the meaning determination was from whole to part, not part to whole. 'Global' doesn't mean that only the whole is meaningful; it is that the parts of the whole gain meaning from the whole. None of these meanings were attached to the hand properties before this immediate gesture but, within it, they have the meanings described.

(McNeill 2012: 12)

In other words, iconic hand gestures actually embody our thinking through bodily action with little or no conscious awareness. We create meaning for other people using our hands without the benefit of a formal lexicon (very different from verbal language and words, or emblems). These iconic gestures may provide us with a glimpse of our hidden unarticulated thoughts. Movements of the hands and arms act as a window on the human mind; they make thought visible. When people are talking, they will often know that their hands have just done *something*, that they have made some movement, but if you ask them to make exactly the same gesture again, they find it very difficult to do this, or if you ask them what exactly the gesture was communicating, they will say 'I have no idea' or something similar. They may even shrug. Many gestures contain a complex of different features, speakers when asked to repeat the movement may make a stab at repeating one of these. They may know where in front of their body they made the movement but usually this is about the only thing that they will get exactly right (unlike speech itself which we are pretty accurate at repeating and reproducing). This makes the spontaneous gestural movements made whilst speaking particularly interesting. In the words of the psychologist Katherine Nelson, writing in 2007, the movements of the hands in everyday talk represent 'a mode of unconscious meaning unconsciously expressed.'

The hands thus articulate ideas that run parallel to those expressed in our speech and in everyday conversation listeners habitually and effortlessly extract the information from these movements and combine it with the information contained in the speech itself. This is done without any conscious awareness that the information contained within the gestural movement is crucial to receiving the full message from the speaker, and thus represents part of the original idea (Beattie 2016a). Most often, the two channels of communications, speech and gesture, are congruent and represent a single idea broken down across the verbal and nonverbal modes. The meaning expressed is most often complementary to that expressed in the speech, quite literally 'combining in such a way as to enhance or emphasize each other's qualities' (see Holler and Beattie 2002, 2003a, 2003b). In Chapter 6, we saw examples when they are not congruent, when people are trying to present false information.

Given the close relationship between speech and these iconic gestures, they are hard (or impossible) to fake, especially given that their form and timing are generated spontaneously and without conscious awareness. But that doesn't mean that people have not tried, and Donald Trump seems to have been *schooled* in the art of generating them to appear 'open' and 'honest' – spontaneously inhibiting these movements would appear to be one possible cue to deception as we have discussed in Chapter 6. But look at some of Trump's 'spontaneous' iconic gesture, which I mentioned in the last section: arms outstretched, arms pointing downwards, palms forward, characteristically signalling his connection with the common man through the distinctive, demonstrative gestures of New York – gestures that work because they speak straight to the usually unconscious nonverbal system. Not an emblem though. It's as if this is a spontaneous and unconscious iconic or metaphoric gesture.

Trump is indeed expert at using some gestures and sequences of gestures in particular but the consistency in their form and timing gives the game away. They are deliberative and conscious ploys to influence the audience subliminally – the barrier signal: arms up, palms out. 'Beware,' it says. 'Danger.' Then he uses a precision hand gesture – a distinctive thumb-and-forefinger position – which alternates with an L-shaped gesture. The danger signal produces an immediate emotional effect, then he reassures the audience with his precision gesture. 'I've got a plan,' he says nonverbally, 'a precise plan. It's time for a change.' They are rehearsed and practised; he is using the brain mechanisms responsible for integrating speech and gesture unconsciously and quickly against us (Beattie 2016a), even speech and more abstract gestures (Beattie and Sale 2012). They are not emblems (which are culturally prescribed, shared, and understood); they are different, mimicking iconic gestures but not quite right in terms of their timing and coordination with what he is stating. They are fake.

But he brings this recrafting and refunctioning of body language into other domains – like the handshake (Beattie 2017). Handshakes are meant to be relatively simple affairs, at least in terms of their signalling function. 'Shake hands on it,' we are told. 'Shake and make up.' We can signal truthfulness and trust that way. They have been used as a civilised and civilising greeting for at least 2,500 years. But soon after he was elected President, Trump began the process of redefining the handshake, transforming it into the opening salvo in a battle for supremacy.

Handshakes date back at least as far as Ancient Greece – and there are artefacts from that period featuring images of Herakles shaking hands with Athena. Glenys Davies writing in the American Journal of Archaeology in 1985 said that this particular scene 'represents the acceptance of Herakles as an equal by the Gods.' On other artefacts, we find images of Hera, the goddess of women and marriage in Greek mythology, shaking hands with Athena, the goddess of wisdom, craft, and war. These handshakes are symmetrical and equal in their execution. The sort of handshake that we would recognise instantly today.

Our common understanding is that the handshake originated as a gesture of peace, demonstrating that the hands are free and not holding a weapon. It is meant to signal cooperation, reflected in the symmetrical nature of the shape of the hands and the movement, not aggressive competition. But tell that to Trump, who uses handshakes as a weapon in his games of one-upmanship.

But Trump's handshakes are not acts of peace, solidarity, and goodwill; they were something altogether different. His handshakes took many of its recipients by surprise. He pulled them forwards into his personal space, unbalancing them, and putting them at an immediate disadvantage. He knew that images of these greetings would be shown around the world – and that they would make it look as if he is the man in charge.

So potent is his technique that one martial arts school had even come up with advice on how to defend it. Consider, for example, Trump's now infamous handshake with Shinzo Abe, the prime minister of Japan. Trump first presented his hand to Abe palm up, inviting Abe to take the dominant position with his hand on top. But Trump then clasped his counterpart's hand for a nineteen-second marathon handshake, patting the back of Abe's hand in several bursts of three pats. Hand patting like this is not a 'comforting gesture' as some might assume. Hand patting, like shoulder touching or back patting, is a dominance signal, asymmetric in its application. Our boss can pat us on the back, we cannot pat them in return. Patting is not marked by the sorts of symmetry that constitute a cooperative handshake.

By the end, Trump's handshake had completely overturned the initial, submissive gesture, and very much made Abe look like the (rather surprised) junior partner. But then Trump is a reality television star – he knows something about the power of iconic images and how moments such as this are perceived by the public.

In a politer forum, a handshake should be firm, but not too vigorous, and should involve around three shakes of the hand with a full grip. It should be accompanied by a natural smile that fades slowly and an appropriate verbal greeting with the position of the handshake in the mid-zone between the two individuals.

We do know that people make judgements about others on the basis of their handshake. Research conducted by William Chaplin and colleagues from the University of Alabama, for example, showed that the characteristics of a handshake can provide accurate information about aspects of an individual's personality. Chaplin reported that handshakes that were "stronger, more vigorous, longer in duration and associated with more eye contact" tended to show that the individual was more extrovert and outgoing, more open to new experiences and less neurotic and shy (Chaplin et al. 2000; Beattie 2011). Those who are particularly concerned about sending out the right signals when they meet people for the first time do think carefully about how to execute their handshake. It is reported, for example, that John F. Kennedy thought that handshakes were so important that he commissioned a study to determine the most effective varieties to use when greeting other world leaders.

Some politicians, however, started giving Trump a run for his money, revealing how the president's infamous handshake can be disarmed. It certainly looks like Canadian prime minister Justin Trudeau prepared himself for handshake war – and we can all learn lessons from how he took Trump on. When they shook hands, Trudeau took hold of Trump's right shoulder to both steady himself and to stop Trump yanking him forward. And later, when Trudeau shook hands with Trump while they were both seated, Trudeau extended his fingers to signal that he wanted to be released. Together, these signal that Trudeau had at least some control over the course of the interaction. They certainly play out better than Abe's attempts in the media clips and show that Trump doesn't hold all the cards.

Trump seemingly believed in using any resource at his disposal to gain some advantage in the political and business worlds. Senior politicians expecting routine and formulaic handshakes have been knocked off guard by Trump's unpredictable behaviour. They find themselves yanked into his personal space, where it is difficult or impossible for them to make eye contact, or to talk coherently without looking away. This gave Trump an advantage in the game of micro-politics.

His handshakes were clearly all about status rather than solidarity. From a psychological perspective, they were arguably self-serving and egocentric, and demonstrated that, as in many aspects of life, the most important thing to Donald Trump is Donald Trump himself. The discomfort on Shinzo Abe's face when his hand was finally released from Trump's nineteen-second shake was plain for all to see, but Trump did not seem to care too much for the discomfort of others. If he did, he would not make them ill at ease in such a calculated way. There's more to life than handshakes, but they did say an awful lot about the new 'leader of the free world.'

They were a form of nonverbal deception in the way he used them, his hand was concealing a weapon that he used against them, a weapon to fight for power, a weapon disguised as something else.

The End in Sight for Donald Trump?

But in 2023, Donald Trump had some very bad days, objectively speaking (Beattie 2023c). A jury in New York found him liable for sexual abuse and defamation in a civil case brought by the writer E. Jean Carroll. This came on top of criminal charges related to a hush money payment to porn star Stormy Daniels, and allegations of mishandling of classified documents. The shame of it all. Just imagine what a die-hard Trump supporter might feel about this. Surely they must be having some second thoughts? The night after the New York court case, Trump was back in action in a town hall meeting in New Hampshire. What would the reaction be? Some held their breath.

Trump stepped on stage to rapturous applause and a standing ovation. He mouthed, "Thank you," and applauded them back. There was no hint of shame or embarrassment, from either side.

In his first presidential campaign, there was a focus on what Trump could do for his white working-class supporters. Now it was all about what was being done to him. But he brought them into his paranoid world – they were all in this together. 'When they go after me, they're going after you,' Trump told supporters during a rally in Waco, Texas in March 2023. 'Either the deep state destroys America, or we destroy the deep state.'

Psychologists Steve Reicher and Alex Haslam, writing in *Scientific American* in 2017, presented an insightful analysis of Trump's 'masterful' use of psychological techniques to manipulate his supporters. They noted that:

> A rally would start long before Trump's arrival. Indeed, the long wait for the leader was part and parcel of the performance. This staged delay affected the self-perception of the audience members: If I am prepared to wait this long, this event and this leader must be important to me. The audience sees others waiting ('it must be important to them') and this establishes a norm of connectedness and devotion in the crowd – the wait for the leader, their applause (spontaneous and in unison, with no delay), their laughing at his jibes and put-downs. Connected behaviours, emotions intertwined.
>
> (Reicher and Haslam 2017: 44)

Sociologist Max Atkinson (1984) has written about charisma, stating that isn't necessarily a gift but rather, behavioural manipulation that produces a demonstrable effect on audiences. Trump supporters all react in the same way, at the same time, and feel as one (many football supporters have similar 'spiritual' experiences at matches). It's about devotion and destiny, and how the benign leader will look after you, no matter what. In the New Hampshire town hall meeting, Trump called the violent riot on the Capitol on 6 January 2021 'a beautiful day.' He said that if he wins the next presidential election, he will pardon a large proportion involved in the riot – even those Proud Boys convicted of seditious conspiracy.

Other politicians lose their backing, so what's different here? Well, Trump fans have invested a lot more in their support – including, in a relatively small number of cases, marching on the Capitol, risking their reputations and even a criminal record. The theory of cognitive dissonance, developed by American social psychologist Leon Festinger in the mid-1950s, might help explain this. Cognitive dissonance occurs when one's beliefs and actions conflict with each other. For example, the belief that the United States needs a strong and moral leader to make America great again conflicts with the action of supporting a man who has committed a serious sexual assault.

Festinger wrote that: 'Dissonance produces discomfort and, correspondingly, there will arise pressures to reduce or eliminate the dissonance.' This conflict might constrain people from acquiring new information that will increase the existing dissonance – for instance, accepting that Trump's court case suggested poor morals. However, seeking new information (from whatever source, including conspiracy theories) that confirms your beliefs – such as about the dark powers behind the supposed election fraud and the 'victimisation' of Trump – would clearly help reduce the dissonance, and make his supporters feel better.

Festinger also analysed an end-of-the-world cult in Chicago in the 1950s that might be particularly relevant here. This cult was waiting for a great flood, scheduled for midnight on 21 December 1954. Many respectable citizens had given up their jobs and families to join the cult. But on that night, the world did not end. So, how did the cult deal with the cognitive dissonance between their expressed beliefs ('The world is going to end with a great flood tonight, but our small group of believers are going to be transported to a distant planet by spacecraft') and the observable real-world events (sitting in a front room waiting patiently, checking the clock)? Festinger wrote:

> The dissonance would be largely eliminated if they discarded the belief that had been disconfirmed, ceased the behavior which had been initiated in preparation for the fulfilment of the prediction, and returned to a more usual existence … But frequently, the behavioral commitment to the belief system is so strong that almost any other course of action is preferable.
>
> (Festinger et al. 1956: 27)

He went on to identify an important way in which the remaining dissonance can be reduced: 'If more and more people can be persuaded that the system of belief is correct, then clearly it must, after all, be correct.'

This is an interesting argument which suggests that if someone commits wholeheartedly to Trump, they may well experience dissonance as they watch the news from that Manhattan courthouse. But they don't necessarily stop supporting him. Instead, they might seek yet more information about the 'deep state' and how it's persecuting Trump, or preach more about his positive attributes and the witch hunt against him. Both are sometimes more immediate ways of dealing with the psychological discomfort than changing support for him.

That's what happened in the case of the end-of-the-world cult, and that's what might well happen here. If so, we can expect to see more conspiracy theories and more proselytising from the hard-core supporters going into 2024 and beyond. Donald Trump may not be finished just yet and it shows the legacy of lies in the political sphere. Its sometimes not so easy to just walk away if you're a hard-core supporter. Not easy at all.

Big Lies and Their Consequences

It was Hitler who came up with the concept of 'the big lie.' He explains how and why in his autobiographical manifesto *Mein Kampf* (*My Struggle*) published in 1925. He wrote this two-volume book whilst in prison following his failed coup in Munich in November 1923. He originally wanted to call the book '*Four and a Half Years of Struggle against Lies, Stupidity and Cowardice*,' but his publisher suggested a punchier title. It became a bestseller in Germany in 1933, following his rise to power.

It is not surprising that 'lies' was in the original title, Hitler was obsessed with lies and the art of lying in politics, but the lies in *Mein Kampf* extend way beyond that. In *Mein Kampf*, he theorises on the utility of the lie in the form of political propaganda, but he also uses lies in his representation of self and in his upbringing and influences. He also inadvertently provides us with some insight into how some big lies can work in action through his own pathological self-deceit and his self-deceit is, in my view, critical to understanding this process. As the sociobiologist Robert Trivers (2011) has noted the best liars, i.e. the really effective liars are those who first deceive themselves or more accurately deceive their *conscious* mind. It makes the lie easier to tell, and more convincing with fewer cues to deception (because it is 'true' for the individual) and Trivers likes to remind us that deception is not some recent cultural phenomenon, a mere product of language use – it is everywhere and ancient. 'Viruses and bacteria often actively deceive to gain entry into their hosts, for example by mimicking body parts so as not to be recognized as foreign' (Trivers 2011: 7). But self-deception is also rooted in our evolutionary history. In the words of Trivers:

> In nature, two animals square off in a physical conflict. Each is assessing its opponent's self-confidence along with its own – variables expected to predict the outcome some of the time. Biased information flow within the individual can facilitate false self-confidence. Those who believe their self-enhancement are probably more likely to get their opponent to back down than those who know they are only posing.
>
> (Trivers 2011: 13)

Self-deception can be very powerful. *Mein Kampf* is a case study in how self-deceit can develop and grow. The book is essentially the quest for a scapegoat – someone or something to blame for Germany's catastrophic defeat in the First World War. It is important to remember that the origin of the term 'scapegoat' comes from that practice, described in the Old Testament, of sending a goat out into the wilderness after the rabbi had symbolically laid the sins of the people upon it. There is always a good deal of symbolic work in the act of scapegoating. The causes of German defeat were complex and interconnecting; scapegoats are not complex and interconnecting; they don't work if they are. In *Mein Kampf*, Hitler constructs his scapegoat – 'the Jews' and related to them the Marxists, which he always viewed as a Jewish conspiracy. I say that he went on a 'quest' but it wasn't much of a quest, he seems to have made his mind up early on, *Mein Kampf* merely builds on this, and documents the emotions and the vitriol.

Scapegoating is always a lie. Life is never that simple; scapegoating pretends that it is. But Hitler tries to present a different more personal, more reasoned picture of how he came to his 'conclusions' about 'the Jew.' He tries to present it as a rational process, beginning with no assumptions about 'the Jew,' with no pre-judgement, with no prejudice. He writes:

> Today it is hard and almost impossible for me to say when the word 'Jew' first began to raise any particular thought in my mind. I do not remember even having heard the word at home during my fathers' lifetime… At the *Realschule* I knew one Jewish boy…There were very few Jews in Linz (his hometown) …. I did not in the least suspect that there could be such a thing as a systematic anti-Semitism. Then I came to Vienna.
>
> (Hitler 1925/2022: 58)

He went to Vienna to take the entrance exam to the Vienna Academy of Fine Arts (he had visited Vienna once previously when he was sixteen). He was, he says, in a state of anticipated excitement, 'proudly confident that I had got through.' But he was not successful, and this devastating failure had a profound effect on his hopes, dreams, and mental well-being, and massively dented his self-confidence. He writes:

> I was so convinced of my success that when the news that I had failed to pass was brought to me it struck me like a bolt from the skies…I fell out of sorts with myself for the first time in my young life.
>
> (Hitler 1925/2022: 30–31)

All of his hopes and aspirations were based on entering the Academy. He writes, 'I was determined to become "something" – but certainly not a civil servant,' [like his father] (Hitler 1925/2022: 29). Entering the academy was a way of leaving his family behind, of changing his position in the social order, of becoming someone that people looked up to, a somebody to be admired. He returned home; his mother was now in very poor health. These were dark days for him. He subsequently returned to Vienna again after her death, the death of the one person he had loved – he explains in *Mein Kampf* that he 'respected' his father, but only loved his mother. But it is interesting from a psychological perspective how later he viewed this period, a period of major disappointment, a period of great loss – of his hopes and dreams as well as personal loss. He says in the book that he saw 'the wise workings of Providence' in all of this and that he was thankful for that period of his life because 'it hardened me and enabled me to be as tough as I now am.' It was in this period, he says, that his eyes were opened, and his views began to change about the world and 'the Jews,' and why things were the way they were. In other words, it was during this period of personal turmoil that preceded the turmoil of the nation after the First World War that he started to build his view of the world – a 'rational' view of the world, directed by reason and analysis. He writes:

> My ideas about anti-Semitism changed in the course of time, but that was the change which I found most difficult. It cost me a greater internal conflict with myself, and it was only after a struggle between reason and sentiment that victory began to be decided in favour of the former.
>
> (Hitler 1925/2022: 58)

Hitler portrays himself as a young man caught between reason and sentiment, between rational thought and emotion, with regard to his attitude towards the Jewish people. But it was reason that won, he says. And yet, what he says in the next paragraph is extraordinary when he describes how he 'no longer passed blindly along the streets of the mighty city, as I had done in the early days, but now with my eyes open not only to study the buildings but also the human beings.' So, what great realisations came when his eyes had been finally opened? What he describes in *Mein Kampf* is not, however, a narrative of the victory of rationality; it is not an account of reason taking precedence over emotion or sentiment. He writes:

> I suddenly encountered a phenomenon in a long caftan and wearing black side locks. My first thought was: Is this a Jew? .... I gazed at the strange countenance and examined it feature by feature, the more the question shaped itself in my brain: Is this a German? ...Cleanliness, whether moral or of another kind, had its own peculiar meaning for these people. That they were water-shy was obvious on looking at them and, unfortunately, very often also when not looking at them at all. The odour of those people in caftans often used to make me feel ill...All these details were certainly not attractive; but the revolting feature was that beneath their unclean exterior one suddenly perceived the moral mildew of the chosen race.
>
> (Hitler 1925/2022: 63)

The Jewish man is no longer a person; he is a 'phenomenon' – the human attributes removed in this broad and ambiguous term. Hitler 'gazed' at it like it was an alien exhibit; he examines it 'feature by feature,' as if trying to make sense of it, like you might examine a dead alien exhibit in a museum where there are no sanctions upon your eye gaze and certainly no constraints on our mutual gaze with your fellow human being. This phenomenon was not clean, he assures us and Hitler says he felt ill, occasioned by disgust at the sight and the smell, and he took this powerful and highly unpredictable emotion (after all there are many things that make us feel queasy, many completely irrational; I have my own list) and extrapolated it from this base physiological frame to something beyond this domain – into morality and philosophy. He 'suddenly perceived,' he says 'the moral mildew of the chosen race.'

This is not what he was saying a few paragraphs earlier in *Mein Kampf*, where he wanted to portray himself as the rational thinker, sensitive to his own psychological functioning, aware of the inner conflict between reason and sentiment when it came to Jewish people, and quite able to articulate it. That inner conflict, he says, was won by reason. But that is not true – this lie is exposed when he describes the process. This is not rationality in action. He lets some odd base feeling direct his judgement; it is a bias in his thinking. He is no great, sensitive thinker; he's prepared to let his emotions take him anywhere they want, and not just take him there, but leave him there, drawing these odd and rigid conclusions, generalisations of an extraordinary magnitude on the basis of what – a momentary feeling? In the very next paragraph, he writes: 'Was there any shady undertaking, any form of foulness, especially in cultural life, in which at least one Jew did not participate' (Hitler 1925/2022: 63): from a sense perception, and a feeling, to inferences about a person, a group, a culture, and all cultural artefacts in one great heave.

There is experimental evidence from psychology that disgust, that emotion which evolved to keep us away from noxious substances and disease, amplifies moral evaluations (Pizarro et al. 2011). This has been shown in experiments in which disgust is experimentally manipulated in a way extrinsic to the moral act being evaluated – inducing disgust in this way can influence people to make harsher judgements of moral violations (Wheatley and Haidt 2005) and to judge the individuals more harshly for other actions. Those individuals who are easily disgusted are also more likely to view certain acts as immoral than those who are less easily disgusted (Horberg et al. 2009; Inbar et al. 2011). Disgust is a powerful emotion, but it is an emotion, not a tool for rational thinking. Individuals who are more prone to this emotion are likely to categorise the world differently as a consequence (for example, moral/immoral). Experimental psychology often leaves description of the process at this point, but the process then continues, as we see in *Mein Kampf*.

But there is another question to be asked here about the origins of the original feeling and the transference effect. Without wanting to sound facetious, I am reminded of Martin Seligman's (1970) research on classical conditioning and the generality of the laws of learning, which show that with certain pairings between two stimuli, you can get one-trial learning in classical conditioning between the unconditioned stimulus and the neutral stimulus (soon to become the conditioned stimulus). Unconditioned stimuli that elicit disgust seem particularly powerful in this domain. Imagine, as Seligman did, that you are sick in a restaurant. You may be sick because of a stomach bug – that is the unconditioned stimulus, but you may go off that curry, that restaurant, that tablecloth for all time! You feel ill when you smell that curry or see similar tablecloths. This is the conditioned response. Disgust is a powerful emotion and many of these 'prepared' associations between stimuli are often associated with disgust and illness. Imagine if that feeling of queasiness was due to the bad food that he was eating (in this 'world of misery and poverty' in Hitler's own words) where one Orthodox Jewish man with black side locks happened to have wandered along. Imagine if this man wasn't the cause of the feeling, but only a *neutral* stimulus but one that Hitler had noticed (and selected in terms of attention from the wide range of alternative stimuli present in that street) because he looked unfamiliar, and therefore one that became 'associated' with the feeling through that basic process of classical conditioning. This man with the black side locks thereby became the conditioned stimulus. I don't want this to sound trivial, but I would expect any rational agent, of the kind that Hitler tries to construct his younger self, might at least attempt to reflect on the process and consider alternatives (after all, Pavlov's work on classical conditioning was known in the 1920s), or think about processes within himself as putative causes of his more general feelings of disgust at the world at large or certain 'phenomena' in it (he had recently been rejected by the Vienna Academy of Fine Arts; he was devastated and no doubt *disgusted* with the world at large). But no, this highly 'rational' agent let odd, uncontrolled feelings run riot and determine his worldview.

He mischaracterised this process throughout *Mein Kampf*. The feeling came first, then the reasons. He misrepresents the kind of person he is. Not such a rational agent. He dissociates his feelings in those early days in Vienna as he entered that world of poverty and misery from his developing ideas. He makes the process of getting over this bolt from the skies and his devastation sound easy ('I had recovered my old calm and reassurance,' Hitler 1925/2022: 31); he doesn't show any self-awareness of how insidious the effects could be. These misrepresentations and lies are critical to the philosophical thrust of *Mein Kampf*.

Of course, many liars do not want to feel immoral in their everyday dealings, even when on a grand political stage, so they justify their lies. Hitler never recognises his description of the inner conflict as at the centre of his anti-Semitism as a lie but he does address the issue of the morality of some of the other lies he tells – the so-called 'big lies' (although the lie about reason taking precedence over emotion in his personal anti-Semitism is probably as big a lie as you can get). How does he justify the big lies in *Mein Kampf*? That is easy, so easy it is formulaic. He says that before he became a user of the big lie, he found that others were using it – they had already recognised its power. This is a standard and classic type of justification, a form of what Scott and Lyman (1968) in their typology of justifications call 'condemnation of the condemners' – the act itself is 'insignificant in comparison with how others behave and what they get away with.' Others were the masters of the lie (the British, the Jew, the Marxist Jew); he was only trying to catch up. He writes:

> In watching the course of political events, I was always struck by the active part which propaganda played in them. I saw that it was an instrument which the Marxist Socialists knew how to handle in a masterly way and how to put it to practical uses. Thus, I soon came to realize that the right use of propaganda was an art in itself and that this art was practically unknown to our bourgeois parties.
>
> (Hitler 1925/2022: 167)

In his view, the failure by Germany to master the art of propaganda (a 'spiritual weapon') was one major reason for their defeat in the First World War (he outlines others as well, mainly focusing on 'Jews…and their fighting comrades, the Marxists'). He writes:

> It was the total failure of the whole German system of information – a failure which was perfectly obvious to every soldier – that urged me to consider the problem of propaganda in a comprehensive manner.
>
> (Hitler 1925/2022: 167)

He describes the propaganda used by Britain and America as 'a real work of genius.'

> By picturing the Germans to their own people as Barbarians and Huns, they were preparing their soldiers for the horrors of war and safeguarding them against illusions. The most terrific weapons which those soldiers encountered in the field merely confirmed the information that they had already received and their belief in the truth of the assertions made by their respective governments was accordingly reinforced. Thus, their rage and hatred against the infamous foe was increased…Thus the British soldier was never allowed to feel that the information which he received at home was untrue.
>
> (Hitler 1925/2022: 171)

German propaganda, on the other hand, made the mistake of ridiculing the worth of the enemy, and Hitler says that the problem with this was that 'when they came face to face with the enemy, our soldiers had quite a different impression.' The consequence of this for the individual soldier was that they felt that they had been deceived by their own government, specifically those in the ministry of information (who employed 'the first ass that came along' in Hitler's words) and this weakened their fighting spirit. The British propaganda was so good, Hitler says, and so clear and consistent, that the German people started to believe it themselves. Hitler wanted to learn from the master of this black art – the British. He drew his own conclusions based on what he had witnessed:

> The great majority of a nation is so feminine in its character and outlook that its thought and conduct are ruled by sentiment rather than by sober reasoning. It is not highly differentiated but has only the negative and positive notions of love and hatred, right and wrong, truth and false-hood. Its notions are never partly this and partly that. English propaganda especially understood this in a marvellous way and put what they understood into practice. They allowed no half-measures, which might have given rise to some doubt.
>
> (Hitler 1925/2022: 173)

Hitler began to create a framework for propaganda to make it 'a weapon of the first order' in Germany as it already was in Britain. He explained that propaganda 'must always address itself to the broad masses of the people.' It must create 'a general conviction regarding the reality of a certain fact....it must appeal to the feelings of the public rather than to their reasoning powers.' It must 'fix its intellectual level so as not to be above the heads of the least intellectual of those to whom it is directed.' He summarises his perspective in the following way:

> The art of propaganda consists precisely in being able to awaken the imagination of the public through an appeal to their feelings, in finding the appropriate psychological form that will arrest the attention and appeal to the hearts of the national masses...The receptive powers of the masses are very restricted, and their understanding is feeble. On the other hand, they quickly forget. Such being the case, all effective propaganda must be confined to a few bare essentials and those must be expressed as far as possible in stereotyped formulas. These slogans should be persistently repeated until the very last individual has some to grasp the idea that has been put forward.
>
> (Hitler 1925/2022: 170–171)

This was his understanding of the psychology of the individual in groups, the masses, and his outline for the future, all described back in 1925. It is at one level a treatise on lies and lying. You must persuade them of the truth of the lie by appealing to their feelings rather than their reasoning; the lie should be simple enough so that everyone can understand it (that way you get critical mass and conformity within the group apart from anything else); you need to repeat it over and over again because they forget; use slogans – they're easy to remember. Be bold! Tell big lies; they're much more effective.

A big lie, in his words, is a lie which is so colossal that no one would believe that 'others could have the impudence to distort the truth so infamously.' Hitler claimed that this technique had been used by the Jews ('the great masters of the lie') to blame Germany's defeat in the First World War on General Erich Ludendorff, a prominent nationalist political leader in the Weimar Republic, a man who Hitler idolised. In *Mein Kampf*, Hitler writes:

> But it remained for the Jews, with their unqualified capacity for false-hood, and their fighting comrades, the Marxists, to impute responsibility for the downfall precisely to the man who alone had shown a superhuman will and energy in his effort to prevent the catastrophe which he had foreseen and to save the nation from that hour of complete overthrown and shame.
>
> (Hitler 1925/2022: 213)

In other words, Hitler explains that he got the idea of the big lie from the Jews (and from others) – he then used the big lie against them. The Jews, he said in his propaganda campaigns, were responsible for Germany's loss and suffering in the First World War (and for causing the war in the first place) and this fuelled his ideology, his justification for the anti-Semitism of the Nazi Party, and, ultimately, for the Holocaust.

But Hitler also speculated on the psychology of the big lie and how it may connect with the more mundane lying of everyday life. The first principle behind the big lie is that 'there is always a certain force of credibility; because the broad masses of a nation are always more easily corrupted in the deeper strata of their emotional nature than consciously or voluntarily' (Hitler 1925/2022: 213). In other words, big lies have to be 'credible,' although credible is perhaps not exactly the most appropriate word here because they don't necessarily have to be primarily *logically* credible as examined by our conscious system of thought but somehow emotionally credible. They have to connect with how we feel, the 'deeper strata' of the human mind, and presumably, they must allow an emotional outlet for these suppressed emotional feelings (the sense of shock, anger, and resentment of Germany after the First World War). Hitler is thinking here in terms of the 'depth psychology' of Freud and others, that the human mind has layers, the conscious mind and the deeper underlying unconscious mind that can and must be targeted for the purposes of persuasion. The big lie has only to be *credible* to the extent that it doesn't provoke instant conscious rejection. When guided by the right emotions which have been targeted by the lie, the idea itself may start to appear more plausible. Emotions can guide our cognitions in this way, as demonstrated by Damasio (1994) and others. One could argue that in the decades to come, new initiatives in advertising guided by psychoanalysts with the same depth psychology approach promoted commercial big lies using the same basic principle (led and developed by the Austrian Jewish psychoanalyst Ernest Dichter [1960] who escaped the Nazis for New York in 1938), including the big lie told in the early twentieth century that smoking is good for you – it reduces bronchial infections and helps you fight stress in everyday life and thereby live longer (Beattie 2018a). This big lie about smoking and its 'positive' health effects certainly appealed to the 'deeper strata' of the human mind giving the public a ready-made justification for their addictive habit.

But it is also interesting to note that although Hitler believed he had identified a psychological truth here, he did not necessarily see this as a positive characteristic of human beings. Quite the opposite in fact. He labels it as 'not masculine,' simple with crude undifferentiated categories and a departure from the reason which should characterise us all and as we have seen, he wrote 'An immense majority of the people are so feminine in nature and point of view, that their thoughts and actions are governed more by feeling and sentiment than by reasoned consideration.' But he knew that he could exploit feeling and sentiment with messages couched in black-or-white terms, messages that did not tolerate ambiguity or subtlety.

But Hitler went on to identify a second principle underlying big lies:

> …in the primitive simplicity of their minds they more readily fall victims to the big lie than the small lie, since they themselves often tell small lies in little matters but would be ashamed to resort to large scale falsehoods.
>
> (Hitler 1925/2022: 213)

He is saying effectively that the success of the big lie critically depends on the fact that we all tell small lies and know what that feels like. It can be unpleasant, shameful even; just imagine how awful it would feel to tell a big lie. Of course, what's also interesting about this extract is that he is criticising (indeed ridiculing) those members of the German public who fell for the big lie that Ludendorff was responsible for Germany's defeat in the First World War (a lie which originated with the Jews in his mind). He refers to 'the primitive simplicity of their minds.' But, at the same time, the penny seems to be dropping – people are simpler than we think, and he may be able to exploit this. They are simple in so many ways. People generally think that other people are like themselves. In other words, they suffer from a false consensus effect (Ross 1977; Beattie 2019). This is a form of cognitive bias. If you are a decent person, then you tend to think that most people are decent. If you hate lying, you assume that others will also hate lying. Most people, he implies, suffer from some degree of shame or guilt when they tell 'small lies in little matters' and assume that others will feel the same way; big lies, therefore, are for the most part inconceivable. Who could cope with that level of shame? How could they stand up there in front of us all and say this? If it wasn't true, that is. We overgeneralise and think that other people are similar to us. Expert liars can exploit this little quirk of human cognition.

Hitler, for one, clearly recognised its importance. He writes: 'It would never come into their heads to fabricate colossal untruths, and they would not believe others could have the impudence to distort the truth so infamously.' Why – because the emotional cost would be unimaginable from their point of view. Hitler goes on to say, 'Even though the facts which prove this to be so may be brought clearly to their minds, they will still doubt and waver and will continue to think there may be some other explanation.' Again, his understanding is that our emotions and the constraints on action that they provide are primary and that we all understand this, and that we will adjust all our other cognitions accordingly. The reason that this is so important is revealed in his next sentence when he writes:

> For the grossly impudent lie always leaves traces behind it, even after it has been nailed down, a fact which is known to all expert liars in this world and to all who conspire together in the art of lying.
>
> (Hitler 1925/2022: 213)

The big lie must appeal to the emotions of the targets so directly, effectively, and unconsciously, that it will guide their thinking about the subject of the lie over a protracted period. That is the challenge for all 'expert liars in this world.'

Hitler was uncovering and developing a strategy for the future, all laid out in *Mein Kampf*, fourteen years before the start of the Second World War and the start of Holocaust. Never again would the Jews or the British be the masters of propaganda, the effective tellers of the big lie. He would never overestimate the reasoning powers of his audience ('I use emotion for the many and reserve reason for the few,' he famously said). He evidently believed that

> the receptive powers of the masses are very restricted, and their understanding is feeble. All effective propaganda must be brought out in the form of slogans until the very last man is enabled to comprehend what is meant by any slogan.

He could copy what had worked and refine it. The slogans would be simpler ('Ein Volk, ein Reich, ein Fuhrer,' 'One People, One realm, One Leader'; 'Free Germany from the Jews,' 'Work and Bread'; 'Blood and Soil'). He did not mind appearing 'lunatic' because of the impudence of his assertions. He was happy to see the big lie become unpleasant. It was a pathway. He told us so himself:

> The masses are in no position to distinguish where foreign illegality begins and our own ends. It confined itself to a few points of view, was addressed solely to the masses, and was pursued with untiring perseverance. Throughout the whole War use was made of the basic ideas and forms of expression, found to be right at the beginning, and even the slightest alteration was never considered. At first it appeared lunatic from the impudence of its assertions – later on it became unpleasant and was finally believed.
>
> (Hitler 1925/2022)

The Office of Strategic Services, OSS, the forerunner of the CIA commissioned the American psychoanalyst Walter Langer in 1943 to profile Hitler based on the language and behavioural evidence in *Mein Kampf* to reveal his motivations and unconscious drivers. This report (finally declassified in 1972) is highly insightful. Langer wrote this about Hitler:

> His primary rules were: never allow the public to cool off; never admit a fault or wrong; never concede that there may be some good in your enemy; never leave room for alternatives; never accept blame; concentrate on one enemy at a time and blame him for everything that goes wrong; people will believe a big lie sooner than a little one; and if you repeat it frequently enough people will sooner or later believe it.
>
> (Langer 1943: Part 11)

The OSS report on Hitler really begins by asking what sort of liar Hitler was. They enquire whether he was sincere in his undertakings or merely a fraud. What was the nature of his self-deceit, his delusion of greatness, and how critical was this? They comment that:

> At times it seemed almost inconceivable that a man could be sincere and do what Hitler has done in the course of his career. And yet all of his former associates, whom we have been able to contact…are firmly convinced that Hitler actually does believe in his own greatness…In each and every field he believes himself to be an unquestioned authority. He says "I am one of the hardest men Germany has had for decades, perhaps for centuries, equipped with the greatest authority of any German leader…but above all, I believe in my success. I believe in it unconditionally."
>
> (Langer 1943: 1–2)

There has been a good deal of speculation as to where this self-deceit and these delusions of greatness came from. Some have suggested that Hitler was a great believer in astrology and that somehow this was all written in the stars, but according to the OSS report, this seems to be contradicted by those who knew him best (and his anger at the use of astrology by his deputy Rudolph Hess would seem to bear this out). The OSS report quotes a number of informants who say that Hitler was in principle against horoscopes because he felt that he might unconsciously be influenced by them. The report also concludes that his feeling of destiny did not emerge only after his great early war-time successes, rather it was present much earlier than that, although these successes undoubtedly consolidated this feeling. In *Mein Kampf*, he reports several critical incidents, including hearing a voice in his head telling him to move whilst he was eating his dinner in a trench during the First World War. 'Hardly had I done so when a flash and a deafening report came from the part of the trench I had just left.' Every member of his group was killed. Hitler believed that he was under Divine protection;

God was talking directly to him, keeping him safe. That internal voice in his head, his unconscious response to the trench itself, the trench shelled by the British, was attributed to an external source, not a 'sense,' not a 'hunch,' not 'a bad feeling.' It was Divine intervention; nothing less, perhaps he was the chosen one. This belief seemed to be growing. In one speech, Hitler said:

> When I came to Berlin a few weeks ago and looked at the traffic in the Kurfuerstendamm, the luxury, the perversion, the iniquity, the wanton display, and the Jewish materialism disgusted me so thoroughly, that I was almost beside myself, I nearly imagined myself to be Jesus Christ when He came to His Father's temple and found it taken by the money-changers. I can well imagine how He felt when He seized a whip and scourged them out.
>
> (see Langer 1943: 6)

He still says that he 'imagined' himself as Jesus Christ, but he goes beyond that psychological gap. He says that he knows how Jesus felt ('I can well imagine'); in the speech itself, he swung his 'whip' violently as if driving out the Jews. He *was* Jesus Christ in the speech. Psychologists often distinguish two different types of the hand gestures that accompany language – 'observer-viewpoint gestures' and 'character-viewpoint gestures' (McNeill 1992). The difference is that with an observer-viewpoint gesture, the speaker plays the role of the observer of the action, the hands enact the topic from a psychological distance just depicting the action, often in broad terms, from an observer's point of view; in character-viewpoint gestures, on the other hand, the hands act out the action from the point of view of the character themselves. These gestures are psychologically 'closer' for the individual – these are how the person you are talking about behaved (Beattie 2003; 2016a). Hitler's gesturing hand is the hand of Christ; he is burnishing the whip; he is whipping them and driving the Jews out of the temple. This is how it felt. Hitler here is identifying with the strong Jesus, not the soft and weak Jesus, which is often how he viewed him (he once referred to Christianity as 'the Jewish Christ-creed with its effeminate, pity ethics'). He was the Jesus 'who recognised these Jews for what they were' and was prepared to take brutal action to deal with them. He is in the role, but he's no sham actor; he knows how Jesus really felt; he knew what it all meant. When Jesus eventually realised the mendacity of the Jews, he and Hitler were as one, Hitler too had woken up. He wrote:

> The Lord rose at last in His might and seized the scourge to drive out of the Temple the brood of vipers and adders. How terrific was the fight for the world against the Jewish poison.
>
> (Langer 1943: 7)

One major conclusion from the OSS report was that Hitler believed himself 'destined to become and Immortal Hitler, chosen by God to be the New Deliverer of Germany and the Founder of a new social order.' The report says that Hitler's conviction 'is not rooted in the truth of the ideas he imparts.' Rather it is based on 'the conviction of his own personal greatness.' Hitler famously said 'I cannot be mistaken. What I do and say is historical.' So, here we had a man with delusions of grandeur, knowing how Christ really felt, a man who believed in his own greatness and in his destiny who had according to the OSS report 'extraordinary abilities… to unearth and apply successfully many factors pertaining to group psychology.' These include the importance of the masses and the importance of winning the support of women and youth. 'The ability to feel, identify with and express in passionate language the deepest needs and sentiments of the average German and to present opportunities for their gratification.' He also had the 'Capacity to appeal to the most primitive, as well as the most ideal inclinations in man, to arouse the basest instincts and yet cloak them with nobility, justifying all actions as means to the attainment of an ideal goal' (Langer 1943: Part 11). Of course, this necessarily depends on deceit and self-deceit. Arousing the most basic instincts but cloaking them in nobility is propagating a falsehood. And how was this achieved? We've already considered his views on the big lie. Who would have the impudence to tell such a lie? But he must connect this with his audiences, and many have commented that this was his greatest gift – his ability to move audiences, to connect with them emotionally – to convince them of the power of his message and what actions needed to be taken, regardless of the usual human constraints.

The OSS reports on one important dimension of the communicative process within the context of the 'dramatic intensity' of the large political meetings, rallies, and festivals:

> The ability to portray human forces in vivid, concrete imagery that is understandable and moving to the ordinary man. This comes down to the use of metaphors in the form of imagery which, as Aristotle has said, is the most powerful force on earth.
>
> (Langer 1943: Part 11)

But these metaphors may be more than mere vehicles to appeal to the ordinary person through their vivid imagery. Their significance and their effects may run much deeper than that as the cognitive linguist George Lakoff and others have discussed (Lakoff and Johnson 1980; Lakoff 1993). What is immediately obvious from *Mein Kampf* (and his numerous speeches) is that they are full of metaphor (see Rash 2005; Musolff 2007). They are relentless particularly regarding certain core targets. We have already seen Jewish people portrayed as snakes (adders and vipers), and the reference to Jewish poison, but there are other recurrent metaphors that occur repeatedly, the Jew as 'germ,' 'germ carrier,' 'agent of disease,' 'fungus,' 'vermin,' 'rats'…. For example:

> The Jew is and remains the typical parasite, a sponger who, like an infectious bacillus, keeps spreading (der typische Parasit, ein Schmarotzer,

der wie ein schadlicher Bazillus sich immer mehr ausbreitet) as soon as a favourable medium invites him.

(see Musolff 2007: 27)

Musolff raises the important point:

> We might ask in what sense a 'view' of humans as *germs* can be deemed to be 'metaphorical', especially when considering that the Nazis matched their actions to Hitler's words and implemented them in the most hor-rifically literal sense. …Racist metaphors used by the Nazis are notorious, but do we understand fully how they 'worked', both for the speakers themselves and for the 'receivers' of their propaganda?
>
> (Musolff 2007: 22)

Neal Gregor (2005) raises a similar point when he wrote that 'we should not regard Hitler's metaphors merely as metaphors: for him, they described reality.' In line with Lakoff, Musolff, Gregor, and others, I do not accept that metaphors are merely 'figures of speech' (as the OSS report seems to assume), traditionally defined as something like 'novel or poetic linguistic expressions where one or more words for a concept are used outside of their normal con-ventional meaning to express a similar concept.' Following Lakoff and others I think that it's important to regard them as 'figures of thought' – major and indispensable ways of construing the world with implications for action and judgement (Lakoff 1993: 202). Analysing and understanding metaphor in discourse and thinking may be an important way to gain some insight into everyday human action (and lying). In classical theories of language, metaphor is seen as a matter of language; in cognitive linguistics, it is seen as a matter of thought, and thought at a deep level, indeed the largely less conscious and unconscious systems of thought.

Let's consider an example. In order to understand the relationship between language and thought, think about how we talk about romantic relationships. Here are some of the things that I may have said recently on this very subject to my nearest and dearest, 'we've reached a fork in the roads,' 'you go your way, I'll go mine,' 'it was always a bumpy ride,' 'we were going along smoothly for a while…until we hit that bump in the road.' My relationship clearly was not going well and the whole discourse about the relationship was coded in a particular way. Lakoff says this about the process:

> The metaphor involves understanding one domain of experience, love, in terms of a very different domain of experience, journeys. More tech-nically, the metaphor can be understood as a mapping (in the math-ematical sense) from a source domain (in this case, journeys) to a target domain (in this case, love). The mapping is tightly structured. There are

ontological correspondences, according to which entities in the domain of love (e.g., the lovers, their common goals, their difficulties, the love relationship etc.) correspond systematically to entities in the domain of a journey (the travellers, the vehicle, destinations etc.).

(Lakoff 1993: 207)

Lakoff goes on to say, 'Such correspondences permit us to reason about love using the knowledge we use to reason about journeys' (Lakoff 1993: 207). That's exactly what we did. My partner and I spent ages talking about our 'journey' so far. We spent a long time arguing about what that (fateful) bump in the road actually was and whether it should have knocked us so badly off track, as it evidently did (although I think I identified two bumps in the road so I'm not sure what bump did the actual damage). My partner lost patience with me (it was me going on about the second bump in the road), she found it very taxing, and eventually said 'the relationship is a total car crash.' That was it; that was the end.

We all know about total car crashes, they change things for all time – the car is a right-off, it is beyond repair, there may be casualties, something may die. When you've hit that bump in the road and that's the result, you spend hours, days even, trying to identify what that bump in the road was and why you didn't see it coming, and why things had to be so final. You blame yourself. What would happen if we'd swerved at the last minute? Would the relationship have survived? We knew the relationship was over because it was a car crash. That's how we can been conditioned, without any conscious decision-making, through our everyday language to think in those terms.

But what if we hadn't viewed it that way? What would have happened if we'd viewed our love relationship as a delicate flower, or a plant, that just need more water, more love poured onto it. We didn't hit a bump in the road (and presumably it was me driving – that was always implied in the arguments), it was just the wind or the rain way beyond our control that had caused some damage as the delicate flower tried to exist in the garden in these days of unpredictable weather. It wasn't anybody's fault – we shouldn't have blamed each other. Plants are capable of springing back to life in ways that cars after a crash cannot. Metaphors, routine and seemingly banal, and used habitually and without any conscious awareness. They are critical for our thinking, for our relationships, for how we run our lives.

Of course, perhaps, it's not that surprising that abstract concepts like love (and love-based relationships) are understood metaphorically in this way. But Lakoff says that these are merely the tip of the iceberg (pardon the metaphor):

What is more interesting, and I think more exciting, is the realization that many of the most basic concepts in our conceptual systems are also normally comprehended via metaphor – concepts like time, quantity, state, change, action, cause, purpose, means, modality, and even the concept of a category.

(Lakoff 1993: 212)

For example, 'time' is understood in terms of a core metaphor TIME PASS-ING IS MOTION (e.g., 'the time will come,' 'that time has passed'). 'Quan-tity' is understood in terms of two core metaphors – MORE IS UP, LESS IS DOWN ('prices rose, interest rates fell'), and 'LINEAR SCALES ARE PATHS' ('I'm way ahead of my classmates in terms of ability'). Categories are understood in terms of the CLASSICAL CATEGORIES ARE CONTAIN-ERS metaphor (in that something can be *in* or *out* of a category; something can be *put into* a category or *removed from* a category), etc.

Lakoff's argument is that these source domains (up/down, paths and dis-tance, in and out of containers) are the stuff of everyday experience and that these 'experiential bases motivate metaphor' with implications for all our loves.

Metaphors operate insidiously and unconsciously affect how we think about things and how we act. Lakoff says that 'Our metaphor system is central to our understanding of experience and to the way we act on that understand-ing' (Lakoff 1993: 245). Metaphors shape social institutions, social practices, laws, even foreign policy. In terms of social institutions, we get stressed be-cause we think we are wasting our time – we'll never be successful; we need to plan more carefully and budget our time (based on the TIME IS MONEY metaphor, no doubt motivated by the Industrial Revolution which happened first in England where people got paid for the amount of time they were at work). In terms of social practice, eye contact and eye gaze are sometimes regulated – in the United States, in the 1940s, for example, black men could not look at white women without sometimes horrific consequences (based on a SEEING IS TOUCHING metaphor where the eyes are limbs and the seen object is touched, 'take your eyes off me'). In law, corporations can be 'harmed' or 'attacked' (based on the CORPORATIONS AS PERSONS meta-phor). In foreign policy, we have *friendly* states and *hostile* states, heroes and villains, with strong states conceptualised as *male* and weak states as *female*. As President Bush said in his address to Congress during the Gulf War 'The issues couldn't have been clearer: Iraq was the villain and Kuwait the victim.' Many talked about the *rape* of *vulnerable* Kuwait by Iraq.

Hitler conceptualised Germany's national crisis after the First World War as an *illness*. Once this metaphor was established and not challenged, then you start to think immediately about the *cause of the illness* (the diagnosis) and the *cure*. That is how metaphor works – you start to make inferences based on the terms used (and you begin to do this without much conscious thought if any). In line with that system of conceptual metaphors known as the *Great Chain of Being* (underpinning the political philosophy of Thomas More, Francis Ba-con, and Thomas Hobbes amongst many others), he regarded the German state (the target domain) as a *human body* (the source domain) that had to be *shielded from disease* (the STATE IS HUMAN BODY metaphor). In Hitler's case, the Jewish people were conceptualised as an *illness-spreading parasite* representing the danger of diseases. Musolff writes:

> The source cluster of *body-illness-cure* concepts is not an arbitrary con-stellation of notional elements but a complex, narrative/scenic schema

or 'scenario', one that tells a mini-story, complete with apparent causal explanations and conclusions about its outcome (...needing a radical cure)...If one accepts the premise of the *illness* scenario, then the necessity of finding a *cure* (and the *healer* to administer it) is assumed as a matter of course...The *healer* is present, the *diagnosis* is clear: the *treatment* is without alternative.

(Musolff 2007: 28–30)

This is the power of metaphor. Recall what the OSS report said again – 'The ability to portray human forces in vivid, concrete imagery that is understandable and moving to the ordinary man. This comes down to the use of metaphors in the form of imagery ... the most powerful force on earth.' But metaphors are not just 'understandable' and 'moving,' although they are certainly that, but in addition to that, they are structured, they are coherent, they form a scenario – an explanatory narrative with attributions about causality built into it, and therefore inferences to be drawn about the issue in question. And, of course, how to deal with it. We think and reason using this source domain (the human body), the human body subject to disease, when we think and reason about the state (the target domain). Of course, we can treat an ill state without the kinds of measures that Hitler proposed (after all during the premiership of Margaret Thatcher, the United Kingdom was often referred to as 'The sick man of Europe' – her proposed cure was economic, in terms of increased competition in the market, and socio-political in terms of an attack on the power of the trade unions and the mining communities in the North of England), which was devastating enough for those involved (see Beattie [1988]). So, Hitler added another level to the illness metaphor, as Musolff so convincingly argues. The illness metaphor gets us thinking about the cause of the illness. But what was the cause of this illness? Here, Hitler integrates anti-Semitic conspiracy theory with the basic illness metaphor. The cause was poisoning, more specifically lethal blood poisoning. In this way, 'the Jew' was constructed not just as a threat to the current generation but future generations (based on Hitler's view, held in common with many others, that blood holds the key to heredity). Musolff says:

At the most basic version, Hitler likens 'the Jew' to a *viper* or an *adder* (*Viper, Kreuzotter, Schlange*), whose *bite* directly introduces *venom* (*Gift, Volkergift, Vergiftung*) into the *bloodstream* (*Blut, Blutzufuhr, Blutlauf*) of the victim. At the second level, 'the Jew' is depicted as a *bloodsucker, leech* (Blutegel, Blutsauger) or generally as a *parasite* (*Parasit, Schmarotzer*). ...At a third, more abstract lever, 'the Jew' is labelled generally as the *germ* or *germ carrier* or *agent of disease* (*Bazillus, Bazillentrager, Erreger*) ...The *infection* concept is also compatible with the scenario of an epidemic (*Seuche*), which Hitler uses to describe Jewish influence in society, specifically *pestilence* (*Pest, Pestilenz, Verpestung*) and syphilis (*Sypjilis, Versyphilitisierung*).

(Musolff 2007: 36–37)

Of course, vipers, adders, leeches, and parasites are not in and off themselves bad creatures, that is just how they have evolved; they are not intentionally evil or deliberately cruel, so Hitler needs to build on the metaphorical frame once more. He needs to put the roof on this whole metaphorical edifice. 'The Jew' is a creature that poisons the blood but worse than the adder, leech, or common parasite, 'the Jew' acts intentionally, deliberately invading the host, with full knowledge and understanding. And how should Hitler portray the host? As the innocent victim, of course, the unsuspecting fair-haired [Aryan] girl. In *Mein Kampf*, Hitler writes:

> This pestilential adulteration of the blood, of which hundreds of thousands of our people take no account, is being systematically practised by the Jew today. Systematically these … parasites in our national body corrupt our innocent fair-haired girls and thus destroy something which can no longer be replaced in this world.
>
> (Hitler 1925/2022: 502)

Mein Kampf was the blueprint of the 'final solution.' Musolff talks about the peculiar metaphorical status of Nazi anti-Semitism, as it is represented in this book. Like layers on an onion. The biological/medical metaphor of the illness affecting the German State, but now identified as a result of deliberate and intentional blood poisoning. Worse than parasites, worse than vipers, worse than leeches, at least these creatures are not conscious of their actions, or so the metaphorical reasoning goes. 'The Jew' was. And where does the madness of the Nazi programme of annihilation come in? After all, how else can we look at the genocide? In Musolff's view – by confusing source and target domains.

> Hitler managed to insinuate that the alleged crime of *blood poisoning* was 'literally' true as well as being the appropriate overarching conceptual frame for the Jewish role in German society …. Within this anti-Semitic 'super-scenario', the conceptual boundaries between source and target domains were erased: for Hitler, and German-Jewish contact *was* blood mixing, hence blood defilement, hence blood poisoning. The conceptual and epistemological difference of source and target levels was short-circuited; the result was a belief system that was no longer open to criticism, as the different levels could be used to corroborate each other. Problematic claims at the target level were 'proven' at the source level, and vice versa.
>
> (Musolff 2007: 41)

Several authors have suggested that the anti-Semitic language of the Nazis is indeed a warning from history. A warning to us all. Their language was based on a system of metaphors that unleashed powerful cognitive forces 'in the service of racist stigmatization and dehumanization leading to genocide' (in Musolff's powerful conclusion). Hitler's Big Lie was dressed up in layers of metaphor, one on top of the others, from a source domain of illness onto the target domain of the State. After the metaphorical *diagnosis*, our mind is now tricked into thinking about the *cure* about the person who could possibly execute that cure effectively. But that was only the start, blood poisoning and *deliberate* blood poisoning with implications for separation, retribution, and protecting the future follow seamlessly because after all the blood does carry our genetic code (or is that too not just another metaphor?). Metaphors are not just linguistic adornments; they affect thought at a deep level, including the unconscious systems of thought. They affect the inferences we draw, the way we reason, even our dreams, and dreaming which Lakoff calls 'unconscious ideation of a symbolic nature.' Indeed, Lakoff contends that:

> The unconscious metaphor system, since it structures ordinary thought, also structures dreams, connecting the hidden meanings of dreams to their overt meanings and images in a systematic way that makes use of what is important in the everyday life, conscious or unconscious, of the dreamer.
>
> (Lakoff 1993: 77)

Hitler always justified the big lie but recognised its effectiveness for the ordinary person. He didn't invent some of the core metaphors about 'the Jew,' many of them had been around for centuries, but he added layers to them and sold this metaphorical frame to a nation. That was his great trick. That was his big lie. And in the process, he undoubtedly convinced himself about his metaphorical way of framing his world, structuring the thought of a nation, including his own. Lies like this depend on self-deceit if they are to be convincing, and he seemed to have managed to convince a nation. He framed the world in a particular way, with his own false version of its poorly examined rational beginnings, and that frame of 'the Jew' and blood poisoning became his reality. These metaphorical frames became part of his unconscious ideation – in talk, in thinking, even undoubtedly in his dreams. And these dreams became the nightmare for so many millions.

8 Closing the Circle

> But although the devil be the father of lies, he seems, like other great inventors, to have lost much of his reputation by the continual improvements that have been made upon him.
>
> Jonathan Swift (1713) in *The Examiner*

Home Truths

I started this book with a description of my life back in Belfast after the death of my father and my relationship with my mother, the first lie she told me and my response. I pretended to be dead. I end the book, I think appropriately returning again to this most important of relationships – that between a mother and a child. A relationship that amplifies the significance of any lies and deceit. Of course, over the years, there were more lies to come in our relationship. I hesitate to say *pay back* because one was quite the opposite – it was an attempt to make my mother feel better. I suspect that it was a lie but a lie of inaction, of silence, of not correcting a misperception. It was in response to yet another family tragedy which occurred soon after my move from Cambridge to that first academic post in Sheffield. Again, we perhaps need more description of the situation to make that lie (if it was a lie) meaningful.

My first impression of the University of Sheffield all those years ago was that the university sat on either side of a dual carriage way with a small but (unfortunately) scalable concrete wall running down the middle to stop students taking shortcuts across the busy road. It worked most of the time. I found it hard to swing my leg elegantly over the wall, so I gave up after a few attempts. I watched many others try in the years ahead. I always thought it an unfortunate accident of place and positioning.

'Sheffield is a great city,' the professor had said at my interview. 'It's very easy to get out of.' He meant, of course, that the Peak District was just on the outskirts of the town. But the dual carriageway up the middle of the university was a constant reminder of departure.

I had been studying at Cambridge for the previous two and a half years, working on a PhD, which I had to still to write it up – I had been offered the

DOI: 10.4324/9781003394563-8

job before my three years of funding were up. That is always considered something of an achievement in academic circles, but I now had to write lectures for the first time and complete my thesis. My older brother Bill knew Sheffield well, he climbed Stanage Edge in the Peak District, he went on endlessly about the virtues of the city – the people, the pubs, the climbing, so I was delighted to be moving there. He would travel down from Scotland to see some of his climbing buddies in the city, they would drink in the Nottingham House in Broomhill. I thought that I might see more of him, and I had images of the two of us climbing together in Stanage Edge, which sat just on the outskirts of the city. We had done a little bit of climbing together in the Mournes, and they were special moments. He didn't seem to have much time for me when I was younger.

I knew I would miss Cambridge, but maybe Spring was a good time of the year to go. For PhD students like me, summer in Cambridge always felt like our long winter, barren and bare, except for the tourists cramming King's Parade, obstacles on the road to pass on my bicycle on the way to the department. Nuisances who swarmed onto the road and got in the way of your bicycle and packed the coffee shops late in the afternoon when you needed some break from your work. You would see them trying to punt on the Cam waving and shouting. You could hear them splashing and giggling under the bridges on the Backs as you cycled home at night in the summer evenings. Cambridge wasn't for me punts and strawberries and King's Chapel at night, it was days spent living in the Gothic darkness of the Downing Site where many of the science departments were situated, in tall, dark brooding buildings with dusty staircases which unlike the colleges, invited no strangers to enter. It was weeks spent on experiments that had a life of their own and had to be tended to keep them alive and functioning through those barren months of summer, when the rest of the world seemed to be having such gay distracting fun almost within ear shot.

But this was all at an end now. The time had come for us to spread our academic wings, to move on, my tutor had said. He had managed to stay there for his entire career. We were all moving on – Oxford, UCLA, Heidelberg, UCL, Stanford, MIT… Sheffield. It was potluck for most, jobs gained on hearsay and academic reputation, which can be a flimsy thing especially at that age, but my journey was more planned than most because of my brother and his climbing tales. I was looking forward to getting to know this northern city.

I had heard all about the redundancies and the unemployment in the North. An economic desert, my tutor in college had called it, questioning why I wanted to move there exactly. I had my reasons, I said, some academic, some personal, I left it at that. My brother had this affinity with Sheffield, that was important to me, but hard to explain to a stranger like my tutor. My tutor had nodded along as I spoke but talked as if he could see through me – 'permanent academic jobs are hard to come by,' he said after a pause, as if he had already read my mind. 'I think you're right to grab the first job that comes along.' It felt a little patronising. The student next in line for this meeting about our planned futures gabbled on about his imminent transition to Oxford, 'the other place,' the student had joked. His father may well have been an MP, I always suspected that, I'm not sure why. He mentioned 'the other place' twice and our tutor had laughed with this tinkling sound that floated towards the open window like a delicately hit glockenspiel. Prince Charles was another of my tutor's students from a previous year.

My first sight of Sheffield was rows of terraced housing on greyish hills stretched out in front of me, like a giant natural amphitheatre. And then, a few minutes later, giant blocks of flats appearing from nowhere. A city famously built on seven hills, like the Eternal City, all the terraced houses looping around meandering hills at the end of the dual carriageway. This was to be my new home; I rang my brother to tell him. 'When are you going to visit?' I asked, but he was always busy, climbing, teaching outdoor pursuits at a centre in the Cairngorms, socialising. He always found it hard to commit.

He did, however, come down to see me in the hall of residence where I was now staying, after I had settled in. I was a tutor there for a few months. Bill looked around at the tutors and the senior tutors and the Warden, the men in what looked like a uniform of brown suits, the women in their tweed skirts, having dinner in this attempt at a High Table in a Redbrick University. I remember that faraway look of his, as if he was slightly puzzled by it all. The conversation was dull; the jokes were tiresome and endlessly repeated. One tutor had had a stroke and was paralysed down one side: his speech was slurred. He had been a very successful ear, nose, and throat specialist; it was tragic what had happened to him. His aphasia made him difficult to understand but everyone listened attentively to his humorous observations on the university, which were just gossip really about people I didn't know. There seemed to be a lot of forced attentiveness generally over the meal; the Warden went on about how some of the female students had significantly put on weight since arriving; a large woman in a tweed skirt explained that it was because they had all gone on the pill.

My brother leaned towards me after a few minutes. 'Do you really belong here?' he said. I'll always remember that. I never asked him to elaborate, with hindsight I think I should have. He had enjoyed visiting me in Trinity ('Jesus,' he would say, 'how did you manage to get in here?' as he gazed at that painting of Henry VIII, the founder of the college, which hung behind Trinity High Table), and perhaps he thought I had proved myself adaptable enough to thrive there. Sheffield was a great university, I explained, and the Psychology Department was full of young lectures with enormous potential. But was I adaptable enough to survive here amongst the men and the women in the brown suits? That's what he was asking.

Perhaps, he thought that these tutors now around me in that hall of residence did not represent the Sheffield he loved. I should have asked. I didn't realise at the time that there were going to be so few opportunities to clear up any misunderstandings between us.

Within a year, my brother had died in a climbing accident in the Himalayas with only vague details about what had happened. It took the other climbers a day to get to his body, perhaps longer, I think they wanted to spare my mother and I some pain. However, the expedition leader did offer to show me photographs of Bill's dead body when they finally returned to England. Bill had fallen three and a half thousand feet. I felt traumatised by his suggestion. Bill was left behind. 'It would have been impossible to get his body down the mountain,' he explained.

He gave me some photographs of the pile of stones covering my brother's body, with his name scratched on the side of a grey slate-looking rock and an ice axe ('Here lies Ben Beattie,' it read. My brother sometimes liked to call himself 'Ben,' from 'Bill and Ben the Flowerpot Men', his best friend earlier in his life in Belfast was a Bill as well; he had to be Ben. But the family never called him that). The ice axe that should have stopped him from falling on Nanda Devi. But didn't.

It was a Sunday morning when I received the news, I got two telegrams – one from my mother and one from my Uncle Terence. One telegram read 'Please phone mother immediately. Urgent.' The other read 'Serious accident to Bill. Please ring Uncle Terence immediately.' I ran to the public telephone box along Fulwood Road (I'd moved out of the Hall of Residence by then, I now lived in an old coach house owned by the university with Carol that was infested with rats; we had a colony living there in the roof of this house, which was level with the main road, or so the pest control people told us). As soon as a quiet voice other than my mother's answered the phone, I knew how serious it was. If my brother had been injured, my mother would have been on the other end of the phone, angry with him and angry with me. I had prepared myself to hear her rage. She had always hated him climbing. But this was some other woman's voice. She told me her name, but I couldn't put a face to it, it was a neighbour. 'I'll put Eileen on,' she said. She was very solemn which told me everything I needed to know. My mother could hardly speak with her sobbing.

'He's dead,' she said, 'your brother's dead.'

In the years ahead, she always said the same thing about this loss. The death of my father had been unbearable, but this was so much worse. A pain like no other, and she never got over it. There were few nights where I didn't see my brother briefly in my dreams (you always seem to dream about the dead). I say briefly because they would often wake me up. At first, he would talk to me, and we would walk together through strange and unfamiliar landscapes, but later, he seemed always to be walking away from me; he had a very distinctive walk from the back – I remember watching him walk down Barginnis Street to get the bus into town to go on one of his expeditions, maybe the Alps, I can't remember, somewhere far more glamorous than rainy Belfast. I was very shy then, too shy to even say goodbye to him. 'Ignorant wee shite,' he shouted upstairs, and I watched him walk down Barginnis Street to get the bus into town. And I noticed his walk. He looked small and vulnerable. And that's how he looked in my dreams. Or he'd be leaving buildings that I was just entering. And in those buildings, somewhere there would be cages and wheels and sometimes fire and the closing curtains of blackness, like the mines and the steel works of Sheffield.

My mother missed him terribly, she was devastated by the loss, and I was away now, in my new life in the city that Bill had loved. 'You're off enjoying yourself,' she would say. 'Out every night, no doubt.'

There was no one to comfort her, the romantic relationships of the past seemed to have fizzled out. She sometimes had to go on what she called 'nerve tablets' after Bill's death. Whenever I was back home in Belfast and the room smelt heavy of whisky, as it sometimes did, she would often burst into great gulps of lugubrious, self-pitying tears that took her breath away. She just couldn't cope, and I wasn't there. And when I was there, I was of no use anyway. I was away across the water giving lectures about theories of learned helplessness and by-stander apathy. I would stand in front of a room of students and say solemnly that if you punish a dog with an electric shock enough that they can't control, they don't learn how to retake control; eventually they just sit there. They give up. I would explain that it works with dogs, rats.... and people. I would look at the students as if this was a profound thought delivered by a profound thinker (even if a twenty-six-year-old profound thinker).

I would describe Martin Seligman's classic research on learned helplessness – dogs were placed in a box with two chambers divided by a low barrier – one chamber of the box had an electrified floor, the other chamber didn't. All the dogs had to do was jump over that low barrier to escape the electric shock. But one group of dogs was given prior experience of being strapped in a harness and given electric shocks but shocks that they could avoid by pressing a panel with their noses. When they were placed in the box with the two chambers, they quickly learned that they had to jump over that barrier to avoid pain. It was easy for them, they knew that they could escape from the pain, that it could be avoided. However, some of the dogs were allocated to a group where they were strapped in a harness and given electric shocks that they couldn't avoid. There was nothing they could do to avoid the pain. They didn't learn how to escape; they just sat there in their pain and their suffering (Seligman and Groves 1970). That was learned helplessness. They had been punished in a way that they couldn't avoid and now they'd given up trying.

Or I would talk about by-stander apathy and the famous case of Kitty Genovese who was murdered in Queens, New York in 1964. Kitty was followed on her way back to her apartment at 3 am after finishing work in a bar and attacked and stabbed by a stranger. Her yelling woke up her neighbours, but none intervened. The story made the front pages of newspapers. 'What is happening to society?' the papers all asked. This, of course, got social psychologists interested. Latane and Darley (1969) analysed how this could happen. There could be no real ambiguity about the seriousness of what the by-standers were hearing on the street down below in this case (which often prevents intervention), but instead there is diffusion of responsibility where the moral obligation to help didn't fall on just one person given that several neighbours were witnessing the tragic event (lots of lights went on in the apartment block overlooking where the incident took place). It was no one person's individual responsibility to act. The responsibility was shared.

When I think about by-stander apathy now, it makes me laugh, in the saddest sort of way. Me standing there in a lecture, *moralising* about by-stander apathy because when you talk about this sort of thing as a lecturer in psychology, a moral tone inevitably slips into your speech (that's just one of my observations). That great psychological distance between New York in 1964 and Sheffield in the late 1970s allows you to look down on those working-class people in Queens, violent and dark, with black and white images of the scene, and think to yourself – what the hell is wrong with those people? We know that when we're in the role of the observer, we understand actions in terms of dispositional characteristics – the people themselves – their personalities, characteristics, and 'dispositions'; actors explain their actions in terms of situational characteristics. That is the great actor–observer discrepancy which applies particularly to negative events (see the meta-analysis in Malle [2006]). Nadelhoffer and Feltz (2008) comment that we hold other people to different moral standards than we would hold ourselves even if we were in the same situation. Perhaps, we have trouble seeing it from their point of view, to imagine life in Queens at that time, witnessing violence, hearing it, out there in the dark, experiencing the repercussions of intervention (because every time you intervene in a violent encounter, there are *some* consequences).

Perhaps, we have trouble imagining generally, or we don't like to, that way we cling on to a different concept of self. Perhaps, that's an act of self-deceit.

Why didn't I try to help my mother more? Her sitting there on her own in her later years, hoping that Brian Keenan, now that his blindfold was off, would somehow drive up to Ligoniel and take her out for a wee drink? She had been punished with two sudden deaths. The two people she loved most in the world (I always thought I was in third place, but there's no disgrace in being third in any competition). Like one of Seligman's dogs, 'strapped in a harness and given electric shocks that they couldn't avoid. There was nothing they could do to avoid the pain.' There was nothing she could do to avoid these psychic shocks. She was undoubtedly now suffering from a form of learned helplessness. And what was I doing to help? Indeed, what sort of by-stander was I? From that lofty office window over in Sheffield overlooking the university playing fields, all that distance away, 'across the water,' as they say in Belfast. I was her son, now her only son. What was I thinking?

The answer is nothing. I didn't see the connections between what I was lecturing about and my personal circumstances. This didn't feel like conscious avoidance on my part; it just seemed that the social psychology I was teaching was to be regarded as a self-contained academic enterprise, to be appreciated mainly for its internal beauty (if it had any) and consistency, and perhaps for its potential application to *other* lives, certainly not to my own. If I must defend my younger self, perhaps it's just that I felt that there was nothing I could do, evoking learned helplessness on my part and not just my mother's. Remembering those painful months and years after my father's death and the fact that my mother had sought solace elsewhere and lied about it. And after my brother's death, perhaps, I thought that her neighbours would be more help; my mother wouldn't move to England after all. I had asked her, she said. 'What would I do in England,' she said. She had grown up with those neighbours. They were there for her every day, if she wanted them, that's what I told myself.

That's the thing about cornerstones of social psychology like learned helplessness and by-stander apathy, they seem a little different when you start to apply them to your own life. I was a lecturer in social psychology, that was who I now was. I was having to pretend to be knowledgeable, to act a part in front of an audience of students, to fake it, to lie if you like. Perhaps, I was also lying to myself about my mother's desperate circumstances.

My mother was quite alone in her grief. She told me that I was no help to a widow woman. My brother would have been more help to her. She made me feel this without saying it directly. And now he had been taken from her. I wanted to tell her that he had also been taken from me, but I couldn't say this to her. She was in enough pain and we still couldn't communicate openly.

I would try to amuse her when she had a drink ('you're never here, you said you would never leave me and now you're away enjoying yourself in England'), and I would see her glance at me sometimes, a glance as vague and as grey and unformed as twilight. She was heartbroken, helpless, puzzled by her fate, defeated by it. And seemingly puzzled by how I was turning out. 'You used to be such a loving boy,' she would say, implying that I was not a loving boy, any longer. I must have got harder, that might have been my way of coping.

She spoke to my brother when she went to bed, just as she had done with my father. It was happening all over again. Sobbing and talking. You could hear her voice rising to ask questions and sometimes you could hear the downward intonation of an assertion appearing in her voice as if she was telling him what he must do. Perhaps, she was warning him. She left gaps in her speech, as if he might be answering back. I don't know if she heard his replies. I tried not to listen that carefully. It felt wrong all over again. My mother sought to find my brother in old tear-stained photographs. Our neighbours always said that he was the most beautiful child they had ever seen, and now he was gone.

I would ring my mother up from Sheffield just to say hello, and for a moment, she would be confused as to which son it was that was calling her so late at night. Sometimes she called me Bill by mistake. I remember the first time. The momentary shock that froze me. I didn't correct her and that perhaps was a terrible lie. I let her have a conversation with her other son for a change. I thought that it might do her some good. I thought that it might be good for her to have her other son back for a while. She started to make this mistake more often. Sometimes, you could hear her coming round on the phone, her mind slowly trying to remember what it was that was blackening and shading her days. She would sound shaken, a little confused. Sometimes I thought that she was getting confused more generally, stuck in that room day in, day out with the dog-eared photographs and the swirly red carpet.

My lies of pretence, by not correcting her, may have helped her, I don't know, that's perhaps what I thought at the time, or it may have helped re-traumatise her further, as she had to recall it all over again. They weren't active lies, I wasn't impersonating my dead brother, I just didn't say anything when she called me 'Bill.'

But I started playing a new role with her, never taking anything too seriously, not consciously but unconsciously. I started to become more outgoing over the years, chatty, far more like my brother, superficial when I had to be, very superficial some of the time. He was always very sociable, I was the quiet one, a bit 'odd' when I was a child, according to my mother, where odd just means socially awkward.

It wasn't a deliberate act, it just seemed to happen. My mother and I went on the train to Wales together. An attractive girl sat opposite. I started talking to her about nothing. My mother sat beside me, not saying anything but taking it all in. The girl got up to go to get a coffee.

'Where did you learn to chat up women like that?' my mother asked. 'You remind me of your brother, that's exactly what he's like' (always still in the present tense). 'I thought you were the wee studious one.' 'I was chatting, not chatting up,' I said, as I glimpsed the girl returning. My mother nudged me in the ribs. Some might have mistakenly taken this as a sign of encouragement, but that's not how it was meant. It meant she was watching me. It meant 'don't overstep the mark.' She was watching me in a puzzled sort of way. She fidgeted in her seat.

'To be honest, I've never met anyone so good at chatting up women,' she said when we were getting off the train. I explained that I hadn't been chatting her up, I was just being pleasant. 'So, you're going to tell me what is and what's not chatting up. I've been chatted up enough my men to know the difference. That was definitely chatting up.' She came to one of my guest lectures at another university. A girl in the front row asked me something in those few moments of uncertainty and excitement before the lecture starts, I can't remember what the question was, but some vague questions about the topic. My mother afterwards accused me of chatting her up as well. She wanted me to be more social but not like this.

'I think you're turning into your brother,' she said, 'he had so many girlfriends, you only had one, now you're making up for lost time.'

My character seemed to be changing, I'll grant you that. I attribute it to being a university lecturer. You must stand in front of large groups and talk. You have to be outgoing and when you're outgoing and friendly you can connect with people. My mother saw this as competition to her, and would scold me for not spending enough time with her. 'You can have lots of women, she would say, 'but you'll only ever have one mother.'

But she liked me going home to Belfast to take her out. I took her to Belfast's top nightclub Pip's, where she got chatted up by some younger man (and that was chatting up). 'Don't tell him how old I am for God's sake,' she whispered. I had allowed her a glimpse of her past. She was out with her outgoing, sociable son in a night full of possibilities. The swotty one would never have done that. I wasn't impersonating anyone, I wasn't deliberately acting or lying, I had just changed, in a way to allow her a different truth. Out with that outgoing son of hers, the charmer, the womaniser, the other one. Where anything can happen.

I never corrected her when she called me Bill. Never. Why would I? What would I have said. 'Bill's dead, have you forgotten that? I'm the other one.' Sometimes, you have to lie, that's what I've discovered over the years, but you can do it in silence. If you're lucky that is.

9 Summary

Lies in Everyday Life (Chapters 1 and 2)

- Lies are everywhere and can have very serious consequences.
- Lies can involve concealment or fabrication, and often the feigning of other emotions to mask the lie. This can make the experience of being lied to feel worse.
- Lies can have significant negative effects on relationships, leading to a breakdown in trust which is the foundation of any healthy relationship.
- Rebuilding trust after a lie can be challenging and may require significant time and effort; sometimes it may never be successful.
- Lies lead to various types of communication difficulties, the person who told the lie may feel the need to continue lying to cover up their initial lie, leading to further dishonesty.
- Lies radiate outwards, for example, in the case of marital infidelity, the individual may have to lie to other people and not just their partner, including their children and others.
- The recipient of the lie may become guarded and hesitant to communicate openly, fearing more deception – this can create significant barriers to open communication and hinder the growth and intimacy of the relationship.
- Lies can cause emotional distress for *both* parties involved – the victim of the lie may experience feelings of betrayal, hurt, anger, or disappointment; the person who has told the lie may feel ashamed, remorseful, and guilty, and anxious or fearful about being caught.
- These emotional responses can strain the relationship and lead to resentment or emotional distance.
- Keeping a lie secret may impact on the physical and psychological well-being of the individual who has told the lie.

DOI: 10.4324/9781003394563-9

- Being lied to can have a negative impact on one's self-esteem. It may make the person question their worthiness or desirability, leading to feelings of inadequacy.
- This can create a cycle of self-doubt and insecurity within the relationship.
- Repeated lying can have long-term consequences on relationships – if lies become a pattern, it can erode the relationship's foundation and make it difficult to rebuild trust. Over time, the relationship may become unsustainable, leading to separation or breakup.
- Many marriages survive the lies associated with infidelity, in the sense that the couple don't get divorced, but the relationships nevertheless can be significantly altered.
- The classic research by Gottman on the 'mathematics' of divorce perhaps should have scored the incidence of lying as a factor underpinning several of the behavioural variables which he did identify as predictive of divorce in his model, like, for example, the display of contempt.
- The impact of lies on a relationship will vary depending on the nature and frequency of the lies, as well as the characteristics and personalities of the individuals involved.
- Many counsellors suggest that open and honest communication, along with a commitment to rebuilding trust, can help address the effects of lies on relationships, and assist in healing and strengthening the relationship. But this is often easier said than done.
- In the meantime, lies can produce some very irrational behaviours in the recipient of the lie, like pretending to be dead (that, I must admit, is a very personal example).
- This would not have surprised the anthropologist Gregory Bateson, who did not study lies directly, but a range of other forms of contradictory communications that put the receiver in an impossible situation where any *rational* response is often not possible because of the power dynamics within the relationship.
- When psychologists write about 'lies in everyday life,' they often fail to consider many of these factors.

Learning to Lie (Chapter 3)

- Children (including Charles Darwin's own son) typically begin to lie between the ages of two and three years old.
- This stage of development marks the emergence of cognitive abilities necessary for lying, such as Theory of Mind and perspective-taking.

- But children engage in more basic deceptive behaviours before that age, like fake crying.
- At around three years old, children start to understand that others can have different beliefs and knowledge from their own. This new-found understanding allows them to engage in intentional deception by manipulating or distorting information to suit their own interests or to avoid punishment.
- Initially, young children's lies tend to be simple and transparent, often accompanied by obvious nonverbal cues like facial expressions or body language.
- However, as they grow older and their cognitive and social skills develop, children become more sophisticated in their lying abilities, refining their deception techniques and becoming better at hiding their dishonesty.
- Lying can be a normal part of child development, but it is also an opportunity for parents and caregivers to teach their children about honesty, trustworthiness, and the importance of ethical behaviour. Charles Darwin himself seemed very keen on this.
- Darwin also encouraged open communication and modelling honesty to help his children develop a strong moral compass as they navigate the complexities of truth and deception.
- Both *Theory of Mind and Executive Function* are positively correlated with frequency of lying, and there is a strong association between Executive Function and the ability to *maintain* lies in addition to the telling of initial lies.
- The association between Executive Function and lying is also strongest for self-protective lies (lies to conceal transgressions to avoid negative consequences) and self-benefitting lies (lies to get a strategic advantage) rather than for white lies (prosocial lies in order to be polite) or lies to protect somebody else.
- In other words, the brightest children, in terms of their Theory of Mind and Executive Function abilities, lie the most and lie most selfishly.
- There is no significant relationship between age and Executive Function ability – rather Executive Function plays a consistent role in children's lying regardless of age.
- Adolescence is a period of transition where teenagers strive for independence and autonomy. Lying can be a way for them to assert their independence, maintain a sense of control, or avoid parental or adult scrutiny.
- Teenagers often face pressure from their peers to fit in or to conform to social norms. Lying may be used to gain acceptance, avoid judgement, or enhance social status.

- Teenagers may engage in lying to test boundaries, challenge authority, or explore their own identity. This can involve fabricating stories or exaggerating experiences to see how others react, or to appear more interesting, experienced or 'hard' (at least in street gangs).
- It is important to appreciate the pressure that teenagers may be under, particularly in certain teenage sub-cultures.
- Certain lies may set up a state of cognitive dissonance in the individuals and we know from the work of Leon Festinger that this can lead to a change in private attitudes and behaviour. Lies, from this perspective, can be part of a mechanism of change.
- We continue to learn to lie after we become adults, sometimes out of necessity, sometimes for ulterior motives, and often, we need to get the approval of our colleagues or accomplices to build a shared representation of the victims as suckers or mugs, who deserve everything they get.
- This can diminish the negative emotional connotations of the lie for the teller of the lie. It makes lying so much easier.
- Those conning the poor, and telling lies about it, may be part of a sub-culture with the same basic mechanisms of approval for deceit as a teenage gang

Expert Liars (Chapter 4)

- Expert liars have developed a series of strategies to allow them to lie without all the negative emotional effects that many of us feel, like guilt, fear, shame, and remorse.
- These strategies include moral disengagement which refers to the cognitive process of justifying or rationalising unethical behaviour (just being 'a good Samaritan'; just being helpful).
- The strategies also involve blaming others, minimising the consequences of the lie, or thinking differently about what they're doing, to detach themselves from the moral implications of their lying.
- These strategies can help alleviate feelings of guilt or remorse.
- Repeated lying can lead to a desensitisation effect, where individuals become less sensitive to the moral and emotional consequences of their actions.
- Over time, habitual liars may experience a diminished sense of remorse, as lying becomes normalised and ingrained in their everyday behaviour.
- When individuals perceive personal benefits or rewards from lying, such as gaining power, avoiding punishment, or achieving social approval, it can overshadow any potential feelings of remorse.

- Expert liars also often have specific strategies, for example, mixing truth with the lie can make the lie more believable. By presenting some true information, the liar gains credibility, making it easier to slip in the false details unnoticed.
- Expert liars often use omission and concealment: rather than telling outright lies, they omit important information. They avoid revealing certain facts that could expose the truth or damage their credibility.
- Expert liars also use misdirection: they divert attention away from their lies by introducing unrelated or irrelevant information, often creating confusion to prevent others from focusing on the critical points.
- They are very good at building rapport: expert liars establish strong rapport and build trust with their targets. People are more likely to believe and be influenced by those they feel comfortable with.
- They feign their emotions: expert liars may pretend to display specific emotions to elicit sympathy, empathy, or trust from their audience. Appearing vulnerable or emotional can make others less likely to question their honesty.
- Expert liars are adept at consciously controlling or suppressing their body language to appear more convincing.
- In contemporary jargon, they may use gaslighting. The expert liar may twist the truth or deny events that have occurred to make the target doubt their perceptions, their memory, or in extreme cases, their very sanity. I highlighted perhaps an instance of this in Chapter 2, but *gaslighting* is a word that is perhaps now often overused in everyday discourse.
- Expert liars attend to the consistency of their lies in order to avoid contradictions. They may rehearse their stories and ensure that all the details align, making it harder to detect deception.
- Expert liars also engage in self-deceit – they often work at convincing themselves of the 'truth' of the lie they are presenting. By fully believing their own lies, individuals can appear more authentic and credible to others.
- Rolls Royce John was a master of self-deceit.
- Self-deceit can play a role in successful lying, especially when it comes to managing one's own emotions and maintaining a convincing facade.
- When someone engages in lying, they may experience guilt or remorse due to the ethical implications of their actions. Self-deceit can help individuals suppress or rationalise these negative emotions, allowing them to maintain a confident and convincing demeanour while deceiving others.

- Self-deceit also helps us overcome cognitive dissonance. Cognitive dissonance occurs when there is a conflict between one's beliefs, attitudes, or values and one's behaviour. When lying conflicts with one's moral values, self-deceit can help alleviate this cognitive dissonance by creating a narrative that justifies or rationalises the dishonesty. This can contribute to a more confident and convincing presentation.
- Self-deceit is not a healthy or ethical approach to social life. But according to the sociobiologist Trivers, it can be highly advantageous.
- As the Roman orator Quintilian noted, many effective lies depend on external sources to make the lie more convincing and expert liars are expert at finding the right sources – the Rolls Royce, the designer suit, the VIP 'friends,' all status symbols with immediate and unflinching effect.
- Sometimes acquiring these also requires considerable skill, which I, for one, clearly do not possess.

Natural Liars and Personality (Chapter 5)

- The absence or reduction of remorse when telling lies can be influenced by various factors, including individual differences, psychological traits, and situational factors.
- Some individuals may have a reduced ability to empathise with others, making it easier for them to lie without feeling remorse.
- Empathy involves understanding and sharing the emotions of others, and individuals with lower levels of empathy may have a diminished sense of guilt or remorse when deceiving others.
- Certain personality traits, such as narcissism or psychopathy, can be associated with limited or no empathy and a reduced capacity for remorse.
- People with these traits may prioritise their own self-interests and lack concern for the feelings or well-being of others, making it easier for them to lie without experiencing guilt or remorse.
- Psychopathy is a developmental disorder, a subset of antisocial personality disorder (ASPD).
- Psychopathy is a continuum; some are higher on this dimension than others. A cut-off on this dimension is used to identify the 'psychopath.'
- Psychopathy tends to be associated with other personality characteristics, specifically *narcissism* and *Machiavellianism*, and psychologists refer to these as the 'Dark Triad' of personality characteristics.

- These other personality characteristics are also associated with lying.
- Narcissists have a grandiose sense of self and crave positive attention – they will lie in order to get attention.
- Machiavellians manipulate social situations and will use lies to do this.
- Psychopaths are callous and lack emotional empathy, and they will be oblivious to the distressing effects of lies on others.
- Dark Triad ratings are correlated with several antisocial behaviours, including higher levels of delinquency and aggression in children, as well as risky and sensation-seeking activities.
- The traits characteristic of the Dark Triad are thought to be associated with a 'compromised' or 'dysfunctional morality,' in that they 'value "self" over "other" in a way that violates implicit communal sentiments in people.'
- All three dimensions are correlated (with the strongest correlation between narcissism and non-clinical psychopathy), and although these dimensions are related, they are not equivalent.
- The one commonality across the triad is 'low agreeableness.'
- There are also significant differences between these dimensions – only psychopaths (but not narcissists nor Machiavellians) are low on anxiety, which is consistent with the general clinical view that psychopaths are very low on anxiety (and resistant to punishment).
- Narcissists and (to a lesser extent) psychopaths exhibit the most self-enhancement in various cognitive tests, whereas Machiavellians show little sign of this.
- Machiavellians are the most 'reality-based' in their sense of self.
- Narcissists exhibit a strong self-deceptive component (with low insight) into their own personality.
- In retrospect, I could apply the criteria of ASPD to almost every member of my gang back in Belfast, probably including myself.
- But it seems odd to me to diagnose a whole group or a community of friends rather than an individual in terms of aberrant *personality*.
- But within that social context itself, deviation from the group norm could be identified. We were sensitive to what behaviours bound us together and what could potentially tear us apart.
- Presumably, that's why psychopathy is described as a *subset* of the broader clinical ASPD classification, which could be applied generally to the group.
- The nature and process of lying in ASPD and psychopathy would seem to be quite different from the norm.
- Any kind of retrospective 'diagnosis' of a condition like psychopathy, even non-clinical psychopathy, is always highly problematic. But sometimes behaviours do stand out *in situ*.

Lie Detection (Chapter 6)

- Human lie detection seems to be highly flawed.
- We are not skilled at accurately identifying lies, despite what most of us think.
- Liars can look you in the eye. Most people across the globe believe that they cannot.
- Lying is a complex behaviour that involves a combination of verbal and nonverbal cues, cognitive processes, and emotional regulation.
- It is challenging for humans to accurately interpret and integrate all these different aspects simultaneously, leading to errors in lie detection.
- Humans rely on a limited set of cues, such as particular facial expressions, certain aspects of body language, and inconsistencies in the narrative, to detect deception.
- However, none of these cues are foolproof and can be masked or manipulated by skilled liars.
- People do differ in their ability to detect lies. Some individuals may have a natural talent for spotting deception, while others may be more easily deceived (although the existing experimental evidence of this is weak, but that is based on lies in the lab).
- Human beings are prone to cognitive biases that can influence their judgement and decision-making.
- Confirmation bias, for example, leads individuals to interpret information in a way that confirms their pre-existing beliefs. This bias can make people more susceptible to believing lies that align with their own perspectives and political affiliations.
- The context in which lies are told can further complicate lie detection. For instance, high-stakes situations, such as interrogations or job interviews, can increase the pressure and stress on both the liar and the detector, making it more difficult to accurately assess truthfulness. The liar may look nervous throughout, for example.
- Most people do not receive formal training in lie detection techniques and rely on their intuition or commonsense (or what they pick up from the media).
- However, research has shown that even with training, lie detection accuracy does not improve significantly.
- This suggests that lie detection is a complex skill that requires extensive training and experience to master.
- Skilled liars are adept at manipulating the cues and behaviours typically associated with deception. They may intentionally display false cues or mask their true emotions, making it difficult for human lie detectors to accurately assess their truthfulness.

- Given these limitations, it is important to approach lie detection with caution and recognise that human judgement is often very fallible.
- The development of technological tools such as polygraph tests and automated systems, which I didn't cover in the book, aim to overcome some of these limitations and improve lie detection accuracy. However, even these methods are not foolproof and have very significant limitations.
- We do seem to know instinctively that our behaviour can leak a great deal when we are lying, so we attempt to inhibit it.
- A meta-analysis of the published literature on deception has found that only three forms of behaviour were reliably associated with lying and they were 'nodding,' 'foot and leg movements,' and 'hand movements.' All three decreased in frequency.
- The structural organisation of the gestural movements that accompany speech seems to be affected by deception.
- There are marked changes in the durations of both the stroke phase of the gesture (the meaningful part of the gesture) and in the post-stroke hold (where the gesture pauses temporarily at the end of the stroke phase).
- Our own research found that the stroke phases of gestures were longer when telling the truth rather than in the deception condition, whilst post-stroke holds were longer when executed as part of the truth than during deception.
- In terms of the form and meaning of gestures, the real underlying representation of an event can sometimes leak out when speakers are trying to deceive.
- The form and structural organisation of gestures are a good deal more revealing during deception than their frequency alone.
- Beats, which are simple stressed-timed movements, are generally much easier to control and considerably less revealing in deception.
- Tony Blair, the former Prime Minister of the United Kingdom, was, on occasion, transparent when he veered away from the truth, showing a significant inhibition of hand gestures.
- It is perhaps a shame (in retrospect) that more people did not study his hand gestures when he was explaining why we had to invade Iraq to eliminate the weapons of mass destruction. It might have had major implications for the stability of the region.
- But we need caution in interpretation throughout.
- Joe Biden would appreciate that (as would so many others) – one single slip (nonverbal or verbal) does not indicate that you are a liar.

Our Masters' Lying Voices (Chapter 7)

- Politics is well known (unfortunately) for its inherent tendencies towards deception and manipulation, and understanding the psychological processes behind lying in this context can provide valuable insights into political behaviour and its impact on society.
- Politicians often engage in strategic deception to achieve certain goals, maintain power, and shape public opinion.
- This can involve making false promises, distorting facts, or deliberately misleading the public to gain support or discredit opponents. Big lies are not rare.
- The motivations behind the lies of politicians can vary, ranging from personal ambition and seeking and maintaining power to various ideological agendae and party loyalty. The personality of the individual politician would often seem to be an important, indeed critical, factor.
- Individuals are more likely to believe and accept lies that align with their pre-existing beliefs and values, which is an example of conformation bias.
- Political leaders often cynically exploit this tendency by tailoring their messages and lies to resonate with their target audience, reinforcing their support and loyalty.
- Trust is a fundamental aspect of political leadership, and when politicians are caught lying, it can erode public trust and confidence in the political system.
- The consequences of lying in politics can have far-reaching effects, including a decline in public engagement, increased polarisation, and a general erosion of democratic norms and values.
- By recognising the motivations, strategies, and consequences of dishonesty in the political realm, citizens can, in principle, become more critical (and perhaps cynical) 'consumers' of political information but better equipped to hold politicians accountable.
- The importance and impact of lying in politics can never be underestimated – from Trump denying that there is such a thing as man-made climate change to Hitler's motivated genocide, driven by lies and deceit.
- Individual politicians have their own methods and techniques for deception.
- Trump uses both language and body language to mislead. He turns the unconscious system of body language against us.
- Putin asserts his power and authority at every level in his communications to force compliance.

- Psychologists talk about lack of empathy, narcissism, failure to take responsibility for actions, and willingness to hurt without remorse or guilt as clear evidence of the Dark Triad of personality characteristics (psychopathy, narcissism, and Machiavellianism). These characteristics would seem to be identifiable in a number of politicians who use lies frequently.
- When it comes to Vladimir Putin, we see how these personality characteristics can operate in his social world and impact on other's behaviour, forcing compliance and demonstrating Putin's authority, feeding back into Putin's own concept of self, so that he then has the impudence to use the big lie.
- Hitler always justified the big lie and recognised its effectiveness for the ordinary person.
- Hitler didn't invent some of the core metaphors about 'the Jew,' many of them had been around for centuries, but he added layers to them and sold this metaphorical frame to a nation. That was his great trick. That was his big lie.
- In the process, he undoubtedly convinced himself about his metaphorical way of framing his world, structuring the thought of a nation, including his own.
- Lies like this depend on self-deceit if they are to be convincing, and he seemed to have managed to convince a nation.
- Hitler framed the world in a particular way, with his own false version of its poorly examined rational beginnings, and that frame of 'the Jew' and blood poisoning became his reality.
- These metaphorical frames became part of his unconscious ideation – in his talk, in his thinking, even perhaps in his dreams.
- And these dreams became the nightmare for so many millions.
- Lying is never trivial. It can have far-reaching and devastating consequences at the level of the individual, family, social group, community, and culture.
- Lies about climate change threaten the whole world.

Chapter 8: Closing the Circle (Chapter 8)

- Lies reverberate within families, societies, and cultures.
- They leave a memory trace and a legacy.
- They can be drawn upon to justify and explain other negative acts.
- The ways in which this is done requires further critical examination because it has serious consequences for society as a whole.

References

Adler, P. A. and Adler, P. (1995). Dynamics of inclusion and exclusion in preadolescent cliques. *Social Psychology Quarterly* 58: 145–162.

Akehurst, L. and Vrij, A. (1999). Creating suspects in police interviews. *Journal of Applied Social Psychology* 29: 192–210.

Alloway, T., McCallum, F., Alloway, R. and Hoicka, E. (2015). Liar, liar, working memory on fire: Investigating the role of working memory in child verbal deception. *Journal of Experimental Child Psychology* 137: 30–38.

Argyle, M. (1973). *Social Interaction*. London: Methuen.

Aristotle (340 BCE). *The Nicomachean Ethics*. Trans. J. A. K. Thomson (1953/1976). Harmondsworth: Penguin.

Asch, S. (1951). Effects of group pressure upon the modification and distortion of judgements. In H. Guetzkow (ed.). *Groups, Leadership and Men: Research in Human Relationships* (pp. 177–190). Pittsburgh: Carnegie Mellon Press.

Atkinson, M. (1984). *Our Masters' Voices: The Language and Body Language of Politics*. London: Routledge.

Bates, E. (1976). *Language and Context*. New York: Academic Press.

Bates, E., Benigni, L., Bretherton, I., Camaioni, L. and Volterra, V. (1979). *The Emergence of Symbols: Cognition and Communication in Infancy*. New York: Academic Press.

Bateson, G. (1972/2000). *Steps to an Ecology of Mind: Collected Essays in Anthropology, Psychiatry, Evolution, and Epistemology*. New York: Paladin Books.

Beattie, G. (1977). The dynamics of interruption and the filled pause. *British Journal of Social and Clinical Psychology* 16: 283–284.

Beattie, G. (1978). Sequential temporal patterns of speech and gaze in dialogue. *Semiotica* 23: 29–52.

Beattie, G. (1979). Planning units in spontaneous speech: Some evidence from hesitation in speech and speaker gaze direction in conversation. *Linguistics* 17: 61–78.

Beattie, G. (1981). A further investigation of the cognitive interference hypothesis of gaze patterns during conversation. *British Journal of Social Psychology* 20: 243–248.

Beattie, G. (1982). Behaviour in the psychological laboratory. *New Scientist* 96: 181.

Beattie, G. (1983). *Talk: An Analysis of Speech and Non-Verbal Behaviour in Conversation*. Milton Keynes: Open University Press.

Beattie, G. (1986). *Survivors of Steel City*. London: Chatto & Windus.

Beattie, G. (1987). *Making It: The Reality of Today's Entrepreneurs*. London: Weidenfeld & Nicolson.

Beattie, G. (1988). *All Talk: Why It's Important to Watch Your Words and Everything You Say*. London: Weidenfeld and Nicolson.

Beattie, G. (1990). *England After Dark*. London: Weidenfeld & Nicolson.

Beattie, G. (1992). *We are the People: Journeys through Protestant Ulster*. London: Heinemann.

Beattie, G. (1996). *On the Ropes: Boxing as a Way of Life*. **London: Victor Gollancz.**

Beattie, G. (1998). *Hard Lines: Voices from Deep within a Recession*. Manchester: Manchester University Press.

Beattie, G. (2002). *The Shadows of Boxing: Prince Naseem and Those He Left Behind*. London: Orion.

Beattie, G. (2003). *Visible Thought: The New Psychology of Body Language*. London: Routledge.

Beattie, G. (2004). *Protestant Boy*. Granta: London.

Beattie, G. (2010). *Why Aren't We Saving the Planet? A Psychologist's Perspective*. London: Routledge.

Beattie, G. (2011). *Get the Edge: How Simple Changes Will Transform Your Life*. London: Headline.

Beattie, G. (2013). *Our Racist Heart? An Exploration of Unconscious Prejudice in Everyday Life*. London: Routledge.

Beattie, G. (2016a). *Rethinking Body Language: How Hand Movements Reveal Hidden Thoughts*. London: Routledge.

Beattie, G. (2016b). How Donald Trump bullies with his body language. *The Conversation*. October 14th.

Beattie, G. (2017). The psychology behind Trump's awkward handshake…and how to beat him at his own game. *The Conversation*. February 20th.

Beattie, G. (2018a). *The Conflicted Mind: And Why Psychology Has Failed to Deal with It*. London: Routledge.

Beattie, G. (2018b). Optimism bias and climate change. *The British Academy Review* 33: 12–15

Beattie, G. (2019). *Trophy Hunting: A Psychological Perspective*. London: Routledge.

Beattie, G. (2021). *Selfless: A Psychologists' Journey through Identity and Social Class*. London: Routledge.

Beattie, G. (2022). Revenge: The neuroscience of why it feels good in the moment, but may be a bad idea in the long run. *The Conversation*. January 26th.

Beattie, G. (2023a). *Doubt: A Psychological Exploration*. London: Routledge.

Beattie, G. (2023b). Joe Biden: Slips of the tongue can project our own hidden thoughts, fears and anxieties. *The Conversation*. April 21st.

Beattie, G. (2023c). Is there a tipping point for Trump supporters to stop backing him? Here's what the science says. *The Conversation*. May 17th.

Beattie, G. and Aboudan, R. (1994). Gestures, pauses and speech: An experimental investigation of the effects of changing social context on their precise temporal relationship. *Semiotica* 99: 221–249.

Beattie, G. and Butterworth, B. (1979). Contextual probability and word frequency as determinants of pauses and errors in spontaneous speech. *Language and Speech* 22: 201–211.

Beattie, G. and Doherty, K. (1995). "I saw what really happened": The discursive construction of victims and perpetrators in first-hand accounts of paramilitary violence in Northern Ireland. *Journal of Language and Social Psychology* 14: 408–433.

Beattie, G. and Ellis, A. (2017). *The Psychology of Language and Communication: Psychology Press Classic Editions*. London: Routledge

Beattie, G., Marselle, M., McGuire, L. and Litchfield, D. (2017). Staying over-optimistic about the future: Uncovering attentional biases to climate change messages. *Semiotica* 218: 22–64

Beattie, G. and McGuire, L. (2015). Harnessing the unconscious mind of the consumer: How implicit attitudes predict pre-conscious visual attention to carbon footprint information on products. *Semiotica* 204: 253–290.

Beattie, G. and McGuire, L. (2016). Consumption and climate change. Why we say one thing but do another in the face of our greatest threat. *Semiotica* 213: 493–538.

Beattie, G. and McGuire, L. (2018). *The Psychology of Climate Change*. London: Routledge.

Beattie, G. and Sale, L. (2012). Do metaphoric gestures influence how a message is perceived? The effects of metaphoric gesture-speech matches and mismatches on semantic communication and social judgment. *Semiotica* 192: 77–98.

Beattie, G. and Shovelton, H. (1999a). Do iconic hand gestures really contribute anything to the semantic information conveyed by speech? An experimental investigation. *Semiotica* 123: 1–30.

Beattie, G. and Shovelton, H. (1999b). Mapping the range of information contained in the iconic hand gestures that accompany spontaneous speech. *Journal of Language and Social Psychology* 18: 438–462.

Beattie, G. and Shovelton, H. (2002). What properties of talk are associated with the generation of spontaneous iconic hand gestures? *British Journal of Social Psychology* 41: 403–417.

Beattie, G. and Shovelton, H. (2005). Why the spontaneous images created by the hands during talk can help make TV advertisements more effective. *British Journal of Psychology* 96: 21–37.

Beattie, G., Webster, K. and Ross, J. (2010). The fixation and processing of the iconic gestures that accompany talk. *Journal of Language and Social Psychology* 29: 194–213.

Bem, D. J. (1967). Self-perception: An alternative interpretation of cognitive dissonance phenomena. *Psychological Review* 74: 183–200.

Berger, A. (1965). A test of the double bind hypothesis of schizophrenia. *Family Process* 4: 198–205.

Blackburn, R. (1965). Emotionality, repression-sensitization and maladjustment. *British Journal of Psychiatry* 111: 399–400.

Blair, R. (1999). Responsiveness to distress cues in the child with psychopathic tendencies. *Personality and Individual Differences* 7: 135–145.

Blair, R. (2005). Responding to the emotions of others: Dissociating forms of empathy through the study of typical and psychiatric populations. *Consciousness and Cognition* 14: 698–718.

Blair, R., Budhani, S., College, E., & Scott, S. (2005). Deafness to fear in boys with psychopathic tendencies. *Journal of Child Psychology and Psychiatry* 46: 327–336.

Bond, C. F. and DePaulo, B. M. (2006). Accuracy of deceptive judgments. *Personality and Social Psychology Review* 10: 214–234.

Bond, C. F. and DePaulo, B. M. (2008). Individual differences in judging deception: Accuracy and bias. *Psychological Bulletin* 134: 477–492.

Bond, C., Kahler, K. and Paolicelli, L. (1985). The miscommunication of deception: An adaptive perspective. *Journal of Experimental Social Psychology* 21: 331–345.

Brown, B. B., Bakken, J. P., Ameringer, S. W. and Mahon, S. D. (2008). A comprehensive conceptualization of the peer influence process in adolescence. In M. Prinstein and K. Dodge (eds.). *Peer Influence in Children and Adolescence*. New York: Guilford.

Brown, B. and Theobald, W. (1999). *How Teens Matter.* Washington, DC: National Campaign to Prevent Teen Pregnancy.

Butterworth, B. L. (1975). Hesitation and semantic planning and speech. *Journal of Psycholinguistic Research* 4: 75–87

Butterworth, B. L. and Beattie, G. (1978). Gesture and silence as indicators of planning in speech. In P. T. Smith and R. Campbell (eds.). *Recent Advances in the Psychology of Language: Formal and Experimental Approaches.* New York: Plenum.

Campbell, J., Schermer, J. A., Villani, V. C., Nguyen, B., Vickers, L. and Vernon, P. A. (2009). A behavioral genetic study of the Dark Triad of personality and moral development. *Twin Research and Human Genetics* 12: 132–136.

Chaplin, W., Phillips, J., Brown, J., Clanton, N. and Stein, J. (2000). Handshaking, gender, personality, and first impressions. *Journal of Personality and Social Psychology* 79: 110–117.

Christ, S.E., Van Essen, D.C., Watson, J.M., Brubaker, L.E. and McDermott, K.B. (2009). The contributions of prefrontal cortex and executive control to deception: Evidence from activation likelihood estimate meta-analyses. *Cerebral Cortex* 19: 1557–1566.

Christie, R. and Geis, F. L. (eds.). (1970). *Studies in Machiavellianism.* San Diego, CA: Academic Press.

Church, R. B. and Goldin-Meadow, S. (1986). The mismatch between gesture and speech as an index of transitional knowledge. *Cognition* 23: 43–71.

Ciotola, P. V. (1961). *The Effect of Two Contradictory Levels of Reward and Censure on Schizophrenics.* Doctoral dissertation, University of Missouri.

Clark, L. F. (1993). Stress and the cognitive-conversational benefits of social interaction. *Journal of Social and Clinical Psychology* 12: 25–55.

Cody, M. and O'Hair, H. (1983). Nonverbal communication and deception: Differences in deception cues due to gender and communicator dominance. *Communication Monographs* 50: 175–193.

Cohen, D., Beattie, G. and Shovelton, H. (2010). Nonverbal indicators of deception: How iconic gestures reveal thoughts that cannot be suppressed. *Semiotica* 182: 133–174.

Coleridge, S. T. (1812/1917). *Table Talk.* Oxford: Oxford University Press.

Cook, S., Wagner, M. and Goldin-Meadow, S. (2008). Gesturing makes learning last. *Cognition* 106: 1047–1058.

Crysel, L. C., Crosier, B. S. and Webster, G. D. (2013). The Dark Triad and risk behavior. *Personality and Individual Differences* 54: 35–40.

Damasio, A. R. (1994). *Descartes' Error: Emotion, Reason and the Human Brain.* New York: Putnam.

Danesi, M. (2020). *The Art of the Lie.* Lanham: Prometheus Books.

Darwin, C. (1872/1955). *The Expression of the Emotions in Man and Animals.* London: John Murray.

Darwin, C. (1877). A biographical sketch of an infant. *Mind* 7: 285–294.

Davies, G. (1985). The significance of the handshake motif in classical funerary art. *American Journal of Archaeology* 89: 627–640.

Davies, M. (1970). Blood pressure and personality. *Journal of Psychosomatic Research* 14: 89–104.

Davis, M. and Hadiks, D. (1995). Demeanor and credibility. *Semiotica* 106: 5–54.

Delgado-Herrera, M., Azalea, R.-A. and Giordano, M. (2021). What deception studies used in the lab really do: Systematic review and meta-analysis of ecological validity of fMRI deception tasks. *Neuroscience* 468: 88–109.

de Montaigne, M. (1602). *Essays.* Trans. J. M. Cohen (1958). London: Harmondsworth.

DePaulo, B. (2018). *The Psychology of Lying and Detecting Lies.* Great Britain: Amazon.

DePaulo, B. and Kashy, D. (1998). Everyday lies on close and casual relationships. *Journal of Personality and Social Psychology* 74: 63–79.

DePaulo, B.M., Kashy, D.A.., Kirkendol, S.E., Wyer, M.M. and Epstein, J.A. (1996). Lying in everyday life. *Journal of Personality and Social Psychology* 70: 979–995.

DePaulo, B.M., Lindsay, J.J., Malone, B.E., Muhlenbruck, L., Charlton, K. and Cooper, H. (2003). Cues to deception. *Psychological Bulletin* 129: 74–118.

de Turck, M. and Miller, G. (1985). Deception and arousal: Isolating the behavioral correlates of deception. *Human Communication Research* 12: 181–201.

Diamond, A. (2006). The early development of executive function. In E. Bialystok and F. Craik (eds.). *Lifespan Cognition: Mechanisms of Change.* London: Oxford University Press.

Diamond, A. and Lee, K. (2011). Interventions shown to aid executive function development in children 4–12 years old. *Science* 333: 959–964.

Dichter, E. (1960). *The Strategy of Desire.* London: Transaction Publishers.

Ekman, P. (1985). *Telling Lies.* New York: Norton.

Ekman, P. (1988). Lying and nonverbal behavior: Theoretical issues and new findings. *Journal of Nonverbal Behavior* 12: 163–176.

Ekman, P. (2001). *Telling Lies: Clues to Deceit in the Marketplace, Politics and Marriage.* New York: Norton.

Ekman, P. (2003). Darwin, deception and facial expression. *Annals of the New York Academy of Science* 1000: 205–221.

Ekman, P. (2009). Darwin's contributions to our understanding of emotional expressions. *Philosophical Transactions of the Royal Society of London* 364: 3449–3451.

Ekman, P. and Friesen, W. V. (1969). The repertoire of nonverbal behavior: Categories, origins, usage, and coding. *Semiotica* 1: 49–98.

Ekman, P. and Friesen, W. (1972). Hand movements. *Journal of Communication* 22: 353–374.

Ekman, P. and Friesen, W. V. (1982). Felt, false, and miserable smiles. *Journal of Nonverbal Behavior* 6: 238–252.

Ekman, P., Friesen, W. and Scherer, K. (1976). Body movement and voice pitch in deceptive interaction. *Semiotica* 16: 23–27.

Ekman, P., O'Sullivan, M., Friesen, W. and Scherer, K. (1991). Face, voice, and body in detecting deceit. *Journal of Nonverbal Behavior* 15: 125–135.

Evans, A. and Lee, K. (2013). Emergence of lying in very young children. *Developmental Psychology* 49: 1958–1963.

Fea, J. (2018). *Believe Me. The Evangelical Road to Donald Trump.* Pennsylvania: Eerdmans.

Fehr, B., Samson, B. and Paulhus, D. L. (1992). The construct of Machiavellianism: Twenty years later. In C. D. Spielberger and J. N. Butcher (eds.). *Advances in Personality Assessment* (pp. 77–116). Hillsdale, NJ: Erlbaum.

Ferber, R, (1991). Slip of the tongue or slip of the ear? On the perception and transcription of naturalistic slips of the tongue. *Journal of Psycholinguistic Research* 20: 105–122.

Festinger, L. (1957). *A Theory of Cognitive Dissonance.* Evanston, IL: Row, Peterson.

Festinger, L., Riecken, H. W. and Schachter, S. (1956). *When Prophecy Fails.* New York: Harper & Row.

Fitzgerald, F. S. (1925). *The Great Gatsby.* New York: Charles Scribner.

Francis, M. and Pennebaker, J. W. (1993). LIWC. *Linguistic Inquiry and Word Count (Technical Report).* Dallas: Southern Methodist University.

Frank, M. G. and Feeley, T. H. (2003). To catch a liar: Challenges for research in lie detection training. *Journal of Applied Communication Research* 31: 58–75.

Freud, S. (1901/2022). *The Psychopathology of Everyday Life*. Harmondsworth: Penguin.

Fromm-Reichmann, F. (1948). Notes on the development of treatment of schizophrenics by psychoanalytic psychotherapy. *Psychiatry* 11: 263–273.

Furnham, A., Richards, S. C. and Paulhus, D. L. (2013). The Dark Triad of personality: A 10-year review. *Social and Personality Psychology Compass* 7/3: 199–216.

Garnham, A., Shillcock, R.C., Brown, G., Mill, A. and Cutler, A. (1982). Slips of the tongue in the London-Lund corpus of spontaneous conversation. In A. Cutler (ed.). *Slips of the Tongue and Language Production*. Berlin: Mouton.

Gladwell, M. (2005). *Blink: The Power of Thinking Without Thinking*. New York: Little Brown and Company.

The Global Deception Research Team (2006). *Journal of Cross Cultural Psychology* 37: 60–74.

Goffman, E. (1963). *Behavior in Public Places*. Glencoe, IL: Free Press.

Goffman, E. (1976). *The Presentation of Self in Everyday Life*. Harmondsworth: Penguin.

Goldin-Meadow, S. (1999). The development of gesture with and without speech in hearing and deaf children. In L. Messing and R. Campbell (eds.). *Gesture, Speech and Sign*. Oxford: Oxford University Press.

Goldman-Eisler, F. (1968). *Psycholinguistics: Experiments in Spontaneous Speech*. London: Academic Press.

Gottman, J. (1994). *What Predicts Divorce?: The Relationship Between Marital Processes and Marital Outcomes*. London: Lawrence Erlbaum.

Gottman, J. (1997). *Why Marriages Succeed or Fail and How to Make Yours Last*. London: Bloomsbury.

Greene, J., O'Hair, H., Cody, M. and Yen, C. (1985). Planning and control of behavior during deception. *Human Communication Research* 11: 335–64.

Greenwald, A. G. and Ronis, D. L. (1978). Twenty years of cognitive dissonance: Case study of the evolution of a theory. *Psychological Review* 85: 53–57.

Gregor, N. (2005). *Nazism, War and Genocide*. Exeter: University of Exeter Press.

Gullberg, M. and Holmqvist, K. (2002). Visual attention towards gestures in face-to-face interaction versus on screen. In I. Wachsmuth and T. Sowa (eds.). *Gesture and Sign Language in Human-Computer Interaction*. Berlin: Springer.

Gustafson, S. B. and Ritzer, D. R. (1995). The dark side of normal: A psychopathy-linked pattern called aberrant self-promotion. *European Journal of Personality* 9: 147–183.

Hare, R. D. (1985). Comparison of procedures for the assessment of psychopathy. *Journal of Consulting and Clinical Psychology* 53: 7–16.

Hare, R. D. (1991). *The Hare Psychopathy Checklist Revised*. Ontario: Multi-health Systems.

Hart, S. and Hare, R. D. (1998). Association between psychopathy and narcissism: Theoretical views and empirical evidence. In E. F. Ronningstam (ed.). *Disorders of Narcissism: Diagnostic, Clinical, and Empirical Implications* (pp. 415–436). Washington, DC: American Psychiatric Press.

Hartshorne, H. and May, M. (1928). *Studies in the Nature of Character, Studies in Deceit*. Columbia: Columbia University Press.

Hartwell, C. E. (1996). The schizophrenogenic mother concept in American psychiatry. *Psychiatry* 59: 274–297.

Heaney, S. (1975/1992). *North*. Faber and Faber: London.

Hendrix, H. (1998). *Getting the Love You Want: A Guide For Couples*. New York: Henry Holt & Co.

Hitler, A. (1925/2022). *Mein Kampf*. Mumbai: Jaico Publishing House

Holler, J. and Beattie, G. (2002). A micro-analytic investigation of how iconic gestures and speech represent core semantic features in talk. *Semiotica* 142: 31–69.

Holler, J. and Beattie, G. (2003a). How iconic gestures and speech interact in the representation of meaning: Are both aspects really integral to the process. *Semiotica* 146: 81–116.

Holler, J. and Beattie, G. (2003b). Pragmatic aspects of representational gestures: Do speakers us them to clarify verbal ambiguity for the listener? *Gesture* 3: 127–154.

Horberg, E. J., Oveis, C. and Keltner, D. (2009). Disgust and the moralization of purity. *Journal of Personality and Social Psychology* 97: 963–976.

Inbar, Y., Pizarro, D. and Bloom, P. (2011). Conservatives are more easily disgusted than liberals. *Cognition and Emotion* 23: 714–725.

Jancovic, M. A., Devoe, S. and Wiener, M. (1975). Age-related changes in hand and arm movements as nonverbal communication: Some conceptualisations and an empirical exploration. *Child Development* 46: 922–928.

Jonason, P. K., Lyons, M., Bethell, E. J. and Ross, R. (2013). Different routes to limited empathy in the sexes: Examining the links between the Dark Triad and empathy. *Personality and Individual Differences* 54: 572–576.

Jonason, P. K. and Schmitt, D. P. (2012). What have you done for me lately? Friendship-selection in the shadow of the Dark Triad traits. *Evolutionary Psychology* 10: 192–199.

Jonason, P. K. and Webster, G. D. (2012). A protean approach to social influence: Dark Triad personalities and social influence tactics. *Personality and Individual Differences* 52: 521–526.

Kahneman, D. (2011). *Thinking, Fast and Slow*. London: Penguin.

Kasanin, J., Knight, E. and Sage, P. (1934). The parent-child relationship in schizophrenia. *The Journal of Nervous and Mental Disease* 79: 249–263.

Kashy, D. and DePaulo, B. (1996). Who lies? *Journal of Personality and Social Psychology* 70: 1037–1051.

Kendon, A. (2004). *Gesture: Visible Action as Utterance*. Cambridge: Cambridge University Press.

Kissen, D. M. (1966). The significance of personality in lung cancer in men. *Annals of the New York Academy of Sciences* 125: 820–826.

Labov, W. (1972). Rules for ritual insults. In D. Sudnow (ed.). *Studies in Social Interaction*. Oxford: New York.

Lakoff, G. (1993). *The Contemporary Theory of Metaphor*. Berkeley: Berkeley University Press.

Lakoff, G. and Johnson, M. (1980). *Metaphors We Live By*. Chicago: University of Chicago Press.

Langer, W. C. (1943/1972). A Psychological Analysis of Adolf Hitler. Reprinted as *The Mind of Adolf Hitler*. New York: Basic Books.

Latane, B. and Darley, J. M. (1969). Bystander apathy. *American Scientist* 57: 244–268.

Lee, V. and Beattie, G. (1998). The rhetorical organization of verbal and nonverbal behavior in emotion talk. *Semiotica* 120: 39–92.

Lee, V. and Beattie, G. (2000). Why talking about negative emotional experiences is good for your health: A micro analytic perspective. *Semiotica* 130: 1–81.

Levine, R., Serota, K.B., Carey, F. and Messer, D. (2013). Teenagers lie a lot: A further investigation into the prevalence of lying. *Communication Research Reports* 30: 211–220.

Levy, D. M. (1931). Maternal over-protection and rejection. *Journal of Nervous and Mental Disease* 73: 65–77.

Lloyd-George, Earl. (1960). *Lloyd George*. London: Muller, Blond and White.

Machiavelli, N. (1513/1977). *The Prince*. New York: W.W. Norton.

Malle, B. F. (2006). The actor-observer asymmetry in attribution: A (surprising) meta-analysis. *Psychological Bulletin* 132: 895–919.

McClelland, J. L. (1979). On the time relations of mental processes: An examination of systems of processes in cascade. *Psychological Review* 86: 287–330.

McHoskey, J. (1995). Narcissism and Machiavellianism. *Psychological Reports* 77: 755–759.

McNeill, D. (1985). So you think gestures are nonverbal? *Psychological Review* 92: 350–371.

McNeill, D. (1992). *Hand and Mind: What Gestures Reveal About Thought*. Chicago: University of Chicago Press.

Meere, M. and Egan, V. (2017). Everyday sadism, the Dark Triad, personality and disgust sensitivity. *Personality and Individual Differences* 112: 157–161.

Meringer, R. and Mayer, C. (1895/1978). *Eine Psychologisch-Linguistische Studie*. London: John Benjamins.

Morris, D. (1979). *Manwatching*. London: Triad Books.

Motley, M. T. and Baars, B. (1978). Laboratory verification of 'Freudian' slips of the tongue as evidence of prearticulatory semantic editing. *Annals of the International Communication Association* 2: 141–152.

Musolff, A. (2007). What role do metaphors play in racial prejudice? The function of anti-Semitic imagery in Hitler's Mein Kampf. *Patterns of Prejudice* 41: 21–43.

Nadelhoffer, T. and Feltz, A. (2008). The actor-observer bias and moral intuitions. *Neuroethics* 1: 133–144.

Nelson, K. (2007). *Young Minds in Social Worlds*. Cambridge, MA: Harvard University Press.

Newton, I. (1672). A letter of Mr. Isaac Newton, Professor of the Mathematicks in the University of Cambridge; Containing his new theory about lights and colours. *Royal Society Philosophical Transactions* 6: 3075–3087.

Nietzsche, F. (1895/1968). *The Anti-Christ*. Trans. R. J. Hollingdale. Harmondsworth: Penguin.

Paulhus, D. L. and Williams, K. M. (2002). The dark triad of personality: Narcissism, Machiavellianism, and psychopathy. *Journal of Research in Personality* 36: 556–563.

Pennebaker, J. W. (1982). *The Psychology of Physical Symptoms*. London: Springer.

Pennebaker, J. W. (1989). Confession, inhibition and disease. *Advances in Experimental Social Psychology* 22: 211–244.

Pennebaker, J. W. (1993). Putting stress into words: Health, linguistic, and therapeutic implications. *Behaviour Research and Therapy* 31: 539–548.

Pennebaker, J. W. (1995). *Emotion, Disclosure and Health*. Washington, DC: American Psychological Association.

Pennebaker, J. W. (1997). Writing about emotional experiences as a therapeutic process. *Psychological Science* 8: 162–166.

Pennebaker, J. W. (2000). Telling stories: The health benefits of narrative. *Literature and Medicine* 19: 3–18.

Pennebaker, J. W. and Beall, S. K. (1986). Confronting a traumatic event: Toward an understanding of inhibition and disease. *Journal of Abnormal Psychology* 95: 274–281.

Pennebaker, J. W., Hughes, C. F. and O'Heeron, R. C. (1987). The psychophysiology of confession: Linking inhibitory and psychosomatic processes. *Journal of Personality and Social Psychology* 52: 781–793.

Pennebaker, J. W., Mayne, T. and Francis, M. (1997). Linguistic predictors of adaptive bereavement. *Journal of Personality and Social Psychology* 72: 863–871.

Pepys, S. (1668). Diaries in *The Shorter Pepys*. Ed. R. Latham (1985). Harmondsworth: Penguin.

Petitto, L. A. (1988). Language in the pre-linguistic child. In F. Kessel (ed.). *The Development of Language and Language Researchers: Essays in Honour of Roger Brown*. Hillsdale, NJ: Lawrence Erlbaum Associates.

Piaget, J. (1932/1948). *The Moral Judgement of the Child*. Glencoe, IL: Free Press.

Pizarro, D., Inbar, Y. and Helion, C. (2011). On disgust and moral judgment. *Emotion Review* 3: 267–268.

Plato. (375 BCE). *The Republic*. Trans. D. Lee (1987). Harmondsworth: Penguin.

Popper, K. (1945/1983). *The Autonomy of Sociology*. Reprinted in *Popper*. Ed. David Miller. London: Fontana.

Potash, H. (1965). *Schizophrenic Interaction and the Double Bind*. Doctoral dissertation, Michigan State University.

Proust, M. (1923–1925/2023). *The Captive and The Prisoner*. London: Yale University Press.

Quintilian, M. (100/1902). *Institutions Oratoriae*. Trans. H. Butler. London: Heinemann.

Rash, F. (2005). Metaphor in Adolf Hitler's Mein Kampf. *Metaphorik* 9: 74–111.

Raskin, R. N. and Terry, H. (1988). A principal-components analysis of the Narcissistic Personality Inventory and further evidence of its construct validity. *Journal of Personality and Social Psychology* 54: 890–902.

Reicher, S. and Haslam, A. (2017). How Trump won. *Scientific American* 28: 42–51.

Richards, I. A. (1936). *The Philosophy of Rhetoric*. New York: Oxford University Press.

Richell, R. A., Mitchell, D.G., Newman, C., Leonard, A., Baron-Cohen, S. and Blair, R.J.R. (2003). Theory of mind and psychopathy: Can psychopathic individuals read the language of the eyes. *Neuropsychologia* 41: 523–526.

Ringuette, E. L. and Kennedy, T. (1966). An experimental study of the double bind hypothesis. *Journal of Abnormal Psychology* 71: 136–141.

Ross, L. (1977). The intuitive psychologist and his shortcomings: Distortions in the attribution process. In L. Berkowitz (ed.). *Advances in Experimental Social Psychology* (pp. 173–220). New York: Academic Press.

Rousseau, J. (1790). *Confessions*. Trans. J. M. Cohen (1953). Harmondsworth: Penguin.

Sai, L., Shang, S., Tay, C., Liu, X., Sheng, T., Fu, G., Ding, X. and Lee, K. (2021). Theory of mind, executive function, and lying in children: A meta-analysis. *Developmental Science* 24: 5.

Saussure, F. de. (1916/1959). *Course in General Linguistics*. Trans. W. Baskin. New York: Philosophical Library.

Scott, M. B. and Lyman, S. M. (1968). Accounts. *American Sociological Review* 33: 46–62.

Schuham, A. I. (1967). The double-bind hypothesis a decade later. *Psychological Bulletin* 68: 409–416.

Sears, D. O. (1986). College sophomores in the laboratory: Influences of a narrow data base on social psychology's view of human nature. *Journal of Personality and Social Psychology* 51: 515–530.

Seligman, M. (1970). On the generality of the laws of learning. *Psychological Review* 77: 406–418.

Seligman, M. and Groves, D. P. (1970). Nontransient learned helplessness. *Psychonomic Science* 19: 191–192.

Shadish, W. R. and Carlson, L. H. (2007). *When Hell Froze Over: The Memoir of a Korean War Combat Physician who Spent 1010 Days in a Communist Prison Camp.* Bloomington, IN: iUniverse.

Shakespeare, W. (1598). *The Merchant of Venice.* London: Wordsworth Classics.

Sporer, S. L. and Schwandt, B. (2007). Moderators of nonverbal indicators of deception: A meta-analytic synthesis. *Psychology, Public Policy and Law* 13: 1–34.

Steele, R. (1712). *The Spectator* 352: 14th April.

Stevens, D., Charman, T. and Blair, R.J.R. (2001) Recognition of emotion in facial expressions and vocal tones in children with psychopathic tendencies. *Journal of Genetic Psychology* 162: 201–211.

Stevenson, R. L. (1881). Truth of intercourse. *Virginibus Puerisque.* Harvard: Harvard University Press.

Stiles, W. B. (1995). Disclosure as a speech act: Is it psychotherapeutic to disclose. *Journal of Clinical Psychology* 15: 212–215.

Sullivan, H. S. (1927). The onset of schizophrenia. *American Journal of Psychiatry* 84: 105–134.

Swift, J. (1713). The art of political lying. *The Examiner* 51.

Talwar, V. and Crossman, A. (2022). Liar, liar…sometimes: Understanding social-environmental influences on the development of lying. *Current Opinion in Psychology* 47: 101374.

Talwar, V and Lee, K. (2008). Social and cognitive correlates of children's lying behaviour. *Child Development* 79: 866–881.

Tedeschi, J. T., Schlenker, B. R. and Bonoma, T. V. (1971). Cognitive dissonance: Private rationalisation or public spectacle? *American Psychologist* 26: 685–695.

Thatcher, M. (2012). *The Path to Power.* London: Harper Collins.

Trivers, R. (2011). *Deceit and Self-Deception.* London: Allen Lane.

Twenge, J. M. and Campbell, K. W. (2009). *The Narcissism Epidemic. Living in the Age of Entitlement.* New York: Atria.

Van Bockstaele, B., Verschuere, B., Moens, T., Suchotzki, K., Debey, E. and Spruyt, A. (2012). Learning to lie: Effects of practice on the cognitive cost of lying. *Frontiers in Psychology* 3: 00526.

Vargas, R. (2011). Being in 'bad' company: Power dependence and status in adolescent susceptibility to peer influence. *Social Psychology Quarterly* 74: 310–332.

Verigin, B.L., Meijer, E.H., Bogaard, G. and Vrij, A. (2019) Lie prevalence, lie characteristics and strategies of self-reported good liars. *PLOS ONE* 14 (12): e0225566.

Vrij, A. (2000). *Detecting Lies and Deceit.* Chichester: Wiley.

Vrij, A. (1999). Detecting deceit via criteria-based content analysis, reality monitoring and analyses of nonverbal behaviour. Paper presented at the Ninth European Conference on Psychology and Law, Dublin, Ireland, July 1999.

Vrij, A., Fisher, R., Mann, S. and Leal, S. (2006). Detecting deception by manipulating cognitive load. *Trends in Cognitive Sciences* 10: 141–142.

Vrij, A., Granhag, P.A. and Leal, S. (2011). Outsmarting the liars: Toward a cognitive lie detection approach. *Current Directions in Psychological Science* 20: 28–32.

Weil, 'Yellow Kid'. (1948). *'Yellow Kid' Weil. The Autobiography of America's Master Swindler.* Chicago: Ziff-Davis Publishing.

Wheatley, T. and Haidt, J. (2005). Hypnotic disgust makes moral judgments more severe. *Psychological Science* 16: 780–784.

Whyte, W. F. (1943). *Street Corner Society.* Chicago: University of Chicago Press.

Williams, B., Ponesse, J.S., Schachar, R.J., Logan, G.D. and Tannock, R. (1999). Development of inhibitory control across the lifespan. *Developmental Psychology* 35: 205–213.

Willis, J. and Todorov, A. (2006). First impressions: Making up your mind after a 100-ms exposure to a face. *Psychological Science* 17: 592–598.

Wiseman, R. (2012). *The Truth about Mind Control. New Statesman* 3rd July.

Wundt, W. (1900). *Volkerpsychologie.* Leipzig: Kroner.

Yealland, L. R. (1918). *Hysterical Disorders of Warfare.* London: MacMillan

Yin, L., Reuter, M. and Weber, B. (2016). Let the man choose what to do: Neural correlates of spontaneous lying and truth-telling. *Brian and Cognition* 192: 13–25.

Zelazo, P. and Müller, U. (2002). Executive function in typical and atypical development. In U. Goswami (ed.). *Blackwell Handbook of Childhood Cognitive Development.* London: Blackwell.

Zuckerman, M., DePaulo, B.M. and Rosenthal, R. (1981). Beliefs about cues associated with deception. *Journal of Nonverbal Behavior* 6: 105–114.

Index